Costly and Cute

School for Advanced Research
Advanced Seminar Series
Michael F. Brown
General Editor

Since 1970 the School for Advanced Research
(formerly the School of American Research)
and SAR Press have published over one
hundred volumes in the Advanced Seminar
Series. These volumes arise from seminars held
on SAR's Santa Fe campus that bring together
small groups of experts to explore a single
issue. Participants assess recent innovations
in theory and methods, appraise ongoing
research, and share data relevant to problems
of significance in anthropology and related
disciplines. The resulting volumes reflect SAR's
commitment to the development of new ideas
and to scholarship of the highest caliber. The
complete Advanced Seminar Series can be
found at www.sarweb.org.

Costly and Cute

Helpless Infants and Human Evolution

Edited by Wenda R. Trevathan and Karen R. Rosenberg

SCHOOL FOR ADVANCED RESEARCH PRESS • SANTA FE

UNIVERSITY OF NEW MEXICO PRESS • ALBUQUERQUE

Library of Congress
Cataloging-in-Publication Data

Names: Trevathan, Wenda, editor. | Rosenberg,
Karen R., editor.
Title: Costly and cute : helpless infants and
human evolution / edited by Wenda R.
Trevathan and Karen R. Rosenberg.
Other titles: School for Advanced Research
Advanced Seminar Series
Description: Santa Fe : School for Advanced
Research Press ; Albuquerque : University of
New Mexico Press, 2016. | Series: School for
Advanced Research Advanced Seminar Series |
Includes bibliographical references and index.
Identifiers: LCCN 2015050137 |
ISBN 9780826357458 (pbk. : alk. paper) |
ISBN 9780826357465 (electronic)
Subjects: LCSH: Infants—Care. | Infants—
Growth. | Parent and child. | MESH: Biological
Evolution | Infant, Newborn—growth &
development | Parent-Child Relations
Classification: LCC RJ101 .C685 2016 | NLM
QH 366.2 | DDC 618.92/02—dc23 LC record
available at http://lccn.loc.gov/2015050137

Text set in Minion Pro; display in Gill Sans
Cover illustration: sashahaltom/Shutterstock

The SAR seminar from which this book
resulted was made possible with the generous
support of the Paloheimo Foundation.

Figures

Tables

CHAPTER ONE

Human Evolution and the Helpless Infant

WENDA R. TREVATHAN AND KAREN R. ROSENBERG

We know from literature, films, and our own personal experience that human newborns are very adept at demanding and occupying the attention of others. They are helpless, dependent creatures who need our care, and they have evolved attractive characteristics and a range of captivating behaviors that are very effective at soliciting and obtaining that attention. This topic has long been of interest to evolutionary biologists and anthropologists. In his influential book *Mankind Evolving*, Dobzhansky was unequivocal in stating that it was humans' helplessness at birth and utter dependence on parents and other caretakers that favored learning and socialization "on which the transmission of culture wholly depends" (1962:196). We agree but argue here that it is more than the transmission of culture that derives from this helplessness. Many of the distinctive characteristics that make us human can trace their origins (or at least their significance) to the fact that we give birth to infants who are highly dependent on others; babies are afforded the opportunity to learn how to be human while their brains are experiencing growth unlike that seen in other mammals, including the nonhuman primates.

In the 1960s and earlier, most models of human evolution featured "man the hunter" (Lee and DeVore 1968) as the key player; in the 1970s (in the context of the women's movement), it became obvious that such an approach examined only a limited part of the human adaptation, and many anthropologists turned their attention to the other half of the species, namely "woman the gatherer" (Dahlberg 1981). The pivotal books that carried those names sought to explain and contextualize a number of distinguishing characteristics of humanness: bipedalism; language; increased reliance on tools and meat eating; expanded kin and other social networks; large, complex, and metabolically expensive brains; prolonged lifespan after menopause for women; sharing of food, childcare, and other resources; art; symbols; rituals; and social and emotional intelligence. While we recognize that single-cause explanations of the human adaptation are simplistic, we propose that an equally important player in the story of human evolution, and one who can account for most of the characteristics listed above, is the helpless, attractive human infant. In a parallel phrase to the previous models, Dean Falk refers to this model as "baby the trendsetter" (chapter 6, this volume).

As anyone who has cared for them will attest, human newborns are truly dependent creatures that arrive in the extrauterine world in an undeveloped, helpless state and that mature even more slowly and over a longer period than any other primate. In spite of these challenges, our ancestors were able to find ways for their infants to survive while maintaining mothers' health *and* reducing the spacing of births relative to apes so that human parents (and alloparents) are able to care for not just one, but several needy offspring at a time (see Lovejoy 1981). This costly developmental pattern is unprecedented among primates and is surely related to other aspects of our biology and behavior and to our adaptation as a cultural species. The chapters in this book examine both the costs and benefits of giving birth to such immature offspring, and the contributors propose that infant helplessness and social and cultural adaptation evolved hand in hand in many significant ways.

We came to our interest in the developmental status of human infants at birth from our work on the evolution of human childbirth. In previous publications (Trevathan 1987, 1988; Rosenberg and Trevathan 2002), we have argued that the evolution of the complex and constrained way in which human babies are born was made possible because of human birth assistance, a behavioral adaptation that may have characterized bipedal hominins even before encephalization. In our early thinking, we saw the timing of birth as one of the variables that can be altered (because of humans' ability to culturally buffer our infants from the extrauterine environment) to mitigate the constraints of the obstetrical dilemma. As a result of a number of developments in the field (reviewed by Dunsworth in chapter 2), our attention has shifted from birth to the developmental status of the newborn. The timing of birth relative to infant development is not only a way to mitigate obstetrical constraints (by being born sooner when head size is smaller and passage through the birth canal easier) but also creates challenges that confer advantages in a species in which the chances of survival and future reproduction are enhanced by attracting the attention (and protection and provisioning) of alloparents. This book investigates the proposition that helpless human infants are costly but that their attractiveness ("cuteness") helps to mitigate those costs and that great benefits balance those high costs. In order to investigate the potential costs and benefits of being born early relative to developmental status, we brought together a group of scholars who we thought could bring fresh perspectives to this issue.

In 2014, the average cost to raise a middle-income American child to age eighteen approached a quarter of a million dollars. This seems expensive to most of us, but costs like these, while not necessarily stated in monetary terms, have been part of the human heritage for millions of years. Infancy is an especially expensive time in the life course, largely due to the extreme dependence and helplessness of the infant. An enduring question is why we have evolved to have such highly dependent infants. Given the costs of pregnancy, childbirth, breastfeeding, and other aspects of caring for these dependent infants, what has our species gained? What have been the trade-offs of this reproductive strategy that have made it worth it? We demonstrate in this book that infant helplessness is central to the human adaptation, and we argue that the only way humans could have adopted such a costly reproductive strategy is with extensive care from others, cooperative caretaking in addition to and beyond that provided by the parents. (Following Hrdy in her chapter in this volume, we define "cooperative breeding" as a characteristic of "any species with alloparental as well as parental care and provisioning of offspring.") Bogin and colleagues (2014) have called this set of behaviors "biocultural reproduction" in recognition of the fact that, unlike most other cooperatively breeding species, human allomothers are not necessarily genetic relatives of the young they care for. Kramer and Otárola-Castillo (2015) have pointed to cooperative breeding as central to the distinctive aspects of human life history.

Human infants are like other primate babies in many ways, but they appear to reach extremes in two significant characteristics: (1) exhibiting a higher degree of helplessness and dependence at birth and therefore (2) needing an inordinate amount, duration, and intensity of parenting and caretaking. The two are obviously related, as has been discussed for centuries. The relationship between the helpless infant and strong family bonds was recognized by Alexander Pope in his *Essay on Man* (1733, noted by Gould 1977), when he observed that most mammals and birds leave their young after a relatively short time to take care of themselves, whereas "A longer care man's helpless kind demands / That longer care contracts more lasting bonds." Bolk, Gould,

Portmann, and Montagu were among the early influential writers who argued that slow development (Bolk's "retarded life course" or "fetalization theory of anthropogeny") was "what is the essential in Man as an organism" (Bolk 1926:469–470). Cohen (1947, cited in Gould 1977) argued that the long period of human infancy is more important than any anatomical differences in distinguishing us from other animals.

Many scholars have written about the significance of extended childhood (delayed maturation or adulthood) for the learning and socialization that are part of our adaptation as cultural animals (e.g., Bogin 1997; Mann 1972; Portmann 1990), but a focus on infant helplessness at the time of birth is less common, and rarely has it served as the focus of an entire book. In this volume we concentrate on late pregnancy to weaning, considering this time period in the human life cycle as a developmental continuum. In this view, birth is neither a beginning nor an end of a developmental stage; rather, it is a point when the neonate leaves the relative isolation of the biological womb of the uterus and enters the larger, more stimulating cultural womb of the mother and her social group.

Historical Overview of Perspectives on the State of the Human Newborn

Across mammals and birds, a continuum of life history patterns is recognized and distinguished by the extremes: altriciality and precociality. Altricial species (like mice) tend to be born after a short gestation, in large litters, with eyes and ears sealed by membranes at birth, without hair, and unable to locomote, regulate their own body temperature, or find food independently. They tend to spend the first period of their extrauterine lives in a nest. Precocial species (like horses) are generally born covered in hair after a long gestation, in small litters, with well-developed sensory organs that are open, and are able to locomote, thermoregulate, and find food on their own (Sacher and Staffeldt 1974; Martin 1992; Harvey 1992). Primates as an order are precocial in the pattern of their development, and humans generally fit this pattern (e.g., Smith and Tompkins 1995). The interesting ways in which humans fail to fit the precocial pattern make it difficult, however, to use either of these terms or even to locate a place along the continuum to describe the state of the infant at birth.[1]

Finding a working phrase to describe this state has been challenging. Terms used by earlier scholars include "helpless," "neotenous," "paedomorphic," "fetalized," "immature," "highly dependent," "secondarily altricial," "semi-altricial," "exterogestate fetus," "altricial-precocial," and "precocial-altricial." Portmann was among the first to write about the significance of the human infant being born in a more helpless and less developed state than the infants of most other primates. In his earliest writings, he used the German terms *Nesthocker* (nest hocker or squatter) and *Nestflüchter* (nest fleer), which were usually translated as altricial and precocial. He recognized that human infants are difficult to categorize in these terms and suggested that, for the human infant to be considered truly altricial, he[2] would have to be born at 5 months of gestation, when the sensory organs are still closed and undeveloped. In contrast, as in other precocial mammals, the sensory organs, locomotor organs, and central nervous system of human infants develop and grow in utero and are largely functional at the time of birth. As further evidence of the precocial state of human infants, Portmann cited the composition of human milk, which is like that of mammals with precocial infants in being very dilute and thus necessitating frequent nursing. Portmann argued that we should see human helplessness at birth in its context: "not as the primitive, somatic immaturity of an altricial infant, but as a very exceptional situation within the mammalian group. In fact, with respect to the full precocial type, humans are secondarily altricial" (Portmann 1990:38; phrase actually first introduced in 1942).

Portmann continued his discussion of the unusual nature of the human infant compared to other mammals by noting that most precocial infants are "miniature versions" of the adults of their species with behaviors and locomotion little different from theirs. But the human infant does not match other primates in relative body proportions, locomotion, and communication until he has matured for approximately 1 year after birth. On the basis of this, Portmann suggested that the functional human gestation period might be considered to last 21 months: "Our preliminary conclusion is only that the actual length of human pregnancy is much less than it should be for typical mammalian development at our level of organization" (1990:51). He further argued that in spite of the fact that our infants are much larger at birth than those of our closest relatives, growth in the first year of life is more like that of a fetus than of an infant: "At the end of the first year of life the moment comes that must be considered as the time of parturition for any true mammal of humanlike organization" (54).

Portmann called the first year of life in humans the "extrauterine spring," referring to the season of growth. It is during this year that the human infant

becomes a walker, a talker, and a doer. The important thing both to Portmann and to the contributors in this volume is that these maturational events
take place in the relatively stimulating cultural and social environment of
the postnatal world, not in the "all-purpose environment of the womb but
under unique circumstances; each phase of postpartum life intensifie[s] this
uniqueness by increasing the possibilities for divergent, individual situations"
(Portmann 1990:91). Portmann concluded this line of thought by proclaim-
ing that it is the existence of this extrauterine spring that accounts for us. "It
will gradually become clear that world-open behavior of the mature form is
directly related to early contact with the richness of the world, an opportunity
available only to the human!" (93). In this sense, we can interpret the term
"spring" in its meaning "to move upward or outward" and as in the root of
"wellspring." (See Dunsworth, chapter 2, this volume, for more discussion of
the extrauterine spring.)

Bostock (1958), a psychologist, proposed that the human infant should have
two birthdays: the first upon leaving the womb and the second when "exterior gestation" ends and quadrupedal movements (i.e., crawling) begin. Perhaps anticipating Washburn's (1960) obstetrical dilemma hypothesis, Bostock
argued that the first birthday occurs when the neonatal head is as big as it can
be and still pass through the birth canal. Recognizing that being born "early"
has costs, Bostock further argued that the exterogestate fetus (referred to by
him as the "neogestate") needs a great deal of care: "The pelvic barrier has been
overcome, but at the cost of all the hazards of keeping alive naked helpless
foetuses under difficult and changing conditions" (1962:1034).

Montagu also wrote a great deal about the state of the human infant
at birth: "man is born as immaturely as he is because—owing to the great
increase in the size of his brain and consequently of his head—if he weren't
born when he is, he wouldn't be born at all" (1961:56). In his view, gestation
is not complete at birth; rather, it consists of "uterogestation" or "interogesta-
tion" in the womb and then "exterogestation" outside the womb. According to
him, the length of uterogestation matches the period of exterogestation, both
at 267 days. He claimed that "it is important that most of the brain growth be
accomplished during the first year, when the infant has so much to learn and
do" (57). Publishing his views in the *Journal of the American Medical Association*, Montagu used a clinical journal for physicians as a platform to decry the
"modern" view of infancy and the disruption in mother-infant interaction:

"The separation begins from the moment of birth, so profound has our mis-understanding of the nature of human beings grown. Perhaps the hypothesis of uterogestation and exterogestation proposed here may cause us to reconsider the meaning of the infant's immaturity and dependency" (57). His concern was that the "symbiotic union" of mother and infant is too frequently disrupted, with potentially negative effects on development. Bostock (1962) also decried the "complete revolution in infant care" that occurred in the first half of the twentieth century; he was particularly concerned for the potential deleterious effects of bottle feeding. He called for an "evolutionary approach to infant care" (1035) and claimed that many social ills could be traced to the first few months of life, when the infant should be treated as an exterogestate fetus and kept close to the mother's body, receiving the same intense nurturing and support as he did in utero.

Although often portrayed for illustrative purposes as a unidimensional continuum, the distinction between altricial and precocial is complex and multidimensional. Despite historical discussions of human infants as altricial or precocial, it is clear that the terms have limited utility when applied to humans. Our babies are not helpless, blind, and hairless/featherless, as expected for altricial young, nor are they able to move about on their own, as expected for precocial young; rather, our babies at birth show a mixture or mosaic of altricial and precocial features.[3] Like other precocial primates, human infants have eyes and ears that are fully open. Also similar to precocial mammals, humans have long gestation periods and usually give birth to one infant at a time. Our babies are large, relative to adult body size, and we reproduce later in life, like other precocial mammals. Human milk is dilute at 88% water, similar to that of other precocial primates, who are able to keep up with their mothers and nurse frequently, in contrast to animals who remain in a nest and can only nurse at discrete intervals (Milligan 2013). Certainly we recognize that infants of many species are rarely completely altricial or completely precocial, but may possess a mosaic of the features usually used to characterize these extremes. The human infant, who is born with eyes fully open but who is utterly helpless in motor skills, has a particularly unusual constellation of features. Rather than describe humans as secondarily altricial, could it be more accurate to say that human infants are simply "precocial babies born at a relatively early stage in their development," as we have suggested elsewhere (Rosenberg and Trevathan 2007:94)?

In an effort to find a single term, most of the contributors to this volume have chosen to use "helpless." It is important to note, however, that this refers only to somatic immaturity and locomotor limitations. Indeed, we argue that it is the precise combination of this helplessness with the fact that human infants are highly engaged with their caretakers and able to manipulate aspects of their environment through their attractiveness (cuteness) and to take in so much sensory stimulation that makes humans unusual and so difficult to place on the altricial-precocial continuum. In addition to motor development, however, there are a number of other ways in which human infants seem to be underdeveloped at birth in comparison with our closest relatives, the monkeys and apes.

What Is Undeveloped about the Human Infant?

BODY PROPORTIONS AND SKELETAL MATURATION

As noted by Portmann (1990:38), human newborns are not "miniature versions of their parents," as in most precocial species. Rather, they are very different from their parents in their body proportions, making them more like altricial infants. In the chimpanzee, the length ratios between infant and adult torsos, legs, and arms are similar, whereas in humans the ratios differ considerably. For example, human legs are much longer relative to the rest of the adult body than they are in infancy.

With regard to skeletal maturation, humans show less ossification at birth than most other primates. In the rates of ossification of long bones and digits, human neonates are as developed as the fetuses of macaques and do not reach the level observed in macaque newborns until several years after birth (Schultz 1949, cited in Gould 1977). Even at 3 months of age, human infants are more immature than newborn chimpanzees with regard to hand and wrist ossification (Watts 1990). Dental eruption also shows similar delays. Cranial plates are open in human infants until several months after birth, when they reach a stage seen in infant monkeys and apes at the time of birth (Gould 1977). The skull bones remain unfused and flexible until brain growth is completed: in early adulthood for humans but in early childhood for apes. This degree of flexibility is important during the birth process because it allows the skull to mold as it passes through the birth canal, reducing the diameter of the head and facilitating birth (Posner et al. 2013). (The occiput is the most developed

Table 1.1. Newborn and Adult Brain Size for Selected Primate Species

	Neonatal Brain Size	Neonatal Sample Size (n)	Adult Brain Size	Neonatal-Adult Brain Size Ratio
Chlorocebus aethiops	47.6	13	66.7	71.4
Macaca mulatta	58.6	79	91.1	64.3
Macaca nemestrina	61.8	93	104.6	59.1
Saimiri sciureus	14.7	43	26.2	56.1
Cercocebus atys	57.5	43	107.9	53.3
Papio anubis	82.9	35	161.4	51.4
Cebus albifrons	33.7	12	71.0	47.5
Callithrix jacchus	3.5	28	7.6	46.1
Pan troglodytes	150.9	22	381.7	39.5
Homo sapiens	373.8	729	1330.5	28.1

Note: Data are courtesy of Jeremy DeSilva and include species for which samples of 10 or more neonatal individuals were available.

of the cranial plates, which is why it can sustain the intense force of uterine contractions during birth; it is also the least likely cranial bone to be damaged during birth; Redfield 1970.) Interestingly, Gould (1991) cited cranial molding as a way to pass a large head through a tight birth canal as an example of something that evolved as an "exaptation" rather than "adaptation." All of these ossification delays are consistent with the overall slowed development in hominins compared with other hominids and haplorrhines.

BRAIN DEVELOPMENT AND GESTATION LENGTH

The average human gestation of 38 weeks is not very different from the gestation periods of the other great apes—32 weeks for chimpanzees and 38 weeks for gorillas and orangutans—making it very unlikely, as some scholars have suggested (Trinkaus 1984; Gould 1975), that the gestation length of our ancestors was significantly greater in either absolute or relative terms compared to humans today (Martin and MacLarnon 1990; Rosenberg 1992). What *is* really different about human newborns is the relative size of their brains compared to adults' brain size. This is achieved by a shift in the position of birth relative to the rapid period of brain growth. In most primates, birth takes place at about the point where fetal brain growth slows down and the brain growth curve shows an inflection. In humans, brain growth continues at fetal rates well past the time of birth (see Falk, chapter 6, this volume, and figure 6.2). This postponement of brain maturation makes human infants helpless in several domains (see Falk, chapter 6, and Semendeferi and Hanson, chapter 7, both this volume). By 18 months of age, brain growth rates for humans and chimpanzees are similar (Leigh 2004). Table 1.1 (from data generously shared with us by Jeremy DeSilva) shows infant brain size as a percentage of adult brain size (what Portmann called the "multiplier factor"). At birth, humans have achieved only about 28.1% of their adult brain growth; the numbers for other primates range from 39.5% (in *Pan troglodytes*) to 71.4% (in *Chlorocebus aethiops*). This means that compared to most anthropoids, human infants have a great deal of brain growth still to accomplish.

Much of the discussion of the human infant brain at birth focuses on size and makes comparisons with adult brain size to highlight the degree of underdevelopment at the end of gestation. But brain size alone does not tell the full story. In comparing neural development during gestation and shortly thereafter in a number of primate species, Clancy and colleagues (2001:14) conclude that human infants have a "precocial brain although somewhat disguised by an unwieldy body." What they mean is that although human infants are motorically undeveloped at birth, they are neurally advanced in comparison to the other species studied. For example, at 7 months' gestation, the human brain has the neural maturation level of a newborn macaque, a week-old kitten, and a 2-week-old rat. This lends further support to the concept of mosaic development in the human newborn, as proposed by DeSilva in chapter 4 (this volume). The extensive neural and cognitive development that takes place in the first year of life is highly dependent on sensory interaction with others in the infant's environment (Bruner 1972; Bjorklund 1997; Bjorklund and Pellegrini 2000; Gopnik et al. 1999; Kinnally 2013). As the contributors to this volume argue, this may be one of the most significant advantages of being born relatively early in the course of brain growth and development. Of course most neural development occurs before birth, but this view emphasizes the importance of the outside world for continuing neurological maturation, which we discuss below, as do Semendeferi and Hanson in chapter 7.

Human infants are not born blind, as would be expected for an altricial mammal or bird, but neither is their vision fully developed at birth (Mercuri et al. 2007). Apparently they can focus on objects 12–18 inches from their faces (conveniently, approximately the distance to their mothers' eyes when they are breastfeeding) (Brazelton et al. 1966). Newborns' preference for the human face has been demonstrated as early as the first 10 minutes of life (Goren et al. 1975), a phenomenon that has been shown for chimpanzees and macaques as well (Tomonaga 2007; Kuwahata et al. 2004). According to Haith (1980), the light and dark areas of a human face are optimal for stimulating maximum neural firing rates. Infants engage in visual searching soon after birth, helping to activate neural areas for further visual development.

Eye contact is important in forming social attachments in humans (Guastella et al. 2008) and appears to be a significant mechanism for forming parent-infant bonds in the first hours after birth (Trevathan 1983). Rivinus and Katz (1971) suggested that as clinging abilities at birth diminished over the course of human evolution, eye contact became more important for maintaining connections between mothers and infants. The ability of human infants to maintain eye contact and to visually follow movements in the early hours and days of life facilitated these attachments, placing a selective premium on the early emergence of visual function even when neural abilities to locomote were limited. Like chimpanzees, right from birth, human infants seek out faces, focusing especially on the eyes, but by 9 months or so, when chimpanzees tend to lose interest, human infants become more interested (Okamoto-Barth 2012; Hrdy 2016).

In considering the various aspects of human development at and soon after birth, perhaps the most conspicuous and consequential undeveloped characteristic is locomotion. Human babies are extremely helpless motorically at birth and are dependent on others for mobility for several years. As a rule, precocial mammals tend to move about in ways very similar to adults, albeit a bit wobblier in the beginning. At birth, human infants can make alternating stepping movements with their legs that are similar to those used in locomotion, but they lack the equilibrium and postural control that is developed embryonically in precocial animals (Muir 2000). These aspects of locomotion develop postnatally in altricial infants and in humans, who are unable to maintain the upright posture of bipedalism until they are at least a year old; it often takes several years beyond that before their movements are smooth and efficient.

At first look, humans appear to be qualitatively different from other primates with regard to when they begin walking, but it turns out that this assessment depends on what point in the life course is selected as a baseline. When measured from birth, humans appear to be greatly delayed in locomotor independence, but if another beginning point is selected, that difference diminishes. Garwicz and colleagues (2009) argue that the onset of walking in humans, when measured from conception rather than from birth, is not different from that of other mammals and is highly correlated with adult brain mass. Their research into the age of walking onset across terrestrial mammals indicates that humans begin walking when their brains reach a certain developmental level and at the time predicted based on adult brain size. They conclude that the neural basis for walking onset is similar across mammalian species with respect to brain development and that it is a highly conserved trait shared by a wide range of placental mammals. So humans walk when their brains reach a maturation level comparable to that of other mammals, but like brain maturation, that point is greatly delayed in the human life course. This observation fits well with the data of Clancy and colleagues (2001), which showed that what is different across mammals is not motor maturation rates but the timing of birth.

GASTROINTESTINAL AND IMMUNE FUNCTION

The human infant's intestinal tract is essentially sterile at birth, but by the end of the first year of life, a baby's intestinal microbiota resemble those of adults (Levy 2007). Most of these come from the vaginal passage during birth, colostrum, and breastmilk (Dominguez-Bello et al. 2010). The birth process provides the first source of gut bacteria via exposure to the perineal region; further colonization comes through breastmilk (Newburg and Walker 2007; Abrams and Miller 2011). The importance of this process is highlighted by the increasing concern today that infants born by cesarean section and fed only formula may find challenges to their GI function in later life (Martin and Sela 2013; Neu and Rushing 2011; Cho and Norman 2013; Mueller et al. 2015; see also Quinn, chapter 5, this volume).

Although human infants are not immunologically naïve at birth (Holt and Jones 2000), their immune systems are far from fully developed, partly due to the very invasive hemochorial placenta (a characteristic of all haplorrhines), which requires immune suppression from both mother and fetus to prevent rejection during pregnancy (Morein et al. 2007). For example, although most immunoglobulins are not expressed until after birth, limiting the newborn's ability to fight off infections (McDade 2005), some (such as immunoglobulin G) can cross from the mother to the infant via the placenta during gestation. Antibodies are acquired from the mother through contact with the vaginal passage during birth and via colostrum and breastmilk early in infancy, as noted above with regard to gut bacteria. There is also evidence that newborn infants acquire bacterial nasal flora directly from their mothers (and others) when their faces are close together. The mother's strains of respiratory organisms develop in the infant's respiratory and gastrointestinal tracts, providing protection from potentially pathogenic bacteria (Klaus and Kennell 1982). It seems that the fact that development of proteins critical for surviving outside the womb is delayed until after birth contributes to the delayed maturation of the infant and his high dependence on the mother and others.

In summary, human infants are undeveloped in several aspects of physiology, anatomy, and neurological development. Although they may not be unique in their state of development (see Robson et al. 2006; Leigh 2004; Finlay and Workman 2013), the needs of human infants for intensive caretaking and inordinate investments of time and energy for a large portion of the life course have both been impacted by and have an impact on almost all aspects of human evolutionary history.

Factors Influencing the Birth of the Helpless Infant

Figure 1.1 proposes a number of factors influencing the helpless state of the infant and factors that flow from that state (originally published in Trevathan 1987:32; factors not in the original model are in italics here). On the left side of the diagram are factors that may contribute to the birth of a helpless infant: an encephalized neonate who must pass through a relatively constricted bipedal pelvis; the deeply invasive hemochorial placenta, which may impact the infant's state in late pregnancy; the advantage of being born before most of brain growth is completed; and metabolic limits to the mother's ability to support the pregnancy. On the right side of the diagram are features that

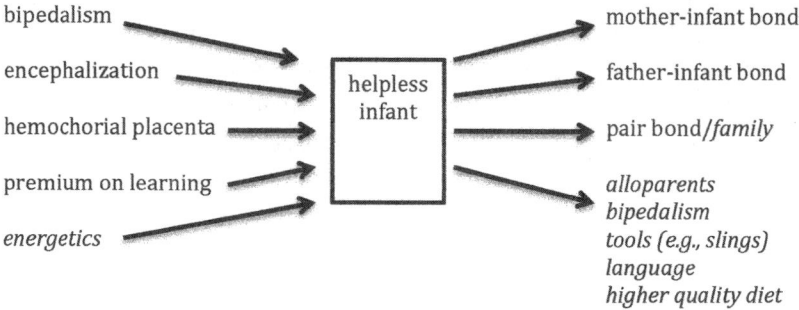

Figure 1.1. Factors in human evolutionary history that have contributed to the birth of the helpless infant. Modified from Trevathan 1987:32.

may flow from the helpless state of the infant at birth: the mother-infant and father-infant bonds; the pair bond and extended family, including alloparents; contributions to selection for bipedalism, tool use, and language; and dietary adaptations that increase diversity, nutrient density, and nutrient quality. Some of these are the subjects of other chapters, but we briefly discuss some features here.

OBSTETRIC FACTORS

For more than half a century, the reigning paradigm to explain why human infants are so helpless at birth has been the obstetrical dilemma, first proposed by Washburn in 1960. If selection is to favor encephalization in a lineage, he reasoned, there must be a way to escape the constraints on brain and body growth imposed by the bipedal pelvis. The dilemma was solved by delivering the fetus at an earlier stage of development. As encephalization evolved in the human lineage, more and more of brain growth had to occur postnatally, placing more and more demands on mothers (and, as we now increasingly recognize, others as well) to care for the increasingly helpless and vulnerable infant. But more than 40 years ago, Epstein (1973) suggested that the pelvis would only have to expand 4 cm (which he described as "readily evolvable") in order to accommodate the birth of an infant with an adult's full brain size. In other words, he concluded that the obstetrical dilemma could not explain why the human infant has only a quarter of its brain size at birth.

The obstetrical dilemma as an explanation for the timing of birth and hence human helplessness at birth has come under further fire from scholars directly assessing the biomechanics and energetics of bipedalism and the metabolic requirements of pregnancy and lactation (Dunsworth et al. 2012; Wall-Scheffler and Myers 2013; Warrener et al. 2015; see Dunsworth, chapter 2, this volume). Length of gestation is determined by a number of proximate and ultimate factors, including both metabolic and obstetrical constraints.

Although maternal metabolism may play an important role in the timing of birth, pelvic shape and size are likely still subject to obstetric selection. Furthermore it is difficult to explain human sexual dimorphism in pelvic morphology (in which females are greater than males, in contrast to body size dimorphism, in which males are larger than females on average) without invoking selection from obstetrical constraints. The discussions about challenges to the birth process usually focus on cephalopelvic disproportion, but there are other maternal and fetal dimensions that pose challenges because of bipedalism and encephalization. Often, midwives are as concerned about shoulder dystocia as they are about cephalopelvic disproportion (Trevathan and Rosenberg 2000) and severe tearing of the vaginal opening and perineum, which may result when a large baby is born through a bipedal birth canal. A third-degree laceration (tearing from vagina to anus), often resulting in what today is called an obstetric fistula, would have had serious impacts in the past on a mother's health and her ability to care for her infant, just as it does today.

As noted above, the cranial plates of human infants do not fuse until several years after birth. This may make the infant somewhat vulnerable to damage if dropped or hit, but the fact that the cranial bones can slide over each other (referred to as "molding" by birth attendants) means that the circumference of the fetal head can be decreased temporarily to allow easier passage through the birth canal. The shoulders of the human infant do not have that degree of flexibility, however, and may actually provide more obstruction to the birth process than do the head and the rest of the body. Monkeys' shoulders are narrower than their heads, so the monkey head provides more resistance to passage through the birth canal than the shoulders do. (Apes, which, like humans, do have broad shoulders, have infants that are much smaller than their mothers' birth canals so shoulders have limited impact in the birth process for those animals.)

ENERGETICS

Although pelvic constraints provide an ultimate factor limiting gestation, most contemporary scholars—beginning at least with Epstein's work (1973) and continuing through Martin's contributions (1983, 2007) and those of Ellison (2001a, 2009)—agree that a primary proximate factor limiting brain growth before birth is the ability of the mother's metabolism to support the fetus in utero. In other words, it is most likely a metabolic trigger that serves as a proximate factor to signal the end of the 38- to 40-week gestation period, which ends with delivery of a highly dependent infant with only about a quarter of its ultimate brain size, a hypothesis proposed by Ellison (2001a), Dunsworth (Dunsworth et al. 2012), and others and discussed further by Dunsworth in chapter 2.

PLACENTAL EFFECTS

Preeclampsia is another constraint on the human developmental state at birth (Rosenberg and Trevathan 2007). Humans, like other haplorrhine primates, have highly invasive placentae with fetal nutrient and oxygen needs met by direct contact with the maternal vascular system (Martin 2003). In the third month of pregnancy, the human placenta undergoes a secondary invasion, or burrowing in, when brain development takes off and nutrient and oxygen needs increase significantly. Sometimes this secondary invasion is incomplete, compromising nutrient and oxygen delivery later in pregnancy and occasionally resulting in preeclampsia. The resulting cost is often a compromised pregnancy or even maternal and/or fetal death. The major indicator of preeclampsia is high blood pressure resulting from resource diversion from the mother to meet increasing fetal needs in the context of limited vascular support of the incomplete invasion. The only cure for preeclampsia is delivery of the infant. Perhaps one of the explanations for a 9-month gestation period is that it prevents a higher rate of preeclampsia than the 10% reported in the world today. (Preeclampsia and the secondary deep invasion of the trophoblast were believed to be unique to humans, but see Crosley et al. 2013 for evidence that preeclampsia is found in other ape species that have the same degree of invasion as humans.)

The deeply invasive placenta is also causally related to the high rate of postpartum hemorrhage (it takes longer to detach from the uterine wall), a prominent contributor to birth-related morbidity and mortality throughout history

(Abrams and Rutherford 2011). Two other placental disorders related to degree of invasiveness and perhaps unique to humans are *placenta abruptio* (premature separation from the uterine wall when invasiveness is too shallow) and *placenta accreta* (invasion is too deep, and detachment does not occur when it should), both of which contribute to maternal and infant mortality today. It is likely, as with other pregnancy and birth complications reviewed here, that preeclampsia and other problems related to the placenta are more common in contemporary populations than they were in the past.

IT IS BETTER OUTSIDE

A great deal of our discussion so far has focused on factors that select *against* developing too long in utero, but there are a number of reasons that it may be better for a species with a cultural adaptation to be outside rather than inside the uterus during important neurological and cognitive development. Oxygen is of utmost importance to brain growth, of course, and the amount of oxygen available to the infant outside the womb is five times what is available in utero (Nathanielsz and Vaughan 2001). Prolonging time in utero may lead to the infant "starving to death" with regard not only to energy, but also to oxygen. Clearly, continued brain growth requires adequate oxygen, so in one view, birth occurs when the fetal lungs are mature enough to utilize the higher levels of oxygen in the environment outside the womb.

Size undoubtedly puts limits on how much brain growth can occur before birth, but the fact that most neuronal and synapse development occurs in the first few months and years of postnatal life suggests that beyond size, there are advantages to having this growth occur in the stimulating environment of the outside world and a dense social network. Miller and colleagues (2012:16482) note that "activity-mediated myelin growth early in human life has the capacity to be shaped by postnatal environmental and social interactions to a greater degree than in other primates, including chimpanzee," suggesting advantages to being born "early."

Costly and Cute

COSTS OF GESTATION

Gestation is costly for all mammals. Human infants are unusually large, and the energetic demands increase dramatically in late pregnancy (see Dunsworth, chapter 2, this volume). At birth, the human infant is notably fatter (around 16% of body weight) than most other mammals (Cunnane 2005; Kuzawa 1998). Fat accumulation in the last weeks of pregnancy is important for maintaining the expensive and rapidly growing brain, for preparing the baby for postnatal life, and for preparing the mother for lactation. The last trimester of pregnancy requires an additional 300 calories a day in the mother's dietary intake to maintain this fat deposition. Cooperative caretaking in the form of provisioning to supplement what she was able to gather herself was probably important throughout human evolution in providing sufficient caloric intake for a late-term pregnant woman (Dufour and Sauthier 2002). Although metabolic efficiency increases in pregnant women, there comes a point when they simply cannot metabolize any more calories, no matter how much food is available (Dunsworth et al. 2012). One way to meet caloric needs is to divert calories from herself to her fetus by reducing physical activity (Dufour and Sauthier 2002). An important contribution that members of her social group can make is to help reduce her workload and physical activity so that more of the calories she consumes go to her developing fetus. In a sense then, cooperative childrearing really begins in the late stages of pregnancy.

COSTS OF GIVING BIRTH

Unlike other primate species, in which females most often give birth in isolation from other members of their social group, it is difficult, risky, and unusual (but not impossible) for humans to give birth alone. Monkey infants have sufficiently developed motor skills at birth that they can help themselves in the birth process (Trevathan 1987, 2015). Human babies have never been reported to use their hands or otherwise actively assist in their own delivery; this is not surprising given the poorly developed motor skills of our infants and the lack of a hairy substrate to cling to. Therefore, delivering a human infant is entirely up to the mother and her birth assistants.

Despite motor immaturity and neonatal brains that are small relative to adult brains, our infants have large brains and large bodies that pose challenges to the birth process. We have argued elsewhere that giving birth to large-bodied, large-brained infants and the way in which the infant emerges from the birth canal have placed a selective advantage for humans on seeking assistance during birth (Trevathan 1987; Rosenberg 1992; Rosenberg and Trevathan 1995, 2002). The costs of complicated childbirth are thus met by another form of social cooperation: assistance during birth, or midwifery. Birth is a time in the human life cycle when the costs of reproduction are shared.

COSTS OF BREASTFEEDING

Like all mammals, humans lactate to nourish their infants, and they incur energetic costs through milk production. As noted above, one of the reasons that caloric intake is so important in the late stages of pregnancy is that it prepares the mother for lactation, which is even more expensive than the late stages of pregnancy (Quinn, chapter 5, this volume). The costs of lactation are balanced by the benefits gained from the provisioning of calories, protein, and immunological protection (Piperata 2009; Quinn, chapter 5, this volume). These costs are shared when other members of the group augment the mother's diet beyond what she can obtain for herself and help to reduce her caloric needs by taking on some of her workload and, in some cases, even serving as wet nurses.

COSTS OF CARE IN INFANCY AND CHILDHOOD

Caring for highly dependent babies during infancy involves more than breast-feeding. Unlike other primates, whose infants can cling to their mothers' fur using four limbs within days of birth, human infants, with only two cling-ing limbs and nearly hairless mothers, must be carried for at least the first year of life in the arms or in a carrying device like a sling. Even after humans begin walking, they cannot do so very efficiently and must be carried when their families cover long distances (Lee 1980). Carrying an infant in her arms is costly for the mother and has the potential to be even more energetically expensive than lactation (Wall-Scheffler et al. 2007). This is another point where cooperation may be important; there is value in having others (e.g., fathers, grandparents, older siblings) help carry the infant (Gettler, chapter 8, and Hrdy, chapter 9, both this volume).

This burden can also be eased by the use of a carrying device, such as a sling (Tanner and Zihlman 1976), which can reduce the energetic costs of carrying by as much as 16% (Wall-Scheffler 2012). Furthermore, traveling long distances while carrying infants has been proposed to increase the interbirth interval by diverting calories from reproduction (Lee 1980). Cooperative caretak-ing in conjunction with long-distance travel probably served to decrease the interbirth interval. There is abundant cross-cultural evidence for family members, including older siblings, and other members of the social group sharing the job of carrying babies.

Certainly, cuteness is, to some extent, in the eyes of the beholder, but by all accounts human infants tend to be immensely appealing to those who matter—not just their mothers but often others as well (Hrdy 1999, 2009). A growing body of neurological, endocrinological, and observational evidence indicates that such caretakers have evolved to find looking at and even caring for infants rewarding and in some cases even socioendocrinologically transformative (Gettler, chapter 8, this volume; Hrdy 2009 and chapter 9, this volume). Returning the favor, human infants enter the world primed to interact with parents and alloparents alike. And why not? From birth, the human infant enters a social world that is not only critical to his survival, but that introduces likely contexts for his ensuing social life. Within months, Hrdy (2009, 2015) argues, human infants are far more capable than chimpanzees with regard to their cognitive and interactive potentials, particularly their interest in monitoring others, assessing their potential to help or hinder, and determining how best to appeal to them.

Human babies exhibit a mosaic of physical helplessness and sophisticated social, manipulative skills. As Turke puts it, human babies exhibit "the combination of physical altriciality and precociality in which children who cannot jump off the ground with both feet can control and manipulate every adult they come in contact with" (P. Turke, pers. comm., 2015). Or, as Trivers (1985:155) has put it, "An offspring cannot fling its mother to the ground and nurse at will. . . . [Rather] it should attempt to *induce* more investment than the parent is selected to give." Human newborns' motor helplessness is paired with socially and emotionally manipulative skills.

It has been argued that the human infant is more helpless at birth than most monkeys and apes, but in the first few hours after birth, the infant has unusual behavioral and physical characteristics that enhance his attractiveness to his mother and others who are present. These behaviors include "primary walking," the Moro reflex, crawling movements, and even smiling. The infant state referred to as the "quiet-alert state" is typically short and fleeting in the first weeks after birth, but it is prolonged in the first hour after birth

(Desmond et al. 1963; Widström et al. 2011). This is the state when the infant is wide awake, can follow voices and faces, and can focus on objects and people, and it is the state in which most learning takes place. It is also a time when the mother is alert and when the baby is highly attractive to her and others. It is an optimal time for social bonds to form. Right after birth, when oxytocin and other socioendocrinological transformations are enhancing the mother's affiliative responses (Carter 2014), is also an opportune time for her infant to engage in ways that "prove" that he is worth the prolonged investment that human young require (Hrdy 1999). In addition to fueling a rapidly developing brain, Hrdy proposes, fetally induced fat accumulation just prior to the infant passing through a tightly constrained birth canal may secondarily serve the neonate as a signal of robustness, effectively saying, "Mom, go ahead and bond. I am a good bet for surviving." Thus, even in his first hour of life, the human infant, seemingly helpless in so many ways, has an array of emotionally and socially manipulative behaviors and characteristics that lead others to invest heavily in him for decades.

Of course, being born early cannot be only costly (and risky), or it would have been selected against. Human babies must gain some advantages to being born when the brain is still undergoing rapid growth, most notably the advantage of being exposed to external stimuli in the environment, which they soak up at a remarkable rate and use to manipulate the world. For example, at a very early stage of life, human babies interact socially and emotionally with those around them. Decades ago, Meltzoff and Moore (1977) showed that newborn babies between 12 and 21 days old imitate a number of different facial and hand gestures that they see in adults. Mandel and colleagues (1995) showed that long before they are able to produce language, 4.5-month-old human infants are able to recognize sound patterns (such as their own names) that have "special personal significance for them." Ferry and colleagues (2013) showed that human infants quickly tune in to the patterns of human language. They are born preferring to listen to primate vocalizations (either human or nonhuman) over artificial sounds, but within months they come to prefer human speech and finally the language most commonly spoken around them. Trevarthen and Aitken (2001:4) claimed that the "existence of specialized innate 'human-environment-expectant' social regulatory and intersubjective functions in the infant mind has been firmly established." Trevathan (1987:149) argued that the advantages that come from being born before much brain growth has occurred include the fact that the infant is exposed to a rich set of sensory stimuli in the environment at an earlier stage in development, encouraging greater plasticity and flexibility, which are important components in learning. Hrdy (2009), Konner (2011), and Martin (2013) all have reviewed literature emphasizing the point that in addition to the adaptive benefits of lengthening (i.e., prolonging) childhood, there are advantages to exposing the human infant to his social, emotional, and physical environments at an earlier stage in brain growth and development and hence at a more helpless and also malleable developmental stage (Semendeferi and Hanson, chapter 7, this volume).

Organization of This Volume

The contributors to the SAR advanced seminar and this book represent a wide range of expertise in human evolution and biological anthropology. We came together to address the question of how infant helplessness evolved and how it has shaped our species in terms of both our biology and our behavior. Our discussions were wide ranging, including such topics as what to call helpless human infants that would fully describe the unusual mosaic of features that they possess, what factors determine infants' developmental state at birth, when infant helplessness began to play a role in our evolutionary history, who takes care of infants and why, in what ways human infants are costly, why people invest so heavily in infants, and whether or not the human infant is as important a player in the story of human evolution as man the hunter and woman the gatherer. As anthropologists, we place great importance on humans' distinctive biocultural adaptation. As seminar participants, we had a high tolerance for provocative speculation (some of which is reflected in the chapters in this volume), hoping it would stimulate investigation and further research.

In chapter 2, "The Obstetrical Dilemma Unraveled," Holly Dunsworth critiques the obstetrical dilemma hypothesis by pursuing three questions: (1) How difficult is it to pass an encephalized baby through a bipedal pelvis? (2) Would a larger pelvis that would make birth easier compromise female locomotion? and (3) Are human babies born early because of pelvic constraints? She argues that there is no evidence that the human pelvis uniquely restricts the length of gestation and neonatal brain growth; rather, gestation length and fetal growth across primates appear to be limited by maternal metabolism (EGG hypothesis). She suggests, as have Wells and colleagues (2012), that difficult birth as we know it today is a somewhat recent phenomenon due to modern technology, medical intervention, improved nutrition and health, and changes in lifestyle rather than due to limits imposed by bipedalism and encephalization. This is clearly an area that deserves further inquiry, since the obstetrical dilemma is invoked in several other chapters in this volume, some of which rely heavily on the original argument that the bipedal pelvis places restrictions on the amount of brain growth that can occur before birth (although certainly all of the contributors recognize the importance of metabolic factors).

Marcia Ponce de León and Christoph Zollikofer further consider the obstetrical dilemma in chapter 3, "Primate Birth at the Extremes." They examine obstetric and metabolic constraints on birth based on three-dimensional fetopelvic relationships in several primate species. Their analysis includes primates whose neonates are large relative to their mothers (e.g., *callitrichids*, *Hylobates*, and *Homo*) and those that have small neonates relative to maternal body size (e.g., *Symphalangus*, and the three great apes). Obstetrical dilemmas are problematic for many of these species, and evolutionary adaptations to solve the dilemmas are varied, including twinning in the callitrichids and rotational birth in *Homo*. Using biomedical imaging technology and modeling the metabolic demands of the fetus and placenta in several nonhuman primate species, they conclude that anatomical constraints are even greater in small primates than in humans and that metabolic constraints probably limit neonatal size for most primate species. While retaining some aspects of the obstetrical dilemma hypothesis, Zollikofer and Ponce de León urge consideration of human birth within the more general framework of maternal-offspring conflict, which accommodates both anatomic and metabolic factors.

An enduring question is, when in human evolutionary history did our ancestors begin giving birth to extremely helpless infants? Answering this question must be grounded in the fossil and archaeological record and may tell us something about the origins of extended families, cooperative childcare, and other characteristics of humans that we argue are traceable, in part, to helpless infants. In chapter 4, "Brains, Birth, Bipedalism, and the Mosaic Evolution of the Helpless Human Infant," Jeremy DeSilva argues that the evolution of habitual terrestrial bipedalism required a form of intergroup interaction, given the inability of the infant to cling to his mother without assistance from her. The helpless infant limited the mother's mobility, and she benefited from assistance from others. DeSilva argues that securing assistance from alloparents meant that humans could afford energetically expensive infants while reducing the birth interval, so that overlapping dependent offspring became possible. He concludes that the behavioral adaptations of alloparenting occurred as early as the Pliocene with the australopiths. This behavioral step allowed the subsequent evolution of the large and developmentally helpless infants of the Pleistocene, and these aspects continue to characterize our species today.

Perhaps the most costly aspect of reproduction for humans is breastfeeding, the subject of the fifth chapter, "Infancy by Design," by E. A. Quinn. As already mentioned, lactation is far more costly in energetic terms than is gestation and, as Quinn notes, represents the bulk of reproductive costs over a woman's lifetime. Quinn documents this and examines variability within and between populations (as well as in individual mothers) in ways of meeting these costs and balancing them with other life demands. We are familiar with the idea that mammalian species produce milk that is tailored to the growth and developmental needs of the offspring, but milk is far more complex than that. Milk is a living substance containing nutrients, probiotics, immune factors, oligosaccharides, and stem cells (to name a few of its components). Furthermore, mothers are able to actively manage (subconsciously, of course) the milk they produce depending on an individual infant's demands, available resources, coexisting factors (e.g., pathogens), and possibly even the sex of the infant. Undoubtedly, these costs and associated challenges have subjected mothers to intense selection on their reproductive physiology throughout human evolution. Although these costs are borne by most mammals, Quinn's research highlights not only the extent of these costs, but also the individuality of mother's milk.

In chapter 6, "Baby the Trendsetter," Dean Falk plays off the titles and concepts mentioned above ("man the hunter" and "woman the gatherer") to focus attention on the role that infant helplessness played in language evolution and in finer nuances of brain development and neurological organization. She introduces three sequential "evo-devo" trends in human evolution that make our species distinctive: (1) the delay in locomotor development that occurred with the origin of bipedalism, which made it impossible for infants to cling to their mothers without support, thus necessitating periodic physical separations of mothers and infants; (2) the seeking of contact comfort by separated infants that included new ways of crying, which led to reciprocal vocal communications with mothers that seeded the emergence of motherese; and (3) the accelerated brain growth during gestation and the first postnatal year due primarily to selection for grammatical language, which sustained the subsequent evolution of hominin brain size and the emergence of higher-order cognitive abilities. Falk suggests that rather than occurring as a direct result of pelvic modifications for bipedalism, the obstetrical dilemma emerged more recently in conjunction with the trend for ongoing perinatal acceleration in brain size. These three evo-devo trends, which continue to be manifested in contemporary neurotypical infants, are conserved in interesting ways in infants with Asperger syndrome.

Chapter 7 by Katerina Semendeferi and Kari Hanson, "Plastic and Heterogeneous," summarizes studies of the developmental plasticity of the human infant brain. The authors argue that postnatal neuronal development depends on input from the environment, especially the social and cultural systems into which humans are born. Human and nonhuman primate brains differ in neural development in ways that reveal humans' capacities for cultural acquisition, including language. In their chapter, Semendeferi and Hanson highlight some of the differences between human and nonhuman primate brain developmental trajectories and propose that certain neurological disorders (e.g., Williams syndrome and autism) can expand our understanding of the evolution of cognition in humans. Their focus takes us well beyond simple differences in brain size and emphasizes the importance of immaturity at birth for providing opportunities for social and cultural growth and maturation.

Recognizing that testosterone is important for reproductive, physiological, and behavioral functions in men, Lee Gettler in "Testosterone, Fatherhood, and Social Networks" (chapter 8) argues that the ability to reduce T production in the presence of dependent and vulnerable infants may have been selected for in human evolution because it contributed positively to reproductive success. Consider that high T production is beneficial in mating competition and mate attraction, but may compromise survival through immunosuppressive effects and increased exposure to dangerous conditions. For most mammalian males, elevated T does not usually contribute to increased paternal care and in fact may be inconsistent with affiliative behaviors toward young infants. In species in which biparental care has evolved, Gettler argues that the ability of males to reduce T production when parenting would have been selected for if the behavior resulted in higher infant survival. In the model he presents, men who were able to reduce T production in the context of male-female affiliation and infant caretaking benefited not only from greater reproductive success, but also from participation in broad social networks and within-group cooperation characteristic of recent human social organization. There is evidence of a great deal of flexibility in this ability, however, which is to be expected given the variety of social and ecological circumstances under which human populations exist. Even with this evident plasticity, it appears that psychobiological factors related to T regulation are involved in increased caretaking by fathers, and thus contributed to the evolution of the helpless infant.

Sarah Hrdy in chapter 9, "Of Marmosets, Men, and the Transformative Power of Babies," focuses on male allomothers (fathers and other males) among marmosets and other callitrichids that engage in extensive care and provisioning of the young. She builds on two decades of work on cooperative breeders to argue that maternal commitment to young varies with the available paternal and alloparental care and is more contingent in primates where mothers must rely on allomaternal care than in primates with exclusively maternal care. Whereas mothers in most primate species, certainly including wild chimpanzees, are highly protective of their young and rarely tolerate contact from other adults, human mothers allow others to hold their infants within minutes of birth.

Hrdy proposes that mothers among cooperative breeders have a stake in exposing others to needy infants so as to take advantage of their responsiveness to infantile signals, such as the down regulation of testosterone in males. These and other transformations induced by exposure to cute babies enhance alloparents' readiness to care for and even provision them. Her chapter describes intricate negotiations as both mother and father assess how much investment the other is likely to provide and adjust their own commitment levels accordingly. For humans and their distant callitrichid relations alike, maternal costs from rearing young are so great that those anticipating low levels of allomaternal assistance may abandon their young altogether. At the heart of this high-stakes coordination game, relying as it does on the highly conserved potentials of nurture present in vertebrate males, lies the magnetic appeal of needy infants and their transformative effects on those in contact with them. When mothers delay, or fail to respond to infant needs altogether, having fathers and others around to pick up the slack further facilitates the evolution of costly infants and accelerates the evolution of cute ones.

In chapter 10, "Forget Ye Not the Mother-Infant Dyad!" James McKenna writes about his work on the legitimacy of mother-infant co-sleeping with breastfeeding (in the absence of known hazards), a sleeping arrangement for which he has coined the word "breastsleeping." His chapter focuses on the challenges of reconciling the preeminence of the mother-infant dyad in a world that must also acknowledge maternal agency and the critical role allo-mothers continue to play in the evolution of the helpless and energetically expensive human infant. Here and in many previous publications, he argues that the mother provides unique physiological regulatory effects, including breastmilk, which is now known to contain components that influence brain architecture in specific ways (see Quinn, chapter 5, this volume). McKenna responds to a particularly thoughtful feminist critique by Bernice Hausman of his evolutionary narrative, which could give rise to, she suggests, untoward consequences for women's reproductive rights. He points out the irony of this possibility, given that he worked purposefully to construct from anthropo-logical and experimental studies scientific research models that empower women by legitimizing their infant care practices. With the complexity of these issues in mind, he explores ways to respond professionally to the legitimate worries that his model inspires, but at the same time to appreciate the ongoing scientific insights that have empowered women through the knowledge that has been acquired because of it, often in the face of medical opposition.

Conclusion

As with any gathering of minds focused on a set of specific questions, the SAR seminar examining the role of infant helplessness in human evolution produced as many questions as answers. Could the inability to cling to the mother help explain selection for bipedalism, as suggested by Etkin (1954) and elaborated upon by many, including Lovejoy (1981)? Can language origins be traced to mothers soothing their helpless infants when they have been "put down," as suggested by Falk (2009)? Did the need to provision helpless infants lead to increased reliance on tools and animal protein consumption, as suggested by contributors to the *Man the Hunter* volume (Lee and DeVore 1968), Lovejoy (1981), and others? Were the first tools the slings that mothers used to carry their helpless infants, as suggested by Tanner and Zihlman (1976)? Is the prolonged lifespan after menopause due to selection for provisioning and other aspects of infant care by "grandmothers," as suggested by Hawkes (1997) and others? Is food sharing causally related to costly helpless infants? Of course the answers to these questions are, to some extent, yes, as discussed by many contributors to this volume, but we all recognize that no human charac-teristic or behavior can be uniquely traced to infant helplessness. In our view, infant helplessness is an important component of a very complex biocultural adaptation that makes humans an unusual, highly prosocial, and cooperatively breeding species.

Is the helpless human infant as significant a player in the story of human evolution as man the hunter and woman the gatherer? Does human helplessness account for many of the features that make our species distinctive? The chapters that follow offer convincing evidence that we are who we are today, in important ways, because of our costly and cute helpless infants.

Acknowledgments

We thank the School for Advanced Research for giving us the opportunity to spend a stimulating week in Santa Fe in beautiful surroundings, working together on the topic of helpless human infants. We are very grateful to the participants at that advanced seminar (who are also the authors of the chapters in this volume) for their collegiality, outstanding intellectual and critical contributions, and good humor. Finally, we thank the two anonymous reviewers of the manuscript for their helpful and constructive reviews.

Notes

1. "Precocial" comes from the Latin *praecox*, which means "mature before its time." The Latin origin for "altricial" is *alere*, to nourish, and its root is feminine. (An *altrix* is a wet nurse in some translations.) If we considered only the literal Latin translation, then the term "altricial" would be all we would need—human infants are highly dependent on nourishment in almost every conceivable form: nutritional, emotional, social, physical, and developmental. Of course these terms have more technical meanings within biology.

2. We use "he" to refer to the infant throughout the chapter to avoid awkward phrases like "he or she" and to distinguish the infant from the mother, who is always "she."

3. A number of authors have investigated these questions from the point of view of evolutionary psychology and came to similar conclusions about the mosaic nature of the human adaptation with respect to the altriciality-precociality continuum (e.g., Alexander 1990; Turke 2013).

CHAPTER TWO

The Obstetrical Dilemma Unraveled

HOLLY M. DUNSWORTH

The obstetrical (or obstetric) dilemma (OD) hypothesis has been the preferred evolutionary explanation for difficult childbirth and for the underdeveloped state of human neonates ever since it was conceived in the mid-twentieth century.[1] Washburn (1960) is commonly credited, but Schultz (1949) and Krogman (1951) also sparked the idea that difficult and dangerous childbirth originated from a unique human evolutionary history. In a culture that has been heavily influenced by interpretations of the book of Genesis, the OD offers a refreshing, scientific explanation for the consequences of the Fall: difficult labor, dangerous childbirth, and sinful, suffering, helpless babies are not Eve's fault, but evolution's.

Several classic observations have been woven together into the formulation and enduring application and dissemination of the OD. For one, humans are encephalized. Also, our bodies metamorphosed for bipedal posture and locomotion, and this included a restructuring of the pelvis. Further, our pelves are sexually dimorphic; on average, women are absolutely larger in many pelvic dimensions compared to men, particularly in the dimensions of the birth canal, and these differences begin with the onset of puberty. On average, women are slower runners and walkers than men, and on average men outperform women in nearly every type of athletic contest. There is a tight fit between neonate and birth canal, and childbirth assistance is culturally universal. The rotational scheme that many human neonates experience in order to exit the birth canal has been well characterized. And, although primates are deemed to be precocial mammals, siding with horses, whales, and others, newborn humans appear to share some developmental commonalities with altricial mammals, including many rodents and carnivores.

As the OD has taken shape in various forms, it synthesizes all or some of those classic observations. It posits that there is antagonism between selection for encephalization and for bipedalism. Thus, natural selection has placed competing demands on the shape of the female pelvis because increasing encephalization in the hominin lineage demanded an adequately capacious birth canal for safe passage of the newborn, while efficient or sufficient bipedal locomotion required a restriction on pelvic dimensions. Multiple consequences—and some "solutions"—were born of this evolutionary dilemma: compromised female locomotion due to sexually dimorphic, childbirth-adapted hips; a difficult and dangerous childbirth; rotational passage of the fetus; universal assistance during delivery; and relatively underdeveloped neonates requiring intensive and prolonged parental investment. In sum, the OD explains both difficult childbirth and the developmental state of human neonates with a uniquely human pelvic constraint, within a tradition of holding apart those two phenomena as uniquely human.

Because the OD is a well-established explanation in medicine, biology, anatomy, and anthropology (Portmann 1990; Martin 1983; Trinkaus 1984; Rosenberg 1992; Rosenberg and Trevathan 1995, 2002; Wittman and Wall 2007; Weiner et al. 2008; Trevathan et al. 2007; Trevathan 2010; Plunkett et al. 2011; Dunsworth et al. 2012; Wells et al. 2012; Martin 2013), it deserves rigorous evaluation in light of the accumulation of evidence since its inception. That is the aim of this chapter.

I break down the OD into its three major components and consider them one by one: (1) the human birth process—a difficult and dangerous labor—results from passing an encephalized baby through a mother's bipedal pelvis; (2) a larger birth canal that could accommodate a larger, more developed neonate would be detrimental to bipedalism; and (3) because of pelvic constraints, human babies are born early or in a state of "secondary altriciality." At the end of the chapter, I consider whether the OD is still a strong hypothesis, worthy of its prevalence and popularity.

OD Component 1

Although there is variation in many aspects of the childbirth experience within individual women as well as between them, our culture tends to focus on and even typify the traumatic end of the birth spectrum, especially as depicted by Hollywood. The relative ease with which other species appear to give birth and the notoriously traumatic births in our own experiences have influenced how scholars write about the evolution of childbirth. For example, within an OD framework, Konner (2010:n.p.) wrote, "The first three months of life, which have aptly been called the fourth trimester, are a legacy of the necessary early expulsion of human fetuses from the womb to avoid an even worse crunch than childbirth already is. Erect posture, followed by brain expansion, made this necessary. The result is a newborn not exactly asocial, but not yet responsive to social cues, and certainly in need of care."

Regardless of our biased impressions, there is strong reason to assert that humans have it worse than other primates when it comes to labor and childbirth. As captive ape births are increasingly filmed and available for observation, it is apparent how much less stressful the experience can be for some apes, at least compared to the worst outcomes for humans.[2] However, it might be hard to argue that humans have the worst parturition of all the mammals given the trauma and mortality risk that spotted hyenas experience. Mothers birth their litters through their clitorises, and for first-time mothers an estimated 60% of pups suffocate (Frank and Glickland 1994).

The anatomy of the human pelvis is likely contributing to childbirth difficulty. The adoption of upright posture and bipedal locomotion is functionally linked to significant alterations in its shape (e.g., Lovejoy et al. 2009b). The ilia are shorter and broader in hominins and face laterally—a change that has shifted the minor gluteals from their roles as hip extensors to hip abductors, which maintain pelvic stability during the single-leg-support phase of walking and running (Hamner et al. 2010). These morphological changes linked to locomotion have reshaped the hominin birth canal from an anteroposteriorly elongated opening, as seen in other apes, to a short oblong passage (Rosenberg and Trevathan 1995; Schultz 1949; Berge and Goularas 2010). Humans also lack the potential to widen the birth canal by extending the tail, if such a thing can be accomplished with a tail.

In addition, the size of the newborn is likely contributing to childbirth difficulty. Relative to neonatal cranium size, the human birth canal is smaller than in many other primates (Rosenberg and Trevathan 2002; Wells et al. 2012). Because of the tight fit and because from inlet to outlet the birth canal shifts from being widest in the mediolateral plane to widest in the anteroposterior plane, many neonates experience a rotational regime during childbirth in order to pass through the birth canal (Rosenberg and Trevathan 1995). As a result, human neonates are predominantly born facing dorsally, unlike what has been observed in other primates (but see Walrath 2003; Hirata et al. 2011).

Human neonates are also relatively large compared to the mother's body size, which is why neonatal shoulders, not just heads, can contribute to dystocia (abnormal labor progression).

Assistance during childbirth is likely, if subtly, contributing to childbirth difficulty. That nearly all women in nearly all cultures have assistance during labor supports the hypothesis that the development of this social behavior facilitated successful birth during human evolution (Rosenberg and Trevathan 1995). By providing more positive birth outcomes, enduring traditions of assistance may have contributed to the evolution of difficult birth because of the reduced selection against any number of contributors to complications, including the tight fit. Today we have a greater frequency of difficult parturitions perpetuating lines rather than ending them, and this trend has only increased with the adoption of increasingly frequent cesarean sections in many human populations. Assistance and intervention during childbirth could potentially explain not only increases in childbirth difficulty, but also some increases in stature: neonatal size is correlated to adult size (Eide et al. 2005), and if larger neonates are more frequently passing safely through the womb, then a higher frequency of larger adults will result. These larger adults can in turn birth larger neonates. Short stature is a well-known risk factor for difficult labor, and the lowest cesarean rates in the world are found in Nordic countries and the Netherlands, where women are often tall and where there is diminished health and nutrition inequality as well (Wells et al. 2012; Liston 2003).

At present, our impressions of childbirth are biased to a degree by the medical industry. In the United States, fetopelvic disproportion is considered to be uncommon, yet it is one of the only, or *the* only, quantifiable cause of dystocia, so therefore it is not uncommon as an impetus for c-section (Scott et al. 1994). Risk of fetopelvic disproportion can be gauged manually, but in the mid-twentieth century, as c-sectioning was beginning to be more prevalent (and as the OD was being conceived in anthropology), pregnant women were sometimes x-rayed in order to predict whether they were at risk for fetopelvic disproportion, and therefore whether they should be induced early or schedule a c-section. In the beginning stages of medical c-sectioning, the rate in the United States was 5.5% but by 1970 it rose to 25%, and it leveled off at 32.8% in 2010 (Hamilton et al. 2011). More experienced doctors perform fewer of these procedures than do their younger colleagues (Scott et al. 1994). Labor and birth position in a restrictive hospital setting (e.g., not taking advantage of the effects of gravity and relaxin, and often working against them), as well as assistance from an obstetrician rather than a midwife, seem to contribute to the difficulty women face in childbirth and recovery (Gupta and Nikodem 2000; Shorten et al. 2002).

Wells and colleagues (2012) have provided an up-to-date, in-depth, and nuanced discussion of the complex contributors to perinatal mortality. It is difficult to hypothesize, let alone quantify, one of these many contributors, fetopelvic disproportion, as a selective pressure across space and time, especially when the available demographic data often include infant deaths up to 1 year of age, and "maternal mortality" statistics can include women's deaths due to abortion and to blood loss from placental and uterine problems that arise after a successful passing of the newborn.

There are several selective pressures acting together on human pregnancy, many of which are unrelated to the fit between neonate and bony birth canal (Brown et al. 2013). However, where c-sections or other interventions are not performed, pelvic morphology determines the maximum size of the neonate that can pass through the birth canal safely. That is, selection acts against neonates too big to fit through the birth canal and against birth canals that are too narrow to birth babies. But there is a significant theoretical difference between describing a proximate selection scenario like that and positing, as the OD does, that difficult childbirth is ultimately due to selection for unique and constrained locomotor traits in the human pelvis, or that constrained pelvic anatomy has required a uniquely shortened human gestation. Support for the OD requires deeper digging.

OD Component 2

The OD hypothesis predicts that the increased mediolateral width of the female pelvis leads to a decrease in functionally adequate walking and running, and that further broadening of the pelvis would be detrimental to efficiency, economy, or performance, or would increase injury risk, or a combination of these negative outcomes. The dilemma this causes when growing large-brained fetuses results in difficult childbirth and gives the appearance of a primary mechanical constraint on gestation length as well (which I consider below). Is the female pelvis, particularly in the dimensions of the birth canal, constrained by selection for locomotion? I consider whether difficult childbirth is ultimately explained by selective constraints for a bipedally sufficient female pelvis.

A strong assumption underlying the OD explanations for difficult human childbirth is that, for mammals, "it is far more efficient to develop brain tissue by transferring resources directly across a placenta. After birth, the mother must first convert her resources into milk, which is then transferred to the infant for digestion. This to some extent explains why human development in the womb is pushed right up to the limit allowed by the dimensions of the birth canal" (Martin 2013:129). So, according to OD expectations, if pelvic morphology were not constrained by the mechanical demands of bipedalism, selection would have favored a change in hominin pelvic shape to better accommodate a prolonged gestation and thus a larger neonate. Presumably, as is commonly vocalized in OD discussions, the pelvis would be large enough to reduce childbirth difficulty so that humans would be more like apes and other mammals that have easier or less risky labors. Of course, there could be some human-specific reason (adaptive or otherwise) to maximize gestation that is absent in other species, causing us to push gestation to the pelvic limit, but that has not yet been identified, and such considerations would have to explain other species that have tight fits between neonate and bony birth canal, like some monkeys (for more on this, see chapter 3).

Regardless of whether humans and other mammals maximize gestation in order to delay costly lactation, for the OD to explain childbirth difficulty (and also gestation length) we need to establish that bipedalism is preventing the birth canal from getting larger. In the updated or revisited terms of the OD, selection favored fetal rotation and childbirth assistance instead of alterations in pelvic shape (Rosenberg and Trevathan 1995; Ruff 1995). But the question remains: Is the size of the birth canal constrained? One way to approach this is to ask whether the female pelvis, which is on average wider in many dimensions than the male pelvis, is worse at bipedal locomotion in any significant aspects.

Since the relevant experiments on humans are difficult or impossible, researchers use several indirect approaches to this problem. The first is to ask whether women are less efficient or less economical walkers and runners, or to ask whether their locomotion is somehow compromised. Studies have measured the metabolic costs of walking and running in men and women with varying results (Warrener et al. 2015). The inconsistency of the results derives partly from methodological differences and the ways in which metabolic costs were normalized across these studies. However, the results highlight that the expectation of the OD hypothesis, that wider pelves negatively affect locomotor economy, is not borne out by laboratory studies of walking and running costs. Multiple studies have shown running efficiency to be equal in males and females when normalized to body mass and distance (Warrener et al. 2015). This contradicts one of the expectations of the OD, which is that because females have wider pelves they should produce higher muscle forces at the hip to stabilize the pelvis, thereby increasing the metabolic cost of locomotion (Hamner et al. 2010; Ruff 1995, 1998; Lovejoy et al. 1973; Berge 1994). However, the OD view is based on static mechanical models of the human pelvis that do not accurately reflect the dynamics of walking and running gaits. When considered part of a dynamic system, pelvic width is a poor predictor of the cost of walking and running, which calls into question the biomechanical relationship between pelvic width, hip abductor function, locomotor cost, and locomotor efficiency (Warrener et al. 2015; Dunsworth et al. 2012). Thus, it is difficult at present to demonstrate that wide or feminine pelves are worse for locomotion. There is also a small but growing literature on the locomotor *adaptations* of female pelvic morphology (Wall-Scheffler 2012).

Constraints on the pelvis could be less obviously or less directly tied to locomotor performance or efficiency. For example, the anterior-posterior dimensions could be constrained for locomotor or other biomechanical reasons. The wider pelvis and greater valgus angle of the knee in females could relate to pelvic tilt and increased hip adduction and knee abduction, which could negatively impact locomotion and increase injury risk (Smith et al. 2002; Cho et al. 2004; Ferber et al. 2003; Hewett 2005). However, the risk of knee injury in females is not as well explained by skeletal morphology as it is by neuromuscular and hormonal processes affecting control and strength (Hewett 2006; Rozzi et al. 1999; Powers 2010). The biomechanics of pregnancy may adaptively constrain pelvic dimensions, because as fetal loads grow, forces on the maternal skeleton change (Whitcome et al. 2007). Further, limitations to tissue strength and other properties of soft tissues of the pelvic floor, for instance, may constrain pelvic dimensions, especially during pregnancy or as a result of it. However, pelvic prolapse also occurs in domestic animals with quadrupedally adapted pelves, not just in bipeds (Noakes et al. 2001). To add to the complexity, thermoregulatory factors may also constrain the pelvis (Ruff 2010), while drift—requiring somewhat lifted constraint—may explain global pelvic variation (Betti et al. 2013).

Arguably, males' dominance in athletic ability has contributed to OD thinking. Elite male runners consistently achieve running speeds about

10% faster than those of women (Thibault et al. 2010): however there is little evidence that the male pelvis is a driving factor. The faster running speeds achieved by men are partly a consequence of anatomical features of the lower limbs (allowing for greater stride length and greater ground force production per step at a given speed), hormonal differences contributing to greater muscle mass and less fat, and differences in the cardiovascular system that contribute to higher VO_2 max (Nelson et al. 1977; Perez-Gomez et al. 2007; Weyand et al. 2000; Daniels et al. 1977; Ramsbottom et al. 1987; Billat et al. 2003).

Many who participate in OD discussions wonder why the birth canal does not widen to make childbirth easier or less dangerous, but perhaps it already has. Sexual dimorphism in the human pelvis is considered to be the result of natural selection for successful childbirth. A mother with too-narrow pelvic genes is not likely to pass on those genes to her children. For any species that gives birth through a bony birth canal, it is a striking example of natural selection constantly in action.

Across human populations, females are, on average, smaller bodied than males but have many absolutely wider dimensions of the pelvis (Simpson et al. 2008; Tague 1992). Differences in aspects of pelvic shape that directly impact obstetric success are the most pronounced—particularly the bispinous diameter (the distance between the bony spine of each ischium) and the mediolateral outlet dimensions. Bi-acetabular width is also greater in females than in males, but the differences are less clear at the pelvic inlet, and males tend to have wider bi-iliac diameters (the maximum distance between the crest of each ilium) than do females. Males and females are relatively monomorphic in pelvic shape until puberty, when differential growth in specific regions of the pelvis acts to remodel the pelvic cavity in both sexes (LaVelle 1995). The resulting sexual dimorphism supports the notion that selection has favored the expansion or maintenance of a wide birth canal in females for successful parturition and is consistent with the observation that in other primates where the neonatal cranium is larger relative to the birth canal, pelvic sexual dimorphism is greater (Ridley 1995). (At present, it does not appear that anyone has demonstrated that female locomotion in these nonhuman primates is lacking or is compromised.) Sexual selection might contribute to pelvic dimorphism as well (Singh and Young 1995), and so might the locomotor benefits to females (Wall-Scheffler 2012).

The obstetric hypothesis for pelvic dimorphism is strong because there is little basis for disputing that selection is acting differently on male and female pelves. For evolution to continue, newborns must fit through the female pelvis. There is also no disputing that selection is maintaining locomotor adequacy in both male and female pelves, despite the variation. However, for the OD to find support, it needs to be shown that the female pelvis is also under constant selection to be constrained for bipedalism. This scenario to explain an upper limit on female pelvis size is harder to demonstrate, as discussed above, and it implies that males with their many smaller dimensions are ideal or more optimized for bipedalism or, alternatively, that locomotion-related selection is different or stronger on the male body (Wall-Scheffler 2012).

One way to examine whether males or females are experiencing stronger selection in the dimensions of the pelvis is to assess variability. When skeletal variation is compared among males and females, overall but particularly in the dimensions of the birth canal, females do not appear to be less variable (Betti et al. 2013; Tague 1989), and thus they do not seem to be experiencing stronger stabilizing selection than are males (Kurki 2013). This kind of evidence does not necessarily refute antagonistic selection acting uniquely on the female pelvis, but it is not support for it either.

Because there is no good reason at present to suppose that the female form leads to suboptimal or compromised locomotion and potentially lower fitness, and because the female form is the gateway to further evolution, it is possible that the male form arose by selection for male-specific locomotor reasons, by relaxed selection, by relatively neutral processes, or as a by-product of selection for seemingly separate but developmentally linked biological traits. And, of course, these hypotheses tend to downplay all the retained overlap between males and females in ranges of variation in both anatomy and locomotor behavior.

Given the current knowns and unknowns, it is possible that when it comes to the OD, sexual dimorphism is a red herring. Sex differences may affect locomotion, but that does not necessarily lead to the conclusion that either form is compromised or lacking in comparison to the other, or that either form is at its limit and cannot evolve any more divergently from the other. Researchers—especially in anatomy, osteology, and paleontology—may be biased by perceptions that the male is the typical or ideal form for a given species, or that such a thing exists at all.

Another approach to the question of a pelvic constraint is to ask how much the bony birth canal would need to increase in order to accommodate a human newborn with a bigger brain, and if that hypothetical pelvis would be a detriment to bipedalism. Modeling the neonatal head as a sphere and accounting for soft tissue, the diameter of a human neonatal cranium would be approximately 3 cm larger at 16 months, which is when the minimum hypothetical developmental equivalent to a chimpanzee newborn is reached (DeSilva and Lesnik 2006). In order to deliver this larger neonate, the maternal pelvis would need to accommodate an additional 3 cm within the dimensions of the birth canal. The most constricted mediolateral dimension of the birth canal, the bispinous diameter, already varies by 3 cm among human female populations (see Simpson et al. 2008), without any obvious or systematic impact on locomotion. This runs contrary to the expectations of the OD that "women couldn't walk" (Small 1998) if the birth canal were widened to accommodate a more developed neonate. Epstein (1973) worked through this same exercise roughly 40 years ago with older estimates of brain size, found that 4 cm more was required, and concluded the same. More recently Wells and colleagues (2012) undertook the same thought experiment, arrived at similar estimates, and concluded that "actual variability in neonatal brain volume and in maternal pelvic dimensions between individuals is massive compared with trivial changes in the same dimensions within mothers or offspring that could potentially reduce the magnitude of the [tight fit at birth]" (10).

In sum, the current evidence does not allow us to conclude that normal variation in the dimensions of the pelvis are significantly affecting locomotion or locomotor-related injury, let alone locomotor-related fitness in space and time. Further, it is unclear whether locomotor performance, economy, efficiency, or sufficiency (or some or all of these) is the appropriate measure for testing the OD. There is currently no strong evidence to support the notion that selection for locomotion prevents selection for increased birth canal dimensions. There could be other constraints on the bony birth canal, but they have not been identified yet. Researchers have yet to establish whether and how average sex differences in locomotor performance should inform reconstructions of human evolutionary history. While sexual dimorphism in the human pelvis appears to be linked to childbirth, the common perception that male pelvic morphology is more advantageous than female morphology for locomotion is not supported by current evidence. This is not to say that pelvic width could expand indefinitely with no consequences to locomotion or to other mechanical issues and soft tissue. However, overall, childbirth difficulty does not presently require the OD as the explanation. Next, I explore whether the developmental state of human neonates does.

OD Component 3

Precociality is ancient. It is as old as, or even older than, placoderm fishes, and it is probably the primitive condition in birds as well (Long 2012). However, for mammals, Martin (2013) asserted—based on embryological evidence and parsimony, given the marsupial strategy—that the primitive condition is to birth altricial young (like present-day carnivores and rodents). Long pregnancies producing precocial and often single offspring (like present-day ungulates and cetaceans) evolved separately in at least 10 mammal lineages, including the order Primates (Martin 2013).

Like myriad life forms, humans are born before they are fully developed and can function as adults. But among precocial primates, humans are often set apart as "secondarily altricial" (Portmann 1990) because our infants are relatively less developed behaviorally at birth than the others are. Some observers have considered human neonates to be premature or even so-called fetal apes that experience an "exterogestation" (Montagu 1961). It has been estimated, and repeated in many publications, scholarly and otherwise, that a gestation length of 18–21 months would be needed for a human baby to be born at an equivalent developmental stage as a chimpanzee neonate—an estimate normally based on relative brain size at birth (Portmann 1990; Gould 1977). This can be modified based on DeSilva and Lesnik's work (2006) to be a minimum of 16 months' gestation since they showed that at 7 months of age a human infant reaches the same relative brain size as a neonatal chimpanzee.

Secondary altriciality has long been hailed as a significant human trait because of the reproductive and social strategies that vulnerable human babies demand. However, comparing humans to altricial mammals (like carnivores, rodents, and lagomorphs) is arguably more poetic than scientific (Martin 2013; Robson et al. 2006; and chapter 1, this volume). Our naked skin is not akin to the furless infancy of rats. Unlike those of pups and cubs, human eyes and ears are open. Altricial mammals tend to have litters, and precocial ones tend to birth singletons. In addition, it appears that humans begin walking just when expected, with age of onset timed like that of other mammals if brain and body size and foot position are considered, running contrary to common perceptions that we begin walking later (Garwicz et al. 2009).

The main element of human development that does not appear to align with precocial placental mammals or primates is our relatively immature nervous system at birth, contributing to the immaturity of infant vision, motor neuronal control, and balance, for example. This condition helps to explain the inability of human neonates to grasp and hold on to their mother (for a deeper consideration of human infants' grasping anatomy and ability, and other perspectives on human helplessness, see Trevathan and Rosenberg, chapter 1, and DeSilva, chapter 4, both this volume). Because humans are not born with absolutely smaller brains than other primates, it could be that some cognitive and emotional connections get established at the cost of a delay of motor neuronal ones. Further, precociality is not a monolithic category against which to contrast human neonatal behavior and development.

Along the spectrum of mammalian precociality, anthropoids as a group are less capable and less independent at birth because they have extended ontogenies related to developing a large brain and its functions. Among anthropoids, chimpanzee infants are even more helpless, with slow development and a long period of dependency. For the first few months of their lives, chimpanzee infants are actively alert for only 10% of the day (see references in Hrdy 2009) and are largely carried, held, and manipulated by their mothers. This is a so-called precocial mammal, but it is hardly precocial in comparison to a horse foal. Chimpanzees are born without tails or relatively large feet, both of which aid developing monkeys, like rhesus macaques, not only in clinging to a mobile mother but in behaving more independently during ontogeny than chimpanzees do (Dunsworth 2006).

Again, among anthropoids, Fragaszy and colleagues (2004) have described capuchins as relatively altricial too, given how they are only able to thermoregulate within a narrow temperature range and have less postural control and locomotor ability just after birth compared to Old World monkeys and many platyrrhines. Infant Old World monkeys are walking quadrupedally within the first few days after birth, but capuchins are incapable of supporting their torsos in such a fashion until after about 5 weeks of age. It cannot be coincidence that neonatal capuchins have the smallest relative brain size (~50%) of all primates, save for chimpanzees (~40%) and humans (~30%), meaning that they, like us, have more postnatal brain growth to accomplish compared to other primates. The prioritization of brain development over muscle development could help explain the general case and also some specific cases of anthropoid immaturity compared to many other precocial neonates, and so could the heterochrony of regional musculature development in the body (Walker 2009; Grand 1992).

Given the trend toward greater altriciality among encephalized primates, humans might be better described as "less precocial" and considered along that spectrum with others in the order, rather than singled out as secondarily altricial. Regardless of how we label it, the relatively greater helplessness of human neonates has been traditionally regarded as an important departure from other primates. Thus, it is neither fundamentally inappropriate nor automatically erroneous to explain this phenomenon along with other differences between us and them. The proximate difference might be explained by the smaller brain, relative to adult brain size, of a human neonate at birth compared to a chimpanzee. But this in turn has traditionally begged for an ultimate explanation, which has been that this decrease in human precociality evolved due to antagonistic selection for bipedalism and encephalization, two prominent, distinctive features of the hominin lineage (OD). While hominins experienced encephalization, they would have experienced increasingly longer pregnancies if the birth canal had not been constrained by selection for bipedal locomotion. Therefore, a relatively short gestation is a solution to this obstetrical dilemma, and a relatively small neonatal brain, causing less precocial neonatal behavior than observed in other primates, is the consequence.

Portmann (1990) offered an alternative to the OD to explain the state of secondary altriciality by coining another term: the "extrauterine spring" (ES) hypothesis. In this hypothesis, an early birth provides a rich period of stimulation and learning that is crucial for the development of human cognitive and neuromuscular function. It is well established that social and environmental stimulation is indeed crucial for child development (Neubauer and Hublin 2012; Bogin 2006), and studies of perceptual and cognitive development in premature infants provide support for the importance of stimulation. The onset of three-dimensional perception appears to occur at the same rate in preterm babies as full-term ones, suggesting that this ability is not a scheduled life history trait but rather an environmentally determined one (Jandó et al. 2012). According to the ES, the pelvis does not limit gestation and fetal growth; the benefits of life outside the mother do. Presumably, persistent selection for slightly premature births, while selection was ratcheting up brain size, led to this so-called extrauterine fourth trimester. Rather than resulting from an adaptive trade-off or a compromise, as in the OD, early birth is adaptive in its own right with the ES.

The OD and ES perspectives emphasize the relatively small human neonatal brain when compared to adult brain size. According to the OD and the ES, additional brain growth would be accomplished through maternal investment in utero if not for their respective adaptive scenarios, requiring it to occur after birth. However, both the OD and the ES are weakened by the fact that human gestation is only short from the point of view of the infant brain. That is, the fetal human brain accomplishes relatively less growth toward adult brain size (30%) than those of all other primates (chimpanzees at 40% are the next closest). But when one looks at absolute gestation length, human gestation, at roughly 38 weeks, is absolutely longer by a few weeks than those of *Pan* and *Gorilla*. Life history comparisons have shown that human gestation length is equivalent to or even slightly longer than expected for a primate of our adult body mass (Dunsworth et al. 2012). Additionally, the idea that human maternal investment in the developing fetus is limited by a shortened time in the womb is incongruent with the observation that both neonatal brain size and body size are as great or greater in human infants than expected relative to maternal body mass (Dunsworth et al. 2012). When these observations are considered, a third explanation for human gestation length and the developmental state of the neonate arises: human gestation is limited by the same overall constraints that limit many other species' pregnancies, regardless of whether they have a tight fit at birth.

What could be limiting gestation and fetal growth if not the pelvis? The EGG (energetics, gestation, and growth) model posits that limitations to gestation and fetal growth are metabolic (Dunsworth et al. 2012). By modeling fetal and maternal metabolism as ever-increasing and competing energetic demands, it appears that a longer human gestation is not feasible because as the fetus develops its energy needs rapidly outstrip the maternal metabolic capabilities, reaching a crossover point by the ninth month in utero (figure 2.1). For humans, the cascade of hormones that triggers birth in response to reaching this limit is described by Ellison's (2001a) metabolic crossover (MC) hypothesis (see also Dunsworth et al. 2012). Evidence to support the MC includes, first, that preterm parturition (that is not the result of infection) is associated with elevated levels of corticotropin-releasing hormone in the maternal circulation, indicating an accelerated trajectory of maternal catabolism. On the other hand, uncontrolled gestational diabetes is commonly associated with postterm parturition. Although substantial variation in the energetic demands of pregnancy and lactation has been documented both between subjects and in population-level comparisons (Dufour and Sauthier 2002), the analysis of metabolic data, based on doubly labeled water studies, shows that the mother's basal metabolic rate remains approximately at late-stage pregnancy levels after

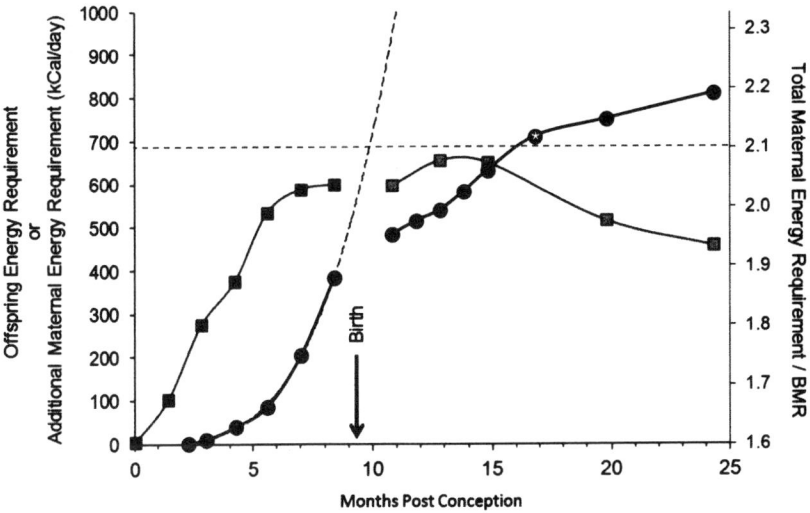

Figure 2.1. Metabolic constraints on gestation length and fetal size (EGG). Fetal energy demands (black circles) increase exponentially during gestation. Maternal energy expenditures (black squares) rise during the first two trimesters but reach a metabolic ceiling in the third, as total energy requirements approach 2.0 × basal metabolic rate (BMR). Projected fetal energy requirements for growth beyond 9 months (dark dashed line) quickly exceed the maximum sustainable metabolic rates for human mothers (horizontal dashed line). After birth (arrow), infant energy demands increase more slowly, and maternal energy requirements do not exceed 2.1 × BMR. The required maternal energy expenditure for a fetus developmentally similar to a chimpanzee newborn (7-month-old infant; circle with star) would entail maternal energy requirements greater than 2.1 × BMR. In humans, the maximum sustained metabolic rate is thought to be 2.0–2.5 × BMR (Hammond and Diamond 1997; Peterson et al. 1990). Adapted from Dunsworth et al. 2012:fig. 3, which includes a table of the data and the sources.

delivery. Sustaining pregnancy beyond 9 months may not reduce maternal metabolic expenditures immediately, but it prevents the infant from surpassing the hypothesized energy threshold her body is able to supply in utero. The EGG hypothesis does not diminish the role of selection on the adequacy of birth canal size. However, contrary to the OD, it does not require that the bipedal-adapted hominin pelvis is exceptional in its effect on human gestation and fetal growth.

Compared to the OD and the ES, an EGG-like view of gestation is old. Medieval preformationists believed that chicks hatch when they deplete all the nutrients inside the egg and likewise believed that humans are born when they deplete their mother's resources (Pinto-Correia 1997). Although EGG has been presented for humans with human data, it is not meant to be tested exclusively in our species, considering how well maternal mass (a proxy for basal metabolic rate) predicts gestation length and fetal growth (singleton or litter mass) in other placental mammals (e.g., Sacher and Staffeldt 1974).

A metabolic limit to human gestation has also been proposed in the specific context of encephalization (Epstein 1973; Martin 1996, 1998). Martin's (1998) maternal energy (ME) hypothesis explains a limit to fetal brain growth according to the metabolic turnover of the mother and the metabolic needs of the developing fetus. The ME can, but not necessarily should, be considered together with the EGG hypothesis, which takes a similar but broader, more holistic view of maternal metabolic capacity and fetal needs. (It is not possible to tease apart direct measures of brain metabolism from the overall daily energetic use data gathered with doubly labeled water.) Brain tissue is an expensive component of the fetus as a whole, so the cost of growing fetal brain tissue is a significant factor in the EGG.

With increasingly available comparative data, variations in gestation length by species may be explained by fetal brain growth (ME), regardless of overall fetal size (EGG). The relative difference in chimpanzee and human gestation lengths might be related to brain growth differences in utero (Sakai et al. 2012). It might also be due to species-level differences in energy throughput (see, e.g., Pontzer et al. 2010; Pontzer et al. forthcoming) during pregnancy, which could be related to or accompanied by differences in energy allocation due to changing energetic requirements of, for example, locomotion (decreased) and encephalization (increased) over hominin evolutionary history (Navarete et al. 2011). As comparative data become available to test EGG on other species, the observed variation between species in gestation length and neonatal size may be explained by interspecies variation in maternal and fetal physiologies as well as maternal behavior and ecology (which includes the increasing energetic demands of locomotion during pregnancy, which may be different in bipedal hominins). If EGG extends beyond humans, then species-specific but similar mechanisms to the MC may be helping to trigger labor in those species as well.

Cetaceans and sirenians lack bony birth canals to limit gestation length and fetal growth, and yet they are born immature, so there is something limiting gestation and fetal growth. These animals should provide insight into what determines gestation length in humans. In a classic paper, using an equation that takes into account neonatal brain weight, litter size, and "brain size advancement" (neonatal brain weight divided by adult brain weight), Sacher and Staffeldt (1974) predicted the gestation length for placental mammals with known gestation lengths at the time. These few variables, which exclude any pelvic dimensions, were successful at predicting gestation length in many of the species in their study, including humans and cetaceans. Similar work in mammalian life history since the 1980s supports a metabolic explanation for placental mammal gestation and fetal development.

The four perspectives on gestation and fetal development seem to be split, with the OD and the ES emphasizing the underdeveloped central nervous system compared to the mother's and with the EGG and the ME emphasizing the shared metabolic constraints in maternal-fetal systems among placental mammals, noting the as great, or greater, human fetal growth and gestation length compared to other primates. Alongside a consideration of gestation length, these four hypotheses can be used to answer the question of why, relative to other closely related species, a greater percentage of human brain growth occurs after birth. For the OD, this postnatal brain growth is due to bipedalism's requirements of the pelvis: the infant must be born before it grows too large to escape the birth canal. For the ES, this postnatal brain growth is a developmental requirement: the infant must be born in order to properly acquire cognitive, motor neuronal, and behavioral functions. For the EGG, postnatal brain growth is caused by metabolic limits to pregnancy: the infant must be born when it becomes too costly for the mother. For the ME, postnatal brain growth is due to the metabolic limits to growing a fetal brain: the infant must be born when its brain becomes too costly for the mother.

Remaining Questions and Future Considerations

Helpless human neonates and their difficult delivery have long been coupled together in the OD scenario for human evolutionary history. Here, these and related phenomena have been considered given the current evidence, demonstrating some difficulty in falsifying it but also revealing weaknesses. That is, the present evidence provides little to support the OD. The tight fit, for example, is not unique to our species. The phenomenon of an impossibly tight fit is just one of today's relatively rare childbirth complications and may be new. Increased pelvic dimensions are not, as far as we know, detrimental to bipedalism. Human gestation is not shortened. Maternal investment in fetal growth is not low. Rather, human gestation length, fetal brain size, and overall fetal size are as great as, or greater than, expected for a primate of our size. A significantly lengthened gestation, with more fetal growth, does not appear to be metabolically feasible, regardless of pelvic dimensions. Human "altriciality" has been exaggerated; the more we learn about other primates, the less outstanding in this regard we are (e.g., most chimpanzee brain growth occurs postnatally too). There is no present evidence for human gestation or fetal growth being uniquely influenced by the pelvis. Thus, from where we stand today, the OD seems to have endured in large part due to incomplete, circumstantial, and biased evidence. The evolution of human gestation and difficult childbirth may be better explained by mammalian physiological limits (EGG and ME) than by uniquely human skeletal (OD) or developmental (ES) constraints. The obstetrical dilemma is an elegant idea and would be an extraordinary example of human exceptionalism if true, but it bears the burden of proof.

The ultimate explanations will largely rely on a detailed understanding of proximate labor triggers in humans and other species, and whether and how they differ. That there appears to be a limited shelf life for the placenta is not support for any one of the hypotheses for the evolution of birth timing, because it shows only that the placenta has evolved to last as long as human pregnancy does. A mechanical labor trigger in the uterus or cervix can be inferred from research that considers the limitations of mammalian uterine space (Hagen et al. 1984), with labor hypothetically occurring when the uterus or cervix is stretched past some limit, perhaps when a certain number of gap junctions are formed (Scott et al. 1994). When uterine space is artificially limited, like in pigs, overall fetal mass may decrease but not always (Hagen et al. 1984). However, it is not known whether uterine stretch, or overdistention, is actually a labor trigger since one study found that fundal measures for mothers of twins were not greater in those who delivered preterm (Neilson et al. 2005).

For a proximate mechanism, the EGG hypothesis relies on the MC hypothesis for humans and something equivalent in other species, like sheep (Thorburn et al. 1991). The ME could rely on the MC as well, but the as-yet-unknown labor triggers required for the OD and ES are weaknesses for those two hypotheses for the timing of birth. It may be possible that late-term mechanical stressors in the pelvis, cervix, uterus, or fetus could induce a process, perhaps like the MC, to trigger labor. If there are species-specific timers in fetal brains (Martin 2013)—for communicating to the mother that gestation is complete and to trigger labor—they would all be unique since species are born at different neurodevelopmental stages. This possibility, which would support both the OD and the ES, has not been ruled out, but it would seem to require a unique adaptive explanation for nearly every species' timing. Perhaps the end of pregnancy should not be categorized as a life history milestone, like the first molar eruption or menarche, or as governed by the same or a similar clock as the menstrual cycle; perhaps instead it should be compared to processes like digestion. From this perspective, a species-specific gestation timer in the fetal brain seems less relevant; a mechanical trigger is not ruled out; and the notion that gestation ends at the limit of maternal metabolic capacity with regard to fetal demands seems most reasonable.

Clearly, gestation and fetal growth are complex processes involving the coordination of numerous aspects of fetal and maternal biologies (Ellison 2001a; Brown et al. 2013). For example, a healthy pregnancy outcome depends not only on an adequate maternal metabolism but on a tolerant maternal immune system and the onset of labor prior to fatal fetal starvation. Furthermore, there are complex contributors, proximately and ultimately, to variation in basal metabolic rate within and between species (Naya et al. 2013), and placental invasiveness, interdigitation, and other placental traits are related to gestation length (Capellini et al. 2011). Future research on whether other species reach a metabolic limit during pregnancy will greatly improve our understanding of whether human gestation has evolved to match pelvic limitations or whether human pelves have evolved to be adequate, secondarily, according to human pregnancies that are primarily limited by energetic and metabolic constraints.

Indeed, birth may have been difficult for millions of years, but it may never have been more difficult than in *Homo sapiens*, considering the number of evolutionarily new contributors to fetopelvic disproportion relating to metabolism, energy throughput and allocation, growth, diet, ecology, climate, and genetic admixture, concomitant with relaxed selection against tightness of fit due to childbirth assistance and, recently, cesarean sections. The frequency of fetopelvic disproportion has probably fluctuated over time and space for these and many other reasons (Wells et al. 2012). The tight fit between the pelvis and the neonatal head may be exacerbated in present-day humans because of nutritional changes associated with an agriculture-based diet, which affects both maternal pelvic shape and neonatal size due to the quality and consistency of nutrition. That is, lower metabolic stress levels throughout pregnancy, whether caused by diet, disease, or other lifestyle factors, can also extend it. Humans have experienced greater effects of admixture in recent centuries, resulting in genomes that are more likely than in the past to carry genes that contribute to relatively large fetuses matched with relatively small birth canals.

In addition, the relatively greater musculoskeletal strength of chimpanzees, not just the relatively smaller neonate, could contribute to the comparative ease of chimpanzee labor. The invasive human placenta may also be extending the human capacity to grow a fetus. Since humans appear to have longer gestations and larger neonates for the mother's size than expected, difficult childbirth could also be due to something particular to human energetic throughput, energetic allocation, and metabolism. Humans might have more energy to put toward processes like gestation and fetal growth than do other primates (Pontzer et al. 2010; Pontzer et al. forthcoming). The fact that apes experience less difficult parturition but show neonatal lines on their teeth, as we do, suggests that EGG is relevant beyond humans, but causal details of perinatal growth cessation have not yet been gleaned from studies of tooth enamel (Zanolli et al. 2011).

Quantifying how the presently rare condition of fetopelvic disproportion has meaningfully influenced fitness over hominin history will be no small feat. The female pelvis has been adequate for birth for a considerable amount of time—witness the 7 billion humans alive at present. Furthermore, that the successful passing of the neonate through the birth canal is now and has always been a selection pressure to some degree is not reason enough to argue that humans are born early due to pelvic constraints nor that, if not for bipedalism and its effect on the pelvis, human gestation would be longer and human babies would be better developed at birth. What is more, even if it is determined that the human pelvis cannot widen without detriment, that still will not constitute evidence that the human pelvis is a unique selection pressure that has modified human gestation length or fetal growth over evolutionary history. These keys to the OD as the ultimate explanation for the timing of birth and the developmental state of human neonates remain unsupported leaps of logic that are difficult to test.

No doubt, future discussions of these issues will be influenced by interpretations of functional morphology and sexual dimorphism in the hominin fossil record. The direction of this debate is also likely to be biased by researchers' aversion or attraction to adaptationism and human exceptionalism. But if further evidence is discovered from extant primates to support the suggestion that humans do indeed have significantly different energetic throughputs or related metabolic traits, then at some point during hominin evolutionary history a shift to larger neonates and longer gestations, which could have been concomitant with encephalization, should be evident. This shift could have acted as a pressure to expand both the birth canal and the overall body size of females to accommodate the metabolic demands of larger fetuses with larger brains, regardless of any body size change in males. This is a reasonable scenario for the evolution of sexually dimorphic pelves and bodies in hominins, but it is unlikely to be this simple, given the complex functionality yet highly evolvable, adaptive, and neutral (Lewton 2011; Grabowski et al. 2011; Grabowski 2012; Betti et al. 2013) morphology of the pelvis. There is not yet professional consensus on an evolutionary explanation for human pelvic dimorphism, let alone overall body size dimorphism, nor is there agreement on functional interpretations of hominin fossil pelvic morphology.

Complexity is a barrier neither to evolution nor to its explanations, but if parsimony is a basis for evolutionary reconstructions, then the EGG and ME hypotheses should be preferred over the OD or ES at present. However, in light of the complex cooperation of maternal and fetal biologies, which evolved over deep time by selection, chance, and phylogenetic constraints, it seems naïve to assert any one hypothesis for the evolution of human gestation length and fetal growth (Lynch 2007). Surely further detailed understandings of the variables that contribute to human skeletal and locomotor variation and of the reproductive energetics, growth, development, and metabolism of humans, their limits, and their genetics, all within a comparative context, will help (see Newman et al. 2014; Thompson 2013).

As we move forward in asking and answering these questions, we must take great care with published mammalian life history data, because primate gestation measures, in particular, may not have been ideally collected (Borries et al. 2013). In addition, research on compa rative primate microbiomes, primate placental function, and the causes of preeclampsia and other pregnancy disorders and anomalies—particularly those dealing with maternal immune function and the irregular onset of labor, or lack thereof—will continue to be crucial for constructing a detailed biology of human pregnancy and fetal growth. Careful investigation of the energetic and metabolic conditions in multiple gestations (twinning and beyond) in human and nonhuman primates, like the callitrichids, will also be key. There is a universe of knowledge waiting for us to discover, particularly from nonhuman primates and other mammals, before we can answer many of these interrelated questions about the evolution of human locomotion, encephalization, and reproduction.

Acknowledgments

I am so grateful to Wenda Trevathan and Karen Rosenberg for inviting me to participate in this thoroughly enriching seminar and to all the participants, especially Jim McKenna, who improved this chapter. For helpful input, I'm grateful to Anna Warrener (especially), Laurel Pearson, Anne Buchanan, Ken Weiss, Pat Shipman, Kathy Jack, John Fleagle, and Herman Pontzer. Any errors are, of course, mine alone. For giving me the opportunity as a postdoc to dig into these fascinating questions, I will always be grateful to Nina Jablonski.

Notes

1. In this chapter, the term "obstetrical dilemma" refers to a human evolutionary hypothesis. However, it is also used elsewhere in this volume and throughout the literature as shorthand for the tight fit between pelvis and neonate at birth in humans and in other species, regardless of the explanation (although, for humans, the OD hypothesis is often implied).

2. Watch a chimpanzee birth at Attica Zoological Park in Greece: https://www.youtube.com/watch?v = 9bF_T3wBE14.

CHAPTER THREE

Primate Birth at the Extremes

Exploring Obstetric and Metabolic Constraints

MARCIA PONCE DE LEÓN AND CHRISTOPH P. E. ZOLLIKOFER

Birth represents a ubiquitous mother-offspring conflict. Insights gained from primate fetal-maternal relationships thus represent an important reference against which specialties of hominin birth evolution can be identified or inferred. Birth in our closest living relatives, the great apes, is comparatively straightforward, because their neonates are small compared to maternal pelvic dimensions. In modern humans, Neanderthals, and possibly earlier hominins, however, birth has been a complex, biomechanically, spatially, and physiologically highly constrained process, because their neonates are large relative to maternal pelvic dimensions (Rosenberg and Trevathan 2002; Ponce de León et al. 2008).

The obstetrical dilemma hypothesis denotes the evolutionary trade-off(s) between neonate body and brain size, developmental state in terms of altriciality, and maternal pelvic size and shape constraints. As demonstrated by A. H. Schultz (1949) and investigated in greater detail by others (reviewed in Rosenberg 1992), the obstetrical dilemma is not restricted to humans, but generally arises in primate taxa in which neonate head dimensions reach the dimensions of the birth canal. Schultz's pioneering research inspired a suite of studies analyzing how neonatal-maternal dimensions and obstetric constraints are related to body size, sexual dimorphism, locomotion, litter size, and life history parameters (Leutenegger 1978, 1979, 1982; Tague 1991, 2005; Ridley 1995; Rosenberg and Trevathan 1995; Abitbol 1996; Tague and Lovejoy 1998; Bouhallier and Berge 2006; Kurki 2007; Wittman and Wall 2007). These studies have yielded important insights into the factors involved in the coevolution of maternal-neonatal (fetopelvic) morphologies. Obstetric constraints are widespread among primates, and various evolutionary strategies have been implemented to solve potential obstetrical dilemmas. Also, obstetric constraints can be expected to cause trade-offs between the evolution of the brain, locomotor system, body size, and life history of primates. The evolutionary interplay between maternal-neonatal morphologies and these factors thus deserves in-depth consideration.

Identifying the factors that influence fetopelvic morphology and birth mechanisms is also a central topic of clinical obstetrics. The availability of biomedical imaging tools, such as computed tomography (CT), magnetic resonance imaging (MRI), and ultrasonography, spurred new 3D analyses of the hard and soft tissue topography of the pelvis, aiming at the diagnosis of birth complications from maternal-neonatal morphology (cephalopelvic disproportion; see Ferguson and Sistrom 2000; Huerta-Enochian et al. 2006; Lenhard et al. 2010; Maharaj 2010). It has become possible to acquire direct MRI data during the human birth process (Bamberg et al. 2012), and similar in vivo methods are used to study fetal development, fetopelvic proportions, and birth in nonhuman primates (Bourry et al. 2006; Kochunov and Duff Davis 2010). As a complement to earlier radiographic studies of primate birth (Stoller 1995), these new data sources have enormous potential for further evolutionary obstetric studies.

Bringing together clinical and primatological evidence in studies on evolutionary obstetrics has a long and successful tradition. Insights gained from primate birth mechanisms have been used extensively in comparative studies of hominin birth evolution (Berge et al. 1984; Tague and Lovejoy 1986; Trevathan 1987; Rosenberg 1992; Rosenberg and Trevathan 1995, 2002; Abitbol 1996; Berge and Goularas 2010), and studies using comparative fetal-maternal data from great apes and other primates have yielded valuable new data, permitting inferences about fossil hominin maternal-neonatal brain and body size relationships (DeSilva and Lesnik 2006, 2008; Whitcome et al. 2007; DeSilva 2011; O'Connell and DeSilva 2013).

Today, methods of 3D image data acquisition (CT, MRI) can be combined with geometric-morphometric methods of 3D form analysis. Geometric-morphometric methods are well suited to quantify patterns of shape variation in complex three-dimensional structures (Dryden and Mardia 1998) and have been applied to human pelvic shape analysis (Marchal 2000; Weaver 2002; Rissech et al. 2003; Pretorius et al. 2006; Gonzalez et al. 2009; Bytheway and Ross 2010; Betti et al. 2013; Betti 2014; Betti et al. 2014). While these studies focus on patterns of sexual dimorphism and climate-related variation, obstetric constraints are being analyzed as well (Bouhallier and Berge 2006; Ponce de León et al. 2008).

The aim of this chapter is to widen the scope of previous studies in two directions: to further explore morphological mother-neonate relationships across the entire size range of extant primates, and to complement and compare these data with new data on the metabolic relationships between mothers and neonates. We use a combination of biomedical imaging, computer graphics, and morphometric methods. We focus here on birth at the extremes, that is, on species that potentially face an obstetrical dilemma for any of the reasons mentioned above. As has been shown by Leutenegger (1979), total neonate body mass (= litter mass) is related to maternal body mass with a negative allometric exponent. As an effect, small primates have relatively larger total neonate body mass compared to maternal body mass than do large primates. DeSilva and Lesnik (2008) showed similar relationships for maternal and neonatal brain mass (and endocranial volume): small primates have relatively larger-brained neonates such that a larger percentage of adult brain size is reached at birth, with important implications for life history evolution. Leutenegger (1979) further suggested that twinning and other multiple births in the smallest primate species represent adaptive evolutionary solutions to the obstetrical dilemma. By partitioning litter mass into several individual neonates, obstetric constraints are mitigated, and later on the costly immatures can be distributed among allomaternal group members.

Here we investigate three species at the lower size range of New World monkeys. *Callithrix jacchus* typically has twin births (with less frequent singleton and triple births) (Tardif et al. 2003), and a similar situation is found in the smallest callitrichid, *Cebuella pygmaea*. The closely related *Callimico goeldii*, with an average adult body mass nearly twice that of *Callithrix*, typically has singleton births. Our current understanding is that the last common ancestor of all callitrichids evolved twinning from a singleton-birth ancestor, while *Callimico* evolved secondary singleton birthing from the last common ancestor of all callitrichids (Harris et al. 2014).

At the middle range of primate body size, we investigate hylobatids as a test case for obstetric constraints. As shown by Schultz (1949) in one iconic graph, neonate head dimensions in *Hylobates* tend to match pelvic obstetric dimensions. Since Schultz, however, empirical data substantiating this observation have not yet been sampled. Hylobatid evolution is typically seen in conjunction with body size reduction ("dwarfing") (Carbone et al. 2014), but compared to most similar-sized Old World monkeys, hylobatids are more encephalized. We thus expect that the obstetrical dilemma in hylobatids results from a combination of small body size (engendering small pelvises but comparatively large neonates) and high encephalization (resulting in larger than expected neonates). Here we investigate fetopelvic relationships in two hylobatid species, *Hylobates lar* and *Symphalangus syndactylus*, which differ in body size (small versus large) and encephalization (high versus low).

Toward the upper range of primate body size variation, maternal pelves tend to be large relative to fetal dimensions. As a consequence, newborn head dimensions in great apes are substantially smaller than the obstetrically relevant dimensions of the maternal pelvis, and there is no indication of obstetric constraints. Obstetric constraints during human evolution are thus typically explained as a conflict between increased neonate encephalization and body size, on the one hand, and decreased maternal pelvic dimensions, on the other. On the maternal side, the evolutionary decrease in obstetric dimensions of the hominin pelvis is interpreted as an optimization for bipedal locomotion (Rosenberg 1992).

The view that constrained fetopelvic relationships and secondary altriciality in modern humans result from an antagonism between neonate encephalization and maternal locomotor efficiency has been challenged on metabolic grounds (Dunsworth et al. 2012, and chapter 2, this volume). On the one hand, it appears that neonate size is limited by the metabolic capacity of the mother; on the other, it appears that secondary altriciality is related to the high degree of human encephalization and its combination with cooperative breeding. Finally, there is evidence that pelvic breadth is not a relevant factor influencing the costs of bipedal locomotion (Dunsworth et al. 2012, and chapter 2, this volume), and evolutionary factors limiting human pelvic obstetric dimensions must be sought elsewhere. Here we follow these lines of argument and explore metabolic maternal-neonatal relationships in a wider range of primate species. While empirical data are still scarce, model considerations can be used to estimate the metabolic load of neonates on their mothers.

Rather than falsifying the obstetrical dilemma hypothesis, however, the new metabolic evidence expands the network of factors that needs to be considered during the study of birth evolution. Human birth is thus best viewed within the more general framework of maternal-offspring conflict. While the offspring is "interested" in exploiting maternal resources as long as possible to its own benefit, the mother is "interested" in birthing the fetus when it reaches her limits in terms of metabolic output and when the fetus starts to interfere with her long-term life history strategy of distributing resources (and thus distributing risks) among consecutive singletons.

Materials and Methods

DATA ON MATERNAL AND NEONATE BODY MASS, METABOLISM, AND LITTER SIZE

Data on primate maternal body mass (M_m), neonate body mass (M_n), maternal basal metabolic rate (P_m), and litter size were collected from the literature (Leutenegger 1973, 1979; White and Seymour 2003; Isler et al. 2008; Jones et al. 2009; Barton and Capellini 2011; van Schaik and Isler 2012).

To obtain estimates of neonate basal metabolic rates (P_n), we used the regression equation relating P_m to M_m, assuming that P_n for a primate neonate with body mass M_n is the same as for an adult with the same body mass, $M_m = M_n$. The validity of this inference procedure can be assessed with empirical data for human neonates. Krauss and Auld (1975) reported values of 378 ± 126 mL $O_2 \cdot h^{-1} \cdot kg^{-1}$ for mass-specific metabolic rates of neonates, whereas our estimate is 376 mL $O_2 \cdot h^{-1} \cdot kg^{-1}$ (the caloric content of O_2 is 0.0048 kcal/ml, and the following conversion applies: 1 mL $O_2 \cdot h^{-1} \cdot kg^{-1} = 6.912$ kcal$\cdot kg^{-1} \cdot day^{-1}$).

Neonate metabolic turnover is tightly linked to placental function. While all maternal-to-fetal energy transfer has to pass the placenta, the placenta itself has its own metabolic demands. Since direct measurements of fetus-free placental metabolism are not available, the specific metabolic rate of the placenta is assumed here to be similar to that of the fetus. A review of the available empirical data on fetal-placental relationships in primates (Digiacomo et al. 1978; Benirschke 2007; Rutherford and Tardif 2008; Salafia and Yampolsky 2009) indicates that placental mass scales approximately linearly with neonate mass and that the placenta weighs $\sim 18 \pm 8\%$ of neonate body mass. Accordingly, neonate plus placental metabolic demands (P_{n+p}) are estimated here as $1.18 \cdot P_n$.

FETOPELVIC DATA

The sample is composed of full-body CT data of neonates and adult females of *Cebuella pygmaea*, *Callithrix jacchus*, *Callimico goeldii*, *Hylobates lar*,

Symphalangus syndactylus, Pongo pygmaeus, Gorilla gorilla, Pan troglodytes,
and *Homo sapiens.* Human data come from the anonymized skeletal database
of the Institute of Forensic Medicine of the University of Zurich and from the
anonymized forensic data archive of the Catholic University of Leuven. All
nonhuman data were acquired through the Virtual Ape Project, which is a
collaborative effort of various research institutions and zoos to acquire high-
resolution biomedical imaging data from fresh and preserved primate cadavers
(Morimoto et al. 2011; Hatt et al. 2013). Compared to data obtained from skeletal
collections, cadaveric data have several advantages for the study of birth-related
morphology. They provide detailed insights into hard-soft tissue relationships,
especially of the musculoskeletal system, and they permit data sampling from
the original, undisturbed morphology. This is especially important for the
neonate head, where bony elements are not yet connected to each other, and
where brain size is a major determinant of head size. It is also important for
the pelvis, because in most osteological collections pelvic three-dimensional
morphology must be reassembled from the isolated ossa coxae and the sacrum.

The sample used for this exploratory study is relatively small but consists
of high-quality CT data mostly from fresh cadavers. Table 3.1 summarizes
the sample structure. To be compatible with earlier studies, we focus here on
skeletal dimensions, assuming that the obstetrically most relevant fetopelvic
dimensions are largely determined by its bony elements. However, it should
be kept in mind that soft tissue structures, such as ligaments and interosseous
sutures, may contribute significantly to the obstetrically relevant morphology
of the pelvis, either by constraining birth canal morphology (e.g., the sacrospi-
nous ligament) or by mobilizing the joints between pelvic elements (e.g., pubic
symphysis and sacroiliac joints).

Volumetric data for adult specimens and for hominoid perinatal specimens
were acquired with multislice helical computed tomography at the Zurich University Hospital, the Institute of Forensic Medicine of the University of Zurich,
the Division of Diagnostic Imaging at the Vetsuisse Faculty at the University
of Zurich, and the Kyoto University Primate Research Institute in Inuyama.
Scanning parameters were as follows: beam collimation: 0.625–1 mm; scan
diameter: 25–70 cm; tube voltage: 110 kV; image reconstruction with matrix
size 512 × 512 or 1024 × 1024; standard and bone kernels: 0.25–0.88 mm within-
plane resolution and 0.2–0.8 mm slice increment. Volumetric data for callitrichid perinatal specimens were acquired with a micro-CT device at an isotropic
voxel volume of 0.36 mm.

Table 3.I. Sample Structure for Primate Birth at the Extremes

Species	Female Pelves[a] (n)	Neonates[a] (n)	Litter Size	Data Source[b]
Homo sapiens	6	6	singletons	IFM, CUL
Pan troglodytes	3	5	singletons	AIM, DMM
Gorilla gorilla	3	3	singletons	AIM
Pongo pygmaeus	3	5	singletons	AIM, DMM
Symphalangus syndactylus	2	4	singletons	AIM
Hylobates lar	5	4	singletons	AIM
Callimico goeldii	5	5	singletons	AIM
Callithrix jacchus	10	10	twins, triplets	AIM
Cebuella pygmaea	5	3	twins	AIM

[a] All data were acquired from fresh or formalin-preserved cadavers. Human data sets were fully anonymized and only represented by skeletal structures.

[b] AIM = Anthropological Institute and Museum, University of Zurich; DMM = Digital Morphology Museum, Kyoto University Primate Research Institute, Inuyama; IFM = Institute of Forensic Medicine, University of Zurich; CUL = Department of Forensic Medicine, Catholic University of Leuven.

Results

Graphing total neonate body mass (M_n) (litter mass) versus maternal body mass (M_m) (figure 3.1A) reveals a characteristic allometric grade shift between strepsirrhine and anthropoid primates, as reported by Leutenegger (1979). Allometric exponents are 0.69 (anthropoid primates without humans) and 0.54 (strepsirrhine primates). Polytocous species (those that produce multiple young in a single litter) are concentrated at the lower end of the neonate-versus-mother distribution. Graphing relative litter mass versus maternal body mass shows that small species have relatively larger neonates than large species do (figure 3.1B). All strepsirrhine and anthropoid primate species with a M_n/M_m ratio >15% are polytocous. It thus appears that total fetal body mass relative to maternal body mass is a critical obstetric factor in these groups and that total litter mass is partitioned among several neonates.

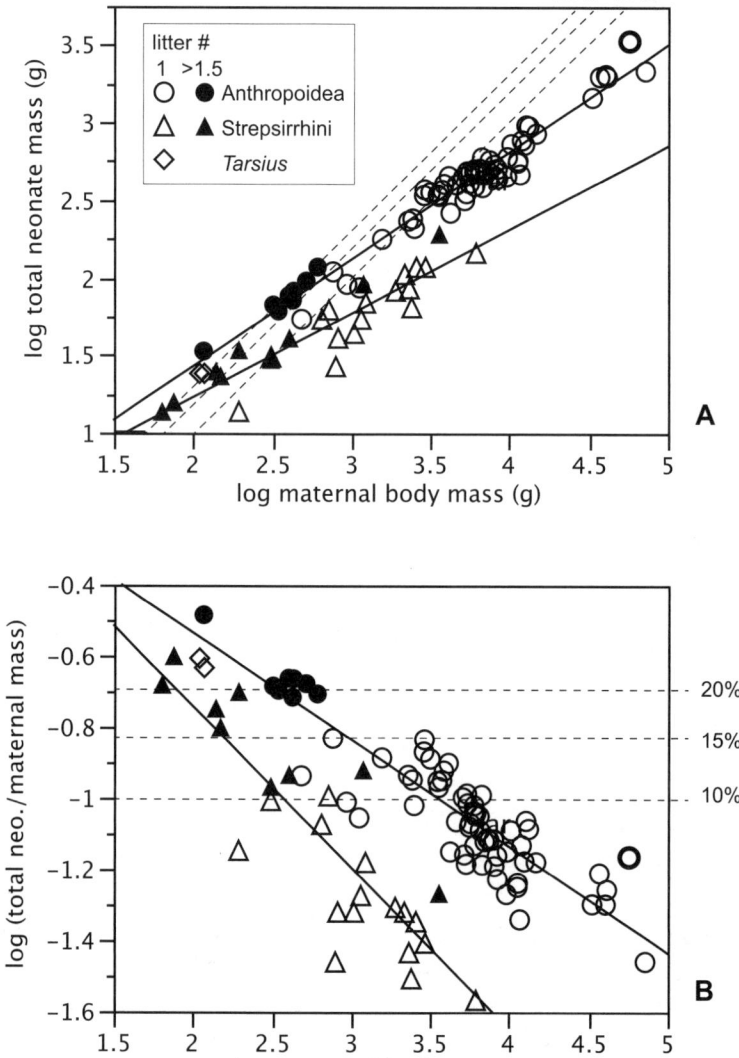

Figure 3.1. Relationship between fetal and maternal body mass. A: log-linear plot of total neonate body mass (M_n) versus maternal body mass (M_m) (anthropoid primates: log M_n = 0.150 + 0.540 log M_m; strepsirrhine primates: log M_n = 0.048 + 0.691 log M_m). B: log-linear plot of relative total neonate body mass to maternal body mass (anthropoid primates: log (M_n/M_m) = 0.164 − 0.453 log M_m; strepsirrhine primates: log (M_n/M_m) = 0.065 − 0.300 log M_m). Bold circle = *H. sapiens*.

To assess the influence of metabolic constraints on primate obstetrics, we used the following model considerations:

- The basal metabolic rate (P_m) (expressed in kcal per day or mL $O_2 \cdot h^{-1}$) represents a measure of the minimum daily energy requirements of the mother to sustain her own basic body functions. Similarly, P_{n+p} represents the amount of energy needed to sustain the fetus and placenta. Combining maternal and fetal perspectives, P_m can be thought of as a measure of the maternal capacity to grow and sustain the offspring in utero, and P_{n+p} can be understood as the minimum amount of energy that the mother has to invest into the growing fetus(es) and placenta(s). Accordingly, the ratio between neonate + placental and maternal basal metabolic rates (P_{n+p}/P_m) denotes the minimum percentage of energy that the mother has to invest in addition to her own P_m to sustain the fetus around the time of birth.

- Empirical data on metabolic rates in human neonates (Reichman et al. 1982) indicate that total fetal energy requirements around birth are 2.2–$2.6 \cdot P_n$. Adding placental energy demands ($P_{n+p} = 1.18 * P_n$; see above), this results in total energy requirements of 2.6–$3.1 \cdot P_n$. Similar measurements for adult human subjects indicate that the sustained metabolic energy production of adults is around 2.0–$3.0 \cdot P_m$ (Peterson et al. 1990; Butte and King 2005). Within the framework of our model considerations, it is thus sensible to assume the same factor, $a = 3.0$, for the average metabolic requirements of the growing fetus and associated placenta around birth ($a \cdot P_n$) and for the maximum amount of sustained maternal metabolic production ($a \cdot P_m$). The ratio $R_{n+p,m} = (a \cdot P_{n+p})/(a \cdot P_m) = P_{n+p}/P_m$ thus represents a tentative estimate of total fetal energy demands prepartum, expressed as a percentage of maximum sustained maternal energy production.

Figure 3.2A shows a negative correlation of $R_{n+p,m}$ with maternal body mass (M_m). This indicates that with increasing maternal body mass, the percentage of energy transferred from the mother to the fetus becomes smaller. The negative correlation between the metabolic variable $R_{n+p,m}$ and body mass is reminiscent of the well-known negative correlation between the specific basal metabolic rate P_m/M_m and M_m. The rate P_m/M_m is a measure of maternal energy density, and it is sensible to assume that this variable limits the

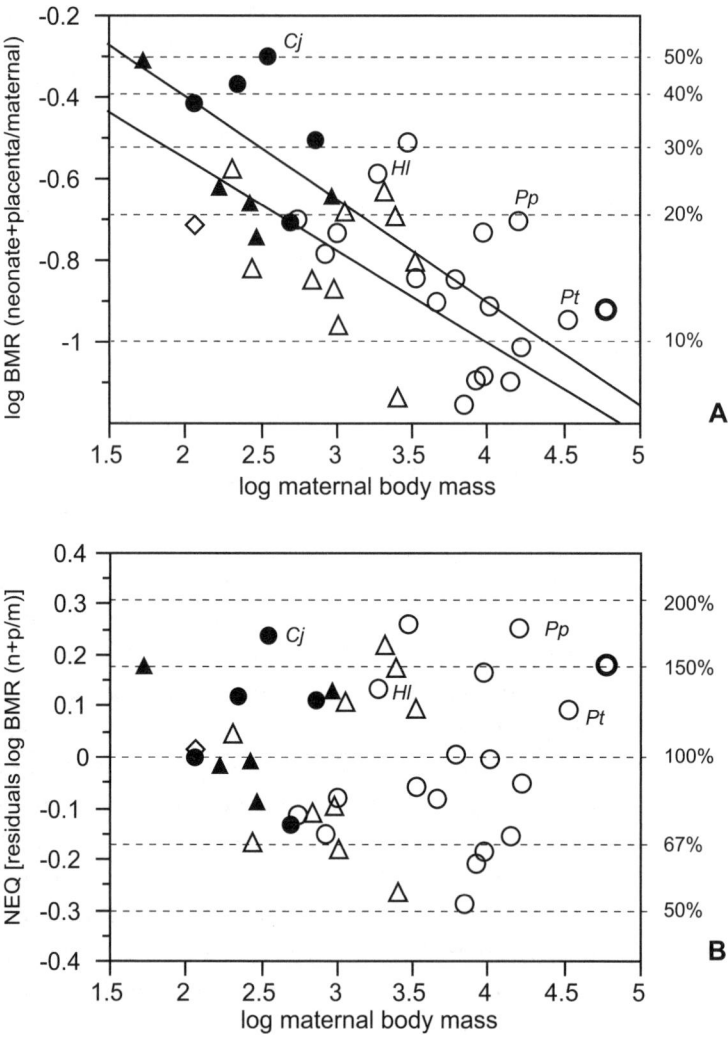

Figure 3.2. Maternal-neonate metabolic relationships. A: plot of relative neonate + placental to maternal basal metabolic rate ($R_{n+p} = P_{n+p}/P_m$) versus maternal body mass (M_m) (anthropoids: log (P_{n+p}/P_m) = 0.106 − 0.253 log M_m; strepsirrhines: log (P_{n+p}/P_m) = −0.098 − 0.226 log M_m). B: plot of NEQ (neonate + placental energy quotient = group-specific residuals of the regressions of figure 3.2A) versus log M_m. White / black symbols = litter size 1 / >1; triangles = strepsirrhines; diamonds = tarsiers; circles = anthropoids; bold circle = H. sapiens. Species abbreviations: Cj = Callithrix jacchus; Hl = Hylobates lar; Pp = Pongo pygmaeus; Pt = Pan troglodytes.

mother-to-neonate metabolic energy transfer. Accordingly, it is also sensible to plot the residuals of the group-specific regression lines of figure 3.2A versus M_m (figure 3.2B). Conceptually, these residuals are similar to encephalization quotients and are thus termed here "neonate energy quotient" (NEQ). Figure 3.2B indicates that NEQ varies considerably around the average neonatal energy demands (NEQ = 100%), ranging from ~0.5 to ~2.0. Great apes and humans are located at the upper range of this distribution (~1.5–1.75), indicating that the preterm fetus represents a metabolic challenge for the mother. The hypothesis that humans have reached the limit of sustained metabolic production needs further testing, however. Interestingly, small and/or polytocous species are equally distributed around the mean.

The data on body mass and metabolism presented here provide a general framework to assess patterns of fetal-maternal covariation and birth-related constraints. Constraints come in two forms: at the lower end of the size distribution of primates, there is a transition from single births (monotoky) to multiple births (polytoky), which is likely related to fetopelvic size constraints and not to metabolic constraints. In great apes, fetal energy demands relative to maternal energy density are high and possibly represent a metabolic birth constraint, while fetopelvic relationships are known to be unconstrained. In humans, metabolic birth constraints are likely to exist in addition to the well-known fetopelvic size constraints.

Figure 3.3 shows preliminary data on fetopelvic relationships in hominids, hylobatids, and callitrichids, all of which were obtained from high-quality CT data sets from the Virtual Ape Project. As a proxy for fetal size, we used the maximum transverse cross-sectional area of the fetal head (greatest width × greatest length of the cranium). As a proxy for the obstetrically relevant (minimum) dimensions of the birth canal, we used the midplane-outlet cross-sectional area (bispinous width × outlet anteroposterior length). Since the specimens in our sample do not represent biological mother-infant dyads, we applied resampling procedures to generate possible ranges of fetal relative to pelvic dimensions. In the great apes, the area of the neonate head is smaller than the birth canal area, and similar relationships are found in siamangs. In the more encephalized gibbons, neonate head area just matches the birth canal area. In the callitrichids, the area of the neonate head is substantially larger than the minimum cross-sectional area of the birth canal.

The dramatic increase of neonate head relative to birth canal size from large to small primates needs further investigation in terms of obstetric mechanics.

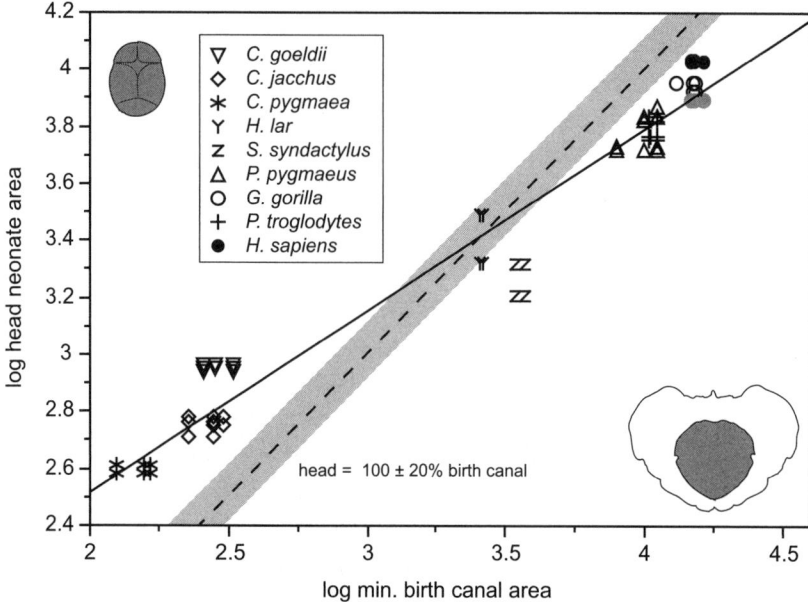

Figure 3.3. Relationship between obstetrically relevant fetopelvic dimensions: maximum fetal head area (greatest width × greatest length of the cranium) and minimum area of birth canal (bispinous width × outlet anteroposterior length). Species-specific data distributions were generated via resampling of mother-neonate dyads (*N* = 20; gray symbols = preterm neonates). Regression line: log neonate head area = 1.236 + 0.638 log birth canal area.

Figure 3.4 shows the results of our first attempts at simulating the birth process in silico. For all species, the neonate is shown in an orientation that minimizes possible spatial constraints during birth. Obviously, in the great apes, the neonate heads are considerably smaller than the corresponding birth canal dimensions. In *H. lar*, neonate cranial dimensions match birth canal dimensions, and the likely birthing trajectory involves oblique rotation of the neonate head. In siamangs, the neonate head is likely oriented in an anteroposterior direction intrapartum.

In all callitrichid species studied here (*Callimico goeldii*, *Callithrix jacchus*, *Cebuella pygmaea*), neonate heads are significantly larger than birth canal dimensions. The age of the neonate specimens typically ranges between 0 and 3 days postpartum, while one of the *Callimico* neonates died 7 days postpartum. However, in none of the three species is neonate head size correlated with age, and we are confident that these specimens represent normal perinatal morphology.

Discussion

The data and results presented in this chapter provide several new insights into fetal-maternal relationships around birth. The smallest anthropoid primates studied here—the callitrichids—represent an interesting evolutionary test bed, because they include both polytocous (*Callithrix, Cebuella*) and monotocous (*Callimico*) species. We showed that for $M_n/M_m > 15\%$ all primate species are polytocous, and we hypothesized that the evolution of multiple births in the callitrichids is related—among other factors—to obstetric constraints. This hypothesis received support by comparing fetopelvic relationships in *Callithrix* and *Cebuella* with that of *Callimico*. In the latter species, the singleton neonate's head is substantially larger relative to the birth canal dimensions than in the twinning species. Twinning thus "reduces" neonate

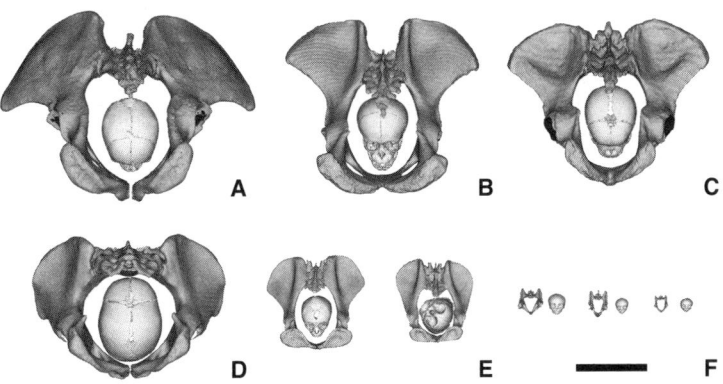

Figure 3.4. Fetopelvic relationships in anthropoid primates. A–C: Great apes (A = *Gorilla gorilla*, B = *Pan troglodytes*, C = *Pongo pygmaeus*); D: *Homo sapiens*; E: Hylobatids (*Symphalangus syndactylus, Hylobates lar*); F: Callitrichids (*Callimico goeldii, Callithrix jacchus, Cebuella pygmaea*). Maternal pelves are shown in inferior (outlet = obstetric) view; neonate skulls are shown in supposed obstetric orientation (except for callitrichids). Scale bar is 10 cm.

head size and potentially facilitates birth. However, even in *Callithrix* and *Cebuella*, the actual neonate head dimensions are still substantially larger than the dimensions of the birth canal as represented by the fully articulated pelvis. The effect of twinning is thus best described as a partial relaxation of obstetric constraints.

Currently, we can only speculate about how the neonate, and especially its head, moves through the birth canal. Judging from video recordings of callitrichid births,[1] it appears that neonates are presented head first and face forward. We used this information to digitally simulate a virtual birth. Possible trajectories of the head involve rotatory movements and substantial deformation of the neurocranium. We thus assume that pelvic joint motility increases substantially toward birth, especially in the symphyseal region.

Overall, these observations are tentative, because the callitrichids used for this study come from multiple-generation lab colonies, in which cesarean sections are carried out routinely, and stillbirths are relatively frequent.

Fetopelvic relationships in the two hylobatid species studied here, *H. lar* and *S. syndactylus*, differ significantly. As noted by Schultz, neonate head dimensions match pelvic dimensions, and a likely birthing trajectory involves rotation of the head while it moves through the birth canal. Following this trajectory, the neonate head is presented in an oblique-lateral orientation, which is in congruence with video observations.[2] Although siamangs are substantially larger than gibbons and concomitantly the pelvic dimensions are larger, figure 3.4 shows that the neonates are smaller in the former compared to the latter species. Accordingly, siamangs do not exhibit obstetric constraints. One possible factor explaining the small neonate head size is that while siamangs belong to the least encephalized hylobatids, *H. lar* is the most encephalized.

As is evident from figure 3.4, fetopelvic constraints in the great apes do not exist, and the birth canal is so spacious that neonates may present in any orientation without birth complications. This is confirmed by direct observations of chimpanzee births (Hirata et al. 2011) and by video sequences of orangutan births;[3] neonates in fact are born in highly variable orientations.

The results presented here also point to an array of unresolved issues, which require further research. Most important, birth in small primates, which seems to be highly constrained by fetopelvic morphology, needs to be investigated in greater detail in order to elucidate fetal-maternal coadaptations to the birthing process. Perinatal survival rates in callitrichids are known to be low compared to larger anthropoid primates (Tardif et al. 2003), and it remains to be tested whether obstetric constraints might be contributing to this pattern.

The role of metabolic constraints on fetopelvic relationships also requires further elucidation. As postulated by Dunsworth and colleagues (2012), human mothers reach the physiological limit of sustained metabolic production when the fetus attains its perinatal body size. The preliminary data presented in figure 3.2B support the notion that intrauterine growth might also be constrained metabolically in other hominoid species, such as *Hylobates*, *Pongo*, and *Pan*. Testing this hypothesis, however, is experimentally demanding, because it must be based on empirical data about maternal and neonatal rates of metabolic turnover. Nevertheless, the growing evidence that great apes and humans have comparatively low basal metabolic rates and low daily energy expenditure (Pontzer et al. 2014) might indicate that both physiological and physical dimensions of the neonate and the mother must be taken into account to understand the complexities of birthing.

Acknowledgments

This study was carried out within the framework of the Virtual Ape Project, a research initiative that emerged from long-term cooperation among various institutions and scientists. We thank Naoki Morimoto, Takeshi Nishimura, Walter Coudyzer, Wim Develter, Patrick Kircher, Michael Thali, and Jean-Michel Hatt for sharing prime (and primate) data and coordinating scanning efforts. The help of our students Alik Huseynov, Marc Scherrer, Arda Leibundgut, and Nathalie Burgener during CT data acquisition, segmentation, and reconstruction is gratefully acknowledged. Also, we thank Holly Dunsworth for her suggestion to integrate placental metabolic requirements into the fetal-maternal energy budget comparisons.

Notes

1. See http://www.arkive.org/black-and-white-tassel-ear-marmoset/mico-humeralifer/video-09a.html.

2. See http://www.youtube.com/watch?v = YFqIM7QAAXs.

3. See http://www.youtube.com/watch?v = 61ae9axuHJY.

CHAPTER FOUR

Brains, Birth, Bipedalism, and the Mosaic Evolution of the Helpless Human Infant

JEREMY M. DESILVA

A human infant is born into the world in a nearly helpless state, without the neuromuscular coordination necessary to actively hold on to her mother. Echoes of our arboreal past are still apparent in newborns who can grasp a parent's pinky finger with unexpected strength or reflexively throw their arms and legs into the air when they are put down on a changing table. In spite of these interesting but essentially useless vestigial behaviors, human infants must be actively carried, and mothers benefit both from the use of slings and from the help of others to balance the costs of carrying large, helpless infants. Furthermore, human newborns continue to experience prenatal rates of brain growth for the first year of life, which puts a considerable energetic burden on the mother as she attempts to gather the necessary high-quality foods to sustain her own needs and those of her infant. It therefore may be no surprise that selection has favored behaviors that mitigate some of the mother's energy burden, such as shared parental care, alloparenting, and technologies that maximize the extraction of energy from food via tools and/or cooking.

Given the exceptionally high energetic burden challenging a new mother and the overall trend of an extended life history in humans, one might expect that the interbirth interval in humans would be longer than that found in the apes. But that is not the case at all. Humans wean our young years earlier than apes typically do and consequently have a shorter interbirth interval. Even our weaned toddlers remain relatively helpless, and there is a period of extended childhood in which they are still highly dependent on their mother, even though the mother may very well become pregnant again at this time. We humans therefore have overlapping dependent offspring, meaning that

mothers (and others) have to care not only for a helpless, energetically expensive infant, but often for a toddler simultaneously (Lancaster and Lancaster
1983; Hrdy 2009).

The human condition contrasts sharply with that found in modern apes.
A chimpanzee, for instance, gives birth to a small and relatively precocial
infant. Although a neonate requires active support from its mother (van
Lawick-Goodall 1967; Mizuno et al. 2006), it has a strong grip soon after birth
(Yerkes and Tomlin 1935) and requires infrequent support during travel in the
weeks following birth (van Lawick-Goodall 1967). The mother can therefore
continue to navigate between the forest floor and the canopy to feed, as the
infant grasps the mother's belly or rides dorsally on her back (figure 4.1). The
typical chimpanzee mother is possessive of her infant and does not let another
chimpanzee inspect her offspring until upward of 6 months after birth. The
earliest observed case of a wild mother chimpanzee sharing her infant was
documented by J. Goodall (1986), who noted that Flo allowed Fifi to inspect
and hold Flint 4 months after his birth. In contrast, a typical human infant is
held, coddled, fed, poked, smiled at, and spoken to by many individuals in the
first 4 months of life (Hrdy 2009). Even after chimpanzee infants can locomote
on their own, mothers continue to nurse them for 4–5 years, so that when the
females do have another infant, their juvenile is usually old enough to forage
on its own.

Assuming that the child-rearing strategy observed in the modern apes is
the ancestral state, how did the human condition evolve? When and why did
human infants lose their gripping abilities? When and under what conditions
did mothers begin to trust others to help rear their children? When and under
what conditions did humans begin to wean their infants earlier and begin to
have overlapping dependent offspring? In this chapter, I review comparative
and paleontological data that help reconstruct these changes over the course of
human evolution—critical changes that have helped make us human.

Brain Development and the Evolution of Secondary Altriciality

The prevailing proximate explanation for human altriciality is the fact that our
brains are not nearly as developed at birth as those of our ape cousins.[1] While
brain maturation is not necessarily the same as brain growth, here I use the
more plentiful data on brain size as a proxy for brain development. Still, few
data exist even on brain size at birth in primates, and often these data are based

Figure 4.1. Two mothers carrying large toddlers. Bipedality turns the gravity vector 90° and eliminates dorsal riding in the absence of sling technology. *Left*: a female chimpanzee from the Ngogo community, Uganda, allows her toddler to dorsally ride as she knuckle-walks terrestrially. *Right*: a modern female human actively carries her toddler, who no longer possesses the anatomies required to cling to her mother. Photo of chimpanzees courtesy of Kevin Langergraber. Photo of mother and toddler courtesy of Nicole Tremblay.

on single individuals (e.g., Sacher and Staffeldt 1974). In fact, prior to Vrba (1998) and Herndon and colleagues (1999), all studies that examined chimpanzee neonatal brain size to infer life history (Sacher and Staffeldt 1974; Hofman 1983; Martin 1983; Harvey and Clutton-Brock 1985; Dienske 1986; Smith and Tompkins 1995; Fragaszy and Bard 1997), brain development and ape cognition (Holt et al. 1975; Passingham 1975, 1982, 1985; Gould 1975), and obstetrics (Leutenegger 1987; Häusler and Schmid 1995; Tague and Lovejoy 1998) were based on 1 or 2 chimpanzee infants. Some studies reported a value of 128 g at birth in chimpanzees, which was based on a single male neonate reported by Schultz (1941). Others have used a value of 150 g at birth, which is the average of the 128 g individual and another young chimpanzee that had a brain mass of 171 g (Schultz 1940). However, this latter individual was already more than 2 months old and presumably had experienced considerable postnatal brain growth already. Herndon and colleagues (1999) and DeSilva and Lesnik (2006) reported the brain masses of 24 newborn chimpanzees, which averaged 150.9 g. Therefore, previous studies that used the 150 g estimate for chimpanzee brain size at birth are supported by larger data sets, while those that used the 128 g estimate should be interpreted with caution or even revisited.

Table 4.I. Great Ape and Human Advancement Factors

Species	Adult Brain Mass (g)	Neonatal Brain Mass (g)	Advancement Factor (%)
Homo sapiens	1330.5	373.8 (n = 729)	28.1
Pan troglodytes	381.7[*]	152.8 (n = 20)	40.0
Pan paniscus	343.3[+]	154.9 (n = 1)	44.9
Gorilla gorilla	494.8[+]	222.0 (n = 2)	44.9
Gorilla beringei	474.5	208.0 (n = 1)	43.8
Pongo pygmaeus	377.8[+]	158.0 (n = 2)	41.8

[*] Data from Yerkes National Primate Research Center; Herndon et al. 1999.

[+] Cranial capacity from Isler and van Schaik 2009, converted to grams using equation in Ruff et al. 1997.

Sources: DeSilva and Lesnik 2006; DeSilva 2011; McFarlin et al. 2013.

Given an average adult brain mass of 382 g, chimpanzee neonates are born with roughly 40% of their adult brain size (DeSilva and Lesnik 2006). This percentage of adult brain size achieved by birth is equivalent to the advancement factor first used by Sacher and Staffeldt (1974) and the reciprocal of the multiplier factor used by Portmann (1990). Humans, in contrast to apes, give birth to infants whose brains average 374 g (n = 729; from DeSilva 2011), and thus newborn human brains are approximately the same size as adult chimpanzee brains. Human brains grow to an average of 1330 g, meaning our brains are only 28% of adult size at birth, despite the large absolute size of the neonatal human brain. While this value can vary depending on the population (DeSilva and Lesnik 2006) or even whether cranial capacity or mass is the metric of brain size (Coqueugniot and Hublin 2012), the point here is that humans have considerably less of our brain volume grown by birth than chimpanzees do. But what about the other great apes? Again, there are few data on brain size at birth in the apes. However, the existing data all indicate that the great apes achieve at least 40% of their brain growth by birth (table 4.1). But the link between brain growth and the state of development of the newborn requires a broader mammalian and avian perspective.

Barton and Capellini (2011) compiled data on neonatal brain mass, adult brain mass, and developmental state for 132 placental mammals. These are graphed in figure 4.2a. Notice that for a given adult brain mass, altricial mammals have a smaller neonatal brain mass. In other words, they are consistently born with a less developed brain than are precocial mammals of the same size. This has long been recognized by researchers (Portmann 1990; Mangold-Wirz 1966; Sacher and Staffeldt 1974; Harvey and Pagel 1988), and the same pattern has been found in birds (Bennett and Harvey 1985), the taxonomic group for which the terms "precocial" and "altricial" were first developed (Portmann 1939). Nevertheless, larger data sets like those compiled by Barton and Capellini (2011) should always be used to retest older ideas that may have been originally proposed based on more limited data.

Figure 4.2b demonstrates that the percentage of adult brain size achieved by birth clearly separates precocial from altricial mammals. The average altricial mammal has grown only 15.5% ± 12.1% of its brain mass by birth. The most extreme case is the brown bear (*Ursus arctos*), which is born having grown only 1.7% of its adult brain mass. The three altricial mammals with higher advancement factors within the range of precocial mammals are all large-bodied bats: the brown long-eared bat (*Plecotus auritus*), the Indian flying fox (*Pteropus giganteus*), and the common noctule (*Nyctalus noctula*). The role that specialized locomotion may play in an otherwise altricial newborn having a relatively large brain at birth is worthy of future study.

Precocial mammals, in contrast to altricial mammals, average 45.7% ± 12.8% of adult brain size at birth. Eisert and colleagues (2013) claimed that the Weddell seal (*Leptonychotes weddellii*) possessed the most developed brain at birth of any known mammal with 70% of its brain grown by birth. But the data presented here suggest that two mammals may exceed this exceptionally high value: the domestic llama (*Llama glama*) grows 72% of its adult brain size by birth, and the newborn harp seal (*Phoca groenlandica*) already possesses an amazing 88% of its full brain size. Eisert and colleagues (2013) suggested that the Weddell seal is so precocial because the pups need to successfully navigate the complex under-ice world immediately after birth; the same selective pressures may have promoted such precociality in harp seals as well.

Primates are not unusual at all in terms of relative brain growth for a precocial mammal. Compared to other precocial mammals ($n = 58$), primates ($n = 34$) have a statistically identical ($p = 0.49$) advancement factor (47.6% ± 12.1%) (figure 4.2b). This is consistent with behavioral studies that characterize newborn primates as precocial, with infants actively grasping their mothers soon after birth. The key observation in this comparative context is the position of modern humans: we possess the lowest advancement factor (28%) of

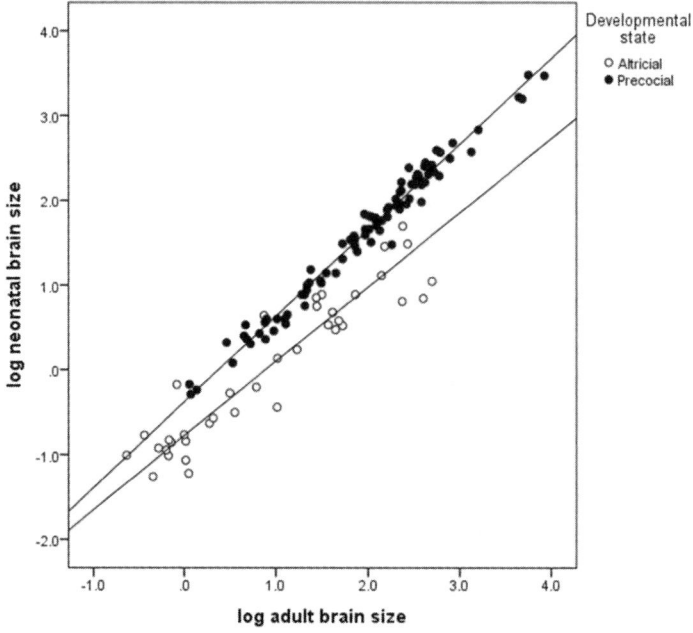

Figure 4.2a. Neonatal brain mass plotted against adult brain mass for
a large sample (*n* = 132) of placental mammals. As long recognized
(Portmann 1990), altricial and precocial mammals can be clearly
distinguished by the amount of brain development that has occurred at
birth. Data from Barton and Capellini 2011, supplemented with data from
Eisert et al. 2013; DeSilva and Lesnik 2008; DeSilva 2011; Isler and van
Schaik 2009.

any modern primate and the fifth lowest of any precocial mammal. Based on
the precocial mammal regression, humans "should be" born with brains that
are 612.8 g at birth, but instead our species typically only achieves 60% of this
expected value. Only four precocial mammals are known to have a smaller
percentage of brain size achieved by birth than humans do: the wild boar (*Sus
scrofa*), sambar deer (*Rusa unicolor*), nine-banded armadillo (*Dasypus novem-
cinctus*), and coypu (*Myocastor coypus*). It is not clear why these four precocial
mammals—quite distinct biologically and phylogenetically—have such poorly
developed brains at birth, and with such limited data on brain size at birth,
there is the possibility that some of these species are being mischaracterized

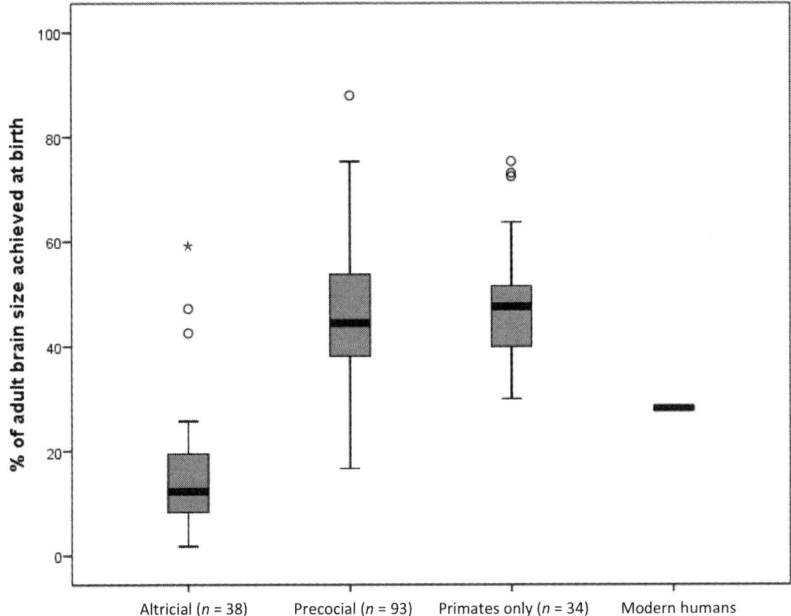

Figure 4.2b. The advancement factor (% of adult brain size grown by birth) in 132 mammals plotted by developmental state. Altricial mammals have on average less (~15%) of their adult brain mass completed by birth, whereas precocial mammals, including primates, have a larger percentage (~45%). Humans have the lowest (most altricial) advancement factor of any primate, though we do not fall within the box plot for altricial mammals. Data from sources listed in figure 4.2a.

based on the brain mass measurement of a single pathologically small-brained newborn. Regardless, modern humans are the least developed (in terms of brain growth) of the precocial primates for which brain data are currently known.

Given these data, it appears as though the proportion of adult brain size achieved by birth is a good metric for inferring the motor helplessness of an infant. Assuming that modern apes represent the primitive condition (~40% of brain size achieved at birth, well within the precocial value), when, why, and how did humans shift to having, as Portmann (1990) called it, "secondary altriciality"? To address these questions, I now turn to the human fossil record.

In order to calculate the advancement factor, or percentage of adult brain size achieved at birth, two data points are required: adult brain size and neonatal brain size. Paleontological work in eastern and southern Africa has resulted in the discovery of dozens of fossil hominin crania with reliable cranial capacities (Falk et al. 2000; Holloway et al. 2004). However, an early hominin neonate has never been discovered, and given the fragility of a newborn skeleton, the likelihood of such a discovery is extremely low. Fossil juveniles of *Australopithecus* are known (Dart 1925; Alemseged et al. 2006), and an infant *Homo erectus*, perhaps as young as 1 year old, has been described and its relative brain ontogeny explored (von Koenigswald 1936; Coqueugniot et al. 2004; Balzeau et al. 2005; O'Connell and DeSilva 2013; Cofran and DeSilva 2015). However, so much brain growth happens in the first year of life in humans that these finds cannot be used to infer much about brain size at birth in early hominins. The oldest known fossil neonate comes from the ~40,000-year-old (Pinhasi et al. 2011) Neanderthal site of Mezmaiskaya, Russia, which includes two infant burials, one of which has yielded a skull preserved well enough to calculate a brain size at birth (Ponce de León et al. 2008). Given the rarity of neonatal fossils, another method is therefore required to reconstruct brain size at birth in hominins.

It has long been recognized that in allometric studies, the slope of the regression line describing the relationship between two variables increases at higher taxonomic levels (Gould 1975). Therefore, although there is an isometric relationship between adult and neonatal brain size in precocial mammals (slope [m] = 1.013; 95% CI of slope: 0.99–1.05), within the more exclusive grouping of catarrhine primates, neonatal brains scale with negative allometry (m = 0.77; DeSilva and Lesnik 2008). As previously recognized (Martin 1983, 1990; Häusler and Schmid 1995) and more recently refined (DeSilva and Lesnik 2008), humans do not stray from the catarrhine regression and have nearly the expected brain size at birth given their large adult brain size. Therefore, for a given adult brain size, one can reasonably estimate the expected neonatal brain size in an extinct catarrhine. Since the adult brain size is known for many extinct hominin taxa, this approach was used to calculate brain size at birth throughout human evolution (DeSilva and Lesnik 2008). Since 2008, new fossils have been discovered that not only permit additional brain size at birth calculations, but provide a test of the regression-based approach. Additionally, here, I calculate neonatal brain size throughout human evolution from the ordinary least squares (OLS) regression equation, which is the recommended approach over using reduced major axis equations as predictors (Hens et al. 2000; Smith 2009).

In 2008, Simpson and colleagues described the first nearly complete female *Homo erectus* pelvis. Though quite small, the birth canal was spacious and would have accommodated an infant with a head of 300–315 cm³ (Simpson et al. 2008). Using the OLS equation and *H. erectus* crania (*n* = 13) of the same geological age as the pelvis from Gona, the predicted neonatal brain for *H. erectus* is 302.1 ± 21.0 cm³. This value is slightly larger than the 270.5 cm³ reported in DeSilva and Lesnik (2008) because it restricts the comparison just to the *H. erectus* individuals known from 0.9–1.4 Ma (the age of the Gona pelvis). Using just the three African crania from this time period (OH 9, BOU-VP-2/66, UA-31), the predicted neonatal skull of a *Homo erectus* is 312.3 ± 20.4 cm³. Given the congruence between the neonatal brain size predicted based on the size of the birth canal in a female *H. erectus* and the predicted brain size from the DeSilva and Lesnik (2008) OLS regression equation, this approach appears reasonable for inferring brain size at birth in extinct hominins. Furthermore, using the OLS equation on adult Neanderthal skulls (*n* = 29) yields a predicted neonatal brain of 405.7 ± 39.3 cm³, nearly identical to the 399 cm³ (382–416 cm³ range) of the reconstructed Mezmaiskaya Neanderthal infant (Ponce de León et al. 2008). This regression-based prediction of neonatal brain size in fossil hominins should continue to be tested as new fossils are discovered, and the equation itself should be refined as data on neonatal brain size in extant primates improve. Until then, the application of this equation to the hominin fossil record yields preliminary insight into the evolution of infant helplessness.

Because neonatal catarrhine brains scale with negative allometry (m = 0.77), the larger an adult brain is, the *relatively* smaller the neonatal brain is. The resulting advancement factor (neonatal brain compared to adult brain, expressed as a percentage) necessarily falls as adult brains get larger. Thus, as hominin brains increased in size through human evolution, the percentage of the adult brain grown at birth became smaller and smaller, resulting in more altricial infants. Figure 4.3 graphs the change in the advancement factor of extinct hominins through time. The ardipithecines (the two crania from *Ardipithecus* and *Sahelanthropus*) are calculated to have been born with brains that were 40.6% of the adult size, well within the range of modern apes. Australopiths (*Australopithecus* and *Paranthropus*) achieved on average 37.7% of their brain growth in utero. If, as argued earlier, this advancement factor is

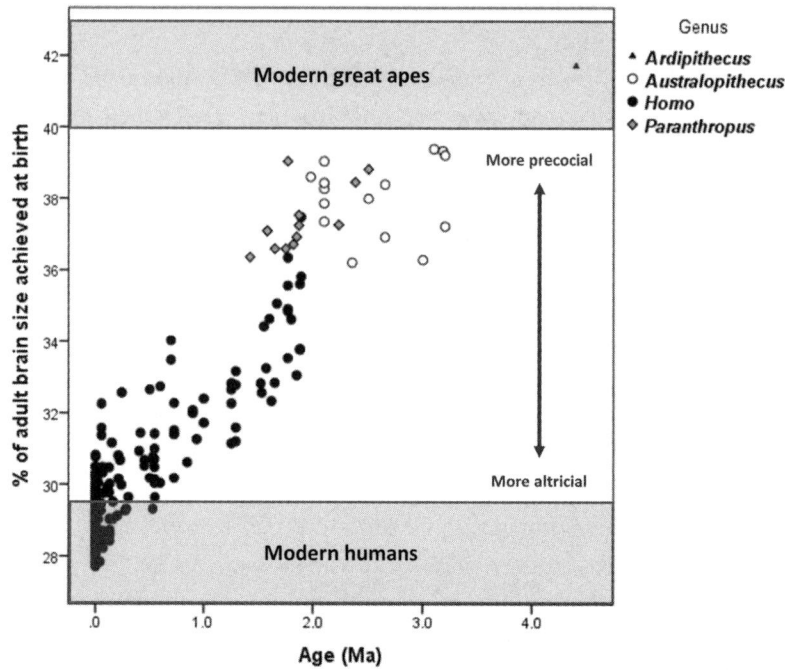

Figure 4.3. The large advancement factor gap between modern humans and modern apes (~12% difference) perhaps helps explain the difference in developmental state (precocial versus altricial) of newborn humans versus newborn apes. Using the conserved relationship between adult and newborn brain size in catarrhine primates (DeSilva and Lesnik 2008), the evolution of the altricial state in the human newborn can be reconstructed from fossil crania. Ardipithecines have apelike developmental patterns, which are presumed to be primitive. However, australopiths (both *Australopithecus* and *Paranthropus*) are more altricial at birth than modern apes are.

related to altriciality, then australopiths would have been slightly more help-less in terms of their motor skills than modern ape infants, but certainly not as helpless as a human infant. Early *Homo* at 35%, *H. erectus* at 32%, and late *H. erectus* (Heidelbergs) at 30% illustrate the gradual trend toward helpless-ness that characterized Pleistocene hominin infants. Neanderthals and Pleis-tocene *Homo sapiens* are both under 30% of brain growth achieved at birth and are within the error range of modern humans. Again, assuming that the advancement factor is a reliable indicator of altriciality, the trend toward infant helplessness began in the Pliocene, but did not reach the modern extent of helplessness present in today's newborns until the middle to late Pleistocene.

There is one final aspect of this scenario that should not be overlooked. Brain tissue is energetically expensive both to grow and to maintain (Leonard et al. 2003). Research has even suggested that the timing of birth in humans is based not on the size of the female pelvis, but on the energetic demands of the neonatal brain outstripping maternal supply (Dunsworth et al. 2012; Dunsworth, chapter 2, this volume), a hypothesis consistent with the close relationship between brain size at birth and gestation length across mammals (Sacher and Staffeldt 1974; Martin 2013). However, by birthing more altricial infants, humans have not by any means eased the energetic responsibilities of the mother. Instead, the energetic needs of a growing brain are shifted to the lactational period (see Quinn, chapter 5, this volume) and beyond, increasing the burden on the mother, who already is expending energy caring for a helpless infant. Given that modern humans approach or reach full brain volume by 6–7 years, the postnatal growth of the brain is concentrated during the infant and early childhood years and may be the driver behind our extended childhood (Kuzawa et al. 2014). Given the calories needed both to grow this much brain tissue and to maintain it, and given that this energetic burden falls almost exclusively on the mother, selective regimes that increase the maternal energy budget either directly (e.g., a higher-quality diet) or indirectly (e.g., shared provisioning) must have evolved coincident with the increase in postnatal brain growth and the gradual development of more and more helpless infants.

Bipedalism and the Helpless Infant

It is tempting to look at the analysis above and regard australopiths as essentially apelike. However, I suspect that this characterization of australopiths is misleading for four reasons that are discussed below: australopiths had larger brains than modern chimpanzees; australopiths had less developed brains at birth than modern apes; australopith neonates were proportionately larger than ape newborns; and australopiths were bipedal. Thus, the paleobiology of australopiths set the stage for many of the critical social and energetic changes necessary to care for an even more helpless infant later in human evolution.

Compared to the 1330 g average of the modern human brain, the measly 450 g average of an australopith cranium is quite small and often characterized as apelike. However, compared to modern chimpanzees (or to the Miocene hominids from which they evolved), australopiths had brains that were 20% larger, making them the most encephalized apes on the planet at the time of their existence. Additionally, given that neonatal brains scale with negative allometry, more brain tissue (~30%) was grown postnatally in australopiths compared to modern chimpanzees. Female australopiths would therefore have had elevated energy requirements compared to female chimpanzees simply in terms of helping to grow and maintain the slightly larger and therefore more energetically expensive brains of their young.

Furthermore, these early hominins had an advancement factor of 37.7%. While this value is certainly closer to the ape condition than to the modern human one, it implies that australopith infants would have been slightly more helpless than a modern ape infant. Unfortunately, there is no ape that has this advancement factor, and thus it is unclear what 37.7% of brain growth at birth would look like in terms of relative helplessness, except that australopith infants would probably have been much more precocial in motor development than modern human infants, but more altricial than a baby chimpanzee. Garwicz and colleagues (2009) have found that the time it takes for a mammal to begin to locomote is a function of adult brain size and gestation length. Assuming that australopiths had a gestation similar to chimpanzees (240 days), the Garwicz and colleagues' equation would imply that an infant australopith would take 6–7 months to begin walking on two legs. And while the appropriateness of the comparison is questionable, it may still be informative to look at another large-brained, social mammal with an advancement factor just under 38%: the African elephant (*Loxodonta africana*). While newborn elephants are quick to get on their feet and join the herd, their survival is dependent not only on their mother, but on other related females, who alloparent and even nurse the calf (Hrdy 2009).

Not only did australopiths have larger brains than do modern chimpanzees and birthed infants with less developed brains than modern chimpanzees, but these infants were proportionately large. Inspired by *Mothers and Others* (Hrdy 2009) and the birth of my own children, I began to wonder what life was like for australopith mothers and their infants. Modern humans give birth to proportionately large babies, which on average are 6% of the mass of the mother and equipped with proportionately high body fat (Kuzawa 1998); modern apes give birth to proportionately small and skinny infants, only 3% of the size of the mother (DeSilva 2011). What about australopiths? As discussed above, regression-based approaches can yield reasonable approximations for the size of the neonatal brain in australopiths. But what about the size of their bodies? Fortunately, the relationship between brain mass and body mass in neonates is conserved in the great apes (~10% of body mass is brain), permitting a reasonable calculation of body mass in australopith neonates. Upward of 12% of the body mass in modern humans is brain, which puts a lower limit on the size of the australopith neonate. My calculations revealed that australopiths (*Australopithecus* and *Paranthropus*) gave birth to infants that were about 1.8 kg. This is considerably smaller than the modern human infant (3.1 kg; weighted average of 11,317 infants from 19 different populations) and only slightly larger than the average mass of an infant chimpanzee (DeSilva 2011). However, australopith females were quite small (average ~31.5 kg) and had smaller weight-bearing joints (hips, ankles) than do female chimpanzees. The result of australopiths having slightly larger infants and slightly smaller females than chimpanzees is an infant:mother mass ratio of 5%. Thus, australopith mothers were carrying proportionately larger infants than chimpanzee mothers do. While it is possible that this 5%–6% actually represents the ancestral condition and that apes independently reduced the relative size of their neonates to more easily and safely carry infants in arboreal contexts, the fact that *Ardipithecus ramidus* (the presumed ancestral condition) is calculated to have an infant 3% of the size of the mother (DeSilva 2011) instead suggests that the enlarged infant in australopiths and early *Homo* is derived.

The relative size of the australopith neonate has energetic consequences in terms of providing sustenance to the infant, but also in terms of transport costs. In the absence of slings, humans exert 16% more energy while walking with an infant in their arms than without (Wall-Scheffler et al. 2007). Undoubtedly, these costs were exacerbated by the fact that australopiths were bipedal. Bipedalism changes the gravity vector acting on a clinging infant by 90° (Amaral 2008). Chimpanzees and other primates experience the same vertical gravity vector when they are climbing (see DeSilva 2011:fig. S3). However, all nonhuman primates have a grasping hallux and other adaptations for clinging to their mother while she is climbing. During quadrupedal locomotion, the infant primate either clings to the underbelly of her mother with powerfully gripping hands and feet, or the infant rides on the mother's back, which is a horizontal platform that requires little effort from either the infant or the mother after the first few weeks, during which the mother does help support the infant during transport (van Lawick-Goodall 1967). Australopiths did not have either option of transport.

Because australopiths were bipedal, dorsal riding was no longer a viable option given that australopith anatomy demonstrates that both the hands and the feet had lost important adaptations for grasping. This is not to imply that australopiths did not still climb trees. They almost certainly did, both for sustenance and for safety from predators at night. However, most researchers would agree that they were less suited for climbing than are modern apes, and their climbing strategy would likely have been slow, cautious, and deliberate—as humans climb today (Venkataraman et al. 2013; Kraft et al. 2014). This mode of climbing is a by-product of the trade-offs between anatomies adaptive for bipedalism and those adaptive for climbing (Ward 2002; DeSilva 2009). Importantly, the very same anatomies that would compromise the climbing abilities of australopiths would render the infants less likely to be able to grip their mother. Furthermore, there may have been little for the infant to grab. Evidence from lice genetic studies indicate that hairlessness may have begun by 3.3 Ma (Reed et al. 2007; but see Knott 2015, who found that at least in orangutans, the infant often grips the loose skin of the mother rather than her body hair). Australopiths may have foraged terrestrially in the heat of the day to avoid the predation that would inevitably occur if they were active during the cool dusk or dawn hours, and therefore the evolution of hairlessness and enhanced sweat glands may have occurred in the Pliocene, concurrent with the drying and cooling of the African savanna, the expansion of grassland environments, and the evolution of obligate bipedality. Next I argue that this combination of features characteristic of australopiths and their environment is a recipe for alloparenting and/or shared parental care.

Consider the following: A small-bodied female australopith has given birth to a relatively large infant (5% of her body mass at birth, and this value only increases as the baby grows). The newborn australopith is more helpless in motor development than a chimpanzee infant since only ~38% of its brain has grown by birth. The mother cannot put the infant on her back since she is bipedal and the gravity vector is now vertical. Furthermore, dorsal riding on her now-vertical back is not a viable option since the infant has reduced grasping abilities both due to its altriciality and due to bipedal adaptations that have either eliminated or at the very least reduced the grasping abilities of the more adducted hallux. There may be little for the infant to grab on to anyway since australopiths may have been losing their body hair as they foraged more frequently in the heat of the day to avoid predation. Assuming a chimpanzee-like gestation of ~240 days, the infant australopith would not take its first bipedal steps on its own for 6–7 months, meaning that the mother would have to actively carry her infant for those months while actively foraging both for herself and for her infant, who has a growing brain (20% larger than a chimpanzee's) to support. The landscape is littered with predators and (at the very least) each evening, the female will need to ascend a tree for safety. Though australopiths retained some adaptations for climbing, their anatomy was not nearly as well suited for life in the trees as an ape's, and therefore australopiths would have climbed slowly and cautiously. But how could a female australopith—already more poorly suited for arboreality than is a modern chimpanzee—get into a tree with one arm (the other arm actively holding her relatively large, relatively helpless, poorly grasping infant)?

There are three possible non-exclusive solutions to this problem. The first is that australopith females invented slings, which if true would be one of the first technological inventions in the human lineage (Tanner and Zihlman 1976; Lancaster 1978; Zihlman 1981). While this is a possibility—and perhaps even likely—it is quite difficult to test given that a sling made of vegetation would not be preserved in the fossil record. The second possibility is that female australopiths parked their infants. While they almost certainly did not do this in the evening, when the little offspring would have attracted predators, female australopiths may have employed this strategy in the daytime, a scenario that may have encouraged vocal contact between mother and child and may have seeded the first roots of language (Falk 2004). The third solution—the one emphasized here—is that the mother and infant (Hrdy 2009) may have solicited and received help from other members of her group. In considering the same set of variables facing australopiths, Stutz (2014:8) wrote, "Virtually the only theoretically plausible behavioral phenotypic compensation that would have co-evolved with the bipedal embodied niche is alloparenting: cooperative offspring care." If true, then the origin of alloparenting and/or shared parental care has its roots not in the genus *Homo*, but in the australopiths. While group care of infants in australopiths may have taken the form of holding an infant while her mother carefully climbed into a tree at night, these simple acts would have required intragroup tolerance, trust, and cooperation, laying the foundation for the more conspicuous acts of alloparenting that likely characterized early *Homo*.

The questions that follow are twofold: Who helped? And how can we detect the presence of helpers in the fossil record? Who helped in australopiths, or even in early *Homo*, is not clear. There is little evidence that australopiths lived long enough for grandparents to assist. While pair bonding and therefore an increased likelihood of male paternal care (see Gettler, chapter 8, this volume) have been hypothesized for australopiths (Lovejoy 1981, 2009; Reno et al. 2003), elevated body size dimorphism may instead suggest male-male competition (Plavcan et al. 2005) and a more limited role of males in caring for the young. Other possible helpers may include maternal relatives and/or older siblings. One potential problem with the maternal relative hypothesis is the possibility that australopiths had chimpanzee-like male philopatry and female dispersal (Copeland et al. 2011). If so, then a female would have had fewer related members in the group that would indirectly benefit from alloparenting her young. Using a mathematical model, Bell and colleagues (2013) have countered that even in the context of low levels of relatedness, female cooperative mothering still would have prevailed in early hominins. And, even if australopiths were patrilocal, there still may have been related female helpers available.

Emlen (1995) proposed that the delayed dispersal of females may lead to alloparenting. Given that high levels of predation are a predictor of delayed dispersal (Emlen 1995) and that australopiths almost certainly were subject to high predation (Pickering et al. 2004), young females not yet ready to leave their natal group may have been recruited as helpers. If related, these individuals would gain indirect fitness benefits. If not related, they still would benefit by learning the skills necessary to raise an australopith baby. This scenario would probably require relaxed female hierarchies (Hrdy 2009) so that the risk of infanticide was low and therefore females would be willing to share their infants with other members of the group.

I suspect that we already possess physical evidence that female australopiths were social with one another and took care of one another in times of need. Based on the size of the birth canal in australopith pelves (AL 288-1, Sts 14, Sts 65, MH2) and on regression-based estimates of brain size in australopith infants, birth was a challenging event early in human evolution (Wells et al. 2012). Although it is not clear whether australopiths experienced the corkscrew rotation through the birth canal that characterizes most modern human births, the cephalopelvic index alone would suggest that australopiths labored during birth. Furthermore, given the width of ape and human shoulders (Trevathan and Rosenberg 2000), even when the head emerged from the birth canal, the wide shoulders still posed a problem. Australopiths probably would have benefited (in a fitness sense) by giving birth in the presence of other females, who could assist during delivery, especially in cases of head or shoulder dystocia (Rosenberg and Trevathan 2002). Additionally, there is growing evidence for frequent conspecific care in early hominins, the most obvious of which is the 1.77 Ma edentulous skull (D4444) of an early *Homo* from Dmanisi, Georgia, which lived for several years despite full tooth resorption (Lordkipanidze et al. 2006). If early hominins were social enough to assist one another during delivery and to keep some elderly individuals from starving to death, how much of a stretch would it be for them to care for one another's offspring after delivery through a form of reciprocal altruism that would benefit all females in the group, related or not?

Early Weaning and Overlapping Dependent Offspring

How can we tell when early hominins started to alloparent? Although the scenarios presented above are reasonable, they do not serve as confirmation of the hypothesis that australopiths and early *Homo* alloparented. To test this idea, I return to the comparative approach.

Before I joined academia, I worked as an educator at the Boston Museum of Science. There, we had on exhibit a family of cotton-top tamarin monkeys (*Saguinus oedipus*). They were in the museum's human biology exhibit to teach visitors about primates and about cooperative breeding. Like humans, tamarins share their young and take turns carrying the infants. The fathers in particular play a crucial role in infant carrying, and there are data demonstrating that male parental care is correlated with survival for infant tamarin monkeys (Garber et al. 1984). Incidentally, they very often twin. After my own twins were born and I spent many hours carrying 15 pounds of helpless babies around, I felt camaraderie with my tamarin cousins. Given the data I presented above about relative body mass, I wondered whether the relative size of the infants was a selective force driving alloparenting, or whether the behavior of alloparenting and the resulting provisioning of the infant drove the increase in body mass. In other words, there existed a chicken-and-egg problem; the arrow of causality could be in either direction.

The comparative data on fish, birds, and mammals confirmed that there was a relationship between litter mass and cooperative breeding, but it was never clear to me which was the driver and which the result. However, there is another variable that appears to be a result of cooperative breeding, not a driver: reduced weaning time. If a female reduces her weaning time and shortens her interbirth interval in the absence of alloparents, then the infant is less likely to survive on her own. This may not be an issue for mammals with large litters, but for those with small litters (including primates), early weaning in the absence of shared provisioning makes little sense from a fitness perspective. What good is resuming the reproductive cycle if your first infant is likely to die on its own? Reduction in weaning time is contingent on some form of shared parental care or alloparenting being in place already. This contention is supported by comparative data that indicate that primates who alloparent are more likely to have shorter nursing times (Mitani and Watts 1997).

Compared to the modern apes, humans have shorter interbirth intervals and wean our infants at a younger age. Modern great apes suckle their young for approximately 4–7 years, with gorillas at the low end and orangutans at the high end of the nursing range (Knott 2001). Humans, in contrast, nurse infants for a shorter period of time. The average weaning age for seven traditional human hunter-gatherer populations is just over 3 years (Konner 2010). The traditional scholarly approach is to ask when this change occurred and why humans have evolved a shorter interbirth interval. However, given suggestions that the great apes are derived morphologically and perhaps also behaviorally (i.e., Lovejoy et al. 2009a), we have to consider the possibility that the apes have all independently extended their weaning age and that humans represent the ancestral condition. Based on body size, humans would be expected to wean infants between 2.8 and 3.7 years (Harvey and Clutton-Brock 1985; Dettwyler 2004), which is close to the actual average weaning age, though there is considerable population-level and inter-individual variation in human weaning age. We may therefore be asking the wrong question. Instead of wondering why the human nursing stage shortened, we may want to consider why the weaning age in the apes—particularly in orangutans and chimpanzees—rose.

However, while the primitive weaning age may bridge the gap between the high ape value and the lower human one, there is some evidence that the interbirth interval either shortened in the australopith clade or was variable among different australopith species. The tantalizing evidence comes from an analysis of tooth wear on two similarly aged australopith juveniles (Aiello and Montgomery 1991) who lived about a million years distant in time. The fossil LH 2 is a juvenile *Australopithecus afarensis* from ~3.6 Ma deposits of the type locality for *A. afarensis*: Laetoli, Tanzania. It possesses an erupted, but nearly unworn permanent first molar, and based on an ape schedule of first molar eruption, LH 2 was approximately 3.5–4.0 years old when it died. The wear on the deciduous molars is minimal. It is informative to contrast LH 2 with the Taung juvenile (*A. africanus*) from ~2.5 Ma deposits in South Africa. Taung is of a similar dental age as LH 2 with a fully erupted, but unworn permanent first molar. It too would have been 3.5–4.0 years old based on an ape schedule of tooth eruption, and this has been independently supported using enamel growth lines (Lacruz et al. 2005). Unlike in LH 2, however, the Taung deciduous dentition is highly worn, with exposed dentin. Given evidence that *A. afarensis* and *A. africanus* had a similar mixture of C3 and C4 plants in their diets (Sponheimer et al. 2013), and the fact that these species had similarly thick tooth enamel (Haile-Selassie et al. 2010), one possible explanation for differences in tooth wear on similarly aged individuals might be that *A. africanus* was incorporating solid foods into its diet in higher frequencies earlier in childhood than *A. afarensis* did (Aiello and Montgomery 1991). While it is recognized that *A. africanus* may not have even descended from *A. afarensis* (Irish et al. 2013) and that tooth wear is at best a crude measure of assessing weaning age (Smith 2013), this comparison still illuminates a possible temporal trend toward earlier weaning in the australopiths, or perhaps suggests variability in weaning age in different australopiths. More work is clearly needed to characterize the patterns of weaning in early hominins.

Even if weaning occurred earlier in australopiths than in modern apes, they still matured rapidly, and it is unlikely that mothers would have had to provision both a nursing infant and a fully dependent toddler. Only when the elongated childhood period evolved did hominin mothers have to face the challenges of overlapping dependent offspring, and it appears likely that the elongated childhood of modern humans may be a relatively recent evolutionary phenomenon, perhaps not reaching humanlike form until the late Pleistocene (Dean 2006; Smith et al. 2010). It is possible that this final shift in human life history—the continuation of helpless infants into still-dependent children and the resultant overlapping dependent offspring—may not have been possible until the energy budgets were sufficient to sustain a mother and her multiple offspring. Food sharing and provisioning by alloparents, including grandparents (O'Connell et al. 1999), combined with the utilization of fire to cook food (Wrangham and Conklin-Brittain 2003) by at least 1.0 Ma (Berna et al. 2012) and the development of more sophisticated technology throughout the Pleistocene would have gradually provided the energetic buffer necessary to extend humans' childhood.

Conclusion

As with many other aspects of human evolution, the shift from an apelike strategy of child-rearing to a human one was mosaic. The very earliest hominins (ardipithecines) likely birthed small-bodied, small-brained infants who could still grip their mothers with a grasping hallux. It is possible that these hominins weaned their young earlier than chimpanzees do, though this hypothesis remains to be tested with fossil and comparative evidence. The evolution of obligate bipedalism in the australopiths eliminated dorsal riding and an abducent hallux, forcing mothers to actively carry their relatively large infants. Australopiths' survival may have depended on intragroup tolerance and some degree of alloparenting given the energetic burdens and predation threats facing australopith mothers. The evolution of helpless infants had already begun by this point since the advancement factor of australopiths was lower than in modern apes, though this gradual trend toward birthing neurologically less developed infants did not reach a modern level until later in the Pleistocene. Therefore, many of the behavioral adaptations to caring for altricial infants and, eventually, overlapping dependent offspring may have taken root in the Pliocene and permitted the evolution of the large, developmentally helpless infants we birth today.

Acknowledgments

Thank you to S. Hrdy and C. Knott for comments on an earlier draft of this chapter. Many thanks to the other SAR participants for the lively, entertaining, and thought-provoking discussions. I am particularly grateful to K. Rosenberg and W. Trevathan for organizing the "Costly and Cute" SAR workshop, for editing this volume, and for providing the SAR participants and the entire biological anthropology community with a model for how to be both great scientists and great people. Finally, many thanks to E. DeSilva, J. DeSilva, and B. DeSilva for inspiring me to think about the role of infants in human evolution.

Note

1. Describing the human infant as "altricial" is problematic for the reasons detailed in Trevathan and Rosenberg, chapter 1, this volume.

CHAPTER FIVE

Infancy by Design

Maternal Metabolism, Hormonal Signals, and the Active Management of Infant Growth by Human Milk

E. A. QUINN

Human milk, like all other mammalian milks, is highly species-specific. Humans produce typical primate milk: high in water content, high in sugar, and low in fat and protein (Hinde and Milligan 2011). There are, however, some noticeable differences, at least based on current evidence: human milk generally has higher concentrations (scaled to milk energy) of oligosaccharides, metabolic hormones, and many immune factors.

As with other aspects of biological variation, human milk and all primate milks have likely been the subject of intense selection. For the majority of human evolutionary history, human milk was the primary food for infants, providing considerable opportunities for selection. Human milk is quite variable outside of the major macronutrients (these show a comparatively high degree of stability), although this variation is poorly characterized since the bulk of research has been conducted in well-nourished, primarily European or European-descent populations.

At present, the majority of studies looking at health outcomes have used simplified, dichotomized comparisons between breastfed and formula-fed infants, reporting decreased morbidity and mortality in breastfed infants. However, commercial infant formula is a relatively recent phenomenon (Stevens et al. 2009), and such comparisons, while important for contemporary public health practice (Sellen 2007), provide minimal illustration of the evolutionary pressures that likely shaped human milk. Instead, comparisons within and between populations, looking at multiple measures of milk composition, are necessary to understand the numerous selective pressures that have shaped human milk (German et al. 2008; Hinde and Milligan 2011; Hinde and German 2012; Oftedal 2012). Equally, understanding the ecological pressures and the ways in which they have shaped infant phenotypes may provide important insights into the capacity of humans to disperse and colonize ecologically challenging environments (Kuzawa and Quinn 2009; Wells and Stock 2007).

Some researchers have argued that infancy is a period of primary selection (Kuzawa and Quinn 2009; Wells 2012b) and that ecogeographical phenotypes may be most important in early life (Wells 2000), since infants and young children are more vulnerable to ecological stressors because of their immature physiology (Cowgill et al. 2012; Wells 2012b, 2014). Maternal physiology, theoretically adapted to the ecological pressures of the local environment because of the successful achievement to adulthood, may promote particular patterns of infant growth through differences in the hormonal content of milk. These early signals may be important regulators of infant growth and may promote the development of specific growth trajectories, such as prioritizing fat mass over lean tissue.

Milk contains numerous hormones and cytokines, many of which function as both metabolic and growth-promoting factors (Melnik et al. 2013; Savino et al. 2009a; Schueler et al. 2013). Several of these hormones, such as leptin and adiponectin, appear to survive digestion and influence infant growth and development (Casabiell et al. 1997; Woo et al. 2012). The understanding of these hormones, especially their association with infant body composition and growth, is still in its early stages. Much of the research has been limited to primarily Western, well-nourished populations (Miralles et al. 2006; Newburg et al. 2010; Whitmore et al. 2012; Woo et al. 2012). This is especially important for investigation of the metabolic hormones in milk and the possible associations with postnatal growth, since the faltering of postnatal growth, commonly experienced in many populations, has not been researched. Infant growth, rather, is studied in the context of optimal infant growth, in very hygienic, often obesogenic environments with comparatively low infectious disease burdens. Understanding the association between growth-promoting hormones in human milk and infant growth under both optimal and suboptimal postnatal growth conditions is necessary to understand the ways in which human milk has itself evolved and contributed to selection during infancy. It is likely that resources and energy for child-rearing were comparatively limited for most of human evolutionary history when compared to their current availability for Western populations, suggesting that "suboptimal" growth patterns may be historically more typical than the pattern seen in contemporary Western populations—or used as a growth reference (Weaver 2011).

In this chapter, I discuss what is known about the associations between selected milk metabolic hormones and offspring growth during the first year of life. Taking the approach that milk is both a maternal phenotype and part of the programming stimuli for infant phenotypes, I examine the current evidence supporting milk as a potential regulator of infant growth. Such management may be important for optimizing maternal reproductive investment, allowing mothers to differentially invest in offspring growth. I also consider the ways in which milk hormones interact with infant growth in nutritionally or ecologically stressed populations.

The Evolution of Human Milk

Mammalian milks are species-specific, with their composition influenced by ecology, maternal water turnover, and maternal behavior (Ben Shaul 1962). This has resulted in considerable diversity in maternal strategies, but also a clustering of specific characteristics within mammalian orders. Primates, with the exception of some species of prosimians (Tilden and Oftedal 1997), generally have dilute, low-fat, high-sugar milks with considerable water content (Hall et al. 2001; Milligan et al. 2008; Power et al. 2002; Power et al. 2008; Tilden and Oftedal 1997; Whittier et al. 2011). Primate milk also varies within species (Hinde and Milligan 2011). Ecological pressures such as food availability, parasite burden, birth order, and even infant sex may influence the composition of primate milks (Hinde et al. 2009).

Humans also show considerable variation across all aspects of milk: from nutritional composition (Prentice 1995), to fatty acids (Smit et al. 2002; Yuhas et al. 2006), to hormones (Quinn et al. 2014), but few factors can explain within- and between-group variation in milk's macronutrient composition. Maternal diet has been rarely associated with milk macronutrients (Anderson et al. 2005). Body composition, measured either as body mass index (BMI) or as maternal triceps skinfold thickness, has been repeatedly demonstrated to show a positive association with milk fat in some, but not all, populations (Brown et al. 1986; Nommsen et al. 1991; Prentice et al. 1981a; Quinn et al. 2012; Villalpando and del Prado 1999). While the direction of the association is always neutral or positive (higher skinfold thickness predicting more milk fat), the magnitude of the association varies between populations. For example, a 1 mm increase in maternal triceps skinfold thickness does not translate into a 0.1 g/dL increase in milk fat in every population. American mothers, for example, may have large triceps skinfold thicknesses and only modest increases in milk fat with each additional millimeter of thickness (Nommsen et al. 1991), while Tibetan mothers have smaller skinfold thicknesses but higher milk fat, with greater increases in milk fat per millimeter of triceps skinfold thickness (Quinn et al. 2014). In addition, lean Bangladeshi women show greater changes in milk fat content with declines in triceps skinfold thicknesses than do women from California (Brown et al. 1986; Nommsen et al. 1991). Overall, however, maternal physiology appears highly capable of buffering milk composition against nutritional shortfalls, and not all populations show associations between maternal adiposity and milk composition (Villalpando and del Prado 1999), although there is good evidence for severe malnutrition limiting volume (Prentice et al. 1994; Rasmussen 1992).

While it is known that compromised maternal nutrition in other mammals may decrease milk energy or volume (Roberts et al. 1985), it is generally thought that for humans, maternal adipose tissue may provide buffering for temporary and transient nutritional shortfalls. Humans are intermediate between capital and income breeders. Capital breeders, such as seals and polar bears, provide milk to their offspring in the absence of maternal food intake, relying on maternal body fat to fuel milk production, whereas income breeders, such as mice, require significant increases in daily food intake to produce milk, and caloric restriction of the mother has a direct impact on milk production and pup growth. Human mothers can produce sufficient quantities of milk during nutritional shortfalls, but there does appear to be a reduction in milk volume in cases of severe or chronic malnutrition (Prentice et al. 1981b; Prentice et al. 1983). It may be, as Vitzthum (2001) has argued for ovarian function, that the association between maternal adiposity and milk fat/energy is based on nutritional signals received across the lifespan, with women who experienced chronic nutritional shortfalls in early life having greater sensitivity to changes in maternal adiposity than do women who grew up with better nutrition.

Not all nutritional aspects of milk show this buffering, however. Milk fatty acids constitute 98% of the fat in milk and are largely derived from the maternal diet either directly from intake or from intermediate storage in fat tissue. The mammary gland can produce fatty acid chains up to 14 carbons in length through de novo synthesis, and the liver produces fatty acids up to 16 carbons, all of which can be incorporated into milk (Czank et al. 2007). However, all long chains (>16 carbons in length) must come from the diet—again, either directly or through intermediate storage in adipose tissue (Czank et al. 2007). Should dietary fat intake be insufficient, de novo synthesis of medium-chain fatty acids in the mammary gland can compensate for nutritional shortfalls with minimal disruption to the fat content of the milk (Hachey et al. 1989; Insull et al. 1959). However, as I discuss in greater detail in the next section, the increased synthesis of milk fatty acids increases the maternal metabolic costs of milk production (Prentice and Prentice 1988).

Appreciation for the signaling capacity of mammalian milk has been growing (Bagnell et al. 2009; Bartol et al. 2013; Hinde and Capitanio 2010). Both animal models and observational studies in humans have provided a wealth of knowledge on the importance of species-specific milk for appropriate offspring growth and development. While experimental designs in animal models have allowed for elegant investigations into the effects of nutrient and hormonal manipulation of milk, observational studies in humans have shown reductions in the incidence of type 2 diabetes, metabolic dysfunction, high cholesterol, high blood pressure, and possible overweight and obesity in infants who were breastfed compared to those who were not (Koletzko et al. 2013; Koletzko et al. 2009). There is also evidence for a close association between the duration of breastfeeding and reduced metabolic risk in adulthood (Gillman 2002; Gillman et al. 2001; Grummer-Strawn et al. 2004; Koletzko and von Kries 2001; Schack-Nielsen and Michaelsen 2006, 2007); again, this duration-based model cannot account for variability in milk composition or volume intake but is an improvement over earlier analyses.

It has been hypothesized that many of the protective benefits of human milk against the development of later disease may stem from the presence of hormonal signals in milk, especially those involved in the regulation of metabolism, growth, and physiological development (Doneray et al. 2009; Donovan and Odle 1994; Gillman and Mantzoros 2007; Koldovsky 1994; Savino et al. 2012b; Schack-Nielsen and Michaelsen 2007). However, since breastfeeding is the evolutionary default state, what these studies are actually capturing is an increase in risk associated with formula use rather than a decrease in risk associated with breastfeeding. Reframing the language to highlight that the associations are not protection by breastfeeding, but rather increases in risk associated with formula feeding, is important in understanding the ways in which human milk—and its nutrients and hormones—has shaped human infancy. Infant formula is inert, whereas human milk—although long treated as equally inert—is full of living cells, immunoproteins, probiotics, bacteria, cytokines, growth factors, stem cells, and other hormones. These vary based on any number of maternal, infant, behavioral, ecological, and genetic factors, and the magnitude and sources of variation are important—and understudied—aspects of human biological variation. To fully understand how such variation has important biological consequences for both mothers and infants, we need to consider the costs of lactation to mothers, unusual aspects of human lactation and milk composition, and the ways in which variation in milk-borne hormones, nutrients, and other factors may have biological implications for human infants. For simplicity, my discussion is limited to macronutrients, hormones, and some immunoproteins and should not be considered exhaustive. The discovery of pluripotent stem cells in human milk, for example, and their capacity to persist into adulthood inside offspring tissues (Hassiotou et al. 2012) suggests that our understanding of milk programming is at best in its infancy (Hassiotou and Hartmann 2014).

Production of Milk and the Costs to Mothers

The onset of milk production is called lactogenesis. In humans, this is split into two general stages, secretory differentiation (formerly called lactogenesis 1) and secretory activation (formerly lactogenesis 2). These stages provide reference frameworks for a number of important cellular changes in the mammary epithelium and the mammary ducts necessary for milk synthesis (Pang and Hartmann 2007). All mammals undergo some form of secretory activation and differentiation prior to the onset of lactation. The transition from secretory differentiation to activation also signals the shift from endocrine to autocrine control (Neville and Morton 2001; Pang and Hartmann 2007). In humans, removal of the placenta, with its production of placental lactogen, is necessary for secretory activation (Anderson 2011). It appears, however, that humans may be unique in that secretory activation may occur as late as 72 hours after birth; comparative primate research is quite rare, but observations in zoo populations suggest minimal or no delay in milk onset.

Evidence from the United States and other industrialized countries has found an increased incidence in delayed secretory activation (Chapman and Pérez-Escamilla 2000). One possible factor that may be contributing to this delay is the increased incidence of type 2 diabetes, gestational diabetes, and being overweight among mothers in the United States (Chapman 2014; Nommsen-Rivers et al. 2010; Nommsen-Rivers et al. 2012). Excess nutrition and associated poor glucose control appear to contribute to delayed secretory activation (Rasmussen et al. 2001).

Secretory differentiation starts during late pregnancy. Breast size increases, capturing both ductal growth and the differentiation of mammary epithelial cells into mature mammary epithelial cells (lactocytes) capable of producing milk. At this stage, lactocytes secrete fat, protein, and lactose in small amounts (Neville and Morton 2001; Pang and Hartmann 2007). The gap junctions between the lactocytes are open during secretory differentiation, allowing for the passage of larger molecules between the cells.

Blood supply to the breasts more than doubles during pregnancy and remains stable during lactation. The increase in blood supply is necessary to provide resources to the individual lactocytes and the surrounding cells, such as myoepithelial cells and adipocytes (fat cells). There is little evidence for nerves extending to the individual alveolus. However, myoepithelial cells and lactocytes have a constant blood supply, allowing for hormonal signaling as well as cellular uptake of glucose, fatty acids, amino acids, and other substances. Geddes and colleagues (2012) estimated that the ratio of milk yield to blood flow is 1:500, which suggests that a large blood supply is necessary for milk synthesis, although the authors cautioned that there is not clear evidence for a direct link between mammary blood flow rate and milk synthesis.

Milk removal is not necessary for secretory activation (Bussmann et al. 1996; Pang and Hartmann 2007) but is necessary to maintain milk supply. While breastfeeding or milk removal is not necessary for the onset of milk synthesis, it is necessary for continued synthesis. Often described simply as a "supply-demand response" (Neville and Morton 2001; Pang and Hartmann 2007), milk synthesis is in fact an elaborate orchestration. Infant suckling stimulates nerves in the nipple, which triggers nerve pulses to the supraoptic and paraventricular nuclei of the hypothalamus. Paraventricular neurons project to the posterior pituitary, where stimulation leads to the release of oxytocin (Rinaman 2007); similar neuron projections trigger the release of prolactin from lactotrophic cells in the anterior pituitary. Oxytocin and prolactin travel through the maternal circulation to the mammary glands, where oxytocin binds to specific receptors on myoepithelial cells and prolactin to prolactin receptors on the lactocytes themselves.

The binding of oxytocin to the myoepithelial cells triggers the cells to contract. These contractions force milk into the ducts. Progressive contractions push milk progressively through the ducts toward the nipple (Ramsay et al. 2005). Blood flow to the alveolus decreases just prior to milk ejection, followed by an increase in blood flow 1–2 minutes later. Prolactin binds to prolactin receptors on the lactocyte, specifically those expressed on the basal membrane side in contact with the maternal blood supply. Binding activates transcription mechanisms in the lactocyte, leading to the activation of genes for the production of milk proteins and lactose (Mohammad and Haymond 2013; Rhoads and Grudzien-Nogalska 2007), as well as for fatty acid synthesis and assembly of the milk fat globule (Maningat et al. 2009). Although prolactin peaks following nipple stimulation, there does not appear to be a direct association between circulating plasma prolactin levels and the rate of milk synthesis (Cox et al. 1996). It was previously thought that human milk synthesis rates ranged from 17 to 33 mL/hour (Arthur et al. 1991), but it is now understood that mammary storage capacity is highly variable between women and that longer feeding intervals and greater milk accumulation predict decreased milk synthesis rates (Daly and Hartmann 1995). Long intervals between feedings, with milk accumulating in the ducts and alveoli, are risk factors for insufficient milk syndrome and problems with having enough product to meet infant demand. Accumulated milk contains an unidentified hormone known to be a feedback inhibitor of lactation (FIL), which theoretically downregulates milk synthesis (Peaker and Wilde 1996). There is some speculation that FIL may be inhibiting the binding of prolactin linked to structural changes of the milk-filled lactocyte.

Costs of Lactation

The energy costs of lactation to human mothers exceed those of gestation. In most populations, the energy costs of milk synthesis are usually estimated at approximately 500 kcal/day, assuming the production of 700 mL of milk (Butte et al. 1988; Butte and King 2005; Butte et al. 2001; Prentice and Prentice 1988), although Sellen (2007) provided higher estimates for these costs in the first few months postpartum. Prentice and Prentice (1988) calculated the costs of milk synthesis at 323–336 kJ/100 mL, depending on the amount of fatty acid synthesis required. At peak lactation, this is a maternal energy cost of 2.87 mJ/day (Sellen 2007); over the course of a 2-year lactation, the energy cost is

2.7 mJ/day during the first 6 months of lactation and 2.3 mJ/day once comple-mentary foods are introduced (Sellen 2007). Total costs are on the order of 220,000 kcal for most mothers and higher in mothers that must synthesize additional fatty acids. These costs are well in excess of those of gestation and represent the bulk of maternal reproductive costs over the lifespan.

Despite these costs, there is little evidence that milk composition is compromised under conditions of negative energy balance, as shown by long-term studies of milk composition in the Gambia (Prentice et al. 1981b) and in the comparisons of "poorly nourished" communities described by Jelliffe and Jelliffe (1978). Pond (1992) argued that the increase in adipose tissue in humans compared to other mammals may be a support mechanism for lacta-tion, with mammary fat stores allowing for maternal buffering of milk com-position—although evidence for volume buffering is less robust, as previously discussed. During the postpartum period, especially the period of exclusive breastfeeding, repeated studies have found that triceps skinfold thicknesses have one of the more robust associations with milk fat. However, there is no consistent association between populations, only within populations (Butte et al. 2001; Prentice et al. 1981b; Quinn et al. 2012; Villalpando and del Prado 1999; Villalpando et al. 1992).

Ecologies and Added Costs of Milk Synthesis

Adaptation to different environments may have significant consequences for milk synthesis and the postpartum costs of infant feeding. For example, I and my colleagues have reported higher mean milk fat in a sample of Tibetan mothers living at high altitudes (Quinn et al. 2014). One potential selective pressure favoring higher-fat milk, and thus increased energy investment in milk synthesis, may be the increased metabolic costs of infancy at high alti-tudes, where both breathing and thermal regulation under chronic cold stress have been hypothesized to increase the daily energy expenditure—and thus energy needs—of infants; other methodological issues cannot be ruled out (Quinn et al. 2016). Alternatively, in a small study of Bedouin mothers, Yagil and colleagues (1986) reported seasonal shifts in milk fat, with the dry season predicting lower milk fat and a higher overall water content of the milk. Wool-ridge (1995) hypothesized that infant thirst, and the need for hydration, may be a primary factor in predicting milk differences; in hot, arid environments infants may need to suckle at a higher frequency to maintain hydration. This may have the overall effect of "diluting" the milk—reducing the fat content and requiring the infant to consume larger volumes of milk to meet nutritional needs. However, as hydration, and not calories, is the primary factor determining feeding frequency in highly arid environments, this may be an adaptive behavioral strategy for infants living in those environments, like the !Kung San. Konner and Worthman (1980) observed feeding frequencies as high as four times an hour—which may be advantageous for meeting hydration needs.

The pathogen load of the environment may be another ecological cost. While considerable evidence shows that human milk's immunoprotein content varies by environment, the overall associations between maternal costs and the innate versus adaptive aspects of human milk are poorly understood. For some of the primary immunoproteins, such as secretory immunoglobulin A (sIgA), there is evidence for feedback between mothers and infants, since infant infection predicts increased milk sIgA compared to milk from the same mother-infant pair in the absence of infant infection (Riskin et al. 2012). As with the milk macronutrients, this association is present within populations, but is not consistent across populations. Moreover, populations living in areas with high pathogen exposure and frequent infectious disease typically have much higher levels of sIgA in their milk than do well-nourished populations with lower disease burdens (Carlsson et al. 1976; Cruz et al. 1982; Lonnerdal et al. 1976). Variation in milk sIgA may be influenced by current environmental pathogenicity (Carlsson et al. 1976) and/or by differences in the environmental pathogenicity experienced by the mother during her own development (Ciardelli et al. 2007; Tomicić et al. 2010), as illustrated by increased sIgA in the milk of Sri Lankan women who migrated to Britain during childhood compared with Sri Lankan women born in Britain (Nathavitharana et al. 1994). Secretory IgA levels were also higher in the milk of mothers who migrated to Italy from Asia or Africa compared to sIgA levels in women from Italy or who migrated from other parts of Europe (Ciardelli et al. 2007). Key aspects of milk, including investment in immune proteins, may be developmentally programmed based on maternal exposures during childhood, although at present this has only been demonstrated at the population level. Miller and McConnell (2015) have argued that sustaining sIgA production in highly pathogenic environments may increase maternal costs and contribute to maternal depletion.

Sex-Dependent Differences in Offspring Costs

A growing body of research investigating differences in maternal costs by off-spring sex should also be considered. It is well established that human male infants are heavier at birth and require slightly more energy than female infants. There is some evidence that human milk composition may vary by infant sex (Powe et al. 2010), but these findings are not consistent and suggest that if sex-based investment in offspring does occur in human milk, it may be an adaptation in some, but not all populations (Quinn 2013). Macaques, however, do appear to have sex-based differences in milk composition (Hinde 2009); comparative data for other primates, especially great apes, are unavailable because of limited sample sizes. For a species such as macaques, where female rank is inherited but male rank must be earned, increased maternal investment in sons may correlate with improved reproductive success in males—and in humans such differences may only be present in populations with a high degree of sexual dimorphism.

Association of Milk Hormones with Maternal Body Composition

Compared to the immunoproteins and macronutrients, research into the hormones of human milk is more recent. Typically, the metabolic hormones and growth factors in human milk are found in correlation with circulating levels of these hormones in mothers, although milk levels are frequently much lower; maternal body composition, usually measured as BMI, is also frequently, but not universally, associated with these factors in milk. There are a few notable exceptions to these associations between maternal circulating levels of these factors and milk hormones and cytokines. This may reflect either preferential recruitment to the mammary gland or mammary synthesis. During lactation many metabolic hormones in maternal circulation, including leptin and adiponectin, are suppressed relative to the levels during pregnancy or nonreproductive states (Butte et al. 1997). The likely mechanism for this is through the action of prolactin and possibly insulin: prolactin inhibits adiponectin and leptin synthesis by adipocytes (Asai-Sato et al. 2006). Suckling also stimulates insulin release in the mammary gland (Travers et al. 1996); insulin is important for the maintenance of prolactin receptors in the mammary gland (Neubauer 1990).

There is also evidence for the mixed recruitment of these hormones—for example, milk insulin is derived exclusively from pancreatic insulin, since mothers with type 1 diabetes who abstained from synthetic insulin for several days had no detectable insulin in their milk but, once they resumed using synthetic insulin, had detectable synthetic insulin in their milk (Whitmore et al. 2012). Levels in milk of the hormone leptin, produced by fat cells, show significant correlations with measures of maternal adiposity and circulating leptin levels (Bronsky et al. 2006; Casabiell et al. 1997; Doneray et al. 2009; Houseknecht et al. 1997; Karatas et al. 2011; Miralles et al. 2006; Savino and Liguori 2008; Schuster et al. 2011; Smith-Kirwin et al. 1998; Uysal et al. 2002; Weyermann et al. 2006), although mammary synthesis has been identified. Another hormone produced by fat cells, adiponectin, sometimes but not consistently shows association with either circulating hormone levels or maternal adiposity (Martin et al. 2006; Newburg et al. 2010; Ozarda et al. 2012; Savino et al. 2012a); this has been interpreted as evidence for mammary synthesis.

Milk leptin is found in variable proportion to maternal circulation, with correlations reported in the range of 0.29–0.56 compared to maternal BMI and 0.43–0.55 compared to circulating maternal leptin levels (Houseknecht et al. 1997; Schuster et al. 2011; Uysal et al. 2002). Leaner populations have lower correlations with maternal BMI than do heavier populations, although the association appears to be more sensitive to changes at the lower end of the distribution than at the higher end (Quinn et al. 2014). This may be a result of receptor saturation, limiting transfer across the mammary epithelium at higher circulating levels of leptin. Mammary epithelial cells have been shown to produce leptin for milk (Smith-Kirwin et al. 1998), and the relative concentrations of leptin from mammary synthesis compared to recruitment from elsewhere in the body is largely unknown. It may be that as overall adiposity declines, the relative contribution of nonmammary leptin to milk leptin also declines, resulting in both the lower leptin content and lower correlations between milk leptin and maternal BMI.

Adiponectin in milk appears to be largely derived from mammary synthesis, although synthesis takes place in mammary stromal cells adjacent to lactocytes, and not in the lactocytes themselves. Less well studied than leptin, adiponectin is sometimes, but not consistently, associated with maternal BMI (associated: Martin et al. 2006; Weyermann et al. 2007; Woo et al. 2012; not associated: Anderson et al. 2015; Ley et al. 2012; Ozarda et al. 2012). Reported population means for milk adiponectin vary from 4.0 ng/mL in

Aeta Filipinos living primarily as foragers and small-scale farmers (Bernstein and Dominy 2013) to 60 ng/mL in mothers from the United States (Martin et al. 2006). In Filipino mothers from Cebu, mean adiponectin levels were 7.5 ng/mL; levels were significantly higher for urban mothers (Anderson et al. 2015). These concentrations are much higher than those reported for other metabolic hormones in milk and suggest that adiponectin may play an important role in neonatal development.

Insulin may also be an important hormone in human milk. In human milk, insulin-like growth factor 1, one of the primary hormones involved in early postnatal growth, declines rapidly over the first few days postpartum. By the sixth week of life, IGF-1 levels are very low, but they are likely still biologically active (Milsom et al. 2008). Insulin in human milk may also be an important growth factor, although it has been historically understudied. Despite the early detection of insulin in human milk, it quickly became medical dogma that the insulin molecule was too large to be present in human milk, since the molecule size would require active rather than passive diffusion into the milk (Whitmore et al. 2012). Insulin levels in milk vary widely within populations and are strongly correlated with circulating insulin levels (Ley et al. 2012). Milk from mothers with type 2 diabetes often shows altered metabolic profiles, including high levels of milk insulin (Whitmore et al. 2012), although it is less clear how other metabolic hormones may be altered.

The hormones discussed above all show age-related declines across the first year of life. Some of this may be driven by changes in milk volume, but the decline is still surprising. One would predict that leptin and adiponectin levels would increase with infant age, since suckling frequency declines and circulating prolactin levels drop. This should, theoretically, reduce prolactin inhibition of leptin and adiponectin synthesis. However, this increase is not observed and instead milk levels of these hormones decline; this may be further evidence for mammary-specific regulation of these hormones.

Milk Intake, Milk Hormones, and Effects on Infants

ASSOCIATIONS OF MILK VOLUME, BUT NOT MACRONUTRIENTS, WITH INFANT SIZE

Although it was originally hypothesized that the amount of protein in human milk may be a limiting factor for postnatal growth velocity, no study has found an association between the amount of total protein in human milk and full-term infant growth. The other macronutrients in human milk, fat and lactose, also fail to show an association with infant growth.

The absence of an association between milk macronutrients—and, subsequently, energy—and infant growth and development is likely reflective of the importance of milk volume in determining infant energy intake. Infants fed at the breast can modulate their daily milk intake in ways unavailable to formula-fed infants, such as modulating consumption based on appetite and metabolic needs, and can compensate for changes in milk's nutritional density by altering volume intake. For example, with decreased breastfeeding frequency, the concentration of fat increases, while high-frequency feedings are associated with lower fat content (Daly and Hartmann 1995; Kent et al. 2006). Infants may receive similar energy despite these different milks simply by modulating how much milk they consume. This may be incredibly important for infant well-being, since milk not only serves to provide infants with nutrition but is also a primary source of water. Given that infants may nurse for thirst as well as hunger, it may be that in some environments, such as arid or semi-arid regions, energy-dilute, high-water milks may be adaptive (Woolridge 1995).

ASSOCIATIONS OF KEY HORMONES WITH INFANT SIZE AND GROWTH

Unlike milk macronutrients or energy, several milk hormones have been shown to have significant associations with infant weight gain during the first and second years of life. While not an exhaustive list, the best-understood hormones as of this writing (2015) that have an association with infant weight, weight velocity, and BMI are largely metabolic hormones: leptin, adiponectin, and insulin. It is highly likely that there is a knowledge bias reflected here: very little is known of other milk hormones, cytokines, and growth factors, such as IGF-2, TGF-β2, resistin, and ghrelin (Aydin 2010; Aydin et al. 2013; Savino et al. 2013). Even for the metabolic hormones, current knowledge is largely limited to primarily Western and well-nourished populations. This serves to limit our understanding of how these hormones may function under conditions of limited nutrition, reduced maternal adiposity, and high energy turnover, which may have been more characteristic of most of human evolutionary history.

As discussed above, not only is there good evidence that these metabolic hormones are actively transported into maternal milk, but there is a growing body of evidence suggesting that they may have important long-term organizational effects on infant biology. Receptors of adiponectin, insulin, the insulin-like growth factors, and leptin have been identified in the gastric epithelial cells in infants' small intestines (Casabiell et al. 1997; Fields and Demerath 2012; Savino et al. 2008). In mouse models, both radiolabeled leptin and adiponectin from maternal milk have been demonstrated to survive digestion, and they are detectable in the circulation of nursing rat pups (Casabiell et al. 1997; Woo et al. 2009). Additionally, specific adaptations appear to protect many of these milk hormones from degradation in the gastrointestinal tract of the infant. Some hormones, such as adiponectin, occur primarily in a highly glycosylated form that is thought to protect the molecule from digestion (Weyermann et al. 2006). Additionally, milk-borne hormones may be protected from degradation in the stomach by the lower pH of infant stomach acid and the high levels of antiproteases found in human milk.

The majority of research into the association between milk-borne hormones and infant growth has focused primarily on weight for age (Doneray et al. 2009; Dundar et al. 2005) and much more rarely on infant BMI (Miralles et al. 2006). While weight for age may be an important growth marker, this overreliance on weight for age as an outcome measure for milk-based developmental signaling may miss much of the phenotypic variation in infant growth.

WHAT IF BODY COMPOSITION WAS TARGETED BY MILK HORMONES?

Buffering infants from environmental pressures, especially those related to cold stress, may be important in promoting long-term infant survival and may be an important aspect of milk-borne hormonal signaling. That is, instead of focusing simply on the associations between milk hormones and infant total weight, other aspects of infant weight, such as relative amounts of lean versus fat mass or change in the allocation to these tissues over time, may be an important outcome of variability in milk-based hormones. For example, among chronically cold-stressed populations, long-term selection on maternal physiology may have favored hormonal patterns that prioritize infant fat mass over lean tissue growth, as a way of buffering infants against the ecological stressors during the early vulnerable periods. As infant motor skills develop and infants become increasingly mobile, thermoregulatory pressures during infancy may decrease. This may explain some of the widespread variation observed in infant adiposity during early life, especially investment in site-specific adipose deposits.

By promoting infant growth in adipose tissue over lean tissue, mothers may be able to promote ecologically better-adapted phenotypes that will serve to increase infant survivorship. Promoting the growth of core, rather than peripheral, adiposity may be more significant in maintaining body temperatures than in serving as an energy buffer. More important, the inverse association between milk-borne hormones, such as leptin and adiponectin, and infant weight gain may be measuring relative gains in fat versus fat-free mass. As milk adiponectin and leptin increase, infant weight gain declines. This may reflect decreased gains in lean tissue mass and an increase in fat mass, as elevated milk leptin and adiponectin should signal good maternal condition and available support for growth during the post-lactation period.

In one of the few detailed studies to date on the association between milk hormones and the compartmentalization of infant growth, Fields and Demerath (2012) reported differential association between key milk hormones and infant body composition at 1 month of age. Although milk leptin, insulin, and TNF-α were all positively correlated in milk, each hormone had a different association with some aspect of infant body composition. All were negatively associated with infant total body weight, but leptin was associated with decreased infant BMI, while both insulin and TNF-α predicted decreased lean mass, but not fat mass. Adiponectin was not measured in the study, but likely would have had its own independent correlation with some aspect of infant body composition.

Bernstein and Dominy (2013) speculated that adiponectin may be important for "mediating the adaptive response of adipose tissue," and the fluctuations may promote adipocyte recruitment from pre-adipocytes as a long-term adaptation to nutritional stressors. The tissue-specific responses of infant physiology to milk hormones may extend to fat patterning, investment in lean versus fat mass, regulation of organ and brain growth, and even the regulation of different types of tissues, such as allocations between lean mass, such as bones, muscle, and brown adipose tissue, and fat mass.

One important aspect of milk in regulating infant growth also appears to occur largely through the maintenance and protection of the infant gastrointestinal tract. While milk is adapted to protect many of these hormones from degradation in the stomach, the presence of receptors in the GI tract suggest that these hormones are transported into infant circulation, where they are biologically active—for example, the "typical" leptin decrease in infants was not found in breastfed female infants (Treviño-Garza et al. 2010). In the GI tract, however, insulin and other metabolic hormones in milk may promote intestinal growth and integrity and help protect the infant from infection. There may even be yet unknown interactions between the hormones in human milk and the microflora in the intestines.

Equally important, and largely missing from the narrative to date, is an appreciation for population-level diversity in milk-borne hormones, especially in non-Western populations with decreased nutritional status and higher workloads. Generally, as with circulating levels of maternal hormones, the levels of many hormones in the milk of these non-Western populations appear to be lower than those of well-nourished WEIRD (Western, educated, industrialized, rich, and democratic) women. In Cebu, Philippines, we found milk leptin levels of 0.26 ± 0.18 ng/mL (Quinn et al. 2014), among the lowest ever reported, and milk adiponectin levels of 7.5 ng/mL (Anderson et al. 2015), also unusually low. These mothers are lean, with relatively low dietary energy intakes. As reported in other populations, both adiponectin and leptin are inversely associated with infant size for age, suggesting that the associations between milk leptin and growth regulation are found across the distribution. However, there is an increased sensitivity to changes in maternal adiposity and milk leptin at the lower, rather than the higher, end of the distribution across populations. Prentice and colleagues (2002) argued that leptin may be best understood as a hormone of scarcity, not excess, and that physiological responses may be more sensitive to changes in leptin levels when levels are lower.

In formula-fed infants, however, this hormonal milieu is largely absent, and infant development occurs without these exogenous signals. This absence of hormonal signals may be meaningful to infant biological development. For the hormones in milk that are positively correlated with maternal adiposity, either directly through established correlations or indirectly through association between maternal adiposity, serum levels, and milk serum levels of these hormones, a complete absence of these hormones may falsely signal maternal nutritional deprivation or severe starvation to infants.

Few populations with very low levels of these hormones in milk have been studied. In Filipino infants from Cebu, who consume milk with average nutritional composition but much lower leptin and adiponectin, milk leptin shows an inverse association with infant weight for age z-score only in female infants, not in male infants (Quinn et al. 2014). Whether this is typical in populations with more milk leptin is unknown, but it does support some of the proposed signaling mechanisms, with milk hormones at very low levels possibly having sex-specific effects on offspring—with females showing conserved patterns of growth. Prior studies of the association between milk adiponectin and infant size for age (either weight, BMI, or change in weight or BMI) reported an inverse association between milk adiponectin and infant weight, with a modest plateau effect at low levels (10–20 ng/mL) of milk adiponectin (Woo et al. 2009). Notably missing from these analyses were data from populations with lower levels of milk adiponectin, such as Aeta Filipinos (4.0 ng/mL) (Bernstein and Dominy 2013) and Filipinos from Cebu (7.5 ng/mL). In Cebu, my colleagues and I reported that the low levels of milk adiponectin (range: 1.3–19.1 ng/mL) showed a positive association with infant weight for age z-score—except at higher levels, where the association plateaued (Anderson et al. 2015). We hypothesize that the association between milk adiponectin and infant weight for age may be U-shaped, with very low levels positively associated with infant growth and higher levels inversely associated with growth, with these associations reflecting differences in the prioritization of adiponectin across populations. For example, in highly stressed populations with both marginal nutritional status and high pathogen exposure, the protective effects of adiponectin on gut barrier function may be growth promoting, while in well-nourished, low-pathogen environments this will not only be less necessary but overall milk adiponectin will be significantly higher, allowing for additional systemic application of adiponectin.

Hinde (2012) suggested that higher levels of milk adiponectin should be energy sparing for mothers—that is, mothers should downregulate infant growth during the period of exclusive breastfeeding to minimize energetic costs to themselves. In later infancy, when supplemental foods can contribute to the costs of growth, offspring growth should accelerate. Building on this, I suggest that mothers in low-resource environments may be investing more in early offspring growth, since there may be less certainty of resources for later growth. Maternal metabolism during the period of early growth may be a more reliable resource—albeit a finite one—and some manipulation of infant growth through changes in metabolic hormones, reflecting changes in maternal adiposity, may be a possible maternal strategy for balancing mother-offspring conflict.

Consuming milk free of these hormones may essentially signal to infants that the external environment is quite poor, and their increased investment in early growth while such growth is still supported by maternal metabolism may be an important phenotypic adaptation for infants. Wells (2003) has further hypothesized that mothers may deliberately confuse signals to infants in an attempt to reduce the nutritional costs of rearing offspring, especially under declining nutritional conditions, by delaying investment in growth until external nutritional resources can support this growth. Mammary synthesis of milk leptin should ensure that there is always some leptin in human milk, but this is under the influence of surrounding maternal metabolic hormones, which may influence mammary-specific synthesis of these hormones and even of milk itself. Milk with few or no hormones may be a sign of severe maternal depletion, and infant growth responses to such milk may be long-term phenotypic strategies to minimize energy expenditure. Alternatively, the increase in milk hormones seen at the onset of maternal weight loss may promote increases in fat mass over lean tissue mass in exposed infants, promoting the development of adipose tissue stores that may be necessary to protect the brain from seasonal or predictable nutritional fluctuations.

Evidence for Signaling

Milk-borne hormones associated with energy, metabolism, and growth have long been hypothesized to play a major role in weight management for breast-fed infants (Locke 2002; Savino et al. 2009b; Weyermann et al. 2007); these predictions were confirmed by the identification of these hormones. However, it may be overly simplistic to think that only these hormones are involved in metabolic regulation and the long-term programming of infant growth.

Adiponectin, leptin, and insulin are each important in the development and maintenance of adipose tissue. Both adiponectin and leptin act to inhibit adipogenesis and may influence total fat mass and energy regulation in infants, including neurological responses to feeding. It is most likely that there are multiple pathways involved in postnatal signaling, with some hormones targeting the intestines and promoting intestinal growth and cellular integrity, which appear to have growth-promoting associations; other hormones possibly involved in the neuroendocrine programming of appetite and satiety; and finally hormones possibly involved in the promotion of specific types of tissue growth, including adipocyte recruitment. Animal models have shown that early exposure to oral hormones commonly found in human milk have long-term influences on adipose tissue mass and cellular activity (Palou et al. 2011; Pico et al. 2007). In humans, the early exposure of premature infants to human milk was shown to reduce leptin synthesis relative to fat mass during late childhood (Singhal et al. 2002).

Over the long term, breastfeeding is associated with decreased risk of being overweight, obesity, type 2 diabetes, and metabolic dysfunction in most, but not all, studies (Dewey 2003; Fewtrell 2011; Gillman 2010). Some of the lack of significant associations may be related to difficulties in measuring early exposure to breastfeeding, since duration, intensity, and other factors are not consistently treated, and studies may group an individual receiving 1 day of human milk with another receiving 18 months of milk, because both were "breastfed"—but they had very different exposures to human milk.

Summary: Optimizing and Promoting Ecologically Sensitive Growth Phenotypes

Humans, as a geographically widespread primate, have considerable phenotypic plasticity. It has been recognized that prenatal influences on growth, metabolism, and later disease risk are quite real and that these processes continue during the postnatal period. Of particular importance during this latter time appears to be the continued hormonal signaling from the mother via human milk.

For formula-fed infants, the hormones, if present at all, may be largely biologically unavailable. Despite higher protein in formula than what is typically found in human milk, the absence of metabolic hormones may mimic conditions of maternal nutrition depletion and may promote the development of specific phenotypes of infant growth, especially those associated with energy-reducing and energy-storing mechanisms.

The plasticity of human milk hormones in response to maternal ecological pressures while maintaining appropriate caloric, fat, and protein density to meet infant needs even under conditions of considerable ecological constraint shows the remarkable buffering capacity of this system. Whereas the metabolic costs of lactation increase dramatically in most other mammals, and maternal nutritional shortfalls often predict decreased milk quality and quantity, human physiology, likely through maternal adipose tissue, is able to effectively buffer the nutrition while maintaining active intergenerational signaling through milk. Promoting through milk hormones the development of specific growth phenotypes, including not only infant size but also the distribution of weight between lean and fat mass, may be an adaptive mechanism for promoting ecologically successful phenotypes through modulations to either body composition or metabolism.

Postpartum lactation is the most biologically expensive aspect of reproduction for mothers, and much of these costs have to do with supporting infant growth and a large and expensive brain concurrently. Maternal regulation of infant growth, through changes to milk hormones, may be important in promoting the development of these ecologically adapted phenotypes. In particular, the regulation and investment in adipose tissue for the infant may reflect a form of physiological bet hedging (Kuzawa 1998), important not necessarily for the thermoregulatory properties often promoted for adipose tissue, but for the energy stores these represent as a buffer for the infant against seasonal fluctuations in food supply, especially those encountered at higher latitudes and altitudes. Signaling via human milk, which is linked with the capacity for phenotypic plasticity in human infants, likely was crucial to the widespread geographical success of anatomically modern humans.

CHAPTER SIX

Baby the Trendsetter

Three Evo-Devo Trends and Their Expression
in Asperger Syndrome

DEAN FALK

In this chapter I describe three evolutionary trends that began in prehistoric hominin infants; their impact on the emergence of grammatical language and other types of advanced cognition in humans; and how these trends are manifested in contemporary infants who have the only form of high-functioning autism characterized by normal to high IQs, the timely development of competent grammar, and superb systemizing skills (Asperger syndrome). Hypothetically, the three trends emerged in association with the following chronological evolutionary framework: origin of bipedalism →[1] changes in infant locomotor development →[2] enhanced mother-infant communication →[3] accelerated brain growth during the first postnatal year associated with neurological reorganization →[4] increased brain size in infants and adults →[5] the obstetrical dilemma. The hominin fossil record suggests that bipedalism may have originated at the inception of hominins ~6.0–7.0 Ma (Senut et al. 2001; Brunet et al. 2002). On the other hand, brain size (indicated by cranial capacity) remained conservative until ~3.0 Ma (Zollikofer et al. 2005; Suwa et al. 2009), at which point it began to increase until it reached a plateau in *Homo sapiens* that is three to four times the brain sizes associated with australopithecines and extant apes (figure 6.1). The lag of roughly 3 million years between the origin of bipedalism and the kickoff in brain size evolution is significant for understanding the relationship between bipedalism and the obstetrical dilemma (OD) (Rosenberg and Trevathan 2001, 2002; Trevathan and Rosenberg, chapter 1, this volume).

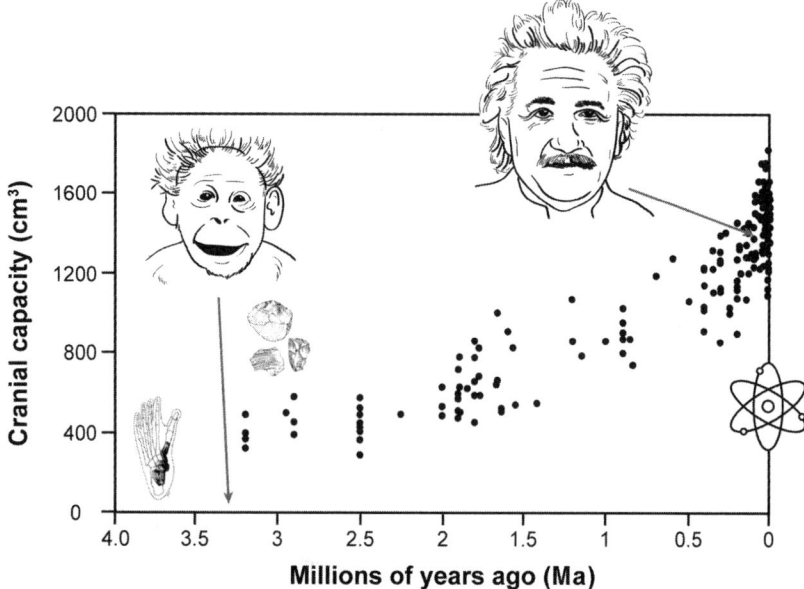

Figure 6.1. The evolution of bipedalism, brain size, and culture. By the time of Little Foot (~3.7 Ma), bipedalism had been evolving for several million years, long before brain size started to increase ~3.0 Ma. Between the time of the Dikika infant (*Australopithecus afarensis*) and Albert Einstein, brains evolved in size and internal connectivity, while material culture blossomed from stone tools to the products of the atomic age. The data for brain size for individuals, represented by cranial capacity in cubic centimeters (cm³), are from Nick Matzke of the National Center for Science Education (www.ncse.com). Reproduced from Falk 2016.

Researchers use various definitions of or criteria for the OD. Here, I adopt the Oxford Dictionaries' definition of a "dilemma" as "a difficult situation or problem," a definition that "is now widespread and generally acceptable."[1] Here, the obstetrical dilemma simply refers to the fact that modern childbirth is difficult (the dilemma) because the brains/heads of term fetuses are too large to pass comfortably through the bony birth canal, which is bordered by parts of the pelvis and coccyx (the obstetrical part of the OD). The size and shape of the bony birth canal reflect demands not only of childbirth, but also of bipedal locomotion, of climatic (thermoregulatory) variables, and for supporting viscera in an upright biped (Warrener et al. 2015). Some versions of the OD require a trade-off in women between increased pelvic width to accommodate childbirth and bipedal efficiency, but this is contradicted by experiments that show that men and women are equally efficient at both walking and running (Warrener et al. 2015). Despite women's uncompromised bipedal locomotion, the fact remains that giving birth is extremely difficult, largely because of cephalopelvic disproportion. As indicated in the above evolutionary sequence, bipedalism did not directly cause the OD, as some suggest—rather, the much later evolutionary increase in brain size did. Nevertheless, selection for bipedalism in hominins caused the shape of the pelvis to remodel in ways that constrained the perimeter of the pelvic outlet, and this remodeled shape was conserved during subsequent hominin evolution. After brain size began its evolutionary increase, the derived morphology of the pelvic outlet limited the maximum head (brain) size that terminal fetuses could achieve and still survive parturition. Bipedalism, thus, had an *indirect* role in setting parameters for the much later emergence of the OD.

The terminal position of the OD in the above sequence does not lessen its importance for hominin evolution. When it finally kicked in, the OD may have primed selection in *Australopithecus* for delayed fusion of the metopic suture, which facilitates the overlapping of the bones bordering the anterior fontanel during parturition (i.e., temporarily constricting fetal head size) (Falk et al. 2012; Schultz 1969). Further, the OD limited the brain size of viable terminal fetuses, which likely impacted gestation length and related homeostatic mechanisms, such as metabolic factors in mothers, fetuses, and newborns (Dunsworth, chapter 2, and Ponce de León and Zollikofer, chapter 3, both this volume). However, despite the suggestions of some researchers, the OD and metabolic requirements do not explain why a greater percentage of human brain growth occurs after birth. Rather, postnatal brain growth is relatively greater in humans because our adult brains are *much* larger than those of other primates. Because of brain evolution, the infant human's brain has further to go (and further to grow) to reach adult size than do the brains of other primate infants. In other words, the greater proportion of postnatal brain growth in humans is the direct result of brain evolution, rather than a consequence of direct selection for associated homeostatic metabolic factors. The interesting question is *why* human brains evolved to be so large and the specific role that prehistoric infants played in this remarkable evolution.

Trend 1: Delay in Locomotor Development (Late Bloomers)

The trend for delayed locomotor development in prehistoric infants occurred at arrow 1 in the above evolutionary sequence (origin of bipedalism →¹ changes in infant locomotor development). It is likely that hominins diverged from the chimpanzee lineage around 6.0 Ma because of selection for bipedalism, probably because it improved their ability to forage (Lieberman 2015). The fossil record shows that by about 3.0 Ma, *Australopithecus africanus* was walking with an efficient, extended lower limb, similar to the walk of contemporary humans (Barak et al. 2013). The transition to bipedalism affected much of the skeleton, including the lower end of the spine, the pelvis, and the foot. The ilia became shorter, broader, and positioned more laterally, while the sacrum and coccyx were pushed down opposite the pubic symphysis, which reduced the relative sagittal diameter of the pelvic inlet. This remodeling constricted the bony birth canal compared to the ancestral apelike condition (Schultz 1969; Rosenberg and Trevathan 2001, 2002). Unlike modern women, female apes have capacious pelvic outlets that easily accommodate the head size of term newborns (Schultz 1969). This was presumably the ancestral condition for hominins, which means there would have been spare room to accommodate small-headed neonates as birth canals became reshaped during selection for bipedalism. As noted, although the derived morphology of the pelvis/lower spine became problematic for birth millions of years later in association with increased brain size, it is unlikely that the OD developed in conjunction with the origin of bipedalism.

As early hominins reduced the time spent in trees in favor of walking on the ground, the anatomy of their hands and feet began to evolve. Compared to the ancestral apelike condition, big toes became longer, more robust, and aligned with the other toes and, subsequently, the other toes shortened and became less curved. These changes facilitated the distribution of body weight along the inside of the foot during the stance phase of walking. The foot thus lost much of its grasping ability as it became primarily a weight-bearing organ. Unlike the foot, selection on the hand was relaxed when it was freed from functions related to arboreal locomotion. Nevertheless, "a common genetic/developmental 'blueprint' in fingers and toes" caused thumbs to become longer and more robust, "largely as a by-product of stronger selection pressures acting on toes" (Rolian et al. 2010:1563–1564). Instead of facilitating bipedalism, however, the parallel changes in the hominin hand were hypothetically preadapted for

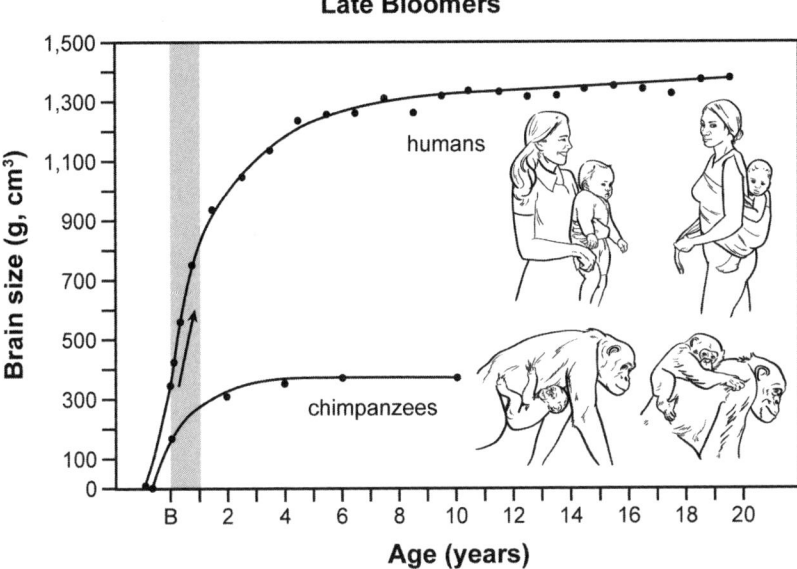

Figure 6.2. Trend 1: Late bloomers. As a result of selection for bipedalism, physical maturation became prolonged (delayed) during early hominin evolution, causing infants to take longer to achieve milestones such as crawling, standing, and walking. Consequently, prehistoric offspring, similar to modern ones, failed to develop an ability to cling unaided to their mothers. This was an evolutionary reversal because all extant monkey and ape infants develop such an ability. The responsibility for attaching infants to caregivers eventually shifted from the former to the latter. B = time of birth. Reproduced from Falk 2016.

the later emergence of dexterous precision grasping, perhaps associated with tool making (Rolian et al. 2010).

Due to especially strong selection on the toes (Rolian et al. 2010), hominin babies (like modern ones) lost the ability to grasp with their feet, a reversal from the apelike ancestral condition. Because the development of hands and feet are genetically coupled and coevolved (Rolian et al. 2010), prehistoric infants' development of posture and locomotion using both extremities changed in ways that become apparent when one compares modern ape and human babies. Pushing off, sitting, standing without support, crawling, and walking bipedally appear considerably later in human than in chimpanzee infants (Plooij 1984; Smith and Tompkins 1995; Adolph and Berger 2006).

When it comes to locomotion, humans are late bloomers (figure 6.2). Partly because of this, human babies have been called "secondarily altricial" (Smith and Tompkins 1995:270) or simply "helpless." It is important to note, however, that human babies are not nearly as helpless when it comes to non-locomotor development. For example, chimpanzee and human infants are remarkably similar in the sequence and timing of other developmental stages, such as distress at separation from the mother, disappearance of blind rooting responses, production of social faces, and fear of strangers (Plooij 1984).

Delayed locomotor development was thus the initial trend kicked (or toe-heeled) off by prehistoric infants. At some point after their feet became adapted for walking instead of grasping, hominin babies failed to develop an ability to cling unsupported to their mothers' bellies and backs, which was an evolutionary reversal because such an ability develops in all living monkeys and apes (Ross 2001). It was not just the lack of grasping ability that made it increasingly difficult for prehistoric infants to remain attached to their mothers, however. With the assumption of upright posture, mothers' vertical backs no longer provided horizontal platforms on which infants could ride with relative ease. Eventually (by at least 3.3 Ma), there was also less hair on mothers' backs and bellies for babies to cling to, as indicated by genetic studies of lice (Reed et al. 2007). (See DeSilva, chapter 4, this volume, for discussion about the impact of infants' loss of grasping ability on their mothers' ability to climb trees.)

Prior to the invention of baby carriers (Hrdy 1999) and perhaps "central place provisioning," which facilitates allomothering in extant hunter-gatherers, such as the Hadza (Marlowe 2005; Hrdy, chapter 9, this volume), hominin mothers probably had a feed-as-you-go foraging lifestyle similar to that of chimpanzees (Marlowe 2006). The inability of infants to cling unsupported to their mothers meant that, for the first time in prehistory, nursing infants had to be actively carried. Laboratory tests have shown that carrying an infant without benefit of a baby sling is an enormous drain on maternal energy, perhaps even greater than that from lactation (Wall-Scheffler et al. 2007). This finding supports the hypothesis that baby slings were probably one of the earliest nonlithic inventions (Zihlman 1981; Hrdy 1999).

Before their invention, however, early hominin mothers likely carried their helpless nursing infants in their arms or on their hips when they traveled. (The milk of prehistoric mothers would have provided a source of hydration in addition to nutrition; see Quinn, chapter 5, this volume.) Although they may have coaxed others into helping, before baby slings were invented ancestral mothers must have put their nurslings down next to them periodically to dig for tubers, pick fruit, or just relax. This component of the putting the baby down (PTBD) hypothesis (Falk 2004, 2009, 2012) has been incorrectly interpreted as suggesting that hominin mothers adopted a prosimian-like practice of "baby parking" their infants and temporarily abandoning them to forage. However, such baby parking was *explicitly* rejected as part of the PTBD hypothesis because frequent nursing required mother-infant proximity and because baby parking would have been maladaptive in predator-occupied hominin habitats (Falk 2004:500). Baby parking is one thing; putting the baby down nearby is another (Falk 2004:open peer commentaries, author's response).

Ancestral mothers probably even put their babies down *after* baby slings were invented. Marlowe (2006) observed that Hadza mothers use slings made of animal skins to transport their nursing infants on their backs when foraging and that they usually keep their infants on their backs while digging tubers, occasionally swinging them to the front to nurse. However, he also noted that mothers sometimes remove their babies from their backs and put them down next to them while they dig (Falk 2009). This strategy, which is used by women in industrialized societies who routinely put their babies down on blankets or in nearby baby seats or playpens in order to go about their business, is not used by monkey or ape mothers with nursing infants. It was invented by prehistoric hominins, and it seems reasonable to suggest that this happened *after* infants lost the ability to remain on their mothers' bodies without support.

Trend 2: Seeking Contact Comfort

The second trend initiated by prehistoric infants occurred at arrow 2 in the above evolutionary sequence (changes in infant locomotor development →² enhanced mother-infant communication). Primate infants who are separated from their mothers yearn for physical contact with them or their surrogates. This need for "contact comfort" was shown experimentally for infant macaques over half a century ago (Harlow 1958), and it accounts for the fact that a major reason human babies cry is to reestablish physical contact with separated caregivers (Small 1998; Wolff 1969; Soltis 2004). Although it may be up to 2 months before newborn chimpanzees are able to cling effectively to their mothers, they fall off infrequently because the mothers support them at this early stage (Plooij 1984). Individual mothers are more or less supportive, however, and infants sometimes become insecurely attached to less attendant mothers. When this happens, the infant becomes agitated and communicates her distress vocally, as illustrated by the following "natural experiment" at Gombe:

> Madam Bee had raised two infants successfully when one of her arms was paralyzed during a presumed polio-epidemic. . . . The two infants that were born afterwards died within a few months. I had the occasion to make observations on the first of these two infants: Bee-hind. Her body was full of wounds and scratches, so she must have fallen repeatedly. Whenever her mother moved about without supporting her, she whimpered and screamed continuously. (Plooij 1984:45–46)

Bee-hind's traumatic experience provides a stark example of how selection may have directly targeted prehistoric infants as their ability to ride unsupported on their mothers faltered during the transition to bipedalism. This is consistent with the observation that, for chimpanzee neonates, "maternal support is of vital importance to the baby. Without it, the baby would surely fall off and may die" (Plooij 1984:45). When prehistoric babies were put down nearby and thus separated from the security, warmth, and comfort of their mothers' bodies, they would have been agitated and expressed their distress vocally, in keeping with the behavior of monkey, ape, and human infants. From such humble beginnings, ancestral infants evolved vocal and visual signals for seeking contact comfort (figure 6.3)—signals that are conserved in modern babies. Who, for example, can fail to understand what the infant on the far right of figure 6.3 wants?

Unlike fossilized hand and foot bones, which provide direct information about trend 1, there is no fossil record of prehistoric infants' signaling, which must be inferred entirely by comparing infant monkeys, apes, and humans. Comparative studies show that human babies have derived facial expressions and ways of crying that are, in large part, adaptations for maintaining proximity with caregivers (Schmidt and Cohn 2001; Small 1998; Soltis 2004; Provine et al. 2009). But crying also evolved "to assure protection, adequate feeding, and nurturing for an organism that cannot care for itself. By definition, crying is designed to elicit a response, to activate emotions, to play on the empathy of another. . . . The caretaker has also evolved the sensory mechanism to recognize that infant cries are a signal of unhappiness, and thus be motivated to do

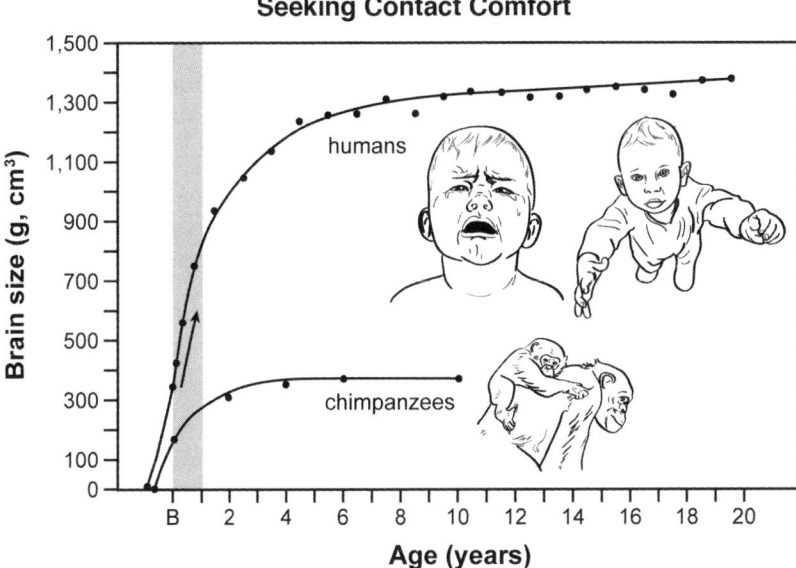

Figure 6.3. Trend 2: Seeking contact comfort. Hominin infants who lost the ability to cling independently to their mothers developed vocal and visual signals (e.g., shedding emotional tears) to prompt caregivers to pick them up or deliver other proxies for contact comfort (e.g., soothing vocalizations, rhythmic bouncing). These signals paved the way for reciprocal communication between infants and mothers and the eventual emergence of motherese, which seeded the first languages. B = time of birth. Reproduced from Falk 2016.

something about it" (Small 1998:156). Small's observation fits with the fact that, unlike all other primates, human infants develop an ability to shed emotional tears (Provine et al. 2009) (figure 6.3). Significantly, the cries of human babies develop more complicated melodies over the first several months of life, which contribute to the eventual emergence of babbling, which in turn paves the way for speaking (Wermke et al. 2007). As Small's research suggests, the cries of ancestral babies likely provoked reciprocal give-and-take gestural (including prolonged eye contact) and vocal communication with their mothers, which would have been an important prerequisite for the eventual emergence of protolanguage (Falk 2004, 2009).

THE EMERGENCE OF MOTHERESE AND PROTOLANGUAGE

Vestiges of the evolutionary old days are seen in human babies who retain a grasping reflex but are unable to cling to their mothers without support (Halverson 1937a, b, c), and in the finding that crying increases the strength of infants' grasping reflex (Halverson 1937a). The past is also evoked when babies respond positively to stimuli that mimic (the lost) constant physical contact with mothers, such as bouncing, co-sleeping (McKenna, chapter 10, this volume), jostling, rocking, swaddling, hugging, soft textures (blankies), and comfort suckling (pacifiers). Infants' favorable responses to vocal reassurances that their mother is near (lullabies and motherese, also known as baby talk) is another evolutionary hand-me-down, as are their reciprocal gestural and vocal interactions (often in the form of play) with caregivers.

Studies of human mothers the world over lend support to the hypothesis that, in response to separated babies' unhappy vocalizations, prehistoric mothers began using melodic intonations to soothe and reassure their infants of the mothers' proximity. Elsewhere (Falk 2004, 2009), I have speculated that give-and-take vocalizations between infants and mothers led to the emergence of lullabies and motherese, which, over time, evolved to their present forms. Compared to the speech that modern adults use with each other, motherese is more melodic, is slower, has a higher overall pitch, is more repetitious, uses a simpler vocabulary, and includes special words like "bye-bye" and "doggie" (Fernald 1994). Once it got under way, prehistoric motherese would have eventually incorporated body language, including facial expressions, touching, patting, caressing, bouncing, rocking, tickling, and laughter, similar to modern motherese.

In a nutshell, the PTBD hypothesis suggests that because of their periodic physical separations, reciprocal vocal communication intensified between prehistoric mothers and infants, which led to the emergence of motherese, and that motherese in turn seeded the subsequent invention of protolanguage, which became conventionalized and transmitted to future generations (see Falk 2004, 2009 for details). These ideas are consistent with data about the invention and transmission by deaf children of Nicaraguan Sign Language (Senghas et al. 2004) and with data about the invention and transmission of protocultural practices by female Japanese macaques and their youngsters, first laterally among group members and then to future generations (Kawai 1965).

The PTBD hypothesis was controversial when it was first proposed for two main reasons. First, some commentators questioned the assertion made long ago (Ferguson 1978) that motherese is universal (Falk 2004:commentaries). However, despite an earlier literature to the contrary (Ochs and Schieffelin 1984; Schieffelin 1990; Ochs 1982), motherese is now documented to exist among Western Samoan, Kaluli New Guinea, and black working-class Americans (Falk 2009:89–95). Further, contrary to the assertions of some (Pye 1991), motherese also occurs among K'iché-speaking mothers from Guatemala's western highlands (Falk 2009). Fieldwork in the societies that supposedly lacked motherese demonstrates that societal norms constrain the form that mother-infant communication may take, but the research does not support the assertion that some cultures completely lack motherese. Motherese is as universal and varied as language itself.

The second reason the PTBD hypothesis was controversial was because some questioned the basic premise that motherese helps babies to learn their native languages. Although mother and infant nonhuman primates sometimes exchange relatively simple contact calls, these primates lack the proclivity of humans to address infants, including newborns in the delivery room (Trevathan 1987), with a more or less continuous stream of a specialized linguistic register of melodious speech. Humanlike motherese, therefore, emerged at some point after the ~6.0 Ma split between the chimpanzee and hominin lineages, as did language itself. Significantly, there is a functional relationship between the two forms of expression. Human babies are born speechless but start to express their native languages by around the end of the first year of life. Among other functions, the motherese that infants are exposed to helps them learn their languages in sequential, age-appropriate steps (Monnot 1999; Dehaene-Lambertz et al. 2006). Baby talk exaggerates vowels, syllables, and certain words, which helps infants learn to parse speech streams. Further, the quality of motherese that neurotypical babies hear is positively linked with their development of speech discrimination skills (Liu et al. 2003). Infants who stand out at perceiving speech sounds at 7 months perform better when they are older on tests that quantify the number of words they can say and the complexity of their speech (Tsao et al. 2004). Motherese helps teach infants the rules for constructing words and correctly combining them into phrases and sentences (grammar) (Karmiloff and Karmiloff-Smith 2001) in English, French, Italian, Polish, Russian, and Serbian (Farrar 1990; Kempe and Brooks 2001).

Although some scholars might object to the suggestion that mothers and youngsters invented the first language on the grounds that it is biased against adult males, it is reasonable to assume that the individuals transporting hominin genes into the future (infants) and the hominin parents most responsible for their survival (mothers) significantly influenced the course of hominin evolution. The hypothesis is also in harmony with the well-known facts that male and female primates pursue different sex-specific reproductive strategies (Lancaster 1985) and that women, on average, tend to outperform men at grasping and producing linguistic, gestural, and emotional communications (Cahill 2006; Andreano and Cahill 2009; see Falk 2016 for discussion).

Trend 3: Accelerated Early Brain Growth (Brain Spurt)

The third trend that emerged in prehistoric infants occurred at arrow 3 in the above evolutionary sequence (enhanced mother-infant communication →³ accelerated brain growth during the first postnatal year associated with neurological reorganization). Prenatal humans have larger brains than chimpanzees, but the pace of brain growth is similar in the two species until 22 weeks of gestation. At that point, the growth of the human fetus's brain begins to accelerate steeply compared to chimpanzees and continues doing so through the end of the first postnatal year (Sakai et al. 2012) (shaded bar and arrow in figure 6.4). After the first year of life, the human brain grows at a less accelerated rate until it levels off at adult size (Passingham 1975) (figure 6.4). The first-year brain spurt propels human brain size higher compared to the chimpanzee growth curve, and human brain growth is also relatively prolonged, which is why adult humans end up with brains that are three to four times the size of adult chimpanzee brains (Passingham 1975; DeSilva and Lesnik 2006, 2008; DeSilva, chapter 4, this volume).

Significantly, the fossil record of hominin cranial capacities shows that modern humans have brains that are also three to four times the size of australopithecine brains and further suggests that developmental brain growth curves were pulled higher during the course of hominin brain evolution. For example, the curve for Taung is slightly above that for living chimps in figure 6.4, whereas the curve for the more recently evolved *Homo erectus* would be higher, but still underneath the human curve. As is well known, brain size in *Homo sapiens* seems to have leveled off (after decreasing a bit) compared to the larger brains of Neanderthals. In sum, once it emerged, the

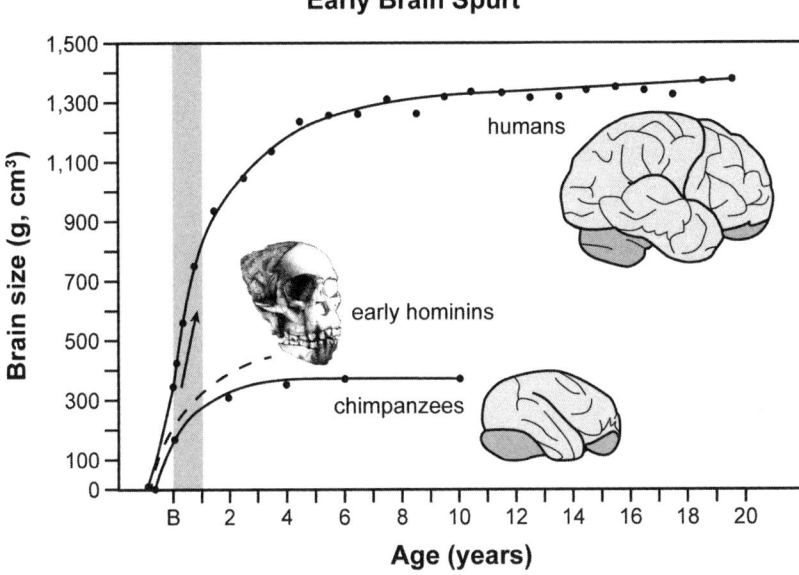

Early Brain Spurt

Figure 6.4. Trend 3: Early brain spurt. Postnatal brain growth in humans (*top*) and chimpanzees (*bottom*). Brain growth is accelerated during the first postnatal year(s) in humans (arrow) compared to early fossil hominins and chimpanzees; adult human brains are more than three times the size of adult ape brains. The dashed line indicates the evolutionary emergence of an accelerated brain spurt in *Australopithecus*, represented here by the Taung child (approximately 2.5 million years old). The brain sizes for chimpanzees and Taung are based on cranial capacities (in cm³); those for humans are in grams. (Because the mass of the brain in grams is approximately equivalent to its volume in cubic centimeters, cranial capacities are an accepted proxy for brain size.) B = time of birth. Data for humans and chimpanzees from Passingham 1975. © 1975 Karger Publishers, Basel, Switzerland. Reproduced from Falk 2016.

trend for accelerated brain growth in prehistoric neonates/infants appears to have been the mechanism that caused hominin brain size evolution.

As Leonard Radinsky (1979:24) remarked long ago, elucidation of the factors responsible for the evolution of extreme brain size in humans "remains a fascinating unsolved problem." But brains did more than just increase in size during hominin evolution. Their internal wiring and architecture became reorganized (Holloway et al. 2004), not in a "mosaic" or modular fashion

(Finlay and Darlington 1995; Finlay et al. 2001; Anderson 2014) but rather across the entire cerebral cortex, including its association cortices (Dart 1929; Semendeferi et al. 2011; Falk 2014; Semendeferi and Hanson, chapter 7, this volume). Because of the current obstetrical dilemma, which emerged on the heels of the third evo-devo trend, future brain evolution is likely to entail the brain's internal (re)organization (Hofman 2014), but without much further increase in brain size. Research carried out since Radinsky's observation, much of it new, goes a long way toward elucidating the factors responsible for increased brain size and the neurological reorganization of the human brain, which entailed selection on the prehistoric infants who had already sparked trend 2 and were thus interacting vocally with their mothers.

GRAMMATICAL LANGUAGE: PROBABLE PRIME MOVER OF BRAIN EVOLUTION

In order to investigate the evolutionary causes of the increased acceleration of brain growth during the last trimester of human gestation as well as the continuation of this spurt during babies' first year(s) (figure 6.4), it is useful to identify features that are unique to the human's developing brain and any associated behaviors. To start with, we can ask what, besides the brain spurt, happens to human fetuses in the third trimester that does not happen to chimpanzees at a comparable stage. Experimental evidence shows that, during the last 3 months of gestation, the human fetus spends most of its waking hours eavesdropping on its mother's speech, which primes it to process linguistic input after birth (Karmiloff and Karmiloff-Smith 2001). Humans thus "perceptually 'map' critical linguistic and prosodic aspects of ambient language beginning in utero, which continues through the first year of life before they can speak" (Kuhl 2000:11850). Concordantly, the structural asymmetries that characterize human brains begin to develop in the third trimester, resulting in a significant asymmetry favoring the left hemisphere for reception of speech-like stimuli in neonates (Dehaene-Lambertz et al. 2006).

The postnatal spurt in brain size is due largely to the development of connections between neurons (synapses) and the formation of insulating material (myelin, or white matter) that surrounds nerve axons. It is important to note, however, that during the first year of life, numerous connections are also eliminated via synaptic pruning, which appears to tune the nervous system "to the particular environment of each individual" (Squire et al. 2008:475).

According to Patricia Kuhl's (2000, 2004) native language neural commitment (NLNC) hypothesis, during a baby's first year, the perception of statistical and prosodic regularities of speech produces neural networks that are dedicated to coding the patterns of native speech, which facilitate the learning of relevant phonemes, words, and (later) grammar. Although 6-month-olds can distinguish the approximately 600 consonants and 200 vowels in all of the world's languages, by the end of their first year their perception becomes selectively tuned to the approximately 40 speech sounds from their native language (Kuhl 2000, 2004). It seems likely that the developmental pruning in infants' perception of speech sounds is related to much of the pruning in their brains' synapses.

Infants' identification and encoding of the subset of phonemes in their native language constrains how they process speech as adults. Listening to speech in adults prompts a representation of its basic elements (phonemes) in neurons of the superior temporal gyrus (STG) of the temporal lobe, a part of the brain that responds to speech over other sounds, in an extremely rapid and complex manner (Mesgarani et al. 2014). Each phoneme causes neurons at different STG sites to fire in response to a particular aspect of the sound, such as voice onset time, manner of articulation (plosive, sonorant, etc.), and place of articulation (labial, dental, etc.). (Rather than responding to one particular phoneme, most STG sites respond to specific groups of phonemes, such as nasals.) Together, the various sites that are activated in response to a particular phoneme "give rise to our internal representation" of it (Mesgarani et al. 2014:1009). Interestingly, a listener's ability to identify a particular phoneme when it is spoken by various individuals under different circumstances (invariance) is due largely to that phoneme's manner of articulation, which is coded in a less distributed manner in the STG than are other phonemic features. This recent discovery is satisfyingly consistent with classical linguistic theory (Grodzinsky and Nelken 2014).

According to Kuhl's NLNC hypothesis, once they have phonemes down, babies use (unconscious) statistical and computational processes to discover words in running streams of speech. In English, for example, most words are stressed on the first syllables, as in the words "jungle" and "monkey" (Thiessen and Saffran 2007). By the time an infant is 7–8 months old, she spontaneously perceives words that have this strong-weak pattern, but not words with the less frequent weak-strong pattern. Thus, when infants hear "guitar is" they perceive "taris" as a unit because it begins with a stressed syllable (Jusczyk et al. 1999).

The singsong prosody of motherese is extremely helpful for marking the divisions between words even before infants know what they mean (Kuhl 2000, 2004). Infants subsequently learn the meanings of words and how to assemble (and produce) them in bigger units (phrases, sentences, etc.) by listening to speech and with help from exposure to motherese. The sequential linguistic processes that create complex (higher-order) combinations from basic units are distributed across wider neural networks than those used to store representations of the basic building blocks of speech perception in the STG (Mesgarani et al. 2014). Although "operations involved in building complex expressions—sentences with rich syntax and semantics—are relatively localized in parts of the left cerebral hemisphere (and distinct from other combinatorial processes such as arithmetic)" (Grodzinsky and Nelken 2014:979; see also Cogan et al. 2014), these parts of the brain also participate in nonlinguistic processes. In other words, there is no language module per se (Anderson 2014).

Elsewhere (Falk 2009), I have suggested that the automatic statistical and computational processes that program infants' wetware (brains) with the fundamentals of their native languages also facilitate their development of other advanced cognitive abilities, such as those related to music, art, mathematics, and science. This idea is consistent with the finding that statistical processes similar to those used to acquire language facilitate infants' learning of visual patterns (Fiser and Aslin 2002; Kirkham et al. 2002). Nevertheless, in light of the third evo-devo trend and its neurobehavioral correlates, it seems likely that selection for enhanced vocal communication between prehistoric mothers and infants provided the initial impetus for accelerated brain evolution and, ultimately, its advanced cognitive derivatives. If this is so, language was the prime mover of hominin brain evolution, and prehistoric infants were the targets that drove our apelike ancestors to become the loquacious species we remain.

Asperger Syndrome and Its Relationship to the Three Trends

In all likelihood, language derived ultimately from extremely ancient contact calls between mothers and infants, which are conserved in many mammals (Newman 2004). Human language is unique, however, because units (phonemes, words, etc.) are combined and recombined based on internalized grammatical rules to express (and understand) a potentially limitless number of ideas. Grammatical rules differ between languages, must be learned, and depend on extremely rapid higher-order (top-down) neurological processing that activates multipurpose networks, which are distributed across the brain (Anderson 2014; Grodzinsky and Nelken 2014). Above all, grammar is inherently systematic and computational in nature—and so, too, are certain other advanced cognitive abilities of humans, such as capabilities in music, mathematics, or physics (Falk 2009).

In this context it is interesting to consider a group of people who have a condition associated with especially proficient linguistic, systematic, and computational skills, namely those with Asperger syndrome (AS) (Falk and Schofield forthcoming). Although Asperger's disorder ceased to be a formal diagnosis when it was merged with other forms of autism in a category called "autism spectrum disorder" in the latest revision of the *Diagnostic and Statistical Manual of Mental Disorders* (American Psychiatric Association 2013), studies show that AS differs significantly from all other forms of autism, including one that is informally referred to as "high-functioning autism" (HFA) (Lai et al. 2013; Tsai and Ghaziuddin 2014; Chiang et al. 2014). The title of one survey is telling—"Asperger's Disorder Will Be Back" (Tsai 2013)—and the startling amount of research that continues to be done on AS suggests it never really went away. One authoritative study suggests that, on average, approximately 10% of all autistic individuals may have AS (Developmental Disabilities Monitoring Network 2014). AS differs from other forms of autism, including so-called HFA, because it is associated with normal or above normal intelligence (Asperger 1944; Chiang et al. 2014), the timely development of grammar (Asperger 1979; Szatmari et al. 2009), distinct traits related to neurophysiology (Duffy et al. 2013), and superb systemizing skills (Baron-Cohen 2012). Aspies (a term of self-affirmation preferred by some people with AS) share the poor communication skills and repetitive and/or stereotypic behaviors associated with other autists, and they typically develop avid but narrow interests, such as a predilection for train spotting, a fascination with classical literature, or a desire to learn everything there is to know about dinosaurs (Attwood 2013). Aspies also tend to speak in a precocious manner and to drone on endlessly about their particular interests, which leads some observers to call AS the "little professor syndrome."

Referring to himself in the third person, the eponymous Hans Asperger compared children with AS to those who have classic autism (Kanner syndrome):

Asperger's typical cases are very intelligent children with extraordinary originality of thought and spontaneity of activity. . . . Their thinking, too, seems unusual in that it is endowed with special abilities in the areas of logic and abstraction. . . . A further important difference . . . is that Asperger children, very early, even before they walk, develop highly grammatical speech and they may be uncommonly apt at using expressions coined spontaneously. . . . However, the children with Kanner's syndrome generally avoid communication, consequently they do not develop speech or develop it very late. . . . The Asperger type of child . . . may continue with his special subject with undiminished vigour and with originality and may in the end find his way into an unusual career, perhaps into highly specialised scientific work, maybe with an ability bordering on genius. . . . Indeed, it seems that for success in science or art a dash of autism is essential. (Asperger 1979:48–49)

In 2010, 1 in 68 eight-year-olds from 11 US sites was diagnosed with autism spectrum disorder (Developmental Disabilities Monitoring Network 2014), which is an increase over previous years. Interestingly, the increase in autism seems to be more pronounced in the milder, high-functioning forms, including AS (Keyes et al. 2012; Beaudet 2012; Mattila et al. 2007). Despite the fact that some researchers believe that this rising prevalence is entirely due to increased awareness and improved diagnostic methods (Grinker 2008), others calculate that about one-half to two-thirds of the apparent increase in diagnoses of autism is real (Dave and Fernandez 2015). Although the causes of autism include environmental factors, such as malnutrition in gestating mothers or advanced age of fathers (Kong et al. 2012), the development of autism is highly influenced by genetic background (Chakrabarti et al. 2009), as shown by familial studies and by comparisons of the prevalence of autism in identical and fraternal twins (Hallmayer et al. 2011; Bailey et al. 1995). This helps explain the well-known fact that neurotypical relatives of individuals with AS have elevated levels of autistic traits.

The so-called geek hypothesis of Simon Baron-Cohen suggests that a relatively high number of infants are born with AS in certain communities because of positive assortative mating between men and women with enhanced technical skills and high systemizing abilities. Although this idea is controversial (Buchen 2011), it is supported by data showing differentially high frequencies of AS in high-tech enclaves, including Silicon Valley in California, Bangalore in

India, and Eindhoven in the Netherlands (Spek and Velderman 2013; Klei et al. 2012). Baron-Cohen suggests that offspring of couples from these communities receive differentially more genes (i.e., from both parents) related to systemizing compared to other infants and, further, that "people with autism, whose minds differ from what we consider typical, frequently display both disability and exceptional aptitude. Genes that contribute to autism may overlap with genes for the uniquely human ability to understand how the world works in extraordinary detail—to see beauty in patterns inherent in nature, technology, music and math" (Baron-Cohen 2012:75).

Among modern neurotypical infants, individuals manifest characteristics associated with the three evo-devo trends to different degrees. Some babies develop physically more slowly, or more rapidly, than average; some cry more than others and may be especially needy (or not) when it comes to seeking contact comfort; and some infants have greater or lesser brain spurts than the norm. In other words, there is a natural range of variation in infants' expressions of these traits. Given Aspies' aptitude for the kinds of analytical thinking described initially by Hans Asperger and quantified later by Simon Baron-Cohen, one wonders how their expressions of the three trends compare to those of neurotypicals.

THE ASPERGER BABY

With respect to the first trend sparked by prehistoric infants, autistic babies are even later bloomers than neurotypicals in achieving developmental milestones, such as gaining control over limbs and head in supine and prone positions, unsupported sitting, crawling, and walking (Ozonoff et al. 2008). For example, Cederlund and Gillberg (2004) reported that the mean age for walking unsupported for 85 males with AS was 13.8 months, compared to a mean of 12 months in the general population. Aspies' motor development may also be out of sync with their sensory development, thus contributing to a tendency to be physically clumsy compared to other high-functioning autistic people (Weimer et al. 2001). Remarkably, some Aspies seem to shed autistic symptoms by adulthood, although this is denied by some and mistaken by others as a "cure" (Padawer 2014), rather than being seen as an extreme manifestation of the evolutionary trend for delayed and prolonged development, as proposed here.

Aspies' manifestation of the second trend (seeking contact comfort) is particularly interesting. Recall that neurotypical babies are soothed by physical cuddling and other stimuli that simulate contact with their mothers (e.g., soft blankies, pacifiers) and by bouncing, swaying, and rocking, which mimics the round-the-clock contact with (frequently traveling) mothers that their prehistoric predecessors enjoyed. Despite the fact that children with Asperger syndrome are known to shun hugs and certain tactile experiences, such as wearing woolly sweaters, they retain an intense need for stimuli that simulate contact comfort, including repetitive stimulation (e.g., bouncing, rocking). Because of their tactile hypersensitivity, however, they find it difficult to tolerate someone else delivering these stimuli. As Temple Grandin put it, "From as far back as I can remember, I always hated to be hugged. I wanted to experience the good feeling of being hugged, but it was too overwhelming" (1995:62). Instead, autistic children provide their own rocking, spinning, hand flapping and other repetitive movements, hugs (Grandin's famous squeeze machine, for example), and contact with soft materials (e.g., the fur of animals). Indeed, one can purchase weighted blankets that are designed to provide soothing tactile pressure to people with autism. Unfortunately, these unusual mannerisms frequently are viewed as undesirable "stimming" rather than as adaptive behaviors that stem from an evolved, deeply engrained need for contact comfort.

As I already noted, the PTBD hypothesis posits that motherese emerged in response to trend 2 in order to soothe infants who were temporarily deprived of direct physical contact with their mothers (Falk 2004). Evidence shows that autistic infants respond positively to soothing vocalizations (Cohen et al. 2013), contrary to the widely held belief that they are impervious to them (Kuhl et al. 2005). Analyses of parental speech (in home videos) directed toward infants, some of whom subsequently developed autism, found that parents of infants who later developed autism increased both the amount of parentese (the term for baby talk when it is used by both mothers and fathers) and the extent of the fathers' interactions with their infants (Cohen et al. 2013; see Gettler, chapter 8, this volume). The researchers concluded that parents of infants who later developed autism increased their use of prosodic infant-directed speech because they may have sensed that doing so increased positive social responses in their infants, and they noted that their findings were consistent with the PTBD hypothesis. Although home video studies have not yet focused on children who later developed AS (David Cohen, pers. comm., 2015), clinicians are beginning to recognize the significance of motherese and its potential therapeutic value for autism (Cohen et al. 2013; Ouss et al. 2014; Saint-Georges et al. 2013; Tanguay 2011).

When it comes to the early brain spurt (third trend), various measures related to brain growth—such as occipitofrontal head circumference (OFC) or brain volume determined by MRI—show that autism, in general, entails an early brain size spurt that frequently, but not always (Green et al. 2015), peaks above that of neurotypicals and then subsides until the curve for neurotypical brain growth catches up with the growth curve of autism spectrum disorder by around age 6 (see graphs in Courchesne et al. 2011). These data suggest that some people with autism may, to a degree, have more accelerated and prolonged brain spurts than neurotypicals (but see Raznahan et al. 2013), which some researchers have interpreted as pathological brain overgrowth associated with increased numbers of neurons, particularly in the frontal and temporal lobes (Courchesne et al. 2011; Dementieva et al. 2005; Fukumoto et al. 2008; Schumann et al. 2010; Green et al. 2015). There is no consensus, however, about whether this acceleration begins prenatally, at birth, or at some point after birth (it seems to vary) (Green et al. 2015).

The results of one study that compared postnatal brain growth (by measuring OFC) at birth and at 16 months in Aspies and other autistic individuals found that, at birth, neonates with AS and autism both had mean OFCs that were somewhat larger than those of neurotypical neonates, although the mean OFC of Aspies was significantly greater than that of other autists. In addition, "one in four to one in five of children with Asperger syndrome, but only one in 10 of those with autistic disorder, have macrocephalus ascertained after age 16 months, which had been present from birth. . . . macrocephalus is rather more typical of the highest functioning variants of autistic spectrum disorders, currently referred to as Asperger syndrome" (Gillberg and de Souza 2002:299). This study is concordant with the conclusion from another investigation that "autistic individuals with accelerated head growth in early childhood displayed higher levels of adaptive functioning and less social impairment" (Dementieva et al. 2005:102). The limited data that are available for Aspies (Gillberg and de Souza 2002) suggest that they have early brain spurts similar to, but sometimes more pronounced than, those of neurotypicals. The fact that the postnatal acceleration in brain growth of neurotypical infants is widely recognized by evolutionary anthropologists as the result of an advanced rather than pathological trend suggests that the hypothesis that the early brain spurt in autism is necessarily pathological (Courchesne et al.

2011) needs reconsideration (Dementieva et al. 2005), at least in the case of AS. (In fact, an argument can be made that the pronounced early brain spurts of Aspies facilitate the development of their particular intellectual strengths; Falk and Schofield forthcoming.)

There is no doubt that Aspies excel at the types of linguistic, systematic, computational, analytical, and creative thinking that evolved in our ancestors on the heels of the three prehistoric trends, which is not surprising given that Aspies seem to manifest pronounced expressions of the trends. (I hasten to add, however, that the origin of these trends, which is extremely ancient, had nothing to do with autism, which apparently emerged during the evolution of modern humans; Green et al. 2010; Meyer et al. 2012; Prüfer et al. 2014.) It is interesting to view AS from the perspective of the neurodiversity movement, which asserts that atypical neurological development is simply a part of natural human variation. This idea contradicts statistical and social concepts of normality and abnormality, which reflect the degree to which individual traits and behaviors coincide with or deviate from average or common traits and behaviors. Although the concept of neurodiversity is clearly problematic when applied to low-functioning autism, ethicists make a convincing argument that it is reasonable to apply it to AS (Jaarsma and Welin 2012). In their opinion, high-functioning autism is neither a disorder nor an undesirable condition per se, but instead represents a condition with a particular vulnerability similar to that suffered by homosexuals before the American Psychiatric Association declared that homosexuality is not a psychiatric disorder and before Western society in general became less homophobic.

Consistent with this view, the data presented in this chapter suggest that AS should be recognized as a natural variation that emerged on the coattails of the trends initiated by prehistoric babies—trends that made us the talkative, technically inclined species we are today. Shouldn't that be reason enough to recognize AS as a condition that is culturally constrained by social vulnerabilities, rather than as a "mental disorder"? After all, our species is currently undergoing an almost unimaginable transformation in technological innovation, and it is a good bet that many of the people who will contribute to future advances in robotics, space technology, artificial intelligence, nanotechnology, quantum physics, and cosmology (plus the arts and literature) will be Aspies (Falk and Schofield forthcoming).

Conclusion

Since at least the time of Darwin, scholars have speculated about whether one particular behavioral "prime mover" was responsible for the remarkable evolution of the brain and cognition in hominins, and whether hominins of a particular gender and age were the targets of natural selection for that behavior. The list of proposed prime-mover behaviors is long (Falk 2016). In addition to language (Jerison 1991; Falk 2004), candidates include hunting (Joseph 2000; Krantz 1968; Lee and DeVore 1968; Washburn and Lancaster 1968), tool production (Darwin 1871), labor in the Marxist sense (Kochetkova 1978), warfare (Pitt 1978), Machiavellian intelligence (Byrne and Whiten 1988), food gathering (Slocum 1975; Lovejoy 1981; Zihlman 1989), and sociality (Dunbar and Shultz 2007). The list of proposed demographic classes of prime movers is shorter—the most prominent nominees being man the hunter (Lee and DeVore 1968) (or man the fill-in-the-blank: tool maker, warrior, Machiavellian intellectual) and woman the gatherer (Slocum 1975). Although both hunting and gathering were, no doubt, hugely important during the vast majority of hominin evolution, neither of these is likely to have provided *the* spark for hominin brain evolution.

Because the rapid acceleration of brain growth in modern fetuses and neonates appears to be a retention of the mechanism that drove brain size higher during hominin evolution (trend 3), it seems reasonable to interrogate development in extant neonates and infants when speculating about the most likely prime mover of brain evolution. As I have discussed, early brain spurts facilitate the development of multidimensional, higher-order cognitive processes that enable infants to acquire language in social contexts, and, further, such evolved circuitry serves other kinds of advanced computational thinking as individuals mature. This is why language is probably the best candidate for a prime mover of hominin brain evolution and why selection on baby the trendsetter is likely to have had a more significant impact on making us human than the occupation of either of her parents.

Acknowledgments

I thank the School for Advanced Research, Wenda Trevathan, and Karen Rosenberg for including me in the advanced seminar "Costly and Cute: How

Helpless Newborns Made Us Human." I am grateful to Daniel Lieberman for helpful discussion about the obstetrical dilemma and to an anonymous reviewer for causing me to rethink its definition and, consequently, completely rewrite this chapter. I thank Rochelle Marrinan at Florida State University for her support and Merryl Sloane for meticulous copyediting.

Notes

1. See http://www.oxforddictionaries.com/us/definition/american_english/dilemma.

CHAPTER SEVEN

Plastic and Heterogeneous

Postnatal Developmental Changes in the Human Brain

KATERINA SEMENDEFERI AND KARI L. HANSON

The adult human brain has expanded nearly three times in size since the divergence from our last common ancestor shared with chimpanzees and bonobos. Evidence from comparative studies suggests that this expansion has been coupled with reorganization in both cortical and subcortical structures at the cellular level. Though evidence from the fossil record (see Ponce de León and Zollikofer, chapter 3, and DeSilva, chapter 4, both this volume) was previously thought to support the notion that the evolution of bipedal locomotion placed constraints on the size of the brain at birth, the neoteny of the human brain may not directly correspond to constraints related to the maternal pelves' changing morphology, but rather to the energetic demands of gestation (see Dunsworth, chapter 2, this volume). Nevertheless, the human neonate's brain is born large and underdeveloped, with a smaller proportion of adult brain size attained prenatally compared to other primates (Trevathan 1987; Leigh 2004; DeSilva and Lesnik 2006).

The development of connections between neurons relies entirely on activity-dependent processes (Greenough et al. 1987). Numerous studies have shown that the development of sensory (Wiesel 1982; Fagiolini et al. 1994; Moore 1985) and motor (Marin-Padilla 1970) faculties depends on input from the environment postnatally to support the development of proper neuronal morphology and distribution. Similarly, the development of areas involved in cognition relies on input from the social and cultural system in highly flexible patterns. Social deprivation experiments performed in a variety of mammalian species have shown departures from typical brain development in structures involved in cognition and behavior (Martin et al. 1991; Braun et al. 1999; Lapiz et al.

2003). In primates, early social deprivation in critical periods results in aberrant social behavior and deficits in behavioral control (Harlow et al. 1965; Harlow and Suomi 1971).

Differences in developmental patterns in cortical and subcortical areas observed in human and nonhuman primate brains likely underlie the enhanced capacities for cultural acquisition and hierarchical social organization in primate lineages. With increased periods of dependence on maternal and allomaternal care and slowed rates of growth and development in areas involved in social cognition, this trend has been magnified, leading to uniquely human capacities for the acquisition of language and for complex cultural behavior and cognition. Here, we outline some of these key developmental differences between humans and nonhuman primates, and we suggest that differences in development likely mediate the emergence of uniquely human cognitive adaptations.

A growing number of studies targeting the physiology of the nervous system show that different classes of neurons fire several distinct patterns of action potentials accompanied by significant variability in energy demands (Moujahid et al. 2014). Studies of the evolution and development of the costly human brain need to take into consideration the distribution of different types of neurons in smaller and larger brains, since the structural complexity of this organ and the associated energetic costs are far from homogeneous. Consideration of overall size alone cannot capture the complex demands of our costly brains, and instead an examination of structural variability is necessary, from the developing brain through adulthood.

General Principles of Human Brain Development

Starting with the embryonic stages and throughout infancy and childhood, the brain changes considerably in both volume and composition (Teffer and Semendeferi 2012). The neural tube is the first brain structure to arise—in the third week of gestation from progenitor cells in the neural plate (Stiles and Jernigan 2010)—and neuron production begins in the sixth week. Numbers of neurons increase exponentially from gestational week 13 to week 20 in the neocortical part of the developing brain (Dobbing and Sands 1973; Samuelsen et al. 2003). Neuronal proliferation and migration continue past mid-gestation (Shankle et al. 1999; Rakic 1988; Sidman and Rakic 1973), when neuron numbers are less than half those in the adult human brain (Pakkenberg and Gundersen 1997). White matter also experiences a significant degree of growth from 13 to 20 weeks, while many regions of the cortex reach their peak cell density between 28 and 38 weeks (Rabinowicz et al. 1996). Neurogenesis slows to a linear rate of increase from gestational week 22 to birth, with total neuron numbers increasing until the full-term infant is born. Prenatally, cortical thickness, a composite measure that includes neurons, axons, dendrites, synapses, and glia, increases linearly throughout the entire brain as a function of age (Rabinowicz et al. 1996), thus serving as a useful gauge of overall maturity.

During early childhood, the brain quadruples in size and grows to roughly 90% of the adult volume by age 6 (Courchesne et al. 2000; Knickmeyer et al. 2008). The initial periods of rapid neurogenesis and synaptogenesis subsequently give way to a period of pruning and neuronal death in order to manage the overproduction of these components. Throughout childhood and adolescence, brain development is characterized by first growth and then decline in gray matter volume and by increases in white matter volume. As the brain increases in size, many microstructural changes occur as well, including dendritic and axonal growth and synaptogenesis. These microstructural changes are also heterochronous; most of these events occur earliest in the sensorimotor cortex and other primary cortices, and latest in the prefrontal cortex and other higher-order association cortices that integrate and process information from the primary cortex (Shankle et al. 1999). Specifically at birth, neuronal density in the frontal cortex is similar to that in many other regions, including the visual cortex; however, adult values are reached by just 5 months of age in the visual cortex and much later in childhood in the frontal lobe.

At the same time that gray matter volume decreases throughout childhood and adolescence, white matter experiences a correlated increase in volume as fiber tracts grow and myelinate. Throughout the cortex as a whole, white matter volume increases 74% from infancy to mid-adolescence (Courchesne et al. 2000). Myelination begins in the 29th gestational week with the brain stem, and the development of white matter also typically follows a caudal to rostral progression (Flechsig 1901, 1920). Humans (Giedd et al. 1999; Gogtay et al. 2004; Klingberg et al. 1999; Levitt 2003; Paus et al. 1999; Pfefferbaum et al. 1994; Watson et al. 2006) and our close relatives the chimpanzees (Gibson 1991; Watson et al. 2006) exhibit a nearly linear white matter volume increase and continued myelination until adolescence or early adulthood. Synaptogenesis begins in utero at around the 20th gestational week. Like many other neurodevelopmental processes, the formation and organization of synapses increases after birth, reaches a peak, and is followed by pruning and decline.

Cellular migration during cortical development (Rakic and Kornack 2007) leads to the formation of minicolumns in the postnatal and adult brain, which have been proposed to function as input-output processing devices that maintain specific connections between cortical regions and subcortical structures (Mountcastle 1979). Variation in minicolumn morphology is present during development and among cortical regions and is related computationally to increasing size and the ensuing connectivity issues. As size increases, brains may become less efficient in terms of connectivity since there is a corresponding decrease in the percentage of neurons to which any individual neuron is linked (Striedter 2005). Subcortical structures first appear early in development, as is the case with the amygdala primordium, which first appears during the embryonic period in humans and is contiguous with the hippocampus and closely related to the striatum. Before the end of the embryonic period, fiber connections develop between the amygdaloid nuclei and the septal, hippocampal, and diencephalic regions (Muller and O'Rahilly 2006).

Morphology and Development of Neurons

The basic unit of cortical microcircuitry is the pyramidal neuron, which determines the pattern of information flow within a particular cortical area or cortical layer (DeFelipe 1997). There is considerable variation in the morphology of pyramidal neurons both within and across species. In the cortices of primate species examined to date, including macaques, chimpanzees, and humans, the morphology of pyramidal neurons varies across functionally distinct cortical areas. Total dendritic length, the complexity of the branching of dendritic trees, and the number and density of dendritic spines (Cupp and Uemura 1980; Bianchi et al. 2012; Jacobs et al. 1997; Jacobs et al. 2001; Elston 2007) have been shown to vary relative to their distribution in functionally disparate cortical areas. Regions of the cortex that integrate information from multiple modalities typically have neurons with more complex dendritic branching and a higher number of synaptic inputs, whereas unimodal cortical areas (i.e., those involved in sensory and motor functions) have neurons that are typically less complex (Jacobs et al. 1997; Jacobs et al. 2001). Additionally, even within the same level of functional hierarchy, pyramidal neurons can differ in their morphological complexity. In the human cortex, for example, although pyramidal cells in upper cortical layer III in some high-integration areas of the prefrontal cortex display more elaborated arborizations and a higher number of spines than those in low-integration areas, there are still differences within them (Jacobs et al. 2001). While some areas, such as BA 10, underwent an increase in size (Semendeferi et al. 2001) and changes in organization (Semendeferi et al. 2011) during the course of human evolution, the evolutionary trajectory of other prefrontal areas remains unknown. Among diverse prefrontal cortical areas, it remains to be explored whether discrete regions may have fulfilled the demand for complex processing differently, with some areas increasing the space available for neuronal connectivity, allowing for greater complexity of pyramidal arbors, and others possibly favoring less branched, but more densely packed neurons (Schlaug et al. 1993; Barbas and Hilgetag 2002). Zeba and colleagues (2008) proposed that, instead of increasing the complexity of dendritic arbors in individual neurons, the need for functional complexity might have been served by increasing the ratio of the most complex neurons. This intriguing observation suggests additional opportunities to test the interplay between the structure and function of pyramidal neurons and the processing demands of particular cortical areas.

Developing neurons are more plastic than adult neurons, and dendritic morphology takes shape at different ages in different species. Research suggests that humans display a delay in the maturation of pyramidal neurons compared to other primates (Bianchi et al. 2013; Petanjek et al. 2008; Petanjek et al. 2011). This developmental delay of neuronal complexity observed in humans may in turn underlie delayed cognitive maturation, allowing additional time for environmental inputs to shape neuronal function. This may facilitate the acquisition of the complex skills and behaviors necessary to navigate an increasingly complex social environment, and the cultural tools required to survive and succeed. Dendritic modifications in response to environmental influences, as well as targeted chemical and behavioral manipulations, have been reported across mammals of various ages (Bryan and Riesen 1989; Cook and Wellman 2004; Brown et al. 2005), with pyramidal neurons responding with highly plastic changes in their morphology depending on their cortical area and layer-specific distribution. Although large-scale changes in the morphology of dendritic trees tend to diminish with age, smaller changes continue to occur throughout life, particularly in the patterning of dendritic spines, thus providing lifelong plasticity in the cortex that seems to be species-specific.

In addition to excitatory pyramidal neurons, which represent the most common neuronal type in the cerebral cortex, a diverse array of interneuron subtypes acts locally to modulate the activity of these pyramidal cells. In the primate cerebral cortex, 15%–30% of neurons are inhibitory, GABAergic interneurons (DeFelipe 1997; Sherwood et al. 2010). Inhibitory interneurons of the cerebral cortex serve a variety of functions in the modulation of excitatory neuronal function, including the control of rhythmic oscillations across assemblages of pyramidal neurons (DeFelipe 1997), which is important for the regulation of spike-timing dependent synaptic plasticity, and thus differentially strengthen the functional connections between neurons. GABAergic interneurons additionally provide for the regulation of subcortical inputs to the cortex (Hendry et al. 1987; Porter et al. 2001). Inhibitory interneurons come in a variety of morphological types classified by their reactivity to calcium-binding proteins, including parvalbumin (PV), calbindin (CB), and calretinin, and to other functional proteins, including enkephalin and substance P (Markram et al. 2004; Harris and Mrsic-Flogel 2013). The exact morphology and pattern of synaptic formation of each class of GABAergic inhibitory interneuron vary relative to the cortical region and layer in which it resides, but general patterns distinguish their morphology and connectivity (Ascoli et al. 2008; DeFelipe et al. 2013).

The distinctive traits of individual cortical neurons owe their differences to their origin and regulation during fetal development (Wonders and Anderson 2006). Similarly, subcortical structures like the primate amygdala are immature at birth, and their development depends on incoming stimuli from the environment (Hrvoj-Mihic et al. 2013a). The differentiation of individual amygdala nuclei continues from the embryonic period through the fetal period and into the postnatal period, with many nuclei exhibiting distinct developmental profiles. For example, postnatally in macaque monkeys, the nuclei of the basolateral complex demonstrate a dramatic enlargement in volume between birth and 3 months of age, with slower growth continuing beyond 1 year. In contrast, the medial nucleus is near adult size at birth, while the volume of the central nucleus is half the adult value at birth and exhibits slow but significant growth even after 1 year of age (Chareyron et al. 2012). At a cellular level, early pyramidal neurons can be distinguished in the human amygdala by the 8th and 9th gestational months. The onset of synaptogenesis is delayed in the basolateral complex relative to the corticomedial complex (Ulfig et al. 2003), with interesting implications for developmental plasticity in the basolateral complex.

Disorders of Typical Development

A comparison of morphological traits across species, while of great interest, requires an understanding of the functional implications of variations in neuronal circuitry. Through the modeling of typical function from pathological dysfunction, neurodevelopmental disorders associated with impairments of specific aspects of cognition and social behavior can be of particular interest to evolutionary studies. Characteristic behavioral phenotypes coupled with microstructural changes in these disorders may provide insights into the relationship between microcircuitry in areas subserving the processing of social information and related behaviors. Pyramidal neurons in people with neurodevelopmental disorders seem to display marked differences compared to control subjects, which may be specific to the particular disorders (Armstrong et al. 1998; but see Kaufmann and Moser 2000 for similarities among different neurodevelopmental disorders). In addition, dendritic organization tends not to be universally affected across functionally distinct cortical areas, with pyramidal cells in specific areas, as well as within particular layers, being affected differently. Pyramidal neurons in patients with autism spectrum disorders (ASDs), for example, tend to display a pathologically increased density of spines compared to typical subjects of the same age (Hutsler and Zhang 2010). Such pathologies are present in layer III across several cortical areas, including BA 7, BA 9, and BA 21, whereas cortical layer V appears affected in BA 21, with no changes between ASD subjects and controls observed in the other two areas (Hutsler and Zhang 2010).

In addition to pathologies in the morphology and number of dendritic spines in autism, deficiencies in Rett syndrome (RTT), a disorder previously classified under ASD but characterized by a specific *MECP2* mutation, include various other modifications. Characteristic morphological increases in complexity across higher-integration cortical areas, as seen in controls, are absent in RTT (Belichenko et al. 1994). In the prefrontal cortex (BA 10), supragranular layers (layers II and III) appear more affected than the infragranular ones (layers V and VI), whereas in the primary motor cortex (BA 4), the effect is the opposite: layers V and VI are more affected than layers II and III. Further, differences between RTT patients and controls appear equally distributed in both supra- and subgranular layers in Wernicke's area (BA 22), which is associated with language processing. The number of spines in RTT patients, however, was consistently reduced across all cortical layers (Belichenko et al. 1994).

Preliminary analyses have suggested that the typical variations in dendritic complexity of pyramidal neurons across functionally different cortical areas may be also compromised in Williams syndrome (Hrvoj-Mihic et al. 2013b), a disorder displaying social and linguistic features in many respects opposite to those of ASD and RTT.

Maintaining the delicate balance between excitatory and inhibitory neuronal activity is essential for proper brain function. Many neurodevelopmental disorders have been shown to involve disruption in the balance between cortical excitatory and inhibitory neuron distribution and function, as revealed through postmortem anatomical studies, and in activity, as measured in vivo in animal models of these disorders (Marín 2012). Many of these disorders differentially affect certain cognitive faculties that may be peculiar to the human behavioral phenotype, including language use and complex aspects of social cognition. Schizophrenia, for example, is a severe psychiatric disorder characterized by major deficits in social behavior and in recognition of affect (Green and Horan 2010). Research has suggested that schizophrenia's unique symptoms may result from selected vulnerabilities associated with recent adaptive genomic changes to the human neurocognitive phenotype (Crow 2000; Crespi et al. 2007; Khaitovich et al. 2008). Specifically, the rapid evolution of certain traits, including language (Crow 1998, 2000), increasingly complex social cognition (Brüne 2005; Burns 2006), and executive function and planning behavior, which are severely affected in schizophrenia, may point to derived substrates among human neuroanatomical phenotypes that support these uniquely derived cognitive and behavioral phenotypes. The cognitive effects of schizophrenia seem to suggest pathologies in the synchronization of gamma oscillations in the dorsolateral prefrontal cortex. Electrophysiological data implicate dysfunction in fast-spiking, parvalbumin-positive inhibitory interneurons, which may be decreased in number and differ in their distribution (Benes 1991). Alternatively, decreased expression of GAD67, an enzyme associated with GABA transmission, in parvalbumin-positive basket cells (PVBCs) may underlie deficits in the inhibitory control of pyramidal neurons (Lewis et al. 2012). A variety of genes may be involved in the dysfunction of PVBCs, and animal models of the disorder have highlighted several promising candidate genes (Marín 2012).

Pathophysiological processing in ASD further seems to point to the involvement of interneuronal dysfunction. Disruptions in oscillatory frequencies

(Orekhova et al. 2007; Dinstein et al. 2011) have importantly been noted, particularly in response to inhibition tasks (Rubenstein and Merzenich 2003; Yizhar et al. 2011) that implicate disruptions in the balance of inhibitory and excitatory neuronal activity. Reductions in GABAergic receptors in the anterior and posterior cingulate cortices and the fusiform gyrus have also been demonstrated in autism (Oblak et al. 2009, 2010; Oblak et al. 2011). Postmortem histological investigations have found reductions in the number of PV interneurons in the dorsolateral prefrontal cortex—specifically BA 9—in a small sample of autistic patients (Zikopoulos and Barbas 2013). Additionally, the same study found that the overall ratio of PV to CB interneurons showed a marked decrease, with significant implications for inhibitory efficacy in local networks. A relative increase of PV interneuron ratios is derived in primates compared to other mammalian lineages (Dombrowski 2001), and this may have interesting implications for derived features of inhibitory control, which may underlie social cognition. Many other cortical areas, including the fusiform face area, show evidence for disrupted synchrony between alpha and gamma oscillatory frequencies in autism (Buard et al. 2013), which further implicates PV interneuron dysfunction. The downstream effects of the decrease in PV interneurons in area 9 are likely systemic in nature (Zikopoulos and Barbas 2013) and contribute to both the local and global dysfunction in mechanisms of attention and cognition that have been noted in autism.

Whereas a variety of molecular and environmental mechanisms have been suggested as contributing to aberrant behavior and cognition in autism and schizophrenia, other disorders with known genetic etiologies show evidence for pathologies of interneuronal function, which can affect social cognition. In fragile X syndrome, for example, a reduction in numbers of several classes of inhibitory interneurons have been noted, as well as a reduction in numbers of GABA receptors, likely mediated by a global reduction in the expression of GAD65 and GAD67 (Mulle et al. 2007; Curia et al. 2009). Similar mechanisms seem to underlie deficits in learning and memory in RTT, where decreased levels of cortical GABAergic transmission may cause impairments in inhibitory neuronal function (Chao et al. 2010). Additional study of the neuroanatomical phenotype and associated perturbations of inhibitory function in disorders characterized by known genetic deletions may further elucidate the mechanisms of interneuronal function that underlie differences in cognition.

Modeling Human Brain Evolution Using Neurodevelopmental Disorders: The Case for Williams Syndrome

Some neurodevelopmental disorders have a more well-defined genetic etiology than do others and thus may provide better models for studying the links among neuropathology, function, and variation in human evolution (Hanson et al. 2014). One such disorder, Williams syndrome, is caused by a known deletion of 26–28 genes on chromosome band 7q11.23, which is of particular interest to evolutionary studies of the nervous system. It is important to note that this deleted region has been compared in typically developing humans; in extant African apes, including chimpanzees, bonobos, and gorillas; and in macaque monkeys. Substantial evidence suggests that this is a region that has undergone a number of sweeps of purifying selection in the hominoid lineage compared to macaques. Along with a very high rate of de novo mutations occurring in this region, this suggests it may be a "hot spot" for genomic change in recent human evolution (Antonell et al. 2005). Thus, Williams syndrome may be considered a sort of "living knock-out model" for studying correlations between atypical genotypes and neuropathological phenotypes (Bellugi et al. 1999; Järvinen-Pasley et al. 2008) in a dynamic and rapidly evolving region of the genome.

Williams syndrome is characterized by multiple somatic effects, including distinctive facial morphology, slowed growth, and cardiac abnormalities (Beuren et al. 1962), in part related to the deletion of the gene for elastin, which is used as the definitive marker for the disorder. Individuals with Williams syndrome additionally display a remarkably consistent cognitive and behavioral phenotype, including global reductions in total IQ, particularly with respect to visuospatial intelligence (Meyer-Lindenberg et al. 2006). Curiously, individuals with Williams syndrome demonstrate a relatively conserved linguistic capacity characterized by elaborate vocabulary and an unusually expressive use of phrases (Reilly et al. 2004), but show deficits in syntax, grammar, and other structural elements of language (Karmiloff-Smith et al. 1997; Brock 2007). Among the most salient features of Williams syndrome, affected individuals tend to be highly gregarious, demonstrating an abnormally high drive to engage in social and affiliative behavior, and they exhibit an unusual willingness to approach strangers (Doyle et al. 2004; Järvinen-Pasley et al. 2008).

This is perhaps the best-described feature of individuals with Williams syndrome: what has been referred to as their hypersociability and their intense drive to engage in social interactions with strangers. Consistent with this exaggerated proclivity to engage in affiliative behavior, as well as a heightened reactivity to emotional stimuli such as music, Dai and colleagues (2012) found increases in basal levels of the social neuropeptide oxytocin in adult individuals with Williams syndrome compared to typically developed control participants. Individuals with Williams syndrome had higher baseline levels of oxytocin, and these results correlated positively with social approach and negatively with adaptive social behavior (i.e., danger avoidance). Given the relationship between oxytocin receptors and dopaminergic input to the nucleus accumbens (Aragona et al. 2006; Insel 2003; Carter 1998), differences in the reward circuitry in Williams syndrome may hint at a functional role of the subcortical systems in modulating social approach and the incentive saliency of social engagement.

Comparative Perspectives on the Costly Brain

Humans and chimpanzees, which diverged 6–7 million years ago (Cheng 2007), are far more similar to each other in terms of brain development than they are to other living primates (Leigh 2004; DeSilva and Lesnik 2006). At birth, the human brain is 26.9%–29.5% of its adult size (DeSilva and Lesnik 2006), while chimpanzees achieve 39.5%–40.1% of their adult brain size by birth (DeSilva and Lesnik 2006; but see also Vinicius 2005). This is a marked departure from macaques, which are born with brains 70% of their adult size (Passingham 1982) and from which extant apes diverged 30 million years ago (Cheng 2007). In humans, adult brain size is reached between the ages of 5 and 7 years (Leigh 2004; Coqueugniot and Hublin 2012) and by 4–5 years of age in chimpanzees (Robson and Wood 2008). An increase in overall brain size is accompanied by discrete changes in the makeup of the nervous system, from the gross anatomical to the cellular and molecular levels, and such neural molding continues in humans especially for years after overall brain size stabilizes. This extended development is likely related to the importance of early social learning for developing proficiency at adult skills, which is evident in chimpanzees (Biro et al. 2003) as well as humans (Tomasello 1999; Boyd et al. 2011).

Longitudinal magnetic resonance imaging (MRI) research suggests that in both humans and chimpanzees, most of the early postnatal brain volume growth is attributable to increases in white matter (Sakai et al. 2011). Additionally, chimpanzees and humans share a long period of synaptogenesis (Bianchi et al. 2013), which occurs in both species throughout the juvenile period; this pattern contrasts with that of macaques, in which synaptogenesis is completed in infancy (Rakic et al. 1986). Comparative neuroanatomical studies of the adult brain suggest (Teffer et al. 2013) that the human prefrontal cortex has increased space available for interneuronal connectivity compared to apes (Casanova and Tillquist 2008; Schenker et al. 2008; Semendeferi et al. 2011; Spocter et al. 2012), and some subtle developmental differences exist between humans and chimpanzees.

The later maturation of both the association cortex and more rostral regions of the human cortex, particularly the frontal lobe, has been established by examining neuronal density (Shankle et al. 1999), dendritic and axonal growth (Schade and Van Groenou 1961; Shankle et al. 1999; Travis et al. 2005), overall gray matter development (Gogtay et al. 2004), and cerebral energy metabolism (Chugani and Phelps 1986). Prolonged rostral prefrontal development also characterizes chimpanzees (Teffer et al. 2013), including the spacing of neuronal bodies and the fact that the dendrites of prefrontal pyramidal neurons of chimpanzees develop later than they do in sensorimotor cortices (Bianchi et al. 2013). Importantly, the regions with later development in humans, like BA 10, are the very same regions that experienced the greatest degree of expansion in human evolution (Hill et al. 2010). Thus, the developmental trajectory up through the juvenile period is prolonged for both species selectively in the frontal pole and likely in other association cortical regions. By the time of adulthood, dendrites in area 10 in both chimpanzees and humans display more complex branching patterns than they do in the sensorimotor and visual cortices (Jacobs et al. 2001; Bianchi et al. 2012), which correlates with the finding that synaptogenesis occurs later in area 10 in both species (Travis et al. 2005; Bianchi et al. 2012) since regions with later development tend to have more complex dendritic branching (Jacobs et al. 1997; Jacobs et al. 2001). There are, however, important developmental differences between the species. In chimpanzees, myelination of area 10 is completed by sexual maturity, while in humans it continues past the time of adolescence (Miller et al. 2012).

Neuroimaging studies have revealed that the uniquely protracted phase of human adolescence is characterized by an extended period of maturation in the brain structures involved in social cognition, executive function, and decision making, particularly in the prefrontal cortex and areas that receive its projections. Increases in white matter consistent with increased myelination have been observed in the frontal and parietal cortices (Sowell et al. 1999). In important fiber bundles connecting cortical and subcortical regions, including the arcuate fasciculus and internal capsule, major increases in myelination have also been found (Paus et al. 1999).

Particularly in regions involved in the inhibitory control of behavior, maturation is slow: frontal and striatal circuitry continues to exhibit major changes into early adulthood (Sowell et al. 1999). Given the role of frontal and striatal circuitry in regulating behavioral inhibition (Aron and Poldrack 2005), the development of these regions is of particular interest for understanding interspecies differences in behavioral control. Behavioral response inhibition has been shown to vary in interesting ways in chimpanzees and bonobos: whereas bonobos experience precipitous gains in their ability to inhibit behavioral responses to stimuli, chimpanzees maintain low levels of behavioral control (Wobber et al. 2010b). The inhibitory control of behavior continues to develop late into adolescence in humans, which is consistent with ongoing developmental changes in the reward circuitry continuing into the third decade of life. Additionally, post-adolescent adult humans have significantly greater minicolumns spacing and neuropil fraction in area 10 than do great apes (Semendeferi et al. 2011; Spocter et al. 2012), which suggests that developmental changes continue in humans after puberty, but not in chimpanzees.

Furthermore, the expression of genes related to synaptogenesis in the prefrontal cortex peaks later in humans than in chimpanzees or macaque monkeys (Liu et al. 2012), suggesting that synaptic refinement may occur over a longer developmental period. Consistent with this idea, it has been reported that dendritic spines in the prefrontal cortex of humans continue the process of pruning into the third decade of life (Petanjek et al. 2011). Such exceptionally slow and delayed neocortical maturation might be associated with the generally protracted growth of humans, who possess an evolutionarily distinct phase of slow childhood growth and a later adolescent growth spurt (Bogin 2009; Crews and Bogin 2010).

The induced pluripotent stem cell (iPSC) technique allows somatic tissue to be reprogrammed into neurons, generating species-specific neuronal cells in vitro. This can be utilized to extend evolutionary analyses beyond morphological descriptions by modeling species-specific patterns of neuronal growth. The technique has been successfully utilized in the analysis of several neural disorders. For example, neurons obtained from the fibroblasts of patients with

RTT successfully replicated the morphology of pyramidal neurons and provided insights into functional characteristics coupled with morphological modification. In addition to the changes in their morphology, reprogrammed RTT neurons displayed electrophysiological deficits and altered calcium signaling compared to controls (Marchetto et al. 2010). The iPSC technique was also applied in disorders of multicausal origin (e.g., schizophrenia) (Brennard et al. 2011) and in Williams syndrome (Chailangkarn et al. 2013), replicating the morphology of neurons and revealing functional implications of the differences in neuronal morphology in the disorders. The combination of the two different approaches—postmortem morphological analyses of cortical neurons and analyses of the neurons using the iPSC technique—provides a fertile ground for evolutionary studies (Hrvoj-Mihic et al. 2014) seeking to surpass the limitations imposed on comparative neuroanatomy in examining the functional correlates of observed morphological differences.

Constraints on prenatal brain size may necessitate that a larger percentage of total brain growth must occur postnatally in humans compared to other primates. At birth, the brain may account for as much as 74% of a human infant's daily energy demands (Holliday 1971). To support the growth and development of such metabolically costly brain tissues, certain adaptations must facilitate these early demands both nutritionally and functionally. Higher levels of adipose tissue have been observed in humans across the lifespan, and this trend is particularly magnified in human babies. In the final trimester of prenatal development, the infant puts on a significant amount of body weight, a very large percentage of which is adipose tissue. It has been suggested that this early fatness may provide an energetic buffer, supporting the early rapid growth of the infant brain by supplying it with glucose and ketones (Cunnane and Crawford 2003). Additionally, the catabolism of maternal tissues as mothers lose the weight gained during pregnancy to support lactation may provide the infant with a large supply of ketones, an optimal source of energy for ATP synthesis and the chemical precursors to the brain's principal functional neurotransmitters, GABA and glutamate.

Models of energy demands for various cell types suggest that there are differences in the energetic costs among them relative to the region in the brain in which they reside. For example, thalamocortical relay neurons are the most energetically efficient among the excitatory neurons, while both the regular and fast-spiking cells from the somatosensory and visual cortices are the most expensive among those measured (Moujahid et al. 2014). Furthermore, since neurons are organized in groups with similar properties in different areas and neural systems in the brain, the metabolic demands of information processing may vary for large populations of interconnected neurons. In light of the structural variability present within and among the brains of humans and the other primates discussed here, it seems reasonable to suggest that our costly brains distribute energy demands heterogeneously in ways that go beyond large brain–small brain dichotomies and issues of encephalization.

Conclusion

Input-dependent changes in the brain occur across the lifespan in important species-specific patterns. Certain structures of the human brain seem to stand out with respect to slow rates of maturation, including areas of the cortex and subcortical structures, such as the amygdala and striatum. With complex roles in regulating aspects of behavior, such as emotion, learning, language, and behavioral control, these regions are of particular interest for study in a comparative context. Ongoing comparative studies have revealed differences in rates of growth and maturation, as well as structural differences in cell distribution and morphology, that provide the substrates for differences in cognitive and behavioral capacities across species. Attempts to infer the functional implications of interspecies variations in morphology can be approached through studies of pathology, particularly in the cases of disorders that affect uniquely human aspects of cognition and behavior, such as autism and Williams syndrome.

From birth to adulthood, our brains are shaped by our experiences. In social species, individuals must learn to navigate their shared environment and encode behavioral repertoires characteristic of their species and group prior to the onset of adulthood. Since human brains are born so immature and since periods of growth and maternal dependence are protracted, so too is the period for learning and cultural acquisition. Thus, the expansion of life histories in primate lineages, particularly our own, may underlie the elaboration of cultural and behavioral systems rooted in the heterogeneity and plasticity of derived neural circuitry.

CHAPTER EIGHT

Testosterone, Fatherhood, and Social Networks

LEE T. GETTLER

Evolutionary perspectives on male life histories and the physiological mechanisms that facilitate life history trade-offs often center on the steroid hormone testosterone (T) because it plays a role in many basic reproductive processes. For example, healthy T production is necessary for spermatogenesis, although the required levels are relatively low (McLachlan et al. 1996). More critically, T contributes to physical characteristics (e.g., skeletal musculature, ornamentation) and social interactions (e.g., competition with conspecifics for territory, resources, dominance, and hierarchy status as well as diverse interactions with females, etc.) that likely shape reproductive success for many vertebrate males (Ketterson et al. 1992; Bribiescas 2001; Ellison 2001a; Gettler et al. 2010; Archer 2006; Gettler and Oka 2016).

However, such T-influenced traits can also adversely impact survival, such as through increased risk of injury and mortality via conflicts with other males as well as increased exposure to pathogens. Males with elevated T likely have reduced capacities to fight off infection and to rapidly heal wounds as a consequence of T's many immunosuppressive effects, although the extent to which this is true probably varies based on a number of factors, for example, age, energetic condition, psychosocial stress (Muehlenbein and Bribiescas 2005), and the specific pathogenic challenge and required immune factors (e.g., Gettler et al. 2014). In the context of vertebrate males' capabilities or inclinations toward paternal care, high T might also facilitate phenotypes characterized by unreliable (e.g., investing heavily in extra-pair matings), volatile (e.g., being intolerant of or negatively responsive to young), or aggressive behaviors. To the extent this is true, elevated T might be incongruent with the behavioral requirements and, in humans, the cognitive demands of investing in highly dependent offspring and cooperating with mothers in that context (Gettler

2014). Thus, for vertebrate species in which biparental investment has evolved, it is hypothesized that selection has led to convergent reproductive physiological adaptations such that male bodies are capable of reducing T in preparation for parenting demands and/or when offspring needs are at their zenith (Wingfield et al. 1990; Gettler 2010; Gray and Anderson 2010; Gettler 2014).

These models, including those for hominins, appropriately focus on the fitness implications related to enhanced male-female relationships (greater likelihood of future mating) and to offspring survival and well-being (greater reproductive success, assuming high paternity certainty) (Gettler 2014). In the hominin lineage—likely more so than in most other vertebrate species with biparental care—cooperation outside of a "nuclear family" unit, across kin, age, and sex categories in diverse productive, social, and protective domains was likely critical to enhanced reproductive fitness (Hart and Sussman 2005; Hrdy 2009; Hill and Hurtado 2009; Burkart et al. 2009; Fuentes et al. 2010; Kramer and Ellison 2010; Gettler 2010). Based on these complex, cooperative social and economic niches in which hominin male reproductive strategies (including transitions toward biparental care) would have evolved, I suggest that there may have been broader fitness implications of the human male's capacity to reduce T production in the immediate context of committed partnering and parenting. Specifically, I propose that hominin fathers with downregulated T might have benefited from resultant prosocial and cooperative tendencies and broad social networks, contributing to selection for or maintenance of this psychobiological capacity.

Testosterone and Biparental Care among Nonhuman Vertebrates

Male birds' T is often higher during the breeding season compared to periods in which males and females pair and cooperatively raise young (Wingfield et al. 1990). Phylogenetic analyses of these data suggest that the selective pressures that gave rise to this physiological responsiveness might have been related to the evolution of male-female reproductive partnerships rather than to the specific demands of direct paternal caregiving in many lineages (Hirschenhauser et al. 2003). Within species, some experimental data are consistent with a mating-parenting trade-off framework, since fathers receiving exogenous T pursued extra-pair matings and male-male competition at the expense of investment in their young and to the detriment of offspring survival (Hegner and Wingfield 1987; Reed et al. 2006). The experimental elevation of male birds'

T also reduced their long-term survival, possibly via the observed increase in competitive and mating behaviors and the associated energetic costs (which divert resources away from investments in survival and in somatic maintenance) (Reed et al. 2006). These ornithological studies provided the primary impetus for testing whether T similarly mediates such reproductive trade-offs in other taxa.

Among mammals, paternal care is relatively more common among rodents relative to most other orders (Kleiman and Malcolm 1981). Wynne-Edwards and Timonin (2007) provide a thorough review of the physiological literature relevant to my purposes here, particularly highlighting that rodent models provide inconclusive or conflicting results as to whether low T is consequential to mammalian paternal care expression. Two of the most thoroughly studied species in this regard are the African striped mouse and the California mouse. Longitudinal data from the former are highly consistent with an avian-like pattern and indicate that the direct care of young contributes to reduced T production (Schradin and Yuen 2011). In contrast, California mice with experimentally reduced or eliminated T do not perform paternal care (Trainor and Marler 2002). Minimally, the highly variable patterns of T and paternal care among rodents suggest that selection does not uniformly converge on reduced T as a key neurobiological-endocrine component of paternal biology (Gettler 2014).

Among nonhuman primates, the most extensive models of male socioendocrinology vis-à-vis roles as cooperative breeders derive from decades of study on multiple species of New World monkeys, particularly cotton-top tamarins, common marmosets, and black tufted-ear marmosets. Similar to the rodent models, data from these monkey species also provide a mixed perspective on whether fathers' T is lower than non-fathers' and whether T has any impact on males' participation in caregiving. Following the birth of their offspring, black tufted-ear marmoset fathers exhibited a nadir in T that coincided with the time period in which their involvement in direct care was highest (Nunes et al. 2000), and males that provided more care had significantly lower T (Nunes et al. 2001). Evidence from common marmoset fathers is less clear. In one study, there was no relationship between marmosets' paternal care and T (Dixson and George 1982), while in a more recent study fathers' T declined from the prepartum to the postpartum infant-care period (correlations to degree of care were not measured) (Ziegler et al. 2009). In the same species, fathers' T rapidly declined when they smelled odors from their dependent infants

(Prudom et al. 2008), while fathers showed no change in T after smelling the scent of an unfamiliar ovulating female, differing from paired and unpaired non-fathers, whose T rose significantly in the latter condition (Ziegler et al. 2005). The studies I have just described evaluate either basal T production or T's acute reactivity to stimuli. Hereafter, I refer to this as the "acute versus basal distinction" (see review in Trumble et al. 2015).[1]

Diverging from the patterns observed among marmoset species, cotton-top tamarin fathers showed rising T throughout their mates' gestation periods (Ziegler and Snowdon 2000), with their T peaking in the early postpartum, that is, during the time frame in which they were highly involved with off-spring care. This finding runs counter to the general theoretical expectations for the socioendocrinology of direct paternal care (Wingfield et al. 1990) but is tightly linked to tamarin life history, since this apex of paternal T coincided with a spike in their partners' luteinizing hormone that signaled ovulation, shortly (2–3 weeks) after giving birth. Thus, the tamarin fathers' T surge likely facilitates a behavioral shift toward the resumption of breeding. Importantly, there is no evidence that higher T interferes with paternal care in this species (Ziegler et al. 2004b; Gettler et al. 2013; Gettler 2014).

The behavioral and physiological data from these marmoset and tamarin species are invaluable in providing a comparative socioendocrine perspective that particularly highlights the diversity of neurobiological-endocrine signals on which selection can act as biparental care evolves. The plasticity of paternal physiological profiles, even among these closely related species with relatively comparable life histories, not only urges caution in terms of over-extrapolating patterns observed in distantly related taxa, but also reflects the challenges of using comparative socioendocrine data to help inform an understanding of shared phylogenetic histories among, for example, hominoids (Gettler 2014).

Among extant primates, the great apes are the most comparable to humans in terms of life history pace and offspring developmental trajectories, though with important differences regarding the timing of weaning, the childhood stage, and the ages at self-sufficiency, among others (Bogin 1999; Kaplan et al. 2000; Robson et al. 2006). The extent to which aspects of great apes' sociality can provide insights on our hominin evolutionary past and, if so, which species is the most relevant model are ongoing debates unlikely to be settled soon. However, germane to my purposes here, males of those species provide little substantive, impactful care to their offspring (Fernandez-Duque et al. 2009; Gray and Anderson 2010), so there are currently no great ape data on T and paternal care or on T and adult male–young sociality from which direct comparisons can be made. There are, however, socioendocrine data on the hylobatids, the "lesser apes," and multiple species of baboon, which are long-lived, large-bodied primate species that generally reside in multi-male, multi-female groups.

Males of multiple baboon species are known to form "friendships" with lactating females and their infants (Smuts and Gubernick 1992; Palombit et al. 1997). In a study of the physiological correlates of such social relationships among olive baboons, Shur (2008) found that friendship-forming males experienced significant declines in T. Specifically, male baboons that were responsible for maintaining contact with a postpartum female and her infant exhibited significant declines in T following the infant's birth, whereas males that participated in friendships that were female-driven did not. The decline in males' T dissipated as the infant developed through the lactation period (Shur 2008). It remains unclear whether this is paternal care, although data from other baboon species indicate that it often is, or perhaps it is a mating strategy (Smuts and Gubernick 1992; Beehner et al. 2009). Regardless, the results from Shur's (2008) study suggest that reduced T might have improved males' effectiveness in social relationships with mother-infant pairs, particularly buffering the mothers and infants from psychosocial stress. Among other baboon species, it has been shown that low T occurs during periods in which older males perform more care and engage less in competition for dominance (Beehner et al. 2009). Whether lower T is causal or contributory in that context remains an open question, but such findings speak to within-species plasticity in the ways in which endocrine function and behavior can bidirectionally affect one another based on socioecological dynamics.

Among hylobatids (i.e., gibbons and siamangs), monogamous pairings are common, but only one species (siamangs) is known to exhibit paternal care (Fernandez-Duque et al. 2009; Malone and Fuentes 2009). In a small, preliminary study of captive siamangs, fathers' T decreased significantly as their young moved through the infancy period, paralleling a rise in father-offspring interaction. In contrast, among gibbon fathers, which are not involved in direct care but are in frequent physical proximity to their offspring, new fathers' T did not shift over the course of the 7-month postpartum study period (Rafacz et al. 2012). Comparable, compelling evidence has emerged from a longitudinal study of free-living white-handed gibbons. Barelli and Heistermann (2012) showed that gibbon males had higher androgen levels (T is an androgen) if they were in residence with a female partner but not other adult males or if they resided in groups with a dependent infant. The authors suggested that those two social groupings are unstable or precarious, requiring males to be primed for aggression and vigilance in defense of the group (Barelli and Heistermann 2012).

BRIEF SUMMARY

The variable patterns of T and paternal care among rodents and primates suggest that there are multiple, complex physiological pathways that can lead to broadly similar paternal care behavioral phenotypes. However, shared evolutionary histories among species also impose limits on the types of novel trait that can arise via natural selection. As comparable niches or opportunities arise (separately) for closely related species, their genetic and phenotypic commonalities increase the likelihood that they will converge on common or similar solutions (Simpson 1967). The evidence from gibbons and siamangs (Shur 2008; Rafacz et al. 2012)—which are comparatively better (than birds, rodents, small-bodied New World primates, etc.), albeit limited, approximations of human life history and more closely related to humans—provides a basis for expanding hypotheses regarding human T in the context of parenting and partnering. Specifically, the lesser ape data suggest that the context of father-offspring interaction and direct paternal care may be a social pathway by which T is reduced in ape species, in addition to or more so than partnering alone.

Human Partnering, Parenting, and Testosterone

WHY TESTOSTERONE IN HUMANS?

Humans facultatively adjust their reproductive strategies, primarily via behavioral flexibility, over reproductive lifespans that last many decades. Testosterone is likely a key physiological mechanism whose production can be flexibly adjusted to help facilitate adaptive behavioral repertoires as new social demands arise, particularly if biparental care evolved in the *Homo* lineage (Gray and Anderson 2010; Bribiescas et al. 2012; Gettler 2014).

The human psychobiological literature on T is consistent with the idea that downregulated baseline T could be generally beneficial in the context of invested, nurturing fathering, particularly when viewed through the lens of evolutionary time. Although T relates to broad measures of "aggressive behavior" only modestly (at best) (Archer 2006), high-T men show tendencies toward angry mood states, and they direct more attention to stimuli that mimic social threats and dominance challenges (van Honk et al. 1999; Wirth and Schultheiss 2007). Studies in which eugonadal men's T was artificially increased over a number of weeks or months provide mixed support for this model, with men's anger, hostility, and aggression (in a laboratory-based, competitive paradigm) increasing with higher T, though the effects were modest (Pope et al. 2000; Dabbs et al. 2002; O'Connor et al. 2004; Archer 2006; see Anderson et al. 1992; Tricker et al. 1996 for studies with null outcomes).

Men with elevated T (both endogenous and experimentally manipulated) experience heightened brain activity in the amygdala, which contributes to emotional processing, when presented with threat-related images. This neural pattern suggests that individuals with high T (subconsciously) attach more salience to such stimuli and are perhaps more likely to respond with reactive aggression (Derntl et al. 2009; Manuck et al. 2010; Goetz et al. 2014; but see Stanton et al. 2009). High T seems to reduce prefrontal cortical connectivity with the amygdala (van Wingen et al. 2010), with implications for the conscious control of vigilance and social behavior (Volman et al. 2011). These integrative hormonal–brain activity studies indicate that men with high T might be particularly oriented to male-male competition and challenge and may be primed to react aggressively in such situations or others involving social threat, which could reduce men's focus and their availability and capability (due to, for example, lost time, injury, or reduced survival) to invest in young or cooperate with their mother (Gettler 2014).

A number of behavioral correlations likewise provide preliminary support for a model in which elevated baseline T might be incongruent with engaged parenting. Men with greater T report more recent and lifetime sexual partners (Dabbs and Morris 1990; Pollet et al. 2011), although in a study of both men and women, only females showed a relationship between recent sex partners and higher T (van Anders and Watson 2007). A large study of military personnel found that married men with high T were more likely to have been unfaithful (Booth and Dabbs 1993), although my colleagues and I tested for a similar effect in the Philippines and found no correlation between men's T and infidelity (Gettler et al. 2013). In some studies, men with elevated T are also more likely to be extroverts and sensation seekers (Gerra et al. 1999; Alvergne et al. 2010), which are personality-behavioral profiles that either have been linked to men's reproductive success (Alvergne et al. 2010) or are hypothesized to contribute to it. Finally, a study found that increases in men's T led directly to increased risk taking, with a strong likelihood of physical injury (acute versus basal distinction) (Ronay and von Hippel 2010). High-T military men also engage in more risky behaviors, such as increased drug or alcohol consumption, and have a greater likelihood of run-ins with law enforcement (Booth and Dabbs 1993; Mazur 1995). In total, these behavioral-cognitive correlates of elevated T are *hypothesized* to conflict with men's willingness or effectiveness to act as committed parents, such that an invested, low baseline T father phenotype, with genetic underpinnings, could have been selected for during hominin evolution. Importantly, most aspects of this model remain to be tested, and some of the best evidence for it stems from experimental hormonal manipulations in birds (see above).

In thinking about whether a low-T parenting phenotype in contemporary populations might reflect past selective pressures, it is important to bear in mind that some form of male-female prolonged social and sexual relationship probably preceded the costly forms of paternal investment (Lukas and Clutton-Brock 2013). As a consequence, selection for reduced T production in the context of these social relationships could have been more strongly related to male-female partnering, males' involvement in parenting, or the concomitant exposure to parenting in the context of partnering. A series of simple predictions arises from that setup: (a) if male-female partnerships were critical, I would hypothesize that T would decrease in that context, with parental investment having no additional effects; (b) if parenting were critical, I would predict that low T would not be expressed in the context of partnering without parenting; and (c) (more likely than a and b) if partnering/parenting co-occurrence were critical, I would hypothesize that the two life history shifts would have additive effects.

PARTNERING AND T

Two large, longitudinal studies of male US military personnel provided the first substantive evidence that life history transitions might interrelate with men's T. Mazur and Michalek (1998) found that men's T declined when they moved from being single to newly married, increased around the time of divorce, and remained stably low if they were married throughout the study period. A second study of military men around the same time suggested possible bidirectional relationships between T and partnered status, showing that married men with higher T at early time points of the study had a greater likelihood of divorce at future data collections (Booth and Dabbs 1993). Other studies (of nonmilitary males) have generally not replicated these results, finding mixed patterns for T and romantic relationship quality (low T, low quality: Perini et al. 2012; high T, low quality: Julian and McKenry 1989; no significant correlation: Gray et al. 2006). The implications of US men's T for marital dynamics might vary based on the stress of the family system. Booth and colleagues (2005) found that when men reported low "role overload" and had elevated T, both they and their partners reported higher marital quality. In contrast, when men reported high role overload, those with low T had higher marital quality (as reported by both partners) (Booth et al. 2005). A well-designed study (Edelstein et al. 2014) also examined relationship quality and T among partnered men and women, finding that individuals (of both sexes) with higher T reported lower relationship quality and that individuals reported reduced relationship quality if their *partners'* T was high (in both sexes but, in fact, stronger for women's T).

Expanding on this foundation, a number of studies have explored other factors that might moderate these patterns, such as the interface among T, partnering status, and commitment levels. Multiple studies of US and Canadian subjects (predominantly middle- to upper-class individuals of European descent) have found that partnered heterosexual men have lower T than do single men (non-fathers) (van Anders and Watson 2006, 2007), with men in more serious, committed relationships (e.g., casual dating versus cohabiting versus married) having lower T (Gray et al. 2004b; Hooper et al. 2011). At our research site (Philippines), my colleagues and I found that newly married/cohabiting non-fathers who had been partnered for shorter durations had significantly greater declines in T compared to men who had been in relationships for many years (Gettler et al. 2013). Other research has shown that partnered US men who maintain interest in sexual activity outside of their immediate relationship or who are polyamorous have high T relative to other partnered men (McIntyre et al. 2006; van Anders et al. 2007; van Anders and Goldey 2010). Therefore, in at least some North American populations, men's T is low in conjunction with long-term, committed relationships to one partner. These results also provide evidence for the plasticity of this system, since it appears that males in these cultural settings flexibly adjust their T based on the specifics of their current partnerships and commitment to them (Gettler 2014).

But see van Anders and Goldey (2010) for a perspective suggesting that men's T drives (rather than responds to) relationship orientation and status. My colleagues and I have demonstrated that such T social dynamics are consistent with bidirectional effects (Gettler 2014; Gettler et al. 2011; Gettler et al. 2013; Gettler et al. 2015).

Variability in the relationship between partnering and T has also been documented cross-culturally in a few studies. For example, Swahili men in Kenya who were monogamously married did not have lower T than unmarried men, while polygynously married men had the highest T of any group (Gray 2003). In contrast, in a similar study, monogamously married Ariaal men in Kenya had lower T than did unmarried men, but polygynously married men did not have higher T than monogamous men (Gray et al. 2007). A study in Japan found a trend toward lower T among partnered men compared to single males (Sakaguchi et al. 2006), mirroring some of the patterns from the United States and Canada described above. Thus, the extent to which T varies between partnered and single men varies both by the cultural patterns of marriage (monogamous, polygynous) and the nature of the bonds/commitment between men and their partners. The studies I have reviewed in this section generally focus explicitly on partnering and do not include parenting status, but parenting sheds further light on this plasticity and variability.

PARENTING AND T

In a series of pioneering papers in the 2000s, Gray and colleagues were the first to test whether both partnering and parenting dynamics had implications for men's T. Focusing initially on samples recruited from Harvard University and broader Boston communities, these studies showed that while married men had lower T than did single non-fathers, married fathers and married non-fathers generally had comparable T. Thus, long-term commitment to a partner appeared to be the more critical social factor contributing to reduced T in these US-based cross-sectional studies (Gray et al. 2002; Burnham et al. 2003; Gray et al. 2004a; Gray et al. 2004b).

Studies of these parenting and partnering correlations with T then expanded to diverse cultural settings around the world, offering suggestive insights into the role that cultural context, political economy, and subsistence practices, among other factors, play in the degree to which the T of partnered fathers and partnered non-fathers look similar (to one another) or differ from the T of single men (Gray and Campbell 2009). In cross-sectional studies that compared men across partnering and parenting demographic categories, scholars found that partnered fathers had the lowest T in both China and the Philippines (Gray et al. 2006; Kuzawa et al. 2009). Additional research by Gray and colleagues highlighted the complexity of these patterns, showing that Kenyan Swahili men with young children tended to have lower T than did fathers with older offspring, but polygynously married men (many of whom were likely fathers) had the highest T of any demographic category measured (Gray 2003). In the Philippines, in the first large-scale longitudinal test of these partnering and parenting dynamics, my colleagues and I observed graded variation across demographic categories. Filipino men transitioning from being single non-fathers to newly partnered new fathers (over a 5-year period) showed declines in T that were substantially greater than those of subjects who remained single non-fathers during the same time frame, and newly partnered non-fathers' T was intermediate between the two (Gettler et al. 2011).

Many of the initial investigations in this domain of human paternal psychobiology were motivated by parental investment theory and predictions based on a definition of reproductive effort in which mating and parenting are mutually exclusive and traded off against one another, though it was long recognized that this model was probably not adequate to account for male primate interactions and investments in young (Smuts and Gubernick 1992). Recent advances have suggested a more nuanced approach that highlights the importance of context-specific competitive and nurturant behavioral and psycho-emotional demands (van Anders et al. 2011; van Anders 2013). There is an accumulating body of literature consistent with this perspective, pointing to intersections among how men are socialized culturally to behave as parents, the extent to which they individually engage in childcare, and their T (Gettler 2014).

The first study to shed light on this issue compared men's T in two neighboring East African groups, with samples drawn from Hadza (foragers, fathers involved in direct care) and Datoga (pastoralists, fathers not principally involved in care) subjects. Among the Datoga, fathers and non-fathers did not differ for T, whereas the Hadza fathers had lower T than did their non-father counterparts, suggesting that cultural norms of parenting and, specifically, degrees of involvement with direct care contributed to variation in male T based on life history (Muller et al. 2009). In studies conducted in Senegal and the United States, which both relied on maternal reports of paternal care, fathers who were highly invested in their children had lower T compared to other fathers (Alvergne et al. 2009; Mascaro et al. 2013b). In the Philippines, my colleagues and I found that fathers who reported involvement in daily physical childcare had reduced T compared to fathers who did not perform such parenting duties (Gettler et al. 2011). Building on this work, we published the first longitudinal evidence for concomitant changes in fathers' caregiving and their T. Over a 5-year period, fathers who increased their weekly childcare effort showed declines in T, whereas fathers' T increased if they became less involved in care (Gettler et al. 2015). Fathers who shared a sleeping surface with their children (co-sleeping), which is the normative cultural practice at our research site, also had lower T than did men who slept away from their offspring (Gettler et al. 2012). Indicating a potential paternal sensitizing effect of diminished T, Canadian fathers with low T reported greater sympathy and a greater need to respond when hearing recorded infant cries, and fathers with past experience directly caring for infants had reduced baseline T (Fleming et al. 2002). In an experimental study, non-fathers who responded to a life-like crying infant doll in a nurturing manner showed declines in T, whereas men who were unable to soothe the doll or who heard infant cries without the opportunity to attend to the "baby" tended to show increases in T (van Anders et al. 2012) (acute versus basal distinction).

Collectively, these data indicate that men's investments in direct childcare contribute to both between- and within-cultural variation in the patterning of men's T based on life history status (Gettler 2014). These data also seem to parallel cross-species results from the gibbons and siamangs (although those data are admittedly limited at this time), indicating that human fathers' physiology is specifically sensitive to their involvement in direct care or, alternatively, that fathers whose T declines when they become parents are inclined toward such behaviors (or the two reinforce one another) (Gettler 2014; Gettler et al. 2015). It is important to bear in mind that fathers' investments in direct care are relatively low in most cultures around the world, paling in comparison to the levels of care provided by mothers on average (Hewlett 1992; Gray and Anderson 2010; Bribiescas et al. 2012). Though clearly difficult to establish, it is possible that the selective micro-environment for direct male care during hominin evolution differed from the socioecological contexts observed today: prior to the rise of language, cultural sophistication, technology, and the highly specialized domestic-economic roles that accompanied the rise of modern humans and, later, settled communities in the Neolithic

(Marlowe 2007; Gettler 2010). The quality of paternal care and its salience for offspring's health and development could have been critical to males' fitness, even if the absolute quantity was not exceedingly high on average. Questions do remain regarding the importance of fathers' childcare (specific behaviors, quantity, quality, etc.) to T and the possibility that a correlate of fathers' care— for example, decreased exposure to male-male competition among invested fathers—is the driver of low paternal T (Gettler 2014).

Adding nuance to this discussion and highlighting humans' psychobiological plasticity, two studies drawing on samples from Poland and the United States showed patterns of elevated baseline paternal T under certain circumstances. Among Polish fathers, education level moderated the relationship between a father's number of children and his T, such that fathers with lower socioeconomic status (SES) with more children had higher T, while the converse was evident among higher-SES fathers (Jasienska et al. 2012). Although they did not test these hypotheses, the researchers suggested that the varying patterns might result from SES variation in the emphasis on male-male competition for resources as well as variable parenting roles and differences in the timing of reproduction. In a large study of US military veterans, Mazur (2014) found that young married fathers had higher T than did married non-fathers. Although specific pathways that might account for this effect were not explored, I have suggested elsewhere (Gettler 2014) that this pattern might align with aspects of competition, protectiveness, or family systems related to military life.

Finally, a study of a contemporary forager-horticultural population (the Tsimane of Bolivia) found that males acutely spike their T during physically demanding tree chopping and plot clearing (acute versus basal distinction) (Trumble et al. 2013). The researchers suggested that this physiological response could enhance men's subsistence productivity, although this was not specifically tested. Alvarado and colleagues (2014) studied Polish fathers' baseline T, muscle mass, and strength in an ecological setting in which males frequently perform highly intensive manual agricultural labor. In this context, men with children had lower T compared to non-fathers, but also engaged in more substantial physical labor and had higher muscle mass and strength. These findings suggest that low basal paternal T is not an impediment to men's subsistence productivity, particularly that which requires high levels of exertion and functional strength (Alvarado et al. 2014). Because male contributions to household/familial/community productivity and energy budgets are key in many ecological settings, the results of Trumble and colleagues and of Alvarado and colleagues add an intriguing layer of complexity to discussions of paternal investment and biology. Integrating the perspectives, it is plausible that human males have the capacity to downregulate their chronic baseline T while retaining the ability to spike their T in the short term when the circumstances might require it (e.g., productivity, competition, protection, aggression) (see also Trumble et al. 2014).

BRIEF SUMMARY

The extent to which human males downregulate T production when they become partnered and/or when they become partnered fathers appears to be contingent on the specifics of those social relationships and men's emotional-cognitive investments in them (e.g., sexual-romantic commitment to one partner) and/or on their behavioral patterns within them (e.g., direct paternal care). Put simply, like many aspects of human adaptability, plasticity appears key here, with male psychobiology having the ability to respond to specific social cues in partnering and parenting contexts but not being inevitably canalized to do so. One of the key questions here is whether this capacity is evolved. Though exploring that is beyond the scope of this chapter, I have previously suggested the possibility that this flexible T responsiveness is an epiphenomenon or "spandrel," emerging from primates' neurobiological-endocrine history of group living and sociality (Gettler 2014). That said, if hominin males were not cooperating with mothers and were not invested in young, with elevated T helping to facilitate male-male competition and inordinate matings as the primary or singular route to male reproductive success, one might predict that this downregulatory sensitivity (to cues from females or young) of the hypothalamic-pituitary-gonadal axis would have been selected *against*.

Models for how hominin fathers that initially cooperated with mothers to raise young could have *benefited* from low T generally focus on fitness implications related to enhanced male-female relationships (greater likelihood of future mating) and offspring survival and well-being (greater reproductive success, assuming high paternity certainty) (Gettler 2014). Yet, we know that cooperation across age and sex classes (not just limited to nuclear families) in labor, transport, foraging, and predator evasion was critical to the success of *Homo* (Hart and Sussman 2005; Hrdy 2009; Hill and Hurtado 2009; Burkart et al. 2009; Fuentes et al. 2010; Kramer and Ellison 2010; Gettler 2010).

Scholars have begun to explore the socioendocrine implications of T for such cooperative, coalitionary dynamics (Flinn et al. 2012).

Building Networks: Testosterone and Social Capital

The human cooperative breeding models that have emerged in the past two decades are clearly necessary to understanding human paternal socioen-docrinology as contextualized in family systems and community networks (Hawkes et al. 1998; Kaplan et al. 2000; Hrdy 2009; Hill and Hurtado 2009; Gettler 2014). In addition, there are a number of human evolution–oriented theoretical frameworks and heuristic models that incorporate concepts of prosociality and social capital accruement that are relevant to the proposal I am outlining here, including Kaplan and colleagues' (2000) embodied capital, Wells's (2012a) capital economy, Hrdy's (2009) mothers and others, and Burkart and colleagues' (2009) cooperative breeding hypothesis. Building from these premises, my final purpose here is to explore whether there might have been (secondary) broader social network and cooperative benefits to hominin males downregulating T (in the immediate context of partnering and parenting), contributing to the selection or maintenance of this psychobiological capacity.

DOES HIGH T INHIBIT PROSOCIALITY? OR, MIGHT LOW T ENHANCE MEN'S CAPACITY FOR CULTIVATING SOCIAL CAPITAL?

I have already reviewed some of the literature relevant to this question, focusing on the implications of T for men's angry/hostile mood states and their evaluation of threats to status, as well as T's relationship to cortex-limbic system functioning, which might affect high-T men's predisposition toward reactive aggression. Other findings likewise suggest that high T could be detrimental to men's ability to forge broad social networks. I have compiled a summary of relevant studies in table 8.1 from a literature search in which I primarily targeted results from studies of male psychobiology, with a notable exception being studies in which human behavior was assessed after exog-enous T administration, which heretofore have focused predominantly on females. I only include results that I have not discussed above. Archer (2006) also provides a rigorous overview of relevant relationships among human T, competition, power motivations, and aggression. His meta-analyses show that the effect sizes between questionnaire-based measures of aggression and T are low to negligible on average, while correlations between third-party (such as staff members or peers) ratings of aggressive behavior and T are generally weak to moderate. Meanwhile, T does relate to aggressive behaviors during some forms of competition (e.g., judo matches), and T often rises in anticipation or during competitive events (Archer 2006). I have generally not included such studies in table 8.1.

Because the review in table 8.1 is not a meta-analysis and, while thorough, cannot be considered explicitly exhaustive, it provides more of a descriptive steering point for this discussion. Consistent with predictions, there are a large number of studies suggesting that reduced T correlates with greater prosocial characteristics or behaviors, such as heightened empathic abilities and enhanced tendencies toward generosity and collaboration. Consequently, men with such a psychobiological profile might have advantages in the forming and sustaining of long-term cooperative coalitions. In contrast, there is also a small body of evidence indicating that under the right micro-environmental social circumstances, elevated T could promote males' social relationships (also see the discussion of cross-primate perspectives below). For my purposes here, I have categorized a number of studies as "hard to interpret" vis-à-vis prosociality and coalition formation. For example, depending on with whom a male is developing social relationships, during what life stage, and in what broader socioecological context, risk taking could be advantageous or detrimental.

It is also important to bear in mind that many of the studies in table 8.1 reflect the exogenous administration of T, often to women. There are likely significant differences on average between men and women in the quantity and sensitivity of androgen receptors in some brain areas that have implications for certain cognitive-emotional functions and behaviors, reflecting developmental neural activational-organizational processes (Schulz et al. 2009; Fernandez-Guasti et al. 2000; Perrin et al. 2008; Herting et al. 2014). Many of the studies in table 8.1 also derive from economic-exchange laboratory-based paradigms, while focusing on samples of limited demographic and cultural breadth (consistent with the WEIRD—Western, educated, industrialized, rich, and democratic—sampling criticisms elsewhere) (Gurven and Winking 2008; Henrich et al. 2010). Questions regarding the application of these results to naturalistic conditions, across the present cultural and ecological boundaries in addition to our hominin evolutionary past, are valid.

Table 8.1. Studies of Testosterone (T) and Prosociality

Source	Sample Size[a]	T Measurement (Baseline, Acute Change, Exogenous)	Prosociality (PS) Measurement	T-PS Finding
LOW T AS PROSOCIAL				
Booth and Osgood 1993	4429	baseline	composite of "social deviance" and "social integration" from self-reports	↑T, ↓social integration; ↑T, ↑social deviance
Harris et al. 1996	155	baseline	personality dimensions from self-report	↑T, ↓prosociality; ↑T, ↑aggression
Johnson et al. 2007	43	baseline	personality dimensions from self-report	↓T, ↑prestige; ~T, ~dominance
Welker et al. 2014	114	baseline	psychopathy dimensions (antisocial behavior, interpersonal relationships, affective traits) from self-report	↑T, ↑psychopathy scores
Flinn et al. 2012	19	baseline (pre–cricket match), acute change (post–cricket match)	team closeness/bond for a given subject from peers' reports of coalitions	↓T, ↑team bond; ~T, ~team bond
Peterson and Harmon-Jones 2012	43 (25F)	acute change (pre- to post-intervention)	emotions from self-reports after an experimental intervention to elicit anger	↑T, ↑anger
Zak et al. 2009	25	exogenous	observed behaviors (generosity, punishment) during an ultimatum game	↑T, ↓generosity; ↑T, ↑punishment
Wright et al. 2012	34 (F)	exogenous	individual and dyadic (cooperative) behaviors in forced-choice tasks	↑T, ↑egocentrism; ↑T, ↓collaboration

Table 8.1 (continued)

Study	N	Type	Description	Result
Bos et al. 2010	24 (F)	exogenous	trustworthiness ratings assigned to photographs of strangers	↑T, ↓trust
Hermans et al. 2006	20 (F)	exogenous	facial expression mimicry (electromyography) of happy and angry faces as measure of empathy	↑T, ↓empathy
van Honk et al. 2011	16 (F)	exogenous	inference of others' emotional/mental states from photographs of their eyes as measure of empathy	↑T, ↓empathy
HIGH T AS PROSOCIAL				
Edwards et al. 2006	12	baseline (pre–soccer match), acute change (pre- to post-match)	self-ratings of social relationships with teammates	~T, ~social connectedness; ↑T, ↑social connectedness
Wibral et al. 2012	91	exogenous	die-rolling game in which subjects could increase monetary payoffs by lying	↑T, ↓lying
Eisenegger et al. 2009	60 (F)	exogenous	observed behaviors (fairness of offers to peers) during an ultimatum game	↑T, ↑social fairness
van Honk et al. 2012	24 (F)	exogenous	observed behaviors during a "public goods game"	↑T, ↑cooperation[c]
Diekhof et al. 2014	50	baseline	observed behaviors during an ultimatum game; in-group and out-group interactions in the context of between-group competition	↑T, ↑in-group generosity; ↑T, ↑out-group hostility
MIXED OR HARD TO INTERPRET RESULTS				
Burnham et al. 2003	26	baseline	observed behaviors (rejection or acceptance of offers) during an ultimatum game	↑T, ↑rejection of low $ offers

Study	N	Condition	Measure	Result
Sapienza et al. 2009	381	baseline	financial risk aversion derived from computer lottery simulation	~T, ~risk aversion
Apicella et al. 2008	98	baseline	financial risk willingness in an investment game with real monetary payoffs	↑T, ↑risk taking
Stanton et al. 2011	78	baseline	risk taking in light of experience of reward and punishment (monetary gains, losses)	↑T, ↑risk taking
Evans and Hampson 2014	67	baseline	risk taking in light of experience of reward and punishment (monetary gains, losses)	T, ↑risk taking
Goudriaan et al. 2010	21	exogenous	risk taking in light of experience of reward and punishment (monetary gains, losses)	~T, ~risk taking
		exogenous	risk taking in which probabilities of failure are unknown	↑T, ↑risk taking
Boksem et al. 2013	54 (F)	exogenous	trust and reciprocity measured via economic exchanges with real monetary payoffs	↓ T, ↓trust; ↑T, ↑reciprocity
Zethraeus et al. 2009	200 (F)	exogenous	multiple economic games to assess altruism, fairness, trust, and risk propensity	~T, ~all measures
Seidel et al. 2013	40	acute change (pre- to post-intervention)	experimental intervention in which subjects were purposely excluded or included by other game players	↓T after exclusion; ↑T after inclusion
Kornienko et al. 2014	74 (69 F)	baseline	social network analysis of friendship network structure (incoming and outgoing ties)	~T, ~all measures

[a] All studies focused on males except those marked with F.

[b] ↑ = high or increased; ↓ = low or decreased; ~ = no significant relationship observed.

[c] Contingent on controlling for the second digit:fourth digit ratio, as a marker for prenatal androgen exposure.

DOES HIGH T IMPINGE ON COALITIONS AMONG THE
GREAT APES OR OTHER OLD WORLD PRIMATES?

While the great apes do not provide direct insights about our last common ancestor with the *Pan* or *Gorilla* genera, since they have also obviously continued to evolve since the hominin-ape split, cross-species comparison can provide perspective on T's correlations to male sociality under the conditions of "ape cognition," prior to the emergence of humans' capacity for shared intentionality (Burkart et al. 2009). Very little is known about male socio-endocrinology among gorillas. Although gorilla groups do commonly have a single silverback alpha male, multi-male groups exist in various configurations (Harcourt and Stewart 2007). The hormonal correlates of behavior in such relationships are understudied (Gettler 2014), but dominant male gorillas appear to have higher T than subordinates do (Robbins and Czekala 1997).

Among chimpanzees, which live in multi-male, multi-female groups, males' T has been linked to conspecific aggression (Muller and Wrangham 2004; Anestis 2006), which is one of the primary means by which males acquire rank and dominance: high-ranking chimpanzees are more aggressive and have elevated T relative to subordinate males (Muehlenbein et al. 2004; Muller and Wrangham 2004). Males' rank and dominance are also related to reproductive success (Muller and Mitani 2005; Wroblewski et al. 2009). In spite of fairly linear social hierarchies, chimpanzees also form male-male (but generally not male-female) coalitions and alliances. For example, alpha males secure support in conflicts from lower-ranked individuals, and males cooperate to mate guard fecund females (Watts 1998; Muller and Mitani 2005; Duffy et al. 2007). Long-term relationships among male chimpanzees are generally more stable among closely related kin and when prosociality (e.g., grooming) is equitable between dyads (Mitani 2009), but, to my knowledge, the socioendocrinology of these relationships has not been explored. In some communities, males also band together to hunt and to patrol the periphery of their territory. Some evidence suggests that males' T spikes upward during patrols but drops during group hunts, especially when meat is shared, which might reflect context-specific, affiliative, prosocial benefits of low T (acute versus basal distinction) (Sobolewski et al. 2012). Using experimental conditions with captive chimpanzees, Wobber and colleagues (2010a) found that males' T acutely spiked when they were placed in a social context in which they had to compete for food with another chimpanzee. In contrast, when the food was portioned in a way that could be shared (or not easily monopolized), males' T acutely declined. Interestingly, bonobos did not exhibit shifts in T in either condition (acute versus basal distinction). Wobber and colleagues (2010a) suggested that these acute physiological responses reflect species differences in competition-related selective pressures since the time when they last shared a common ancestor. In total, high-ranking chimpanzee males have elevated T and are especially aggressive, but they also play a prominent role in maintaining social alliances, including through grooming behaviors and allowing other males access to mating opportunities (Watts 1998; Muller and Mitani 2005; Duffy et al. 2007). These results suggest that high T does not interfere with chimpanzee male coalitions and alliances, and, considering the factors above, higher-T male chimpanzees are likely to be desirable intrasex social partners.

Similar to chimpanzees, bonobos live in mixed-sex communities in which both males and females compete for dominance positions. However, compared to chimpanzees, male reproductive success is based less on physical aggression toward females, females can commonly be dominant to males, and intersexual social relationships have greater significance (Parish and de Waal 2000; Surbeck et al. 2012). Based on their findings, Wobber and colleagues (2010a) also argued that bonobos might have experienced relaxed selective pressure for acute T responses to competition, potentially differing from other hominoids in this regard (acute versus basal distinction). In the absence of selection for high T and competitive behavior (Wobber et al. 2010a), it is possible that low basal T would not be relevant to prosocial, affiliative behavior among bonobos. Preliminary socioendocrine studies have shown mixed results as to whether male bonobos' basal T is correlated with rank (Sannen et al. 2004; Marshall and Hohmann 2005; Surbeck et al. 2012). Relatedly, although high-ranking bonobo males are more aggressive toward other males in mating-related circumstances, this does not appear to correlate to elevated T (Surbeck et al. 2012), differing from chimpanzees. In fact, when competing for mating opportunities, lower-T bonobo males engaged in more grooming with unrelated, potentially fertile females (Surbeck et al. 2012), which the researchers suggested is consistent with an amicability-testosterone trade-off, reflecting the potential importance of intersex social relationships to male bonobo reproductive success.

The utility of comparing bonobos and chimpanzees for T's potential effects on social alliances is limited by the sparse bonobo literature. Studies have tested for other (non-T) endocrine correlates of food sharing among chimpanzees (Crockford et al. 2013), and both bonobos and chimps show context-contingent plasticity in reciprocity during food sharing (reviewed in Jaeggi et al. 2010). Drawing on this variation and building on Sobolewski and colleagues (2012) and Wobber and colleagues (2010a), future research could test whether basal T is implicated differently between the two species in the dynamics of reciprocity and prosociality related to food sharing, and the effects on long-term alliances (Muller and Mitani 2005; Jaeggi et al. 2013).

Though they are our more distant phylogenetic cousins, relative to our fellow hominoids, comparisons with large-bodied, group-living, non-ape Old World primates can likewise prove informative for the model here. Decades of research on multiple baboon species have documented intersections among elevated T, dominance-related aggressive and competitive behaviors, and reproductive success (Sapolsky 1983; Altmann and Alberts 2003; Beehner et al. 2009). Baboon males with higher T tend to rise through the dominance hierarchy and engage in more mating (likely as a consequence of achieving high rank) (Beehner et al. 2006; Beehner et al. 2009). In multiple species, males' T was elevated in conjunction with heightened male-male aggression during periods of instability in which they were jockeying for high rank (Sapolsky 1983; Beehner et al. 2006; Beehner et al. 2009; cf. Gesquiere et al. 2011). In terms of dominance translating to reproductive success, research from the long-running Amboseli study has shown that male rank accounts for up to 50% of the variance in between-male mating success (Altmann and Alberts 2003; Alberts et al. 2003). Moreover, drawing on the same study, Archie and colleagues (2012) demonstrated that there are health benefits to being at the top of the baboon social hierarchy, perhaps providing high-ranking males with longer average reproductive lifespans. In total, these results suggest fairly unequivocally that the shortest and most reliable route to high reproductive success among baboons is to pursue social dominance, which is sometimes facilitated mechanistically via elevated T, likely through its influence on behavior (Beehner et al. 2006).

In spite of these rigid status hierarchies and male-male aggression, there is some evidence that male baboons also engage in coalitionary and cooperative behavior with each other, such as to gain access to a female who is consorting with another male. Multiple studies have found that older and middle- to low-ranking males were most likely to form coalitions, often allying against younger and/or higher-ranking males (Bercovitch 1988; Noë and Sluijter 1995).

To my knowledge, the hormonal correlates of baboons' alliance formation have not been tested. A few preliminary observations can be pieced together, however.

First, it has been proposed that coalition-forming males ally on the basis of fighting ability (i.e., two modestly competent fighters combine forces to challenge a highly effective fighter) (Noë and Sluijter 1995). To the extent that higher T might relate to baboons' fighting ability, likely through psychobehavioral pathways more so than somatic effects (Bercovitch 1989), males with especially low T might be at a disadvantage for alliance formation. However, in multiple species, T declines in male baboons as they age (Beehner et al. 2009) and as they drop in the hierarchy. Thus, compared to younger and higher-ranking males, those older and lower-ranking males who form alliances are likely to have reduced T. Noë and Sluijter (1995) found modest evidence linking coalitionary behavior and friendships between males; they hypothesized that the causal arrow went from temporary coalitions to the formation of longer-term affiliative friendships. Thus, a testable hypothesis is that changes in T related both to aging and to declining rank could predispose males to behavioral or psychological phenotypes that tend toward coalition formation and prosocial affiliative relationship maintenance.

Comparatively less research has been conducted on geladas, which are closely related to baboons. However, differing from most baboons, geladas tend to live in large groups with a single breeding male or in all-bachelor groups. Gelada males' T spikes during their reproductive prime and declines with age (Beehner et al. 2009), and breeding "leader males" appear to have higher T than do the males living in all-bachelor groups (Pappano 2013). Among bachelors, males with greater T are more likely to subsequently take over units and become leader males. However, Pappano (2013) found that males in the all-bachelor groups were rarely aggressive toward one another and formed highly affiliative social bonds, which included extensive grooming; these male-male friendships were often made with related individuals. Geladas begin to form these relationships after they disperse from their birth group and before they become reproductively mature (Pappano 2013). At that time, they have low T compared to adults (Beehner et al. 2009). However, they maintain these affiliative relationships during the life history stage in which their T is peaking (Beehner et al. 2009) and when they move to become leader males (Pappano 2013); thus, this would be an interesting test case for the intersections among T, affiliative male-male relationships, and prosocial behavior among Old World monkeys.

MALE STATUS AND SOCIAL NETWORKS

Studies examining the pathways through which human males attain social status have focused on the domains of "dominance" and "prestige" (von Rueden et al. 2011; see also Kruger and Fitzgerald 2011).[2] Briefly, in these contexts, dominance is generally characterized by the accrual of status via overt aggression, intimidation, and the threat of force or coercion. In contrast, prestige results from factors such as operationalizing prosocial skills, cultivating cooperative social networks, and conferring benefits to members of one's community (Henrich and Gil-White 2001; von Rueden et al. 2011; Kruger and Fitzgerald 2011).

In a series of studies sampling Tsimane (Bolivia) horticulturalists, von Rueden and colleagues demonstrated that men who were physically larger and/or were rated as good fighters by their peers had more social support (i.e., allies) in their community. Men with high dyadic fighting ability were rated as more likely to get their way during group disputes, while larger men were thought to wield more community-wide influence, via their broader ally networks. In a potentially divergent status pathway, men with prosocial personality characteristics were also rated as having community-wide influence and holding sway during group disputes, likely acting through prosocial men's greater levels of social support. Finally, excellent hunters were afforded high levels of respect, but this did not necessarily translate to social status independent of other factors (von Rueden et al. 2008). In a separate analysis, dominant (i.e., high fighting prowess) and prestigious (i.e., those with wide community influence) Tsimane men were both shown to have more offspring, and prestigious men's children survived at higher rates (von Rueden et al. 2011). Von Rueden and colleagues (2014) also showed that politically influential Tsimane men had lower cortisol (commonly associated with psychosocial stress) and reduced risk of respiratory infections. Politically influential men had more social support, including labor- and food-sharing partners, and this partially mediated their healthier physiological and morbidity profiles. Finally, elevated social status conveys similar reproductive fitness advantages to males in many other small-scale societies. Successful big-game hunters, especially, have heightened reproductive success in many foraging societies (reviewed in Smith 2004; von Rueden et al. 2008).

While one cannot draw explicit inferences about our evolutionary past via studies of modern cultural groups, these results do provide a framework for thinking about the dynamic interfaces of social status, social networks, cooperation, and components of male reproductive strategies. Testosterone helps to facilitate skeletal growth and fat-free muscle accretion across adolescence and into adulthood (Bribiescas 2001), contributing to sex differences. Fat-free mass could plausibly be beneficial when functional strength increases subsistence productivity. To date, there is no evidence that basal T increases subsistence productivity, through strength or otherwise, but it has also rarely been tested (Worthman and Konner 1987). Notably, healthy reproductive-aged males' T is generally not correlated to variation (between males) in musculature and strength (Gettler et al. 2010). Alvarado and colleagues' (2014) study of men's T, strength, and work output among Polish subsistence agriculturalists also runs counter to this model. Analyses of ethnographic and anthropometric data from a sample of Hadza foragers (Apicella 2014) showed that upper body strength was perceived to be the most important trait contributing to hunting success, and men with more muscular upper bodies had greater reproductive success, largely mediated by their reputations as better hunters. T was not measured. However, Muller and colleagues (2009) showed that Hadza fathers have lower T than non-fathers do, and Marlowe (2003) found that Hadza fathers increased their provisioning rates during the periods in which their partners' foraging returns were low due to breastfeeding (see also Wood and Marlowe 2013). The cross-sectional nature of these results, across multiple studies, prevents definitive inferences, but it seems that reproductive success, hunting reputation, foraging productivity, a muscular body, *and* low T all tend to co-occur, on average, among Hadza fathers. Finally, Trumble and colleagues (2014) showed that successful hunting caused an acute increase in T among Tsimane men (acute versus basal distinction). While this reverses the order of causation (hunting → elevated T), consistent with a "winner effect" on T, the researchers suggested that higher T could have a reinforcing effect on provisioning, based on T's interactions with "reward" pathways in the brain.

Larger body size could be advantageous in the context of male-male physical confrontations or could simply serve as an outward signal, enhancing social intimidation. As I have reviewed above and as outlined in Archer (2006), high T is also related to competitive behavior and heightened attention to status threats and challenges from other males, including activity in the limbic system (i.e., amygdala). Thus, high-T men are likely more circumstantially aggressive in male-male physical confrontations, a contention that receives some nominal support from studies of combat sports (Salvador et al. 1999).

While levels of sexual dimorphism in modern humans suggest that male-male fighting diminished in importance during our evolutionary past compared to many other primates (Marlowe and Berbesque 2012), these T-facilitated factors could serve a role for males in establishing alliances, which appears to be a pathway to elevated social status.

Testosterone peaks in young adulthood (Mazur 2009), when males form critical inter- and intrasexual social relationships that are often important over the life course. Germane to my purposes here, men in certain cultures do not exhibit lower T when they become partnered or fathers (Muller et al. 2009), and there is also within-culture variation in such T declines (e.g., Gettler et al. 2011). Thus, at minimum, T is unlikely to interfere with the formation of alliances or social networks in such contexts—or researchers have yet to uncover the specifics of its facilitatory role therein. A life course perspective, including how men's social relationships and the demands to forge and maintain alliances may shift as they age, along with careful attention to cultural context, is paramount here. Consistent with the literature showing that T is often low among married men and fathers in the United States, my colleague and I (Gettler and Oka 2016) were the first to show that US men also have lower T in the context of emotionally supportive relationships beyond their own spouse and children. While our research focused on older men in the United States and thus needs to be replicated for men in their reproductive primes and in other cultural contexts, the results are consistent with the predictions I outline in this chapter.

Specifically, lower-T men appear more inclined toward nurturance (partnering and parenting), empathy, and prosociality (see table 8.1), which, through other means, can also seemingly increase the breadth and strength of male social networks. In evolutionary terms, the extent to which this could be fitness enhancing would likely rest on the extent to which low-T, prosocial men could forge social-economic relationships with similar individuals (rather than being exploited) and thus derive benefits. A large set of social network analyses from a long-running study of Hadza subjects tested many assumptions that are at the core of models for the evolution of human cooperation (particularly among non-kin). Specifically, Apicella and colleagues (2012) showed that cooperative individuals tend to associate with one another, while noncooperators also tend to establish homophilic connections. A separate meta-analysis (Jaeggi and Gurven 2013) examining food sharing among multiple forager-horticulturalist societies found that reciprocity (food shared ←→ food received) explained a substantial portion of the variance in exchange relationships, independent of kin relatedness and other pathways. Reflecting the potential benefits of prosociality, a population-based panel study in the United States found that subjects who engaged in greater prosocial community activities had more robust social networks, which correlated to better health (O'Malley et al. 2012). Similarly, a study of Quechua (Peru) agropastoralists (Lyle and Smith 2014) showed that individuals who engaged in "collective actions" that benefited all in the community at a cost to themselves were held in higher esteem and were seen as more generous. Such highly regarded household heads had more substantive social networks, and their households reported better health.

There have been few explicit tests of fathers' social capital on their reproductive outcomes. In addition to von Rueden and colleagues' (2011) study, Scelza (2010) showed that Martu Aboriginal (Australia) fathers accelerated their sons' reproductive trajectories, enabling them to marry and become parents themselves at younger ages. Scelza argued that fathers were able to draw on interpersonal relationships to advocate for their sons in community discussions related to initiation rituals (a precondition for marriage) and to acquire resources from kin networks to support their sons' initiation.

Conclusion

There is substantial between- and within-culture variation in the extent to which men's T responds to partnering and fatherhood and the factors that seem to mediate or moderate that effect. In light of this and the plasticity across and within other primate species, it is reasonable to suggest that hominin males' psychobiology and behavior would have similarly flexibly adjusted to social and ecological circumstances during our evolutionary past (Gettler 2014). By no means am I arguing that a low-T, invested father, prosocial phenotype is the sine qua non of males' reproductive strategy as they move through young adulthood to mid-adulthood. That said, as researchers attempt to model the dynamics of human cooperative breeding, it will be useful to consider the socioecological contexts in which this "biology of fatherhood" was likely to have been expressed and how these broad social-capital pathways could have contributed to stabilizing or positive selection thereof.

Acknowledgments

I am very grateful to Drs. Karen Rosenberg and Wenda Trevathan for honoring me with an invitation to this seminar and to contribute here. I thank them for the enormous amount of time and effort they put into this process, which facilitated the production of this volume. I offer my gratitude to Dr. Sarah Hrdy, for whom I have much admiration, for her thorough review of my chapter during our time in Santa Fe. Dr. Ben Trumble generously offered his time as an external reviewer on my chapter, and his many insightful comments and critiques improved the quality of this contribution. Lastly, Dr. Jim McKenna provided many helpful remarks on multiple drafts of this chapter.

Notes

1. It bears mentioning that these two study designs looked at acute, short-term hormone responsiveness (i.e., minute to minute), whereas most of the research I review here pertains to basal or chronic hormone production. A review of the distinctions between these two perspectives on physiology is beyond the scope of this chapter, but it is worthwhile to keep in mind that for a given species there could have been selective pressure on long-term adjustments to T's baseline production based on life history, on T's acute responsiveness to specific stimuli or social contexts, or both.

2. This final section of my chapter overlaps and draws from components of the discussion section of Gettler and Oka (2016:39–40). This conceptual chapter and that (2016) empirical data-based testing of the ideas presented here emerged together across 2014 and 2015 and thus share their grounding in the literature and their phrasing.

CHAPTER NINE

Of Marmosets, Men, and the Transformative Power of Babies

SARAH B. HRDY

A survey across some 64,000 species of mammals, birds, reptiles, and mostly fish in the vertebrate subphylum, focusing only on that minority with any parental care at all, would reveal fathers as likely as mothers to be involved. With the emergence 200 million years ago of mammals, this class of vertebrates embarked on a different evolutionary trajectory. Gestating mothers' certainty of maternity together with their offspring's reliance on milk led to the evolution of females being peculiarly responsive to signals of need from nearby infants.

Rising levels of estrogen and prolactin, peaking near the end of pregnancy, along with declining progesterone, act on maternal brains to diminish aversive responses and to increase attraction to infantile cues. During pregnancy, receptors to oxytocin and opioids in maternal brains are upregulated, promoting the formation of emotional bonds with the tiny aliens emerging from their bodies (Decety and Svetlova 2012:5–7; Rilling 2013). Over time, through suckling and intimate contact, these ties grow stronger still (Konner 2010). Among humankind's closest great ape relations, mothers alone carry and nurture new infants. But in over half the other species in the primate order, caretaking is shared by others, providing novel evolutionary opportunities for the latent nurturing potentials in males to become expressed and rendered visible to Darwinian social selection (West-Eberhard 2003).

In quite a few primate species, mothers allow others (typically, relatives) to take and carry even very young infants. There may also be brief bouts of allomaternal suckling (Hrdy 2009), a common occurrence among traditional humans (Hewlett and Winn 2014). However, provisioning infants with food that allomothers can consume themselves is limited to some 20% of primate species (Hrdy 2010).[1] Physiological and emotional thresholds for responding to infantile signals of need (e.g., cries) (Newman 2007) vary with circumstances. Relevant factors include an allomother's own reproductive status, past experience, and probable relatedness to the mother. Through the repurposing of highly conserved vertebrate potentials, fathers and perhaps other male allomothers not only respond to infants but, like mothers, can over time become neuroendocrinologically transformed by such experiences (Abraham et al. 2014; Gettler 2014 and chapter 8, this volume; Rilling 2013).

In line with an ongoing paradigm shift in evolutionary anthropology, the care and provisioning of immatures by male and female allomothers (prereproductive, reproductive, and/or postreproductive group members, mostly but not always kin) are now viewed as essential among Pleistocene ancestors rearing slow-maturing young who remained nutritionally dependent on others for years after weaning (Burkart et al. 2009; Hawkes and Paine 2006; Hawkes et al. 1998; Hewlett and Lamb 2005; Hill and Hurtado 2009; Hrdy 1999; Konner 2010; Meehan and Crittenden 2016; Meehan and Hawks 2013). Twenty-first-century research on the developmental trajectories of human brain growth reveals energy demands peaking around 4–5 years, after the age when youngsters would have been weaned and by which time their mothers might be nursing another infant (Kuzawa et al. 2014). Kuzawa and colleagues argued that the massive increases in brain size between australopiths and *Homo sapiens* needed to be accompanied by slower growth, increasingly long childhoods, and, with these, more sustained allomaternal subsidies (see also Isler and van Schaik 2012).

Elsewhere (Hrdy 1999) I have documented unusually contingent levels of maternal commitment, which coevolved in cooperatively breeding hominins as mothers juggled demands from current and future offspring and in the process became increasingly sensitive to cues of social support. In monogamous primates with biparental care, paternal assistance is almost as obligate as maternal investment. But among cooperative breeders (any species with alloparental as well as parental care and provisioning of offspring), paternal nurture varies along a continuum from fathers highly motivated to care and provide for offspring, at one extreme, to uninvolved fathers, at the other (Hrdy 2008, 2009).

Given how much help mothers need, such facultative fathering seems paradoxical. But compared with infants' obligate need for mother's milk, male provisioning of peri- and post-weaning offspring among cooperatively breeding callitrichines, and especially hunter-gatherers, represents a more fungible commodity. Fathers are freer to adjust their investment in line with alternative reproductive options and with alternative sources of provisioning and care. For example, even if a human father defects or dies, compensatory nurture from alloparents might pull his offspring through (Hrdy 2008; Sear and Mace 2008).

In other apes, infants arrive widely spaced and, once weaned, provision themselves. Mothers can afford single-minded dedication to each infant until the arrival of the next. By contrast, among modern humans and probably also earlier hominins, infants tend to be more closely spaced and take far longer to mature. Since earlier hominin mothers gave birth to a new infant before an older child was nutritionally independent—their staggered "as-if litters" with multiple dependents vying for investment—her new infant could no longer rely on the ape mother's single-minded dedication. These hominin infants had to appeal at birth (Hrdy 1999). Infants needed to monitor and engage mothers while also ingratiating themselves with other potential caretakers. Over the course of development, hominin infants were conditioned to become more other-regarding, resulting in neurologically novel ape phenotypes. Over successive generations these novel ape phenotypes were subjected to Darwinian social selection (sensu West-Eberhard) favoring the survival of youngsters better at assessing the thoughts and feelings of others and eliciting their succor (Hrdy 2009, 2016).

In this chapter I explore the dynamic interactions between the more contingent responsiveness to infant signals among mothers and the facultative commitment elicited from male allomothers, often possible fathers, supporting their reproductive enterprise. I hypothesize that the ensuing "negotiations" or adjustments between strategizing parents reconfigured opportunities for Darwinian social selection to promote and elaborate the highly conserved nurturing potentials present in males.

None of us can go back in time to observe the processes transforming comparatively aloof ape males into nurturers who under some conditions behave so prosocially and generously as to volunteer prized commodities like meat to others. However, there is at hand a potentially informative comparison with other cooperatively breeding primates: marmosets and tamarins belonging to the subfamily Callitrichinae (figure 9.1). I have been inspired to imagine my way into this exercise by the work of Judith Burkart (Burkart et al. 2007;

Figure 9.1. Among callitrichines, such as these golden lion tamarins, mothers typically bear twins, which are carried by the father and other allomothers most of the day and then transferred back to the mother for suckling (*upper left*). Males take the initiative, but access to infants is controlled by the mother. The timing of the first transfer varies between species and with circumstances. As weaning approaches, male allomothers catch prey to deliver to infants. Drawing by Sarah Landry, a gift to Sarah Hrdy, reprinted with permission.

Burkart et al. 2014) documenting the humanlike readiness of marmosets to provide food to others, sometimes even including unrelated group members. My argument relies on the emerging evidence for socioendocrinological responses to infants among male allomothers in biparental and cooperatively breeding species, well summarized by James Rilling (2013) and Lee Gettler (2014 and chapter 8, this volume).

Whether marmosets or men, it is increasingly clear that males in intimate contact with infants can be neurobiologically transformed by the experience. Prolactin levels rise (Dixson and George 1982; Storey et al. 2000), often accompanied by marked declines in testosterone. Decreases in testosterone are found among males caring for infants in both humans (Alvergne et al. 2009; Gettler et al. 2012; Gray et al. 2002; Gray et al. 2006; Gray and Anderson 2010) and marmosets (Nunes et al. 2001; Prudom et al. 2008), while circulating levels of oxytocin, a neuropeptide long associated with birth, lactation, and female orgasm, also rise in baby-tending human fathers and in pair-bonded tamarin and marmoset parents (Abraham et al. 2014; Gordon et al. 2010; Snowdon et al. 2011). These hormones are implicated in paternal responses to infantile signals of need (Mascaro et al. 2013a). Unfortunately, little is known about how intimate exposure to infants affects males in other great apes. My prediction is that infantile need and familiarity will matter, but that the effects will be less pronounced than in humans.

Rationale for Comparing Cooperatively Breeding Homininae and Callitrichinae

In spite of obvious differences between small-bodied, tiny-brained, arboreal New World monkeys and their far larger, brainier, terrestrial, more visually oriented, longer-lived hominin relations, and in spite of marked differences in reproductive physiologies, callitrichines and humans have converged on remarkably similar modes of rearing young. These distantly related cooperative breeders share a distinctive combination of traits found in few primates and no other extant ape. These include maternal responsiveness to infant cues being contingent on social support, and variable or facultative paternal care, which is often accompanied by the direct or indirect provisioning of immatures with highly nutritious and preferred animal prey during prolonged periods of peri- and post-weaning dependence. Comparisons between human and callitrichine responses to immatures permit the exploration of how such extremely "unprimatelike" behaviors may be linked.

Anthropoid mothers long ago opted for life in the slow lane. Compared with other mammals, they utilize less energy per day, take longer to gestate, and lactate longer, resulting in longer intervals between births (Charnov and Berrigan 1993; Konner 2010:chap. 2; Pontzer et al. 2014). In the case of primarily folivorous/frugivorous hominoid apes, the intervals between births stretch out for four or more years, and as long as eight among orangutans. Challenged by anthropocene habitat loss and ongoing climate change, such a slow reproductive pace spells extinction for today's great apes, a predicament reminiscent of the "demographic dilemma" Lovejoy (1981) postulated for ancestral apes moving out onto Plio-Pleistocene savannas. But at some point, a line of bipedal and increasingly omnivorous apes switched lanes, starting to produce offspring who were weaned earlier even though they were costlier and even slower maturing (DeSilva, chapter 4, this volume). This switch was rendered feasible by allomaternal provisioning, which buffered immatures challenged by highly variable Pleistocene rainfall and fluctuating resources (Magill et al. 2013; Potts 1996; Wells 2012c). The allomaternal provisioning of young permitted at least some populations to bounce back after local

population crashes and also migrate into new habitats. Although allomaternal provisioning is widely accepted as a defining feature of cooperative
breeding, it is not known how the routine sharing of such highly valued
resources as animal prey got under way in an ape.

Like humans, the phylogenetically distant callitrichine males also volun-
tarily share animal prey with others. Like humans, these New World monkeys
are adapted to boom-and-bust ecologies and readily colonize new habitats.
Like humans, tamarin and marmoset mothers exhibit extraordinarily flexible breeding behavior. Females mate with one or several males, sometimes
including extra-group males, in groups containing one to several breeding
females (Digby and Ferrari 1994; Goldizen 1988; Hilário and Ferrari 2009;
Smith et al. 2001). Like humans, callitrichines produce costly babies at unusually (for their taxon) rapid rates. Relative to maternal body size, no anthropoid
primate has a longer gestation period or higher birth mass (Digby et al. 2011;
Tardif et al. 2013). The callitrichines' shift toward smaller size accompanied by
multiple relatively large young probably occurred *after* substantial allomaternal (including paternal) assistance was already available, rather than the other
way around (Dunbar 1995; Goldizen 1990; Harris et al. 2014). It is unlikely that
allomaternal provisioning could have evolved if these tiny monkeys had not
(like hominins) already been adept extractive foragers adapted to fluctuating
food supplies—both voracious hunters (arthropods, lizards, nestling birds)
and reliable harvesters of plant foods, in the callitrichine case mostly fruits,
seeds, and exudates (Garber 1997).

Callitrichine twins weigh up to 20% of the mother's weight, yet birth in
one season rarely diminishes maternal fertility in the next. The more offspring
Leontopithecus rosalia mothers produce one season, the *more* they bear the
next (Bales et al. 2001). This is feasible because males carry the infants and help
to provision them. In some cases, these allomothers provide nutritious prey
between the (relatively early) onset of weaning and the youngsters' attainment
of the strength and the hunting, gathering, and processing skills essential for
nutritional independence. Provisioning peaks around 12 weeks after birth. At
16 weeks, allomothers still provide up to 90% of solid foods (Hoage 1982; Rapaport 2011). Not surprisingly, offspring survival is correlated with the number
of male helpers (Bales et al. 2000; Culot et al. 2011; Garber 1997). Over evolutionary time, therefore, selection should have favored maternal sensitivity to
available help.

Contingent Commitment in Callitrichine Mothers

Almost from the first discovery of marmosets, European naturalists were struck by their peculiar combination of attentive fathers and nonchalant, even rejecting mothers. The first published illustration of marmosets was accompanied by primatology's first-ever description of male care (Edwards 1758). Two decades later, French zoologist M. Siret described a marmoset mother that was curiously unmoved by infantile signals of need.

> It seemed that the mother cared less for the [twins] than did the father. When seen neglecting her charges the mother was warned by the father with a cry.... After suckling [the twins] the mother made every effort to rid herself of them. She would free herself by kicking them off or by rolling on her back and tearing them away as they scurried to her underside. Each time the father came to the rescue and invited the twins to mount his back. Once when one of the young fell from a perch and lay stunned below, the [colony proprietor] thinking it dead reached into the cage and picked it up. At this intrusion the father became furious, threw himself upon his lordship, and shrieked until the master of the house returned the young to the floor where he found it. The father then picked up his offspring and placed it on his back where it recovered. (Siret 1778:453, translated in Hershkovitz 1977:551)

Under pressure to reduce the metabolic costs of carrying and nursing babies, mothers in cooperatively breeding and biparental care genera (e.g., *Callithrix*, *Saguinus, Callicebus, Aotus*) reduce their load by scraping infants off, sometimes biting their hands and feet (Hoffman et al. 1995:402; Huck and Fernandez-Duque 2013:378; Cooper 1964, cited in Hershkovitz 1977:788; Ross et al. 2005). Unless fathers come to the rescue, complaining neonates may be left on the floors of cages (e.g., Epple 1970:66). Even parous callitrichine mothers may ignore infants who cease to move or vocalize, sometimes abandoning still-vocalizing ones. For primatologists accustomed to the obsessive protectiveness of Old World monkey and ape mothers, such nonchalance, particularly in experienced mothers, is surprising. Old World monkeys born missing limbs or with cerebral palsy are still picked up, carried, and suckled (Berkson 1974; Turner et al. 2005). Comatose or dead infants continue to be carried for days.

Tiny arboreal monkeys are difficult to observe in the wild, thus most reports of abandonment come from captivity (Bardi et al. 2001; Epple 1970:66; Johnson et al. 1991; Rothe 1975:316–317). Interpreting the high frequencies of maternal rejections in callitrichines is therefore complicated because even monkey and ape species never observed to reject infants in the wild may do so in captivity. Yet even compared to other captive primates, there is an unusually high incidence of rejections among these monkeys dependent on allomaternal assistance. Furthermore, rejections are also reported from the wild, which represents a marked contrast with experienced mothers in other monkeys and apes, who virtually never reject or abandon, and *never* wound, their own infants. In the far fewer hours during which tamarins and titi monkeys have been observed in the wild, there are multiple reports of females biting infants to death. In three cases (detailed below) the mother almost certainly killed her own infant. These represent the only known cases from nature in which a mother was sufficiently unmoved by infant signals of distress as to not only push her baby away but to actually kill it. All of these incidents occurred in species with obligate (or nearly obligate) dependence on allomaternal care and provisioning.

Although uncommon, infanticide is widely reported for primates (Hrdy 1979; van Schaik and Janson 2000), witnessed in 56 populations in 35 different species and inferred in 16 more (Palombit 2012). Almost always, the killer is a male or female *other* than the victim's own parent. Under unfavorable conditions, primate mothers may spontaneously abort prior to birth (e.g., Roberts et al. 2012), display lower investment after it (e.g., Fairbanks and Hinde 2013), or rebuff infants to facilitate early weaning (Altmann 1980), but the outright rejection of full-term infants is rare. Exceptions involve captive, socially deprived mothers; mothers under extreme duress (e.g., repeated stalking by an infanticidal male); or inexperienced young mothers inadequately tending firstborns (e.g., Schino and Troisi 2005). No primate fieldworker has ever reported a mother killing her own infant *except* in species with obligate allomaternal care.

Female infanticide is particularly common among cooperatively breeding callitrichines, with many cases reported in captivity, nine well-documented cases among wild populations (Bezerra et al. 2007; Culot et al. 2011:table 1; Digby and Saltzman 2009; Tirado-Herrera et al. 2000), and one case in monogamous biparental care, *Callicebus nigrifrons* (Cäsar et al. 2008). In seven of the ten wild cases, the female killed another female's infant, but in the

Callicebus and two tamarin cases, living babies were almost certainly bitten to death by their own mothers, unheard-of behavior for anthropoid primates.

In field primatology's first report of maternal infanticide (Tirado-Herrera et al. 2000), a saddle-back tamarin (*Saguinus fusicollis*) gave birth in a group containing several males and a second pregnant female. On its first day of life, the infant was dropped several times only to be retrieved, usually by one of the males, until when once again reunited with its mother, she "took a vertical position on a [tree] trunk, gripped the infant, and bit into its face. The infant moved its arms and legs. Further bites were directed to the face and to the brain case" (155). After the corpse fell to the ground, it was determined that the baby's brain had been entirely consumed. In the second case, a moustached tamarin (*S. mystax*), who had successfully reared three sets of twins during periods when four or five males were on hand to help, gave birth when there was a second breeding female in the group, but only two or three males were present. This mother also was observed biting and eating the head of her baby. Although the infant was vocalizing shortly before, observers could not be absolutely certain that her son was still alive when she began biting (Culot et al. 2011:182). In the third case, a black-fronted titi mother (*Callicebus nigrifrons*) gave birth to a healthy son, who was then carried mostly by her mate until the third day. When the vocalizing infant was returned to her, she began to bite his face, eventually dropping the corpse to the ground (Cäsar et al. 2008). Under duress, other mammals are known to cull or cannibalize their infants or abandon whole litters (e.g., Hoogland 1994), but most primate mothers go to extraordinary lengths to keep their babies safe, becoming especially protective when danger threatens. Only in primates with obligate allomaternal care have wild-living mothers been observed to deliberately wound their own infants.

Experiments with *Callimico goeldii* (marmoset-like monkeys that, although they produce singleton young, are sometimes classified with Callitrichinae) reveal mothers surprisingly quick to put their own safety ahead of their infants'. *Callimico* fathers are interested in their infants right from birth, but in the wild it is usually day 11 before mothers allow them access. In captivity, the first transfer is later still, around day 27. But when a "predator" (someone's pet ferret) was experimentally introduced near their cages, instead of holding their baby closer and moving away, six of seven mothers turned their infants over to the fathers days earlier than they ordinarily would have (Schradin and Anzenberger 2005). The experimenters hypothesized that mothers sought to protect their infants in this way. But since *Callimico* males are nearly the same size as the females and little better at defending young against predators than the mother would be, her behavior is better explained by an urgent desire for unencumbered escape.[2]

Have Callitrichines Evolved Neural Overrides to Maternal Commitment?

Although uncommon, maternal infanticide is widely documented for humans in both the ethnographic and historical records (Hrdy 1999), but it is not known to occur among wild primates. Only among those New World monkeys with extensive allomaternal (including paternal) involvement do we find mothers sufficiently unmoved by *Kindchenschema* as to pass infants off when danger threatens or deliberately mutilate or kill one, even focusing on the vocalizing face. Obviously, the survival of any mammalian species depends on mothers being motivated to care for offspring. Usually mothers, especially primate mothers, are. Nevertheless, systematic analyses of the circumstances surrounding a large sample of callitrichines' rejections reported for a breeding colony in the United States suggest a method to this seeming madness.

Massimo Bardi and colleagues (2001) used stepwise multiple regression to evaluate factors affecting survival to 1 year for 1,093 *Saguinus oedipus* born between 1984 and 1993 at the New England Primate Research Center. Fifty percent (546) were rejected while an additional 12% (134) were killed before they could be removed and hand reared. In 89% of these cases, termination of the mother's investment ended within 3 days of birth. Infanticide in these instances could not be attributed to pathological individuals since virtually all parents that abused or rejected offspring had on other occasions successfully reared them. Interestingly, the postpartum timing of these rejections echoes the timing of infanticides among traditional and modern human societies (Hrdy 1999:chaps. 12–14). Of 3,312 infanticides recorded by the US Centers for Disease Control between 1989 and 1998, 82.6% of cases occurred on the first day, and the incidents peaked in the first week, with mothers almost certainly present and implicated (Paulozzi 2002; see also Overpeck et al. 1998).

Since mothers are the major caretakers right after birth, it is assumed that the callitrichine mothers are primarily responsible for the "decisions" to reject

(Bardi et al. 2001:167). But mothers might also be responding to signals of paternal willingness to help, or to the availability of male help generally. In the Bardi sample, the single most important predictor of rejection was the availability of helpers. When older siblings were available, 54.9% of infants were accepted, compared with 17.2% when older siblings were absent. Mothers in poor health and those bearing triplets were more likely to abuse infants. The rates of rejection were also higher for inexperienced (64.1%) compared with experienced (39.5%) mothers and for younger parents of either sex than for older ones. These trends parallel maternal competence in primates generally (reviewed in Hrdy 1999). Thus it is surprising that the tamarin mothers *without* prior caretaking experience were *less*, not more, likely than experienced mothers to mutilate babies they rejected. Compared with the 8.2% of inexperienced mothers who abused infants, the rate for parous females was nearly double (15.2%), suggesting that mutilations were not due to inexperience or incompetence.

Firsthand observations of maternal rejections raise the possibility that some of the mutilated, often headless, infants found on the floors of breeding cages were bitten by mothers. Quite possibly, a nonresponsive infant is simply reclassified as "prey," inviting the consumption of its delectable brain. But the contrast with other primate mothers, who remain protective of comatose or dead babies for days, leads me to suspect some neurophysiological dampening of bonding mechanisms in postpartum callitrichines. This might help explain why some marmoset mothers fail to discriminate between their own infant and unfamiliar infants matched for age (Saltzman and Abbott 2005). Dampened responsiveness would facilitate rejection under conditions with insufficient allomaternal support. Possibly, maternal distancing even helps mothers to "poll" the available assistance.

Callitrichine males (especially probable progenitors?) are highly responsive to infant cues (Sánchez et al. 2014), often retrieving rejected babies and carrying them until returned to their mother for nursing. Males with experience or in good condition are especially responsive as measured by both behavior and higher prolactin levels (Ziegler et al. 2004a). Gauging her mate's responsiveness is valuable feedback for a mother to have so that some maternal rejections may be strategic rather than terminal. If she repeats or escalates rejection and no other allomother intervenes, the father too may terminate his investment, information that is worth having sooner rather than later.

Some Highly Derived Specializations for Ensuring the
Availability of Caretakers

Obviously, callitrichine mothers do not conceive and gestate babies in order to discard them. Abandonment is a last resort. Under most circumstances, mothers proactively line up allomaternal assistance in advance by mating polyandrously with several males. Not only do females mate throughout the cycle (as human women also do), but callitrichines ovulate again shortly after birth, while lactating. To inseminate her, a male needs to be nearby in the postpartum period and will thus be exposed to stimuli from her newborns. Furthermore, tamarin fathers may join mothers in consuming the placenta, ingesting an extra cocktail of nurture-promoting hormones, a predilection also documented in other mammals with obligate male care (Gregg and Wynne-Edwards 2005).

Callitrichine mothers can produce twins or triplets sired by *different* fathers, and placental fusion permits the transfer of cells, possibly even germ cells, between multiply sired siblings in utero (Ross et al. 2007; Sweeney et al. 2012). Thus researchers can rarely know which male or males sired which offspring. Interestingly, chimeric infants known to carry DNA from more than one father are more attractive to and more often carried by male allomothers compared to non-chimeric young. Mothers, however, carry chimeras less (Ross et al. 2007), possibly because they count on males to compensate. Callitrichine mothers also increase the availability of babysitters by eliminating the offspring of rival mothers (Digby 2000). Over generations, the threat of infanticide led to selection on females to suppress their own ovulation when in the presence of a more dominant female. Imposing this threat requires a pregnant or postpartum female to override the special responsiveness to signals of infant distress that ordinarily emerges during mammalian pregnancy (Numan and Insel 2003; Barrett and Fleming 2011).

Across mammals, including humans, postpartum mothers exhibit diminished responsiveness when stressed. But an increased aversion to babies in *pregnant* females is one of the stranger overrides to maternal responsiveness on record. Even multiparous marmosets that have successfully raised young and that were attracted to infants early in pregnancy exhibit *longer* latencies to approaching infants during late pregnancy. Experiments reveal that some pregnant marmosets are so averse to infants that they reflexively attack them (Saltzman and Abbott 2005). Of the seven wild females that bit another female's infant to death, five were pregnant (Culot et al. 2011:table 1). Furthermore, considering all ten cases (including maternal ones), four involved cannibalism with brains preferred—a risky appetite for pregnant or just-delivered mothers (Bezerra et al. 2007). My suspicion is that this aversion to infants *during* pregnancy is a highly derived trait that could only evolve in primates with neural systems already predisposed to override maternal responses to infantile cues.

A Common Overall Strategy with Major Human-Callitrichine Differences

Callitrichine and human mothers have converged on a similar decision rule: proactively line up allomaternal assistance, but if that fails, bail out. A human forager whose new infant is born before an older child is sufficiently independent or who finds herself short on allomaternal support will terminate contact before lactation upregulates her responsiveness (Hrdy 1999:472), making neglect or abuse less likely (Strathearn et al. 2009) and abandonment harder. Nevertheless, having evolved as cooperative breeders for far less long, humans presumably never evolved such highly derived callitrichine adaptations as postpartum estrus, and except in the rarest instances, women do not bear chimeric offspring. Nor is there any evidence from foraging societies of pregnancy-related baby aversion or the murder of babies born to other women.

It may be relevant that callitrichine infants are relatively less costly for a mother to produce than are human infants. Rejecting callitrichine mothers may go beyond increasing males' exposure to infantile magic and move into the realm of "extortion": "Help me, or I'm bailing out." After all, a callitrichine mother might produce twins or triplets as often as twice a year. Even already pregnant with the next batch, a tamarin mother loses little weight during lactation (Bales et al. 2002). Measured in weight loss, caring callitrichine fathers expend far more energy. Males prepare by gaining up to 15% of their body weight prior to birth, starting to "show" even before their pregnant mates do (Ziegler et al. 2004a), and, as mentioned, tamarin fathers further prime themselves by consuming the placenta. Among humans, by contrast, each newborn represents a tremendous energetic and opportunity cost, and especially with the onset of lactation, mothers are on a "mammary leash," endocrinologically incentivized to nurture and far less inclined to abandon an infant than the father is (Hrdy 1999).

Among humans, neither mother nor father consumes the placenta. But a mother can lower thresholds for nurturing responses in nearby allomothers by allowing trusted candidates to hold her baby right after birth, something no other ape does. Nevertheless, if they are short on social support, both callitrichine and human mothers may reduce or terminate their investment right after birth. Women also exhibit some specializations of their own. Never having evolved the physiological equipment for truly partible paternity, human mothers in many parts of the world use culturally generated fictions about paternity to line up extra provisioners. Sexual partners in addition to a woman's husband who *believe* they are possible progenitors help to provision her and her offspring (Beckerman et al. 1998; Hrdy 2000; Walker et al. 2010). Prolonged lifespans also make available experienced, hardworking, postreproductive kinswomen to help care for and provision offspring (Hawkes et al. 1998; Hawkes and Coxworth 2013).

Refining What Counts as "Cute"

With the accelerating relevance of culture among behaviorally modern humans, conditional emotional responsiveness may have provided windows of opportunity for mothers to consciously discriminate between infants kept versus those abandoned by using real (physical defects, prematurity) or more arbitrary (culturally invented) criteria relevant to the child's prospects. Over time, millions of women have eliminated perfectly healthy infants born the "wrong" sex so as to try again for the preferred sex (reviewed in Daly and Wilson 1995; Hrdy 1999:chap. 10). The topic is sensitive and understudied, but I am convinced that preferences for well-timed, robust offspring, those most likely to survive and mature into healthy adults, have characterized humans long enough that unconscious as well as conscious biases have shaped maternal responses. (See Swamy et al. 2008 for the long-term implications of low birth weight; Frodi et al. 1978 for aversion to the cries of premature babies; Glocker et al. 2009 for preferences for plumper, full-term-looking baby faces; Leckman et al. 1999; Mann 1992; Overpeck et al. 1998 for maternal responses to cues correlated with prematurity; Barden et al. 1989 for maternal aversion to babies born with facial disfigurements.) Whether callitrichines ever discriminate based on infant attributes is unknown.[3]

Thermoregulation and especially the need to fuel costly brains would have favored fatter newborns in the line leading to the genus *Homo* (Kuzawa 1998). As increasingly discriminating mothers came to associate full-term, plump neonates with healthier outcomes, selection would also have favored babies born looking full term and robust, since such babies would be more likely to appeal to mothers. One result was the otherwise maladaptive-seeming accumulation of white adipose tissue just prior to passage through a bipedal mother's narrow birth canal (Trevathan and Rosenberg, introduction, this volume). The combined outcome of such selection pressures was human neonates born with four times the body fat of other apes (15% versus 4%), newborns advertising to their mothers, "I'm a good bet; keep me" (Hrdy 1999:chap. 20). Maternal retrenchment's most portentous effects, however, may operate on fathers.

Paternal Care in Cooperative Breeders Even More Facultative than Maternal Care

Paternal care is essential for infant survival among monogamous New World *Callicebus* and *Aotus*. Among cooperatively breeding Callitrichinae, however, infant survival is correlated with the total number of adult males in the group because, as in humans, paternal shortfalls can sometimes be compensated for by alloparents (Gettler 2014; Hrdy 2008). In one well-studied group of wild tamarins, *Leontopithecus rosalia*, paternal effort varied inversely with how many other males were present. Short on alloparental help, paternal participation increased even as the mother's time spent carrying the infant remained constant (Bales et al. 2002:454).

Anthropologist Courtney Meehan (2005) documented a similar dynamic among Central African foragers. Among the Aka, residence patterns are typically flexible, and people move between groups. During periods when parents resided matrilocally, the mother's kin engaged in much direct childcare, permitting the father to do little. When parents moved to be near his family, however, patrilineal kin proved less helpful. Yet, with little change in how much the mother held her baby, the *total* time infants were held remained more or less constant because fathers compensated by doing exponentially more (figure 9.2).

Those who assume that such well-calibrated adjustments to parental investment can only be explained by uniquely "practical reasoning" in cognitively sophisticated humans (e.g., Driscoll 2005:287) should consider the similarly opportunistic calibrations of parental care reported for tiny-brained callitrichines (Bales et al. 2002), which lack anything like sapient-grade foresight or perspective (e.g., Burkart and Heschl 2007). Among captive marmosets, fathers as well as mothers were more likely to push 6- to 9-week-old infants

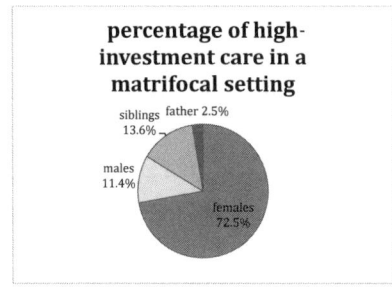 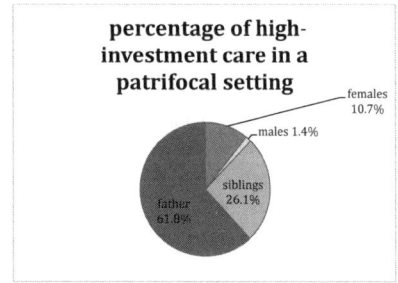

Aka Allomothers

Figure 9.2. Aka babies were held by allomothers for roughly the same amount of time in matrilocal and patrilocal settings, but in a matrilocal setting with matrilineal kin offering to help care for a mother's infant, the father engaged in relatively little direct care, even less than the combined care from other male alloparents. However, in patrilocal settings with less alloparental assistance on offer, fathers cared far more. Adapted from a diagram provided by Courtney Meehan, reproduced here with permission.

off if experienced alloparents were on hand (Fite et al. 2005). Similarly, as group size (and the availability of alternate care) increases, a wild tamarin male reduces his invitations to infants to climb aboard. Indeed, reproductive males may benefit from additional help even more than mothers do since allo-parental participation reduces the father's energetic expenditures while also enhancing the group's defense, potentially extending a given male's reproductive tenure in the group (Bales et al. 2000:fig. 1 and elsewhere).

Although early evolutionary psychologists were convinced that primate males would only nurture infants whose paternity they could be certain of (e.g., Symons 1982), it has become increasingly clear that fathers as well as mothers may benefit when mothers mate polyandrously if offspring *possibly* a male's own thereby garner extra provisioning (Beckerman et al. 1998; Diaz-Munoz et al. 2014; Eliasson and Jorgensen 2014; Hrdy 2009; Starkweather and Hames 2012; Walker et al. 2010). Among hunter-gatherers such as the Hadza, fathers are reported to put more effort into hunting than do unmated, childless men (Wood and Marlowe 2013). Clearly, probable genetic relatedness matters. Yet even when men manage to channel resources to their own families, more than half the meat men bring back gets distributed to other group members (Hawkes et al. 2010; Hawkes et al. 2014). Furthermore since better-fed mothers resume ovulation sooner (Marlowe 2001), more meat brought into camp not only enhances the well-being of offspring possibly a man's own, but also increases the availability of fertile women in his group generally and the viability of the community upon which he and his kin depend.

Why Would Male Apes Voluntarily Share Food?

Regardless of just how closely chimpanzee breeding systems do or do not resemble those of humankind's last common ancestor with other apes, common chimpanzees still provide the best-studied proxies for estimating their sociocognitive capacities. Experiments on the "altruism" of *Pan troglodytes* suggest that when food is presented, chimpanzees are "overwhelmed" by the incentive before them and display little interest in the mental states or desires of nearby others, rarely engaging in spontaneous sharing or reciprocal exchanges (Yamamoto and Tanaka 2009). Chimpanzees will respond to persistent solicitations, but rarely initiate voluntary donations (see esp. Silk et al. 2013). In the wild, successful hunters may proffer scraps after persistent begging by other adults, but almost never give any food to youngsters. With the exception of mother-to-infant transfers (rarely involving commodities so prized as meat), there is no increase in allomaternal provisioning around weaning, the life stage when youngsters are most at risk of starving (Boesch and Boesch-Achermann 2000). Although less well studied, bonobos are genetically as closely related to humans as common chimpanzees are, and bonobos are both more tolerant and "xenophiliac" (Hare 2014; Hare et al. 2007). Nevertheless, even bonobo males are rarely reported by fieldworkers to offer food to others.

In contrast to either species of chimpanzee, callitrichines readily volunteer food, with marmoset breeders more willing than nonbreeders to pull in a tray delivering food to another adult (Burkart et al. 2007; Martin and Burkart 2013). Experiments by Judith Burkart reveal that adult *Callithrix jacchus* share with infants 53% of all food items they obtain, with provisioning peaking when youngsters are 10–16 weeks of age. The more difficult it was to obtain a food item, the more likely it was to be delivered to a nearby begging immature. Interestingly, as in Marlowe's Hadza sample mentioned above, breeding male marmosets tried harder to provision than did nonbreeding helpers (offering 61% of food items obtained compared to 46%) (Burkart and Finkenwirth 2015). Among wild tamarins (*Leontopithecus rosalia*) as well, allomothers (usually male) were four times *more* likely to share animal prey than (less coveted) vegetable foods. Amazingly, the hunter himself refrained from eating any meat. Seventy-one percent of the time, the male allomother accompanied his gift with a special call designating "animal prey" (Rapaport 2006:217–218).

Callitrichine food transfers seem calibrated both to meet infant nutritional needs and to selectively transfer information. Lab experiments confirm that adult male tamarins monitor emerging competence in juveniles, ceasing to respond to their begging once immatures learn to operate a food-delivery apparatus for themselves (Humle and Snowdon 2008). The delivery of novel fruit or prey that youngsters have not previously encountered is accompanied by special staccato food calls (Rapaport and Brown 2008). Humans aside ("Here, sweetie, try this"), callitrichines are the only primates known to accompany gifts with context-specific vocalizations. Once "mentors" locate potential prey, they vocalize, luring 4- to 12-month-olds to that location. Novices then set about foraging for themselves, learning where to search and, through trial and error, how to hunt.

As youngsters mature and learn to process more plant foods for themselves, the proportion of animal prey delivered actually increases. This counterintuitive result suggests that male provisioning really does function to promote faster growth and earlier weaning, buffering youngsters from starvation around this vulnerable time. Rapaport and colleagues (2013) have even hypothesized that inclusive fitness benefits from male provisioning might explain the overproduction of sons that has been documented for various tamarin species (Hershkovitz 1977:table 89B). Whether provisioning by opening hard-to-open fruits (Garber 1997), by teaching young to forage in the forest for themselves (Rapaport 2011), or by pulling in trays of food for others in captive experiments (Burkart et al. 2007; Cronin et al. 2011), callitrichines tend to be remarkably prosocial, generous where food is concerned (Burkart et al. 2014) as well as rescuing infants from danger (e.g., Graetz 1968).

Among human foragers, energetically rich foods (meat and honey) obtained by males also are routinely shared. But even leaving aside language and culture, there are major differences. In particular, callitrichines lack sex-defined divisions of labor in either infant care or hunting. Callitrichines' prey are small, located in circumscribed geographic ranges, caught on the fly in one hand or extracted from tree holes by nimble fingers, so the young are nearby, and male hunters hand prey *directly* to immatures (Brown et al. 2004). Among humans, by contrast, captured prey are divided and prepared by other group members.

Rarely do men directly offer meat to immatures. Instead, when asked, ethnographers recall men "helping a young child eat soupy stuff from a gourd" or "fathers helping kids eat small fish with bones" (R. Hames discussing Amazonian hunter-horticulturalists, pers. comm., 2014); New Guinea highlander men delivering premasticated food via kiss-feeding (I. Eibl-Eibesfeldt's photo archives); and Hadza men sharing bits of cooked meat or highly desired honey (A. Crittenden, pers. comm., 2014). !Kung children begging food from fathers are rarely rebuffed (Konner 2010:462). The only quantitative data come from Courtney Meehan and Jessica Collins (pers. comm., 2014). Of 78 Aka children between birth and 4 years of age, six were given food by their fathers while four received food from other men. Such instances sound more like demonstrations of affection than routine provisioning yet nevertheless appear symptomatic of high levels of tolerance and nurturing intent.

Setting the Stage for Male Tolerance

Food sharing among primates ranges from nonexistent to "tolerated theft" to voluntary and frequent. Humans and callitrichines fall at the extreme end of such "donative intent," spontaneously proffering food, including meat, to kin and even non-kin (Burkart et al. 2009). Once established, the routine division of labor accompanied by food sharing and long-term exchange relationships between groups allowed human foragers to lower the risks of unpredictable resources (Cashdan 1990; Wiessner 1982). Among slow-maturing, intelligent apes already characterized by incipient divisions of labor (e.g., Boesch and Boesch-Achermann 2000; McGrew 1979 for chimpanzees), behaviorally modern *Homo sapiens'* increased recourse to cultural solutions (including language) made it increasingly possible to reduce starvation risks through pooling and sharing resources (Cashdan 1990; Kramer and Ellison 2010; Wiessner 1982). Such exchanges generate their own hypersocial sequelae, which are beyond the scope of this chapter. But how does voluntary sharing get started?

Relatively few primates hunt, but among species that do, meat's concentration of protein and lipids is highly prized. Wresting meat from a possessor risks aggressive retaliation. Humans and chimpanzees, typically males, are the only apes really interested in hunting (e.g., McGrew 1979; Marlowe 2010), but only in human apes does meat constitute an important part of the diet. Given how self-centered great ape males tend to be, and how little caretaking beyond generalized protection they do, how did apes in the line leading to the genus *Homo* become sufficiently tolerant as to allow others to partake of prized commodities?

In tracing the origins of hominin male tolerance, it is worth keeping in mind how dangerous to infants males can be. Infanticide by males is widespread among primates, rodents, and other animals. Tolerance-producing mechanisms were essential to reduce the likelihood of males harming offspring possibly their own. In some house mouse strains, ejaculation during mating activates a time-delayed neural inhibition of infanticidal responses beginning 3 weeks (the mouse gestation period) later, and spontaneously reemerging 2 months after ejaculation, long enough for offspring possibly the male's own to be weaned (Perrigo and vom Saal 1994). In other mice, testosterone implants in virgin, castrated males were enough to switch their response to neonates from tolerant to infanticidal (Perrigo and vom Saal 1994:372). Among mammals, including nonhuman primates, most infanticidal males only attack infants cared for by females they have not mated with (Hrdy 1977).

Male mice encountering stray pups either ignore or attack (and possibly cannibalize) them, but repeated exposure to pup after pup elicits tolerance, even nurture.[4] It has been discovered that immature mice secrete a pheromone from the lacrimal gland that, when released in the tears of 2- to 3-week-old mice, inhibits sexual behavior in adult males (Ferrero et al. 2013). In species where males find themselves in proximity to infants likely to be close kin, neural overrides to the attack impulses would be essential fail-safes, especially if accompanied by thresholds for responding to infantile cues sufficiently low to promote nurture under the right circumstances.

Not only do males become more tolerant and affiliative after intimate exposure to infants, but with or without recent histories of direct male care, primate males appear preadapted to recognize, look out for, and behave affiliatively toward possibly related youngsters (Fox et al. 2014; Hrdy 1979). For example, polygynously mating male baboons preferentially respond to distress calls from mothers with infants only possibly their own (Palombit 2000) as do Barbary macaque males (Small 1991). Even ordinarily aloof, promiscuously mating male chimpanzees care for orphans likely to be relatives (Boesch and Boesch-Achermann 2000; Goodall 1986). My speculation is that the neuropeptides and other hormones enlisted by natural selection here are "recycled" from molecules and neural circuits already on hand because they promoted maternal nurture. Whatever the physiological basis, it behooves primate mothers to seek to remain near males with whom they mated (Altmann 1980; Hrdy 1979).

Initially, maternal preferences might involve nothing more than remaining near those males—males predisposed to be tolerant and protective toward her infant rather than infanticidal (Hrdy 1979). Under the right circumstances, however, phylogenetically ancient, highly conserved male proclivities can reemerge (e.g., West-Eberhard 2003; Wu et al. 2014; Dulac et al. 2014; Rilling and Young 2014). As Gettler (2014 and chapter 8, this volume) explains, intimate contact with infants is correlated with the downregulation of testosterone, predisposing males to be more tolerant toward immatures and others. Presumably, such tolerance extends to the immatures persistently importuning males for animal prey. Elevated oxytocin and prolactin would promote affiliative emotions as well as tolerance (Carter 2014), increasing the likelihood that beggars get some food. For example, when Saito and Nakamura (2011) administered oxytocin into the central nervous system of male marmosets, begging youngsters were more likely to be fed rather than rebuffed. Meanwhile, mothers remaining close to previous mates would find they could minimize care in the expectation that someone else would pick up the protective slack, further increasing males' exposure to infant signals of need. Since former mates have a stake both in possible offspring's well-being and in reducing the interval until the mother's next conception, Darwinian selection should favor lower and lower thresholds of male responsiveness—sometimes including a greater willingness to share food.

In the first phylogenetically controlled examination of food sharing's evolution among primates, Jaeggi and van Schaik (2011) analyzed data from 68 different species. They concluded that "food sharing among adults only evolved in species already sharing with offspring" (2125). Their phylogenetic analysis is consistent with available natural history. For example, when a tamarin male who has been carrying infants on his back and providing them occasional snacks returns the twins to be nursed, he may tolerantly permit their mother to remove food from his hands or chew on insects he has caught (e.g., Graetz 1968). Presumably, success obtaining food in this way conditions and emboldens youngsters and their mothers to beg more. The provisioning of young is most likely to occur when the available foods require strength or processing skills beyond those immatures ordinarily possess (Jaeggi and van Schaik 2011; see also O'Connell et al. 1999 for hominins). The elaboration of other-regarding capacities among slow-maturing, long-dependent youngsters that need to ingratiate themselves with nurturers is one corollary of this mode of child-rearing (Hrdy 2009); the enhanced tolerance among male caretakers is another (Burkart et al. 2009).

How Cute Babies Catalyze Self-Reinforcing Feedback Loops

Allomaternal care and provisioning enhance the inclusive fitness of collateral kin and in some cases the direct fitness of fathers through offsprings' survival. A male's provisioning also increases his mate's lifetime reproductive outputs by shortening interbirth intervals (e.g., Marlowe 2001). If exposure to infants coincides with the downregulation of testosterone, reducing aggressive inclinations, and with even a slight upregulation of oxytocin-enhanced tolerance, the stage is set for more prosocial responses. Instead of responding with irritation, the possessor of a preferred food item allows another to take it. If tolerated snatchings enhance the survival of offspring likely to be related, there is all the more reason for selection to favor lower and lower thresholds for males responding to signals of infantile need. This becomes, quite literally, a self-reinforcing feedback loop with profound implications for ongoing evolution in the genus *Homo*.

There is general agreement that scavenging and hunting played important roles in human evolution and that meat was shared. However, debate persists over *why* men hunted. Some researchers emphasize fathers' motivations to provision their families (Lovejoy 1981; Kaplan et al. 2000; Wood and Marlowe 2013). Others emphasize sexually selected female preferences for good providers (Darwin 1871; Lancaster and Lancaster 1987; Lawrence and Nohria 2002:182). Still others stress socially selected quests for prestige (Hawkes 1991; Hawkes et al. 2010). While Wood and Marlowe (2013) emphasize that Hadza men with children put more effort into bringing back food for the community, doing so on 41% of days (married men without children: 31%; unmarried men without children: 21%), attempting to channel it to their own relations, Hawkes and colleagues (2014) question whether delivering protein to the mothers of their own children is men's only, or even primary, motivation for hunting. They point out these hunters' preference for targeting more elusive and obligately shared but also reputation-enhancing large game rather than smaller prey that would more reliably provision their own families. Any combination of these explanations seems plausible, but I am not qualified to weight them.

Sidestepping these debates, I focus here on how ape males became sufficiently tolerant toward others for food sharing to occur at all. Once meat
was shared, generosity might subsequently be further favored for all sorts of
reasons, including the punishment of selfish, aggressive, or self-aggrandiz-
ing behavior (Boehm 2012). Indeed, Hare and colleagues (2012) propose that
the more tolerant bonobos became "self-domesticated" through selection
disfavoring male aggressiveness. But primate-wide—so presumably a basal
condition—the most common context in which group members mob and
punish offending males is *not* when some male behaves selfishly by hoarding
a resource for himself, but rather when a male responds inappropriately by
threatening an infant. Thus I favor the hypothesis that hominin males were
rendered more tolerant by increased exposure to infantile solicitations, essentially *Kindchenschemized* and already preadapted for prosocial responses,
before routine food sharing got started.

A High-Stakes Coordination Game with Cute Babies at the Center

Little is known about the sequence of events that by the beginning of the
Pleistocene (Hrdy 2009) and possibly earlier (DeSilva 2011 and chapter 4,
this volume) led to the evolution of full-fledged cooperative breeding with
both parental and alloparental provisioning of groupmates. To date, the most
carefully worked-out scenario for the evolution of cooperative breeding in a
primate is for callitrichines (Goldizen 1990:fig. 1) rather than hominins.

Goldizen's model (1990) assumes an obligately monogamous starting condition that encouraged the evolution of paternal investment, followed by
increased fertility (twinning), selection favoring increased alloparental assistance from kin, and increasingly facultative (polyandrous) mating by females.
Chimerism and suppressed ovulation emerged later, as highly derived features
of this cooperative breeding system (Hrdy 2009). Whether or not the earliest
hominins were also characterized by pair bonding, as suggested for *Australopithecus afarensis* (Lovejoy 1981) and *Ardipithecus ramidus* (Lovejoy 2009), is
not yet knowable. Both Goldizen's proposal and explanations for pair bonding,
including mate guarding, antagonism toward same-sex rivals over resources,
and forestalling infanticide, continue to be debated and bleed into discussions
over how allomaternal provisioning got started. Were monogamously paired
males hunting to provision needy offspring (Marlowe 2010)? Was alloparental

provisioning initiated with plant foods donated by postreproductive matrilineal kin (Hawkes et al. 1989; Hawkes and Paine 2006), by older siblings or co-suckling co-mothers, or some opportunistic combination thereof (Hrdy 2009)? The reliance on male provisioning among some obligately monogamous primates (e.g., Huck and Fernandez-Duque 2013) is consistent with paternal provisioning arguments, while correlations between female philopatry and shared infant care in anthropoid primates underscore the importance of nearby matrilineal kin (Hawkes et al. 1998; Hrdy 2010). Any resolution must await more and better paleontological evidence. My aim here is to highlight how the increased exposure to infantile signals of need affects males.

Until recently most researchers focused on human maternal responsiveness, leaving the effects of babies on group members other than mothers unexplored. Twenty-first-century experiments using recordings played to parents revealed that yes, mothers respond more readily to mild infant distress (cries of a just waking baby), but fathers responded just as fast if cries signaled real distress (Stallings et al. 2001; Fleming et al. 2002). As with most primates, men tend to be protective of infant group members, with probable fathers especially so. Assuming he is within earshot, if the mother fails to respond, the father eventually will, resulting in his increased exposure to infantile stimuli. Researchers have also discovered the socioendocrinological effects on male allomothers. As mentioned, prolonged proximity to an infant leads to decreased levels of testosterone in men while prolactin and oxytocin are likely to go up; the enhancement of affiliative emotions and social tolerance are likely corollaries (Carter 2014). Any fitness payoffs from increased offspring survival would produce self-reinforcing feedback loops favoring even lower thresholds of male responsiveness.

Humans are not as specifically adapted to cooperative breeding as callitrichines are. Human mothers are not so prone to filter out signals of infant distress and are rarely as rejecting as tamarin mothers. Nevertheless, in both taxa, when mothers fail to respond, the father or other relations may pick up the slack. By ignoring or even rebuffing infants desperate to cling to them, mothers increase males' exposure to the infantile equivalents of "sex appeal." Furthermore, as in the cases of both tamarins and some foragers, how much care is required from fathers varies with the amount of alloparental assistance on offer. Just as fathers signal their probable commitment to mothers, fathers need to monitor the intentions of others.

Weeks before birth, in anticipation of the extra exertion required, a marmoset male signals his future commitment by gaining weight. After birth, mothers informally poll paternal commitment by monitoring how readily males retrieve the infants. A highly motivated father will persist in retrieving the baby whenever the mother pushes it off, returning it to her to nurse. However, if their mates' responses appear inadequate and no other allomother intervenes, mothers may terminate their investment. I suspect that as weaning approaches, fathers themselves are scanning how readily others provision infants. Certainly, the infants are doing so. In spite of the fact that people are embedded in far more complex communities with very different criteria at issue, humans and callitrichines alike are engaged in what economists call a "coordination game." The optimal strategy for each player depends on what other players do. But this coordination game has a special twist. Cues emitted by the needy baby can profoundly alter the internal motivations (neuroendocrinology) of the other players.

Human mothers of course also make conscious, culturally influenced calculations informed by their age, past experiences, current and future reproductive prospects, and specific attributes of their infant. And *both* parents consciously and unconsciously process signals of likely social support beginning even before mate choices are finalized. That fathers as well as mothers take alloparents into account is captured by a traditional African proverb, advice given to a son in search of a wife: "First, find yourself a good mother." The advisor here is not referring to the mother of a man's future children, but to his prospective wife's own mother and her kin, the suite of potentially available alloparents. In worlds without safe nurseries, food markets, or institutionalized social safety nets, how much help his mate can command impacts how much energy the father himself will have to expend and what opportunities he may have to forgo in order to ensure that at least some of his offspring survive. Still, today, the most rational parental calculations are colored and occasionally overridden, by responses far older than the human neocortex. Consider the case of a mother who consciously decides to reject but ends up so captivated by an infant that she changes course, or of adoptive parents who end up more committed than genetic parents (Hrdy 1999:chaps. 12–14, 20–21).

Conceptualizing the interactions among cooperative breeders as coordination games provides useful frameworks for interpreting both the behavior of care-delegating, occasionally rejecting, modern mothers and the highly facultative levels of commitment exhibited by human fathers. This perspective also changes the way infantile cues are interpreted. A case in point would be the discovery by researchers in Israel that men sniffing pads wetted with women's odorless emotional tears instead of a saline control "experienced reduced self-rated sexual arousal, reduced physiological measures of arousal, and reduced levels of testosterone" (Gelstein et al. 2011:226). Some have assumed that this must be nature's way for women to communicate "turn-off" messages to unwanted sexual partners (e.g., Zimmerman 2011). But if one assumes that crying babies long provided the likeliest context for encountering tears, it makes more sense to view reduced sexual arousal in tear-exposed men as another highly conserved neurobiological retention (possibly one further elaborated by millions of years of breeding cooperatively) through which men in intimate proximity to infants become less aggressive, more tolerant, and prone to nurture.

Selection in this coevolving feedback loop falls heaviest on vulnerable immatures. Infants play for higher stakes with the most to lose. But as the currency of fitness, "cute" babies also hold a trump card. Over hundreds of millions of years, selection would have favored myriad sensitivities to the signals babies broadcast. In the primate case, conditional maternal investment opened novel opportunities for others to respond, to be drawn in, and through the resulting experiences, to be transformed. The expression of nurturing potentials in male phenotypes renders highly conserved vertebrate legacies newly visible to natural selection, which has favored lower and lower thresholds for tolerant, affiliative, and perhaps even generous responses in men intimately exposed to babies. Those interested in fostering calmer, gentler societies might do well to keep in mind this transformative power of babies.

Acknowledgments

I am indebted to Karen Bales, Judith Burkart, Sue Carter, Leslie Digby, Lee Gettler, Kristen Hawkes, Lisa Rapaport, James Rilling, and Mary Jane West-Eberhard for valuable discussion and criticisms; to Jessica Collins, Alyssa Crittenden, Ray Hames, and Courtney Meehan for ethnographic input; and to Paul Seabright for suggesting the relevance of coordination games. Thanks also to participants at SAR's "Costly and Cute" seminar and CARTA's "Birth to Grandmotherhood" symposium.

Notes

1. Note that "allomother" here refers to any female or male group member other than the mother, possibly including the progenitor. The designation "alloparent" is only used when there is sufficient information to be confident that a given male is "other than a parent," which without DNA evidence can be tricky.

2. Anecdotal reports suggest that fathers are *more* vulnerable to predation than mothers because they are more encumbered by carrying infants (L. Rapaport, pers. comm., 2014).

3. One *Saguinus geoffroyi* mother abandoned the twin with a harelip but not the other (Epple 1970:66), and Mallinson (1965) reported the abandonment and partial cannibalism of premature twins among captive *S. nigricollis*. But against a backdrop of frequent abandonment in captive tamarins, who knows what these isolated cases mean?

4. Such experiments, with their resulting levels of mayhem, are no longer ethically acceptable.

CHAPTER TEN

Forget Ye Not the Mother-Infant Dyad!

In a World of Allomothers and Maternal Agency, Do Mothers Still Stand Out?

JAMES J. MCKENNA

Birth no more constitutes the beginning of the life of the individual than it does the end of gestation. Birth represents a complex and highly important series of functional changes which serve to prepare the newborn for the passage across the bridge between gestation within the womb and gestation continued out of the womb.

—Montagu 1986:57

I was between lectures at a lactation conference in Perth, Australia, having spoken on the evolution of mother-infant attachment and what anthropologists have learned about pediatric sleep and breastfeeding, and I was casually perusing the book exhibit section, taking a break while another speaker was on. I was feeling pretty good about how both lectures had fared and was resting a bit, but excited about my plans for the next set of lectures to follow after lunch, lectures that would focus on moving beyond the theoretical, evolutionary foundation of infancy and mothering to my own empirical, data-based studies of solitary and co-sleeping breastfeeding mother-infant dyads.

But at the moment, I was welcoming a chance to look over the latest books on breastfeeding and lactation research. I did not choose any particular book title, but I just grabbed one randomly and opened it to the middle of a chapter. Staring me in the face was a most intriguing chapter title: "Stone Age Parenting." I chuckled a bit, since just 15 minutes previously in the lecture hall, this was exactly what I had been talking about, absent such a clever title. Imagine my surprise when I saw my name, repeatedly, and realized that the ideas, concepts, and perspective that Professor Bernice Hausman in her remarkable book *Mother's Milk: Breastfeeding Controversies in American Culture* (2003) was critiquing were none other than my own, and that the very evolutionary narrative and rhetorical strategy I was purposefully constructing to combat medical authoritative knowledge, in order to empower mothers, could itself, according to the author, be used in ways that potentially are harmful to protecting and arguing for women's reproductive rights.

Starting with what prompted Hausman's response, two plenary lectures she attended at a La Leche League conference, in this chapter I explore her critique of my SIDS (sudden infant death syndrome) and mother-infant co-sleeping and breastfeeding research in the context of an evolutionary narrative and what can be inferred from it. I review the structure and content of my lectures in relationship to my goals and the context in which my research has taken shape over the years, reflecting the integration of anthropological with psychobiological and epidemiological medical research on infant sleep, specifically solitary versus bedsharing-breastfeeding mother-infant dyads (hereafter referred to as "breastsleeping dyads") and SIDS (McKenna and Gettler 2016). As much as possible I expose my rhetorical strategy and pedagogy, aimed at convincing pediatricians that understanding what promotes more optimal human neonate/infant health will not be achieved by concentrating on the infant. Rather, I argue that normative human infant physiology and development can only be understood if viewed in contact with and in relationship to its mother's body, the only micro-environment to which the infant is adapted. My overall purpose is to stress the significance of the mother-infant dyad as the critical analytical unit, and my overall goal is to show skeptical pediatricians how and why breastsleeping is to be both supported and encouraged.

I explain in this chapter why I place such an emphasis on the mother's role more than that of allomothers (individuals other than the mother who help care for the infant and who remain critical for a variety of important reasons). But my fundamental beginning point is that anything an infant can or cannot do (or needs) is best and more thoroughly explained by referring to what the mother, more so than any other individual, provides. I also explore whether, as Hausman suggests, the evolutionary narrative on parenting that emerges (however inadvertently) too heavily privileges the unique contributions mothers make, portraying women as without agency and forever constrained by a seemingly frozen ancient biological legacy, which seems by comparison not to have hindered the evolution of male bodies (or behavior) in the same ways.

Relatedly, in addition, I ask if by appreciating the dyad and the mother's specific role in it, we necessarily diminish an appreciation of the critical role played by allomothers, without whom raising such energetically expensive infants would likely not be possible (see Hrdy, chapter 9, and Gettler, chapter 8, both this volume). I do not argue that the mother has no choice as to whether or not to "invest," nor that her role is not supplemented by needed helpers, since allomothers, especially fathers and grandmothers, particularly shape and regulate the infant's biology, as has been proposed and documented (Christensson 1996; Gettler 2014). But especially in light of studies on breastmilk and breastfeeding by Quinn (chapter 5, this volume), Hinde and Milligan (2011), and Hinde (2013), I think it necessary to stress that only a mother's breastmilk and its delivery system can provide to the infant ongoing neurohormonal signals regarding what type of infant brain to grow, including its underlying dense interconnectivity, alongside tailor-made immunities specific to the infant's habitat. Similarly, the fact that breastmilk's energy yields and/ or hormonal glucocorticoids may potentially program brain growth toward the expression of behavioral phenotypes provides an even richer context and a reason to appreciate the uniqueness of the mother-infant dyad.

From the Beginning

Considering Hausman's comments, it is not surprising that suddenly the structure, content, and rationale of the lectures I had just given were of concern in quite an unexpected way. Not just what I said, but why and how I said it seemed important. Could my research really be doing something I was actively working against? In developing a new model of the role of maternal biology as it shapes infant biology, was I at the same time providing ammunition that could weaken arguments for women's full reproductive rights or freedoms of choice?

To avoid being too anthropocentric, I began my lectures by discussing what a primate is, stressing the degrees of relative neurological immaturity at birth, prolonged childhoods, and the importance of learning in the context of intense, enduring contact, carrying, breastfeeding, co-sleeping, and general sociality. I then described what Myron Hofer (1994) once called the hidden "neural traffic" that underlies and supports the mammalian mother-infant relationship. To illustrate I presented a synthesis of the negative physiological and behavioral effects associated with separating primate infants from their mothers or other important attachment figures for both short- and long-term durations.

For example, I explained the work of René Spitz (1945, 1951), who first described, filmed, and documented the anaclitic depression characteristic of abandoned human infants who lose their mothers or who fail to develop attachments in foundling homes ("hospitalism") and the process by which, after 5 months, institutionalized human infants suffer lifelong psychosomatic damage. This particular depressive syndrome was first documented among human infants in terms of three distinct phases following the loss of the mother: first, the bereft abandoned infant engages in hyperactivity, vocalizing distress coos or crying as he or she searches frantically for the lost caregiver; the second involves withdrawal, which is characterized by the infant refusing to engage in any and all interactions; finally, in the third phase, either recovery or possibly death from failure to thrive ensues.

Much later, this exact behavioral sequence alongside physiological changes was experimentally induced and documented among "attached" laboratory bonnet and pigtailed macaque mother-infant pairs (and other species) when the mothers were removed from the infants' group, as Rosenblum and Kaufman (1968) beautifully described. Many studies have shown that the effects of short-term separation are intensified where there are no allomothers to which infants can transfer attachment or from whom they can receive any physical contact while the mother is missing (Reite and Field 1985; for diverse examples, see Reite et al. 1978a; Reite et al. 1978b).

Surely, these data reveal the extent to which maternal contact for neurologically immature primates, especially human infants, is much more than just a nice social idea. Rather, maternal contact (holding, embracing, carrying), including co-sleeping, influences everything from sleep architecture to breastfeeding frequency (McKenna et al. 1997), from breathing patterns, including the distribution, duration, and types of apneas (Richard et al. 1998), to daily weight gain, growth, and other physiological variables discussed below.

Field's work (1995, 1998; Field et al. 1987) showed, for example, that among human infants weight gain correlates positively with the amount of massage or daily touch human infants receive. Massaged human infants on average experience a remarkable 44%–47% increase in daily weight gain compared with a non-massaged group of infants. Since mothers are in contact with their babies far more than any other individuals are, surely they play a primary role as regards touch, infant growth, and the mosaic of interacting neurohormonal transactions that all seem to be involved, though in less understood ways (Field 2001; Field et al. 1986; Matthiesen et al. 2001; Uvnäs-Moberg 1989, 2003; Uvnäs-Moberg et al. 1987).

Consider, as I pointed out in the lecture, that growth enhancement through increased touching is likely mediated synergistically by oxytocin, which can be released by way of social stimulation. According to Field (1998), reduced levels of cortisol, a stress hormone, have consistently been observed among massaged infants, and increased oxytocin levels appear to play a central role in this generalized relaxation and growth response.

It may seem odd, as I point out to my pediatrician colleagues, that maternal touch is linked to the infant's digestive process in the sense that touch stimulates the vagus nerve, and parasympathetic vagal activity in general facilitates gastric activity, such as the release of gastrin and insulin. Indeed, the enhanced touching and holding of infants might make the absorption of calories more efficient by speeding up digestion itself (Field 1996, 1998).

I would be remiss not to also point out the numerous studies showing the benefits of maternal-infant skin-to-skin contact ("kangaroo care") following birth. For example, in several studies, contact with the mother's ventrum acts as an analgesic for newborns, helping them to recover rapidly from birth-related fatigue (Gray et al. 2000; Ludington-Hoe et al. 2005). Moreover, among human infants spontaneous breastfeeding often occurs with immediate skin-to-skin contact, potentially leading to longer durations (in months) of breastfeeding, especially when breastfeeding and bedsharing are practiced in tandem (Ball 2002, 2003, 2006; Blair and Ball 2004).

Extended contact with mothers following birth likely provides the scaffolding for the optimal development of a broad array of cognitive, emotional, and somatosensory systems during what is (especially for altricial mammals) a particularly sensitive critical period, as Clancy and colleagues (2013) so eloquently address. This scaffolding likely takes the form of the mother's body simultaneously regulating a suite of sensory systems, each of which contributes to the effectiveness of the others. For example, the mother's body is known to keep the human infant's body temperature higher, helping infants to conserve energy and boost immunities. Especially for preterm infants, skin-to-skin contact promotes longer infant sleep duration, less agitation, greater heart rate stability, variability (always a sign of vigor), and less periodic breathing (see Schone and Silven 2007 for review). Fardig (1980) compared newborns placed directly on top of the mother's ventrum with separated infants placed in closed incubators with ambient air temperatures matching their mother's body temperature, and found that the incubator was not sufficient to prevent the infants from losing at least a degree of body temperature. The researcher opined that separation likely led to the production of stress hormones, which were responsible for that temperature decline.

After showing my audience photos of a variety of extremely sad-looking, distressed, recently separated infants, I moved to a classic demonstration of how infants are apparently presensitized to respond specifically to breathing sounds, movements, and gases, that is, signals or cues given out by their mothers that may function to compensate for the human newborn's immature respiratory system (McKenna 1986; McKenna et al. 1993). Thoman and Graham (1986) placed a "breathing companion" in the incubator with premature babies with the objective of facilitating more stable breathing among seriously apnea-prone newborns. The companion was a teddy bear that was made to breathe by a pump connected via plastic tubing to a rubber bladder in the bear's torso. Each breathing teddy bear was set to the most stable breathing each infant had exhibited. The results showed that the breathing companions reduced the rates of apnea by as much as 60% in the infants and increased the amount of quiet sleep. Not only did the newborns' breathing become trained to the rhythm provided by their companions, but the tested infants migrated in their cots to lie in contact with their breathing partners—essentially snuggling with them (see also Stewart and Stewart 1991). Without a mother or other sleeping companion, infants experience increased numbers of apneas, and there is a shift toward longer apneas in deeper stages of sleep. Arousal to terminate those apneas during that stage of sleep can make it more difficult for the infant, potentially leading to more serious oxygen desaturation (Richard et al. 1998).

The increased cortisol production associated with separated infants, I added in the lecture, reduces infant appetites too, while simultaneously increasing heart rates and blood pressure. Both deprivation and sleep fragmentation are likewise correlates of maternal separation, with infants becoming more susceptible to viruses and bacteria due to the reduced production of antibodies (Schone and Silven 2007; McKenna 1986; Reite and Field 1985 for reviews).

It is highly likely that allomothers also regulate infants' physiology and behavior in ways documented to occur in the maternal- and paternal-infant dyad (Gettler 2010, 2014; Schone and Silven 2007; Gray and Campbell 2009;

Field et al. 1986). But it seems fair to suggest that during the first 3 critical months, when infants are transitioning to the extrauterine environment, including establishing a breastfeeding relationship, it is the mother who plays the most prominent role (Schone and Silven 2007; McKenna et al. 2007; McKenna and Gettler 2007). Ethnographic studies support this contention: even where grandmothers and fathers act as solid backups when the mother is attending to other activities, it is still the mother who is in association with the infant the most and who spends the most time with her infant (Hardyment 1983; Fildes 1986; Konner 2010; Hrdy 1999).

The Composition of Mother's Milk

The role that the mother plays in the physical regulation of her infant's body was followed in the lecture with an explanation of further reasons that, from a biological (very practical) perspective, the human mother-infant dyad evolved to be in relatively continuous contact and proximity (Clancy et al. 2013). Nonhuman primates (but not human infants) have the ability to cling to their mothers' ventrums and are rarely absent from them. Aside from the emotional need for contact, as previously discussed, both human and nonhuman primate neonates and infants require frequent feeding, producing short breastfeeding intervals, due to their mothers' calorie-light breastmilk (Ben Shaul 1962; Blurton-Jones 1972), I explained to the highly interested audience.

Pediatricians are always surprised to learn that human milk contains relatively more fast-burning carbohydrates (and less fat and protein) compared with many other mammals, which is why we are considered by Blurton-Jones (1972) to be a "carrying" species, in contrast with "nested" mammalian species, where mothers park and/or conceal their infants before they leave to forage. In nested species, breastmilk contains much more fat and protein, and thus infants can sustain longer periods of time between feedings and are content to be alone. Unlike the primate infants who cry in their mothers' absence, signaling their need for contact, and who have no problems defecating at any time, nested infants do neither. To cry upon the mother's departure (calling attention to itself) or to defecate in the mother's absence (creating a scent trail) would most assuredly attract predators, leading to the infant's destruction. In this way, mammalian milk composition is determinative of how infants are cared for and is associated with a suite of other supportive adaptations.

Mother's Breastmilk and Breastfeeding: A Postnatal Umbilical Cord Influencing Behavioral Phenotypes

There is no doubt that I presented in my lecture a strong case for the pivotal contribution that mothers make in producing and delivering breastmilk, which is, after all, a singular role and an intrinsic part of what goes on in the specific mother-infant dyad. Among nonhuman primates, I pointed out, breastmilk is not typically shared with another female's offspring, whereas among humans it can be. But still, all mothers do not make exactly the same breastmilk, especially as regards providing "homegrown" antibodies for the specific infectious microbes a particular infant will confront.

Moreover, twenty-first-century work suggests that specific energetic yields, corticosteroids, and other bioactives produced by different mothers stimulate certain brain nuclei and growth patterns in intriguingly different ways, potentially producing specific behavioral phenotypes (Clancy et al. 2013; Hinde and Milligan 2011; Quinn, chapter 5, this volume; Chen and Rogan 2004; Dettmer et al. 2013). A convergence of old and new studies on a variety of mammals led me to catch the audience off guard by sharing that breastmilk does not just stimulate growth in general but determines what *kind* of brain to grow.

Hinde's (2013) pioneering work with rhesus monkeys affirms that components in breastmilk essentially "signal" the infant brain nuclei via glucocorticoids for what appears to be a kind of bending or inclining (at least) rhesus infants toward particular behavioral styles, temperaments, or emotional responses, including being less fearful in different kinds of social engagements (Hinde and Milligan 2011). A study by scholars at the University of California's Primate Research Center in Davis (Capitanio et al. 2005) demonstrated that among 44 rhesus monkey infants, especially males, a higher concentration of cortisol found in their mothers' milk seems to have made them more "confident," at least when a multivariable ranking system using adjectives like confident, bold, active, curious, and playful was employed.

In her own study of that same group, though switching to a new variable (available milk energy), Hinde (2013) found that both sons and daughters of rhesus mothers who produced higher available milk energy yields showed behavioral activities and exploration levels that similarly ranked them as confident. That breastmilk may indeed have an organizing effect on building certain types of primate brains leads Rutherford (2013:531) to suggest that "the physiological pathway from mother to infant is not restricted to the role of the placental interface experienced only during prenatal life but continues post-natally in the form of mother's milk."

Relatedly, Deoni and colleagues (2013) found that exclusively breastfed infants experience enhanced neurological white matter development, potentially optimizing interneuronal communication (with more prolific and dense receptor sites inducing increased intercellular communication). This study compared the amount of white matter, which facilitates the rapid and synchronized brain messaging required for higher-order cognitive functions, in the brains of 133 healthy human children from 10 months to 4 years of age using magnetic resonance imaging scanning. The group was divided into infants who were exclusively breastfed for 3 months, those who were exclusively formula-fed, and those who were fed a mix of breastmilk and formula. The results of this study describe some of the earliest changes in human white matter development specifically in an area of the brain associated with higher-order cognition, such as planning, social-emotional functioning, and language. Surely Rutherford's observation is in evidence here, yet again, indicating a unique contribution mothers alone can make.

Rutherford's (2013) observation is likewise, I pointed out, illustrated by McKenna and Mosko's (1990) study of the apparent physiological entrainment of mother-infant respiratory signals while bedsharing, further illustrating what being an exterogestate actually means for an infant. In this case mother-infant pairs could be distinguished from other pairs based on the complementarity and potential patterns of each partner's breathing (breaths per minute) in relationship to the other. Surely infants breathe much faster than their mothers, and yet, from both infrared videotapes and polysomnographic recordings it was determined that each partner's total breaths per minute was influenced by partner-induced arousals that often precipitated overlapping apneas, changing the oxygen saturation levels, which would have been different had each partner slept alone. Moreover, bedsharing mothers and infants exhibited more "simultaneous activity time": compared to when they slept in separate beds, about 12% of their sleep architecture (i.e., what stage of sleep they were in and when they were in it) was determined by the sleep behavior of the other partner (McKenna at al. 1994).

Challenging the Biological Behavioral Anomaly of Westerners Who
Regularly Separate Infants for Nighttime Sleep

Because infant sleep and breastfeeding are functionally interdependent, generally where there is breastfeeding, one need not look hard to find mother-infant co-sleeping (however culturally variable) and the many emotional and cognitive benefits that each confers. Indeed, so functionally integrated is maternal and infant sleep architecture with breastfeeding that neither can be correctly understood or modeled without reference to the other, which is one reason I have coined the new term "breastsleeping" (see McKenna and Gettler 2016). Indeed, I have argued through the years in similar lectures to the ones Hausman responded to that any study of either infant sleep or breastfeeding that claims to be extracting and quantifying normal, healthy human infant sleep data must use breastsleeping mother-infant pairs (McKenna et al. 1993; McKenna and Mosko 2000). Breastsleeping sets in motion a cascade of mutually regulating behavioral and physiological subsystems involving practically every sensory modality, which is consistently confirmed in every culture in which it has been studied (McKenna et al. 1997; McKenna et al. 2007; Ball 2006; Blair and Ball 2004; Baddock et al. 2004, 2006).

Having made the connection between social sleeping arrangements and feeding method, I presented in my lecture the available cross-cultural (ethnographic) data to provide evidence of its universality (Barry and Paxson 1971): it is the default, species-wide infant sleeping arrangement. Many slides of diverse co-sleeping arrangements from around the world were shown along with the various sleep structures and/or objects used to keep babies close. These data provided a new insight for pediatricians unaware of the extent to which Western assumptions of what constitutes "normal infant sleep" have been exclusively focused fallaciously on the solitary sleeping, formula- or bottle-fed infant, a form of infant sleep that is historically unique, exceedingly recent, and completely anomalous biologically.

It was at this point in the lecture that I stated my major contention: the way infants have been "put down to sleep" in Western societies (alone, bottle-fed, and separated) is neither "normal" nor "healthy" at all. Indeed, the shifts from social to solitary infant sleep, from breastfeeding to bottle feeding, and from supine (back) to prone (stomach) sleep, all untested cultural innovations, have all proved to be independent risk factors for SIDS, leading to the deaths of approximately a half million infants in Western industrialized societies over a 50-year period (McKenna et al. 2007).

An appreciation of evolutionary concepts and processes is then the center-piece of my research and hypotheses. Specifically, I maintain that parent-infant sleep separation devoid of breastfeeding makes it easier for human infantile deficits to find expression in the form of SIDS, apparently pushing some number of infants beyond their adaptive limits (McKenna 1986; McKenna et al. 2007). Obviously, I assume in many of my writings and presentations (something I became keenly aware of by speaking to pediatric research com-munities) that medical audiences are not at all familiar with evolutionary ways of thinking, in this case as evolution pertains to human infant development and to biologically more optimal nighttime maternal care. Nor are physicians generally aware of why the maternal-infant dyad is much more than an expres-sion used to emphasize who mostly cares for whom; in addition the phrase denotes a critical initial micro-environment, a habitat within which the imma-ture human's developmental systems are primed to respond and directly regu-lated, hour to hour, minute to minute, second to second, all in relationship to its mother's presence.

Pediatricians have been told by their major professional organization, the American Academy of Pediatrics (Moon 2011), about the dangers of bedshar-ing. In one notorious anti-bedsharing public poster in Wisconsin, a metal cleaver (substituting for a mother's body) is pictured in an adult bed next to a sleeping infant; the text above it reads, "Sleeping with Your Baby Is as Dangerous as This." Given that this poster is not an anomaly—many others were produced—there is no reason to think that pediatricians might have any conceptual scientific-based knowledge as to how to counter such rhetoric or other similar public health messaging unless fortuitously they encountered or had some exposure to evolutionary models of human development, including evolutionary medicine.

As a nonthreatening, user-friendly means to challenge the validity of this inappropriate image and to redefine the biological functions and place of human breastsleeping as seen from an evolutionary perspective, I created a set of con-trasting cartoons (figure 10.1). These panels are meant to push the point that when infants less than a year old enter the pediatrician's office for a well-baby checkup, understandably pediatricians will have a very different perspective of who any given infant is, what it needs as regards infant care, and why. Given especially that pediatricians' first goal is to keep babies healthy, it would seem less important or likely for them to be thinking about what inherent, species-wide, evolutionary-based legacies or traits human infants do or do not possess as their mothers carry them into their offices. And yet, knowledge of such attributes could surely be used to explain how and why infants respond as they do to differing caregiving practices, especially why they often refuse to sleep alone and/or prefer their mother's (or allomothers') company to nighttime separation.

In reality, pediatricians will base their assessments of an infant's developmental progress (often unknowingly) on cultural expectations and not on the full range of evolutionary-based developmental perspectives. Take, for example, a 4-month-old infant who is not sleeping through the night and refuses to sleep alone. These ubiquitous complaints by parents will more times than not be interpreted by the pediatrician in the top panel of figure 10.1 as "problematic," and suggestions could be made as to how to correct the "problem." The pediatrician might, for example, suggest that the mother sleep train the infant, forcing it to self-soothe (i.e., go back to sleep on its own without parental intervention) perhaps through a cry-it-out technique (after Ferber 2006), because self-soothing and sleeping through the night unattended by parents (i.e., sleep consolidation) remains a Western cultural ideal. This is often confused with an important developmental advantage or necessity (McKenna et al. 2007), where there is none.

The point is that solitary infant sleep promotes deeper sleep and is thus not an advantage due to the increased risk of SIDS (McKenna et a. 2007). It would seem that any given pediatrician is not likely to be familiar with the polysomnographic-based research showing how, compared with bedsharing, solitary infant sleep significantly increases the number of minutes per sleep cycle infants spend in the deepest stage of sleep, which has a very high arousal threshold, making it hard for babies to wake up quickly should they need to overcome a cardiopulmonary crisis. That is, uninterrupted, sensory-deprived solitary sleep leads over time to an infant spending significantly more of its nighttime sleep in prematurely accelerated "mature" (stages 3–4) deep sleep rather than more time in the lighter sleep of stages 1–2 (see Mosko et al. 1996), which breastsleeping infants naturally experience (Mosko et al. 1997). Insofar as arousals in deeper sleep to terminate apneas may be more challenging for solitary sleeping infants born with congenital arousal deficiencies, this kind of sleep potentially places them at increased risk of dying, as our research team has proposed (McKenna 1986; McKenna et al. 2007; Kinney and Thach 2009).

Figure 10.1. Culturally based notions of infants' developmental milestones. *Top*: "What you see is what you get," or what the physician assumes the infant brings to her office when no evolutionary legacy is used to assess the infant's behavior. *Bottom*: "What you see is NOT all you get." Knowledge of the evolution of the human mother-infant dyad is used to assess infants. The mother's evolutionary ancestors are imagined sitting in the waiting area, having helped produce the contemporary infant's behavior and biology. This information is used to interpret why human babies respond as they do to what they experience.

In contrast, the pediatrician in the bottom panel of figure 10.1, whose beginning assumptions about infants are guided less by cultural and more by evolutionary considerations, might chuckle at the irony of the fact that it is the infant that fails to protest sleep separation from its mother that should raise health concerns, and not the infant that protests a lonely, companionless night's sleep, which puts it at risk. This is because in the environment within which the human infant's emotional proclivities evolved, reflecting its vulnerabilities, separation from the mother (however brief) appropriately signaled danger. By crying, the infant can ameliorate what amounts to a lifethreatening situation, assuming that the infant's cry elicits the mother's retrieval. Indeed, a mother's desire (and the father's as well) to respond to her infant, to settle and please it, also reflects evolved reciprocal and appropriate sensitivities that benefit infants (Feldman 2004; Feldman et al. 2002; Feldman et al. 2003; Gettler 2014).

In sum, these cartoons illustrate two contrasting kinds of assumption that Western pediatricians might make, depending on their backgrounds and education. The first panel represents a view of an infant in which the physician assumes "what you see is what you get," and no doubt represents the most common reaction for pediatricians not schooled in evolutionary sciences. Here, depending on the infant's age (note the sign on the wall in the waiting room), what the infant should be doing developmentally is evaluated only in terms of what the physician sees or is told by the mother or father and always in comparison to culturally based developmental timetables and/or cutoff points produced from Western assumptions devoid of infantile evolutionary considerations. The specific assessment given reflects the belief that the infant carries into the pediatrician's office no noteworthy species-wide or evolutionary-based adaptations that can help explain why the baby responds behaviorally (or medically) as it does to modern Western versions of proper nighttime care (among other things), which purports to condition infants to sleep through the night without requiring intervention or contact with the parents or caregivers. The infant is seen as having no past except for the very few weeks it has been alive, but no inherent, evolved responses inclining it to reject (for its own good) the emotional feelings that come from sleeping alone without a body next to it, feelings that evolved because it always was and still is dangerous for infants to sleep alone (Mitchell and Thompson 1995; McKenna 1986; McKenna et al. 2007).

This view contrasts with the physician in the bottom panel who, enlightened by evolutionary considerations, understands that the infant presents to the world "more than what meets the eye." The infant expresses (and reflects) a prehistory and attributes that may or may not be complementary or congruent with recent cultural expectations and the caregiving practices recommended, which are not necessarily responsive to the physician's attempt to nullify or override them. The panel suggests that both mothers and infants are prepared (not in any robotic way, of course) to engage with each other in particular ways, reflecting a rather conservative set of complementary, evolved emotional needs designed by natural selection. Together, the cartoons point to the fact that the two differently educated physicians' beginning point for understanding who the infant and mother are will make a huge difference in how each physician interprets what is and is not normal and expectable for the human infant.

The Fossils Say—and Prove—What?

What followed in my lecture was a picture of what this evolutionary legacy specifically looks like, the larger context that complements or provides the physical evidence at different evolutionary times that is relevant to the physician's perspective in the bottom panel of figure 10.1. A brief, fossil-based photo display of evolving hominins is always useful, if not powerful, to remind the audience of the existence of real "live" fossil skulls and quickly move notions of human evolution from an abstraction (to medical audiences) to the reality that human evolution did occur, and what we are talking about represents (however imperfectly) the human story. It was here that I brought into view a colorful sketch of a cute little *Australopithecus* toddler playing in front of its mother under a tree. I asked the audience to seriously wonder, as an anthropologist must, what a day in the life of an *Australopithecus* mother-infant pair might have been like 2 million years ago. It shocked them when in the following slide under the caption "Meet the Neighbors" I showed one of the many predators with which our ancestors shared their environment: a ferocious saber-toothed cat species, an ancestral felid with six-inch canines protruding from each side of its mouth whose family members and friends no doubt, as Hart and Sussman (2005) so carefully documented, placed many unwanted holes in the crania of many of those cute little toddlers and their parents.

Thinking about what parenting might have been like beginning in the Paleocene, about 65 million years ago, up through the Pleistocene, about

2 million years ago, certainly provides justification for viewing mother-infant co-sleeping with breastfeeding as being anything but a passing parenting fad. Rather, breastsleeping is an important human behavior, phylogenetically old, relevant, and fundamental to our species, past and present; and judging from the behavior of contemporary neonates and infants it cannot be overturned or suppressed by recent cultural proclamations such as those made by the American Academy of Pediatrics, which claims that infants should not sleep next to their mothers' bodies (Moon 2011). Such a culturally inspired recommendation contradicts human emotional proclivities and the neurohormonal physiology underlying them in mothers and fathers (and other allomothers) as well as the needs of infants for contact, which suggests why recommendations against breastsleeping have failed (Gettler and McKenna 2010).

The Mighty Obstetrical Dilemma Remains a Powerful Heuristic

It was here in the lecture that my audience learned why the human infant struggles so long and so hard to be born, to show its sweet little head at birth, which reflects remnants of the obstetrical dilemma. This was much to the surprise and, I daresay, delight of my medical audience, most of whom had never heard of such a thing before but seemed thrilled to have another scientific justification for the concepts to which they were being introduced. The basic idea of the obstetrical dilemma is that in concert with encephalization (increased brain size relative to body size) and maternal energetic constraints, upright locomotion required extremely neurologically immature, energy-draining human infants to be born (Trevathan 1987; Trevathan and McKenna 1994; Trevathan et al. 2007; see also Trevathan and Rosenberg, chapter 1, and Dunsworth, chapter 2, both this volume). In effect, selection *rolled back* the developmental age at which all humans and our immediate ancestors are born, leaving us, in Montagu's (1986) phrase, "exterogestates," premature neonates in need of a fourth stage of gestation. Essentially, after humans are born, we need parents and allomothers who can share the excessive energetic expense of the most needy, slowest-developing primate infant of all: the cute but costly human baby.

Preparing for Attachment

My rhetorical strategy for the audience up to this point consisted basically of presenting diverse lines of anthropological evidence, all coalescing around and supporting the importance of the mother-infant dyad. I did this in order to establish the dyad as a powerful biological beginning point for understanding why John Bowlby's mentor, D. W. Winnicott, was the first to suggest (but certainly not the last) that there is "no such thing as a baby, but a baby and someone." This well-used phrase connotes a way of thinking about human infants in which their development is argued to be inseparable from the caregiver, comparable to their gestational dependence, except that the degree of regulation by the mother is more contingent on her choices, itself another proposition unfamiliar to the medical world. Both in popular culture and in several different scientific paradigms, the almost sacred notion of the *essentialism* of maternity (mothers without their own agendas or choices) is often too uncritically accepted and applauded, despite Hrdy's (1981, 1999) exquisite critique that not only did no such woman evolve, she would not have been possible.

The point is that these lyrical but accurate descriptions of the ecological setting within which the postnatal mother-infant relationship develops hint at the necessity (and reality) of ongoing neurobiological continuities between pre- and postnatal life that follow the infant as it moves through the birth canal and into its caregiver's enveloping arms and body. Maternal agency notwithstanding, this image offers an appropriate sequel to Bowlby's description of the infant's evolution on the African savanna and the mother's role, half mimicked (he erroneously or naïvely thought) by contemporary !Kung hunters and gatherers who, from his point of view, exemplify the way all humans are primed (however diversely) to seek contact and to "attach" with the help of the infant's "perceptuo-motor mechanisms" to protect, carry, feed, and generally care for infants (Bowlby 1969).

Perhaps no scholar before him more successfully understood the meaning of the infant's tie to its mother than did John Bowlby. What he proposed at the time was, of course, a radical shift away from psychoanalytical theorizing to ways of thinking about, observing, studying, acknowledging, and describing attachment in the context in which it evolved, at least as Bowlby imagined, which was clearly outside of therapists' offices. Grounded as it was in empirical evidence, Bowlby's simple conclusion that "the infant and young child should experience a warm, intimate, and continuous relationship with his mother (or permanent mother substitute) in which both find satisfaction and enjoyment" (Bowlby 1951:13) is certainly as relevant now as it was almost 70 years ago (see McKenna and Gettler 2012).

In more recent years appropriate corrections to Bowlby's (1969, 1982) seminal concept of attachment and the context within which it occurred, the environment of evolutionary adaptiveness, have been made (Foley 1996; Irons 1998; Hrdy 1999; McKenna and Gettler 2012), and yet Bowlby's idea of the mother's central role is still very much appreciated. Many of my esteemed colleagues continue to agree with me that the place and role of each primate in the dyad provide key insights into how and why human life history evolved as it did. Hrdy (1999:69) wrote, "For species such as primates the mother is the environment," and I co-opted Theodosius Dobzhansky's famous statement on the importance of evolution to biology to add: "There is nothing that an infant can or cannot do that makes sense except in light of the mother's body" (McKenna et al. 2007:134).

Could All This Be the Wrong Place to Start?

Hausman's "Stone Age Parenting" chapter certainly gave me unexpected insights about my lectures, including their structure, content, and potential uses. Hausman caused me to reflect and realize just how much my own research relied on a specific, limited evolutionary narrative in which the critical importance of the mother-infant dyad was being elevated yet was removed, for rhetorical purposes, from the larger social context within which it actually functioned. Above all else, by using a very powerful scientific rationale and currency, I believed I could demonstrate to a skeptical medical audience a legitimate argument with a wealth of empirical support behind it, which would allow me to persuade them within the intellectual medical domain in which I had to operate. But what Hausman made me realize was that mine was not only an evolutionary narrative but a rhetorical strategy too, and it might be coming with a price I had not anticipated.

As mentioned, my aim is and always has been to demonstrate that the main analytical unit for pediatric study is not the human infant per se but rather the mother-infant dyad and how the mother's body represents the infant's habitat and is the only micro-environment to which the infant is adapted, a theme throughout most of my writings in one way or another (going back to McKenna 1986). That said, I also know that the maternal energetics associated with this intense dyadic relationship could never have existed or evolved outside the context of other hominin adaptations, specifically the rise and coevolution of allomothering and sharing food, in combination with a theory of mind, empathy, behavioral plasticity, and emotional mind-reading intelligences, as so well articulated by Tomasello (2009), Hrdy (1999, 2010), and others. The question I had to ask myself is: could I sell both ideas or should I settle for one at a time? I favored the former because I did not want to diminish the impact of what, for pediatric medical communities, would be the most radical concept, that is, Winnicott's idea that "there is no such thing as a baby, there is a baby and someone," referring not to allomothers, but to the mother herself.

For the most part, I felt I could not build my model up only to knock it down by introducing to my audience the larger, more complete, and more accurate model of cooperative breeding, a model that makes it not only possible but necessary for mothers always to assess what they can and cannot do for their offspring. I recognize that at any given time, mothers need to calibrate the extent to which their time, resources, and efforts can be committed to their infants. Ironically, the very worries Hausman had about maternal agency and the possibility that my message could complicate or diminish it pointed out to me that this was the opposite of what I thought my approach was doing. I still see the convergence of the lines of scientific evidence as strongly positioning women and empowering them against a very powerful medical, authoritative knowledge system that is attempting to erode or diminish mothers' agency.

As Jordan describes so ably in *Birth in Four Cultures*, medical knowledge succeeds at legitimizing one way of knowing as "authoritative" by devaluing and often totally dismissing all other ways of knowing. Those who reject authoritative knowledge systems, she says, are seen as "backward, ignorant, or naïve troublemakers" (1993:152). She concludes: "The power of authoritative medicine is not that it is correct but that it counts" (153). In other words, and what I have found to be so true as regards the bedsharing debate in the United States, Western medical authoritative knowledge is successfully controlling the institutional and public discourse. That is, we do not talk about how to minimize bedsharing risks but only about how dangerous it is, which means we should not practice it as opposed to making it safer. In the process of condemning bedsharing, medical professionals dismiss altogether the validity and importance of alternative knowledge systems, but more important, they dismiss maternal/paternal instincts and the legitimacy of co-sleeping from a biological vantage point, especially when based on acquired parental knowledge reflecting what their own family needs and wants.

The public health messages have failed to distinguish breastsleeping from well-known dangerous kinds of bedsharing, with the authorities choosing instead to reduce the diverse forms of bedsharing to one singular, unacceptably high-risk behavior. The American Academy of Pediatrics' seven-person subcommittee, working alongside a small group in the National Institutes of Health, has placed millions of federal dollars into a nationwide "safe-to-sleep" campaign (one size must fit all) waged against any and all bedsharing families, effectively depriving them of safety information and stigmatizing them. But millions of parents, thousands of lactation scientists and professionals, many SIDS and developmental researchers, and organizations such as UNICEF and the World Health Organization remain in staunch disagreement. And, as Hausman (2003) pointed out, and rightly so, this imposed system of knowledge, the medical one, is often experienced by women giving birth in Western hospitals, where physicians running on different priorities and time limits disempower parents by taking away informed decision making and by limiting and belittling their understandings, roles, preferences, and/or procedural choices. This is exactly applicable to the issue of where infants should sleep and who has the right to decide.

Hausman's Critique

Being a La Leche League member and ardent breastfeeding, co-sleeping mother herself, Hausman (2003) stated great sympathy for, support for, and appreciation of the legitimacy of my pediatric sleep research and my ongoing defense of mothers' rights to bedshare. She suggested, however, that my narrative (and my rhetorical strategy, and she was not sure which of the two it was) came with an unintended downside: it could be used equally well to paint a picture of contemporary women as tied to their biologically based, maternal, reproductive roles because of their "unevolved" 400,000-year-old Pleistocene bodies. Hausman pointed out that a woman's body, based on such scientific narratives, could be portrayed as retaining a biological "primitiveness" since the discourse perhaps unintentionally suggested that her body has not evolved to the same degree as a man's body, whose contribution to reproduction she described as limited to genetic transfer.

Hausman (2003) was especially critical of Dettwyler's (2004) evolutionary perspective on breastfeeding, particularly her suggestion that it is "sensible" for all women to breastfeed for longer than 6 months, based on the !Kung hunter-gatherer model. Hausman responded by pointing out that it is not surprising that most US mothers who nurse their babies for extended periods, usually longer than 6 months, are white, educated, and middle class. It is here that Hausman is at her best, I think, pointing out what really is at stake if the evolutionary narrative fails to include reference to the critical importance and role of maternal agency and maternal resources. What she is referring to as regards maternal resources includes money limitations, time, energy, and the choices about the timing and form of parental investment faced by mothers, along with the role and availability of allomothers in helping to shape maternal investment.

Hausman (2003) suggested that women who have the resources, both personal and financial, can effectively mimic the "ancestral pattern of extended breastfeeding" (if there was just one, which seems unlikely). She claimed that this is the paradox of the evolutionary perspective at least as regards more "optimal" breastfeeding. Dettwyler (2004) argued, for example, that all women should space out births and nurse their children for years, a suggestion that Hausman found especially problematic. Hausman opined that Dettwyler thinks that women should choose this strategy because, in the evolutionary scenarios in which it is discussed, this is said to represent the "best" adaptation. But what is really at stake, in Hausman's view, is that mothers' options are being threatened: evolutionary discourse privileges certain choices over others. "Expert advice," she asserted, "seems always to have as its goals, whether inadvertent or not, control over women's actions as mothers" (Hausman 2003:148). The evolutionary narratives articulated in breastfeeding advocacy discourses operate to promote specific behaviors on the part of the privileged, white American woman based on interpretations of the practices of "primitive," non-Western others. American culture loses, Hausman said, because its cultural practices are deemed maladaptive for infants, "but it also wins because it can incorporate the evolutionarily appropriate practices of other cultural traditions through scientific rationales" (2003:148–149).

Middle-class American white women, Hausman (2003:148–149) contended, "can be both primitive and modern" and thus always in their "proper place." But poor American women, white or black, cannot afford to be "primitive" in the same way that better-resourced women can, even though such behavior might be economically beneficial in terms of health care costs for their infants. "It is one thing for a black woman to nurse her baby for years in a context where that is not unusual; it is another to consider how black women in America might negotiate this highly charged field of symbolic meanings and material consequences" (Hausman 2003:149).

The important critical observations Hausman made about the way I framed my sleep research and justified it could be seen to add a new, unintended, disturbing meaning to Hrdy's 1981 book, *The Woman That Never Evolved*. Writing as a feminist biological anthropologist, Hrdy provided in her book a myriad of compelling examples and a conceptual model demonstrating to skeptical feminists that biology need not be used always against women. She showed that the female passivity and inherent, irrepressible nurturing tendencies attributed to women throughout some periods of history (material expanded on in Hrdy, *Mother Nature*, 1999) could truly never have evolved in any primate lineage, including our own, and that natural selection did not operate just on males. Female bodies and mental faculties are most certainly not frozen in time. If only researchers cared to look, Hrdy (1981) pointed out, it is clear that among women evolution produced necessarily a distinctly broad and flexible biological legacy of many different behavioral phenotypes, facilitating female rank differences in the context of female-female competition, risk taking, protective interventions, aggression, the hoarding and sharing of resources, including mates, and promiscuity—all of which find expression when and if the conditions require it and if it is advantageous.

Does My Evolutionary Narrative Deny All of This? Making Choices

Trying to reconcile what amounted to a clash of purposes, I realized just how much the traditional medical paradigm and its larger cultural-historical context was shaping, if not constraining, my professional world. It affected how I structured my presentations, decided what journals outside my discipline I needed to submit my research to, and what professional groups, societies, and associations I was participating in. It also influenced where I was invited to give lectures, which included many hospitals where I presented pediatric grand rounds. To be most effective in this professional context, outside my normative anthropological purview, in front of non-anthropologists (who were suspicious of my credentials for doing research on SIDS), I was proactively planning and thinking about how to frame my arguments, I realized, to show them what I knew, providing foundation and purposefully emphasizing some points at the expense of others.

The experience of encountering Hausman's insightful discussion of my work has proved productive because it led me to consider just how much I had given up in developing certain aspects of the narrative so as to not reduce or diminish my impact on medical cultures. My emphasis had required introducing pediatric researchers and pediatricians to a variety of lines of evidence with which they have little or no familiarity (cross-cultural, cross-species, psychobiological, and evolutionary data), and they have much doubt as regards how these lines of evidence might pertain to redefining what constitutes normal, healthy human infant sleep and how these normative assumptions might in fact be related to the rise of SIDS in Western industrialized societies. The whole idea that in addition to providing nutrition, the presence of the mother next to her infant positively changes the infant's sleep physiology in clinically positive ways (as discussed earlier) and involves neurobiological pathways and/or mechanisms relevant to maximizing infant well-being is for SIDS and pediatricians a radical proposition. That important neurohormonal signals are passed through the mother's milk, changing brain architecture and the infant's developmental trajectory, is even more challenging to them.

What Hausman Worried About and Hrdy's Proposed Way Out

While Hausman described my work as being done by a "formidable" researcher with arguments correctly directed against injurious if not inappropriate cultural norms, she suggested that in the end the arguments might not necessarily "serve women and children well" (2003:131). She pointed out that "dependence on scientific discourse to promote breastfeeding [or co-sleeping] even when such discourses are obscured by references to natural mothering, can serve ultimately to subordinate women's practices to the paradigm of 'scientific motherhood' in which mothers' own views and experiences take second place to the advice of (usually male) experts" (Hausman 2003:153). This is the very thing I was arguing against, in my own way.

Especially with regard to breastfeeding advocacy (rather than co-sleeping per se), Hausman (2003:135) saw a dramatic tension between evolution as "a random process that rewards better adaptations and a medical perspective bent on promoting not simply survival but optimal infant health" at the expense of the mother. Hausman saw this as permeating evolutionary discourses on both breastfeeding and co-sleeping. She critiqued a more medicalized view (ironically, the same term I use in my critique of Western obstetrics and pediatric sleep research). Especially, she was concerned with the idea of "added protection" to the infant that increased breastfeeding offers, for example, described as "dose-specific," a reality that has potential negative costs for mothers. She suggested that this view of breastfeeding is itself "medicinal," and insofar as this is true it moves from ensuring infant survival, to optimizing infant health with increased costs to maternal resources that women either cannot provide or may choose not to.

We know now that infants sleeping in rooms by themselves are at higher risk of dying than those sleeping in the proximity of a committed caregiver, and the risk is compounded if the baby is bottle feeding (Blair et al. 1999; Vennemann et al. 2009; Forste et al. 2001). But this is not all. A synthesis of the more limited but documented longitudinal effects of co-sleeping on children is beginning to show that there may well be associated psychological benefits too (that is, behavioral phenotypes), which can be identified at different time points leading to adulthood. Children who had the opportunity to co-sleep as infants are less fearful earlier on, are able to be alone, and can solve problems (on their own) more easily compared with enforced solitary sleeping children. As young adults, the co-sleepers may well be more comfortable with affection and their bodies in general and, as adults, have a more optimistic view of their lives (McKenna et al. 2007).

While Hausman did not dispute the research, she pointed out that caring about the "psychological benefits" to infants is a relatively new phenomenon in Euro-American cultures, dating back to the nineteenth century. Here she worried again, like she did about "dose-specific" breastfeeding, about the emphasis on the emotional benefits of extended co-sleeping, which she called an "optimizing" paradigm that results when evolutionary ideas are used to support medical practices and advice. That is, "sleeping with baby is not merely about survival but about creating babies healthier than those maladaptive infants who somehow survive sleeping on their own in cribs" (Hausman 2003:137).

And the Good News Is . . .

Hausman (2003) relied greatly on Hrdy's (1999) astute critique of the environment of evolutionary adaptiveness; Hrdy and others have questioned Bowlby's lack of appreciation of the diverse ecologies within which not one but a number of different hunters and gatherers beyond the !Kung should be considered. Hrdy and others provided relevant evidence that blurs the accuracy of Bowlby's original vision, including the singular importance of seeing the !Kung as representing the perfect Pleistocene poster family from whom all of us can draw insights as to how to engage with our children. Most of the critics of Bowlby's work (with whom very likely he would agree, if he were alive), including his romantic vision of the ever-devoted, isolated mother, argue that it is overly simplistic. As Hrdy (1999:233) put it: "The extended half decade of physical closeness between a mother and her infant supposedly typified by the !Kung [and] so typical of other apes tells us more about the harshness of local conditions and the mother's lack of safe alternatives than the natural state of *all* Pleistocene mothers." The cultural differences, including infant care practices, between contemporary hunters and gatherers, such as the Efe and the Aka, are proof of this.

Hausman (2003) warned that the particular evolutionary narrative and lecture structure I settled on *could* be co-opted to support a larger, unwanted political conversation that stresses what could be interpreted as biologically based limitations to what mothers can and should be doing as regards what infants need. Should this occur, it would trump the critical other half of my intended purpose, which is to help legitimize and protect a woman's right to choose how to care for her infant based on her own needs, circumstances, and purposes. To diminish the potential misinterpretation, what I can do in my work going forward is more conspicuously speak to the critical role that maternal agency plays. I can also recognize that a "goodness of fit" is critical for shaping and supporting the quality of the relationship that develops between a mother and her infant, the nature of which determines the extent to which the maternal-infant regulatory effects described above can benefit both.

But to include what we have learned about the significance of the dyad in relationship to allomothers and the evolution of cooperative breeding, I still maintain, would seriously compromise a perspective new to medical audiences. Of primary importance is the mother-infant dyad specifically as regards the infant's innate sensitivities and physiological responses to its mother's consistent regulation, whether through her breastmilk or through the array of maternal-infant sensory exchanges that regulate the infant's physiology and neurodevelopment in critically important ways (figure 10.2).

My argument about the legitimacy of breastsleeping, for example, is intended specifically to subvert the contemporary view of the inherent, allegedly unmodifiable dangers argued to be associated with forms of co-sleeping, such as bedsharing, and to expose the American Academy of Pediatrics' unqualified recommendation against it as being both ethically and scientifically unsupportable and not likely to be accepted in any event. Recall that this recommendation was made by a small, insular group that continues to dismiss the needs, desires, and disagreements of those for whom the recommendations

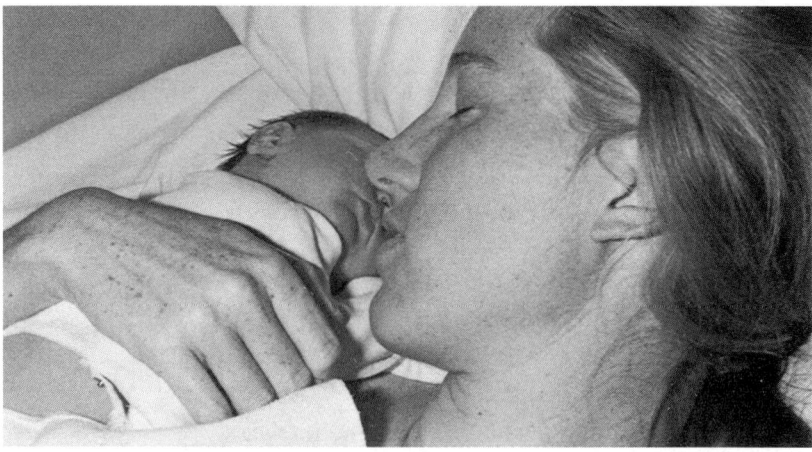

Figure 10.2. This mother knows exactly what the mother-infant dyad is all about and its place in the larger context of maternal agency and shared care by allomothers. Photo by Dan Hrdy, reproduced with permission of Sarah and Dan Hrdy and their daughter, Katrinka, born in December 1977.

are being made. This is a serious breach of evidence-based medicine, which begins by respecting the values of those for whom recommendations are intended, according to Sackett, who is referred to as the "father" of evidence-based medicine (e.g., Sackett et al. 2000). Aside from dismissing the views of millions of mothers, this committee has turned its back on the work of a sizable cadre of well-published (and well-reputed) scientists and lactation researchers, all of whom have demonstrated in much peer-reviewed research the important functional connections between healthy infant sleep and breastfeeding, and this has been done to promote a recommendation that simply does not work for the majority of mothers (Gettler and McKenna 2010). Redefining and reemphasizing the inherent political rights of mothers to be in charge of their own caregiving choices, and empowering them, will continue to be an important part of my work (see Gettler and McKenna 2010; McKenna and Mosko 2000).

That said, I recognize the potential misuse of the scientific model that frames and justifies my written work and oral presentations, which have been interestingly reviewed, critiqued, and discussed by Hausman. Her critical review already has led me to clarify components and make additions to my arguments and presentations that should make it more likely to achieve the goals to which both Hausman and I are equally committed.

Acknowledgments

I thank my wonderful friends and colleagues all, not only Wenda Trevathan and Karen Rosenberg, whose efforts (both creative and organizational) were ever heavy and continuous and outstanding, but my newer friends and colleagues too, whose insights and conversation during the seminar made me a better scholar. Best of all, these new but no doubt enduring friendships will go well beyond our immediate efforts. It was an extraordinary seminar with extraordinary people, and I will always be grateful for my inclusion.

Abitbol MM. 1996. Birth and human evolution: anatomical and obstetrical mechanics in primates. Westport, CT: Bergin and Garvey.

Abraham E, Handler T, Shapira-Lichter I, Kanat-Maymon Y, Zagoory-Sharon O, Feldman R. 2014. Father's brain is sensitive to childcare experiences. Proc Natl Acad Sci USA 111(27):9792–9797.

Abrams ET, Miller EM. 2011. The roles of the immune system in women's reproduction: evolutionary constraints and life history trade-offs. Am Phys Anthropol 146:34–154.

Abrams ET, Rutherford JN. 2011. Framing postpartum hemorrhage as a consequence of human placental biology: an evolutionary and comparative perspective. Am Anthropol 113:417–430.

Adolph KE, Berger SE. 2006. Motor development. In: Kuhn D, Siegler RS, editors. Handbook of child psychology. New York: Wiley. 161–213.

Aiello LC, Montgomery C. 1991. The natural history of deciduous tooth attrition in hominoids. J Hum Evol 21:397–412.

Alberts SC, Watts HE, Altmann J. 2003. Queuing and queue-jumping: long-term patterns of reproductive skew in male savannah baboons, *Papio cynocephalus*. Anim Behav 65(4):821–840.

Alemseged Z, Spoor F, Kimbel WH, Bobe R, Geraads D, Reed D, Wynn JG. 2006. A juvenile early hominin skeleton from Dikika, Ethiopia. Nature 443:296–301.

Alexander RD. 1990. How did humans evolve? reflections on the uniquely unique species. U Mich Mus Zool Spec Publ 1:1–38.

Altmann J. 1980. Baboon mothers and infants. Cambridge, MA: Harvard University Press.

Altmann J, Alberts SC. 2003. Variability in reproductive success viewed from a life-history perspective in baboons. Am J Hum Biol 15(3):401–409.

Alvarado LC, Muller MN, Thompson ME, Klimek M, Nenko I, Jasienska G. 2014. Seasonal fluctuation of men's testosterone levels and body composition in rural Poland. Paper presented at: American Association of Physical Anthropology meeting, Calgary, Canada.

Alvergne A, Faurie C, Raymond M. 2009. Variation in testosterone levels and male reproductive effort: insight from a polygynous human population. Horm Behav 56:491–497.

Alvergne A, Jokela M, Faurie C, Lummaa V. 2010. Personality and testosterone in men from a high-fertility population. Pers Indiv Differ 49(8):840–844.

Amaral LQ. 2008. Mechanical analysis of infant carrying in hominoids. Naturwissenschaften 95:281–292.

American Psychiatric Association. 2013. The diagnostic and statistical manual of mental disorders: DSM-5. Arlington, VA: American Psychiatric Association.

Anderson AM. 2011. Disruption of lactogenesis by retained placental fragments. J Hum Lact 17(2):142–144.

Anderson J, McKinley K, Onugha J, Duazo P, Chernoff M, Quinn EA. 2015. Lower levels of human milk adiponectin predict offspring weight for age: a study in a lean population of Filipinos. Mat Child Nutr. doi: 10.1111/mcn.12216.

Anderson M. 2014. After phrenology: neural reuse and the interactive brain. Cambridge, MA: MIT Press.

Anderson NK, Beerman KA, McGuire MA, Dasgupta N, Griinari JM, Williams J, McGuire MK. 2005. Dietary fat type influences total milk fat content in lean women. J Nutr 135(3):416–421.

Anderson R, Bancroft J, Wu F. 1992. The effects of exogenous testosterone on sexuality and mood of normal men. J Clin Endocrinol Metab 75(6):1503–1507.

Andreano JM, Cahill L. 2009. Sex influences on the neurobiology of learning and memory. Learn Memory 16(4):248–266.

Anestis SF. 2006. Testosterone in juvenile and adolescent male chimpanzees (*Pan troglodytes*): effects of dominance rank, aggression, and behavioral style. Am J Phys Anthropol 130(4):536–545.

Antonell A, de Luis O, Domingo-Roura X, Pérez-Jurado LA. 2005. Evolutionary mechanisms shaping the genomic structure of the Williams-Beuren syndrome chromosomal region at human 7q11.23. Genome Res 15:1179–1188.

Apicella CL. 2014. Upper-body strength predicts hunting reputation and reproductive success in Hadza hunter-gatherers. Evol Human Behav 35:508–518.

Apicella CL, Dreber A, Campbell B, Gray PB, Hoffman M, Little AC. 2008. Testosterone and financial risk preferences. Evol Human Behav 29(6):384–390.

Apicella CL, Marlowe FW, Fowler JH, Christakis NA. 2012. Social networks and cooperation in hunter-gatherers. Nature 481(7382):497–501.

Aragona BJ, Liu Y, Yu YJ, Curtis JT, Detwiler JM, Insel TR, Wang Z. 2006. Nucleus accumbens dopamine differentially mediates the formation and maintenance of monogamous pair bonds. Nat Neurosci 9:133–139.

Archer J. 2006. Testosterone and human aggression: an evaluation of the challenge hypothesis. Neurosci Biobehav Rev 30(3):319–345.

Archie EA, Altmann J, Alberts SC. 2012. Social status predicts wound healing in wild baboons. Proc Natl Acad Sci USA 109(23):9017–9022.

Armstrong DD, Dunn JK, Antalffy B. 1998. Decreased dendritic branching in frontal, motor and limbic cortex in Rett syndrome compared with trisomy 21. J Neuropath Exp Neur 57:1013–1017.

Aron AR, Poldrack RA 2005. The cognitive neuroscience of response inhibition: relevance for genetic research in attention-deficit/hyperactivity disorder. Biol Psychiatry 57(11):1285–1292.

Arthur PG, Kent JC, Hartmann PE. 1991. Metabolites of lactose synthesis in milk from women during established lactation. J Pediatr Gastroenterol Nutr 13(3):260–266.

Asai-Sato M, Okamoto M, Endo M, Yoshida H, Murase M, Ikeda M, Sakakibara H, Takahashi T, Hirahara F. 2006. Hypoadiponectinemia in lean lactating women: prolactin inhibits adiponectin secretion from human adipocytes. Endocr J 53(4):555–562.

Ascoli GA, Alonso-Nanclares L, Anderson SA, Barrionuevo G, Benavides-Piccione R, Burkhalter A, Buzsáki G, Cauli B, Defelipe J, Fairén A, et al. 2008. Petilla terminology: nomenclature of features of GABAergic interneurons of the cerebral cortex. Nat Rev Neurosci 9:557–568.

Asperger H. 1944. Die "Autistischen Psychopathen" im Kindesalter. Archiv Psychiatr Nerven 117:76–136.

Asperger H. 1979. Problems of infantile autism. Commun: J Natl Autistic Soc 13:45–52.

Attwood T. 2013. The pattern of abilities and development of girls with Asperger's syndrome. http://www.tonyattwood.com.au/index.php?Itemid=181&id =80:the-pattern-of-abilities-and-development-of-girls-with-aspergers-syndrome&option=com_content&view=article.

Aydin S. 2010. The presence of the peptides apelin, ghrelin and nesfatin-1 in the human breast milk, and the lowering of their levels in patients with gestational diabetes mellitus. Peptides 31(12):2236–2240.

Aydin S, Kuloglu T, Aydin S. 2013. Copeptin, adropin and irisin concentrations in breast milk and plasma of healthy women and those with gestational diabetes mellitus. Peptides 47:66–70.

Baddock SA, Galland BC, Beckers MG, Taylor BJ, Bolton DP. 2004. Bed-sharing and the infant's thermal environment in the home setting. Arch Dis Child 89(12):1111–1116.

Baddock SA, Galland BC, Bolton DPG, Williams S, Taylor BJ. 2006. Differences in infant parent behaviors during routine bed sharing compared with cot sleeping in the home setting. Pediatr 117:1599–1607.

Bagnell CA, Steinetz BG, Bartol FF. 2009. Milk-borne relaxin and the lactocrine hypothesis for maternal programming of neonatal tissues. Ann NY Acad Sci 1160:152–157.

Bailey A, Le Couteur A, Gottesman I, Bolton P, Simonoff E, Yuzda E, Rutter M. 1995. Autism as a strongly genetic disorder: evidence from a British twin study. Psychol Med 25(1):63–77.

Bales K, Dietz J, Baker A, Miller K, Tardif S. 2000. Effects of allo-caregivers on fitness of infants and parents in callitrichid primates. Folia Primatol 71:27–38.

Bales K, French JA, Dietz JM. 2002. Explaining variation in maternal care in cooperatively breeding mammals. Anim Behav 63:453–461.

Bales K, O'Herron M, Baker AJ, Dietz JM. 2001. Sources of variability in numbers of live births in wild golden lion tamarins (*Leontopithecus rosalia*). Am J Primatol 54:211–221.

Ball HL. 2002. Reasons to bed-share: why parents sleep with their infants. J Reprod Inf Psychol 20(4):207–222.

Ball HL. 2003. Breastfeeding, bed-sharing and infant sleep. Birth 30(3):181–188.

Ball HL. 2006. Parent-infant bed-sharing behavior: effects of feeding type, and presence of father. Hum Nature 17(3):301–316.

Balzeau A, Grimaud-Hervé D, Jacob T. 2005. Internal cranial features of the Mojokerto child fossil (East Java, Indonesia). J Hum Evol 48:535–553.

Bamberg C, Rademacher G, Güttler F, Teichgräber U, Cremer M, Bührer C, Spies C, Hinkson L, Henrich W, Kalache KD, et al. 2012. Human birth observed in real-time open magnetic resonance imaging. Am J Obstet Gynecol 206:e501–e506.

Barak MM, Lieberman DE, Raichlen D, Pontzer H, Warrener AG, Hublin JJ. 2013. Trabecular evidence for a human-like gait in *Australopithecus africanus*. PLoS ONE 8(11):e77687.

Barbas H, Hilgetag CC. 2002. Rules relating connections to cortical structure in primate prefrontal cortex. Neurocomputing 44:301–308.

Barden RC, Ford ME, Jensen AG, Rogers-Salyer M Salver KE. 1989. Effects of craniofacial deformity in infancy on the quality of mother-infant interactions. Child Devel 60:819–824.

Bardi M, Petto A, Lee-Parritz D. 2001. Parental failure in captive cotton-top tamarins (*Saguinus oedipus*). Am J Primatol 54:150–169.

Barelli C, Heistermann M. 2012. Sociodemographic correlates of fecal androgen levels in wild male white-handed gibbons (*Hylobates lar*). Int J Primatol 33(4):784–798.

Baron-Cohen S. 2012. Autism and the technical mind: children of scientists and engineers may inherit genes that not only confer intellectual talents but also predispose them to autism. Sci Am 307(5):72–75.

Barrett J, Fleming A. 2011. Annual research review: all mothers are not created equal: neural and psychobiological perspectives on mother and the importance of individual differences. J Child Psychol Psychiatr 52(4):468–397.

Barry H, Paxson LM. 1971. Infancy and early childhood: cross-cultural codes 2. Ethnol 10:466–508.

Bartol FF, Wiley AA, Miller DJ, Silva AJ, Roberts KE, Davolt ML, Chen JC, Frankshun AL, Camp ME, Rahman KM, et al. 2013. Lactation biology symposium: lactocrine signaling and developmental programming. J Anim Sci 91(2):696–705.

Barton RA, Capellini I. 2011. Maternal investment, life histories, and the costs of brain growth in mammals. Proc Natl Acad Sci USA 108:6169–6174.

Beaudet AL. 2012. Neuroscience: preventable forms of autism? Science 338(6105):342–343.

Beckerman S, Lizarralde R, Ballew C, Schroeder S, Fingelton C, Garrison A, Smith H. 1998. The Bari Partible Paternity Project: preliminary results. Curr Anthropol 39:164–167.

Beehner JC, Bergman TJ, Cheney DL, Seyfarth RM, Whitten PL. 2006. Testosterone predicts future dominance rank and mating activity among male Chacma baboons. Behav Ecol Sociobiol 59(4):469–479.

Beehner JC, Gesquiere L, Seyfarth RM, Cheney DL, Alberts SC, Altmann J. 2009. Testosterone related to age and life-history stages in male baboons and geladas. Horm Behav 56(4):472–480.

Belichenko PV, Oldfors A, Hagberg B, Dahlström A. 1994. Rett syndrome: 3-D confocal microscopy of cortical pyramidal dendrites and afferents. NeuroReport 5:1509–1513.

Bell AV, Hinde K, Newson L. 2013. Who was helping? the scope for female cooperative breeding in early *Homo*. PLoS One 8:e83667.

Bellugi U, Lichtenberger L, Mills D, Galaburda A, Korenberg JR. 1999. Bridging cognition, the brain and molecular genetics: evidence from Williams syndrome. Trends Neurosci 22:197–207.

Benes FM. 1991. Deficits in small interneurons in prefrontal and cingulate cortices of schizophrenic and schizoaffective patients. Arch Gen Psych 48:996–1001.

Benirschke K. 2007. Comparative placentation. http://placentation.ucsd.edu.

Bennett PM, Harvey PH. 1985. Brain size, development and metabolism in birds and mammals. J Zool 207:491–509.

Ben Shaul DM. 1962. The composition of the milk of wild animals. Int Zoo Yearb 4:333–342.

Bercovitch FB. 1988. Coalitions, cooperation and reproductive tactics among adult male baboons. Anim Behav 36(4):1198–1209.

Bercovitch FB. 1989. Body size, sperm competition, and determinants of reproductive success in male savanna baboons. Evol 43:1507–1521.

Berge C. 1994. How did the australopithecines walk? a biomechanical study of the hip and thigh of *Australopithecus afarensis*. J Hum Evol 26:259–273.

Berge C, Goularas D. 2010. A new reconstruction of Sts 14 pelvis (*Australopithecus africanus*) from computed tomography and three-dimensional modeling techniques. J Hum Evol 58:262–272.

Berge C, Orban-Segebarth R, Schmid P. 1984. Obstetrical interpretation of the australopithecine pelvic cavity. J Hum Evol 13:573–587.

Berkson G. 1974. Social responses of animals to infants with defects. In: Lewis M, Rosenblum ML, editors. The effect of the infant on its caregiver. New York: Wiley. 233–249.

Berna F, Goldberg P, Horwitz LK, Brink J, Holt S, Bamford M, Chazan M. 2012. Microstratigraphic evidence of in situ fire in the Acheulean strata of Wonderwerk cave, Northern Cape province, South Africa. Proc Natl Acad Sci USA 109:e1215–e1220.

Bernstein RM, Dominy NJ. 2013. Mount Pinatubo, inflammatory cytokines, and the immunological ecology of Aeta hunter-gatherers. Hum Biol 85(1–3):231–250.

Betti L. 2014. Sexual dimorphism in the size and shape of the os coxae and the effects of microevolutionary processes. Am J Phys Anthropol 153:167–177.

Betti L, von Cramon-Taubadel N, Manica A, Lycett SJ. 2013. Global geometric morphometric analyses of the human pelvis reveal substantial neutral population history effects, even across sexes. PLoS ONE 8(2):e55909.

Betti L, von Cramon-Taubadel N, Manica A, Lycett SJ. 2014. The interaction of neutral evolutionary processes with climatically-driven adaptive changes in the 3D shape of the human os coxae. J Hum Evol 73:64–74.

Beuren AJ, Apitz J, Harman D. 1962. Supravalvular aortic stenosis in association with mental retardation and a certain facial appearance. Circulation 26:1235–1240.

Bezerra BM, Da Silva Souto A, Schiel N. 2007. Infanticide and cannibalism in a free-ranging plurally breeding group of common marmosets (*Callithrix jacchus*). Am J Primatol 69:945–952.

Bianchi S, Stimpson CD, Bauernfeind AL, Schapiro SJ, Baze WB, McArthur MJ, Bronson E, Hopkins WD, Semendeferi K, Jacobs B, et al. 2012. Dendritic morphology of pyramidal neurons in the chimpanzee neocortex: regional specializations and comparison to humans. Cereb Cortex 23:2429–2436.

Bianchi S, Stimpson CD, Duka T, Larsen MD, Janssen WG, Collins Z, Bauernfeind AL, Schapiro SJ, Baze WB, McArthur MJ, et al. 2013. Synaptogenesis and development of pyramidal neuron dendritic morphology in the chimpanzee neocortex resembles humans. Proc Natl Acad Sci USA 110(2):10395–10401.

Billat V, Lepretre PM, Heugas AM, Laurence HM, Salim D, Koralsztein JP. 2003. Training and bioenergetic characteristics in elite male and female Kenyan runners. Med Sci Sports Exerc 35:297–304.

Biro D, Inoue-Nakamura N, Tonooka R, Yamakoshi G, Sousa C, Matsuzawa T. 2003. Cultural innovation and transmission of tool use in wild chimpanzees: evidence from field experiments. Anim Cognit 6:213–223.

Bjorklund DF. 1997. The role of immaturity in human development. Psych Bull 122:153–169.

Bjorklund DF, Pellegrini AD. 2000. Child developmentand evolutionary psychology. Child Dev. 71:1687–1708.

Blair P, Fleming P, Bensley D, et al. 1999. Where should babies sleep: alone or with parents? factors influencing the risk of SIDS in the CESDI study. BMJ 319:1457–1462.

Blair PS, Ball HL. 2004. The prevalence and characteristics associated with parent-infant bed-sharing in England. Arch Dis Child 89:1106–1110.

Blurton-Jones NK. 1972. Comparative aspects of mother-child contact. In: Blurton-Jones N, editor. Ethological studies of child development. Cambridge: Cambridge University Press. 305–328.

Boehm C. 2012. Moral origins: the evolution of virtue, altruism and shame. New York: Basic.

Boesch C, Boesch-Achermann H. 2000. The chimpanzees of the Tai forest: behavioral ecology and evolution. Oxford: Oxford University Press.

Bogin B. 1997. Evolutionary hypotheses for human childhood. Am J Phys Anthropol 104(S25):63–89.

Bogin B. 1999. Patterns of human growth. 2nd ed. Cambridge: Cambridge University Press.

Bogin B. 2006. Modern human life history: the evolution of human childhood and fertility. In: Hawkes K, Paine RR, editors. The evolution of human life history. Oxford: Currey. 197–230.

Bogin B. 2009. Childhood, adolescence, and longevity: a multilevel model of the evolution of reserve capacity in human life history. Am J Hum Biol 21:567–577.

Bogin B, Bragg J, Kuzawa C. 2014. Humans are not cooperative breeders but practice biocultural reproduction. Ann Hum Biol 41:368–380.

Boksem MA, Mehta PH, Van den Bergh B, van Son V, Trautmann ST, Roelofs K, Smidts A, Sanfey AG. 2013. Testosterone inhibits trust but promotes reciprocity. Psychol Sci 24(11):2306–2314.

Bolk L. 1926. On the problem of anthropogenesis. Proc Section Sci Kom Akad Wetens 29:465–475.

Booth A, Dabbs JM. 1993. Testosterone and men's marriages. Soc Forces 72(2): 463–477.

Booth A, Johnson DR, Granger DA. 2005. Testosterone, marital quality, and role overload. J Marr Fam 67(2):483–498.

Booth A, Osgood DW. 1993. Influence of testosterone on deviance in adulthood: assessing and explaining the relationship. Criminol 31(1):93–117.

Borries C, Gordon AD, Koenig A. 2013. Beware of primate life history data: a plea for data standards and a repository. PLoS ONE 8(6):e67200.

Bos PA, Terburg D, van Honk J. 2010. Testosterone decreases trust in socially naïve humans. Proc Natl Acad Sci USA 107(22):9991–9995.

Bostock J. 1958. Exterior gestation, primitive sleep, enuresis and asthma: a study in aetiology. Int Med J Aust 45:185–188.

Bostock J. 1962. Evolutional approach to infant care. Lancet 279(7238):1033–1035.

Bouhallier J, Berge C. 2006. Analyse morphologique et fonctionnelle du pelvis des primates Catarrhiniens: conséquences pour l'obstétrique [Morphological and functional analysis of the pelvis in Catarrhines: consequences for obstetrics]. C R Palevol 5:551–560.

Bourry O, Ouwe-Missi-Oukem-Boyer O, Blanchard A, Rouquet P. 2006. Fetal ultrasonography: biometric data from four African primate species. J Med Primatol 35:38–47.

Bowlby J. 1951. Maternal care and mental health. World Health Organization monograph, no. 2. Geneva, Switzerland: WHO.

Bowlby J. 1969. Attachment. New York: Basic.

Bowlby J. 1982. Attachment and loss. Vol. 1. 2nd ed. New York: Basic.

Boyd R, Richerson PJ, Henrich J. 2011. The cultural niche: why social learning is essential for human adaptation. Proc Natl Acad Sci USA 108:10918–10925.

Braun K, Lange E, Metzger M, Poeggel G. 1999. Maternal separation followed by early social deprivation affects the development of monoaminergic fiber systems in the medial prefrontal cortex of *Octodon degus*. Neuroscience 95:309–318.

Brazelton TB, Scholl ML, Robey JS. 1966. Visual responses in the newborn. Pediatr 37:284–290.

Brennard KJ, Simone A, Jou J, Gelboin-Burkhart C, Tran N, Sangar S, Li Y, Mu Y, Chen G, Yu D, et al. 2011. Modelling schizophrenia using human induced pluripotent stem cells. Nature 473:221–225.

Bribiescas RG. 2001. Reproductive ecology and life history of the human male. Yearb Phys Anthropol 116:148–176.

Bribiescas RG, Ellison PT, Gray PB. 2012. Male life history, reproductive effort, and the evolution of the genus *Homo*: New directions and perspectives. Curr Anthropol 53(S6):S424–S435.

Brock J. 2007. Language abilities in Williams syndrome: a critical review. Dev Psychopathol 19:97–127.

Bronsky J, Karpisek M, Bronska E, Pechova M, Jancikova B, Kotolova H, Stejskal D, Prusa R, Nevoral J. 2006. Adiponectin, adipocyte fatty acid binding protein, and epidermal fatty acid binding protein: proteins newly identified in human breast milk. Clin Chem 52(9):1763–1770.

Brown EA, Ruvolo M, Sabeti PC. 2013. Many ways to die, one way to arrive: how selection acts through pregnancy. Trends Genet 29(10):585–592.

Brown G, Almond R, van Bergen Y. 2004. Begging, stealing and offering: food transfers in nonhuman primates. Adv Study Behav 34:265–295.

Brown KH, Robertson AD, Akhtar NA. 1986. Lactational capacity of marginally nourished mothers: infants' milk nutrient consumption and patterns of growth. Pediatr 78(5):920–927.

Brown SM, Henning S, Wellman CL. 2005. Mild, short-term stress alters dendritic morphology in rat medial prefrontal cortex. Cer Cortex 15:1714–1722.

Brüne M. 2005. "Theory of mind" in schizophrenia: a review of the literature. Schizophr Bull 31:21–42.

Bruner JS. 1972. Nature and uses of immaturity. Am Psych 27:687–708.

Brunet M, Guy F, Pilbeam D, Mackaye HT, Likius A, Ahounta D, Beauvilain A, Blondel C, Bocherens H, Boisserie JR, et al. 2002. A new hominid from the Upper Miocene of Chad, central Africa. Nature 418(6894):145–151.

Bryan GK, Riesen AH. 1989. Deprived somatosensory-motor experience in stump-tailed monkey neocortex: dendritic spine density and dendritic branching of layer IIIb pyramidal cells. J Comp Neurol 286:208–217.

Buard I, Rogers SJ, Hepburn S, Kronberg E, Rojas DC. 2013. Altered oscillation patterns and connectivity during picture naming in autism. Front Hum Neurosci 7. http://doi.org/10.3389/fnhum.2013.00742.

Buchen L. 2011. Scientists and autism: when geeks meet. Nature 479(7371):25–27.

Burkart JM, Allon O, Amici F, Fichtel C, Finkenwirth C, Heschl A, Huber J, Isler K, Kosonen ZK, Martins E, et al. 2014. The evolutionary origin of human hyper-cooperation. Nature Comm 5. doi:10.1038/ncomms5747.

Burkart JM, Fehr E, Efferson C, van Schaik CP. 2007. Other-regarding preferences in a nonhuman primate: common marmosets provision food altruistically. Proc Natl Acad Sci USA 104:19762–19766.

Burkart, JM, Finkenwirth, C. 2015. Marmosets as model species in neuroscience and evolutionary anthropology. Neurosci Res 93:8–19.

Burkart JM, Heschl A. 2007. Perspective taking or behaviour reading? understanding visual access in common marmosets (*Callithrix jacchus*). Anim Behav 73:457–469.

Burkart JM, Hrdy SB, van Schaik CP. 2009. Cooperative breeding and human cognitive evolution. Evol Anthropol 18:175–186. doi:10.1016/j.neures.2014.09.003.

Burnham TC, Chapman JF, Gray PB, McIntyre MH, Lipson SF, Ellison PT. 2003. Men in committed, romantic relationships have lower testosterone. Horm Behav 44(2):119–122.

Burns JK. 2006. Psychosis: a costly by-product of social brain evolution in *Homo sapiens*. Prog Neuropsychopharmacol Biol Psych 30:797–814.

Bussmann LE, Bussmann IM, Charreau EH. 1996. Role of receptors for epidermal growth factor and insulin-like growth factors I and II in the differentiation of rat mammary glands from lactogenesis I to lactogenesis II. J Reprod Fertil 107(2):307–314.

Butte NF, Garza C, Smith EO. 1988. Variability of macronutrient concentrations in human milk. Eur J Clin Nutr 42(4):345–349.

Butte NF, Hopkinson JM, Nicolson MA. 1997. Leptin in human reproduction: serum leptin levels in pregnant and lactating women. J Clin Endocrinol Metab 82(2):585–589.

Butte NF, King JC. 2005. Energy requirements during pregnancy and lactation. Public Health Nutr 8(7A):1010–1027.

Butte NF, Wong WW, Hopkinson JM. 2001. Energy requirements of lactating women derived from doubly labeled water and milk energy output. J Nutr 131(1):53–58.

Byrne RW, Whiten A. 1988. Machiavellian intelligence: social expertise and the evolution of intellect in monkeys, apes, and humans. Oxford: Oxford University Press.

Bytheway JA, Ross AH. 2010. A geometric morphometric approach to sex determination of the human adult os coxae. J Forensic Sci 55:859–864.

Cahill L. 2006. Why sex matters for neuroscience. Nat Rev Neurosci 7(6):477–484.

Capellini I, Venditti C, Barton RA. 2011. Placentation and maternal investment in mammals. Am Nat 177(1):86–98.

Capitanio JP, Mendoza SP, Mason WP, Meninger N. 2005. Rearing environments and hypothaamic-pituitary-adrenal regulation in young rhesus monkeys (*Macaca mulatta*). Dev Psychobiol 46:318–330.

Carbone L, Harris RA, Gnerre S, Veeramah KR, Lorente-Galdos B, Huddleston J, Meyer TJ, Herrero J, Roos C, Aken B. 2014. Gibbon genome and the fast karyotype evolution of small apes. Nature 513:195–201.

Carlsson B, Ahlstedt S, Hanson LA, Lidin-Janson G, Lindblad BS, Sultana R. 1976. *Escherichia coli* O antibody content in milk from healthy Swedish mothers and mothers from a very low socio-economic group of a developing country. Acta Paediatr Scand 65(4):417–423.

Carter CS. 1998. Neuroendocrine perspectives on social attachment and love. Psychoneuroendocrinol 23:779–818.

Carter CS. 2014. Oxytocin pathways and the evolution of human behavior. Ann Rev Psychol 65:17–39.

Casabiell X, Pineiro V, Tome MA, Peino R, Dieguez C, Casanueva FF. 1997. Presence of leptin in colostrum and/or breast milk from lactating mothers: a potential role in the regulation of neonatal food intake. J Clin Endocr Metab 82(12):4270–4273.

Casanova MF, Tillquist CR. 2008. Encephalization, emergent properties, and psychiatry: a minicolumnar perspective. Neurosci 14:101–118.

Cäsar C, Franco ES, Soares GCN, Young RJ. 2008. Observed cases of maternal infanticide in a wild group of black-fronted titi monkeys (*Callicebus nigrifrons*). Primates 49:143–145.

Cashdan E, editor. 1990. Risk and uncertainty in tribal and peasant economies. Boulder, CO: Westview.

Cederlund M, Gillberg C. 2004. One hundred males with Asperger syndrome: a clinical study of background and associated factors. Dev Med Child Neurol 46(10):652–660.

Chailangkarn E, Hrvoj-Mihic B, Stefanacci L, Marchetto C, Yu D, Bardy C, Bellugi U, Gage F, Semendeferi K, Muotri AR. 2013. Williams syndrome:

a closer look into the dish. Paper presented at: 43rd Annual Meeting of the Society for Neuroscience, San Diego, CA (abstract).

Chakrabarti B, Dudbridge F, Kent L, Wheelwright S, Hill-Cawthorne G, Allison C, Banerjee-Basu S, Baron-Cohen S. 2009. Genes related to sex steroids, neural growth, and social-emotional behavior are associated with autistic traits, empathy, and Asperger syndrome. Autism Res 2(3):157–177.

Chao H-T, Chen H, Samaco RC, Xue M, Chahrour M, Yoo J, Neul JL, Gong S, Lu H-C, Heintz N, et al. 2010. Dysfunction in GABA signalling mediates autism-like stereotypies and Rett syndrome phenotypes. Nature 468:263–269.

Chapman DJ. 2014. Risk factors for delayed lactogenesis among women with gestational diabetes mellitus. J Hum Lact 30(2):134–135.

Chapman DJ, Pérez-Escamilla R. 2000. Maternal perception of the onset of lactation is a valid, public health indicator of lactogenesis stage II. J Nutr 130(12):2972–2980.

Chareyron LJ, Lavenex PB, Amaral DG, Lavenex P. 2012. Postnatal development of the amygdala: a stereological study in macaque monkeys. J Comp Neurol 520:1965–1984.

Charnov EL, Berrigan D. 1993. Why do female primates have such long lifespans and so few babies? or, life in the slow lane. Evol Anthropol 1:191–194.

Chen A, Rogan W. 2004. Breastfeeding and the risk of post neonatal death in the United States. Pediatr 113:e435–e439.

Cheng K. 2007. Visualizing columnar architectures using highfield fMRI. Prog Nat Sci 17:19–23.

Chiang HM, Tsai LY, Cheung YK, Brown A, Li H. 2014. A meta-analysis of differences in IQ profiles between individuals with Asperger's disorder and high-functioning autism. J Autism Dev Disord 44(7):1577–1596.

Cho CE, Norman M. 2013. Cesarean section and development of the immune system in the offspring. Am J Obstet Gynecol 208:249–254.

Cho SH, Park JM, Kwon OY. 2004. Gender differences in three dimensional gait analysis data from 98 healthy Korean adults. Clin Biomech19.145–152.

Christensson K. 1996. Fathers can effectively achieve heat conservation in healthy newborn infants. Acta Paediatr 85(11):1354–1360.

Chugani HT, Phelps ME. 1986. Maturational changes in cerebral function in infants determined by F-18-DG positron emission tomography. Science 231:840–843.

Ciardelli L, Garofoli F, Avanzini MA, De Silvestri A, Gasparoni A, Sabatino G, Stronati M. 2007. *Escherichia coli* specific secretory IgA and cytokines in human milk from mothers of different ethnic groups resident in northern Italy. Int J Immunopathol Pharmacol 20(2):335–340.

Clancy B, Darlington RB, Finlay BL. 2001. Translating developmental time across mammalian species. Neuroscience 105:7–17.

Clancy KBH, Hinde K, Rutherford JN, editors. 2013. Building babies: primate development in proximate and ultimate perspective. New York: Springer.

Cofran Z, DeSilva JM. 2015. A neonatal perspective on *Homo erectus* brain growth. J Hum Evol 81:41–47.

Cogan GB, Thesen T, Carlson C, Doyle W, Devinsky O, Pesaran B. 2014. Sensory-motor transformations for speech occur bilaterally. Nature 507(7490):94–98.

Cohen D, Cassel RS, Saint-Georges C, Mahdhaoui A, Laznik MC, Apicella F, Muratori P, Maestro S, Muratori F, Chetouani M. 2013. Do parentese prosody and fathers' involvement in interacting facilitate social interaction in infants who later develop autism? PLoS ONE 8(5):e61402.

Cohen M. 1947. The meaning of human history. La Salle, IL: Open Court.

Cook SC, Wellman CL. 2004. Chronic stress alters dendritic morphology in rat medial prefrontal cortex. J Neurobiol 60:236–248.

Cooper RW. 1964. Experimental breeding of subhuman primates. In: Quarterly and annual reports of the primate colony. San Diego, CA: Zoological Society of San Diego.

Copeland SR, Sponheimer M, de Ruiter DJ, Lee-Thorp JA, Codron D, le Roux PJ, Grimes V, Richards MP. 2011. Strontium isotope evidence for landscape use by early hominins. Nature 474:76–78.

Coqueugniot H, Hublin JJ. 2012. Age-related changes of digital endocranial volume during human ontogeny: results from an osteological reference collection. Am J Phys Anthropol 147:312–318.

Coqueugniot H, Hublin JJ, Veillon F, Houët F, Jacob T. 2004. Early brain growth in *Homo erectus* and implications for cognitive ability. Nature 431:299–302.

Courchesne E, Campbell K, Solso S. 2011. Brain growth across the life span in autism: age-specific changes in anatomical pathology. Brain Res 1380:138–145.

Courchesne E, Chisum HJ, Townsend J, Cowles A, Covington J, Egaas B. 2000. Normal brain development and aging: quantitative analysis at in vivo MR imaging in healthy volunteers. Radiol 216:672–682.

Cowgill LW, Eleazer CD, Auerbach BM, Temple DH, Okazaki K. 2012. Developmental variation in ecogeographic body proportions. Am J Phys Anthropol 148(4):557–570.

Cox DB, Owens RA, Hartmann PE. 1996. Blood and milk prolactin and the rate of milk synthesis in women. Exp Physiol 81(6):1007–1020.

Crespi B, Summers K, Dorus S. 2007. Adaptive evolution of genes underlying schizophrenia. Proc Biol Sci 274:2801–2810.

Crews DE, Bogin B. 2010. Growth, development, senescence, and aging: a life history perspective. In: Larsen CS, editor. A companion to biological anthropology. Hoboken, NJ: Blackwell. 124–152.

Crockford C, Wittig RM, Langergraber K, Ziegler TE, Zuberbuhler K, Deschner T. 2013. Urinary oxytocin and social bonding in related and unrelated wild chimpanzees. Proc R Soc B 280(1755). doi:10.1098/rspb.2012.2765.

Cronin K, Schroeder KKE, Snowdon CT. 2011. Prosocial behaviour emerges independent of reciprocity in cottontop tamarins. Proc Roy Soc B 277:3845–3851.

Crosley EJ, Elliot MG, Christians JK, Crespi BJ. 2013. Placental invasion, preeclampsia risk and adaptive molecular evolution at the origin of the great apes: evidence from genome-wide analyses. Placenta 34:127–132.

Crow TJ. 1998. Nuclear schizophrenic symptoms as a window on the relationship between thought and speech. Br J Psych 173:303–309.

Crow TJ. 2000. Schizophrenia as the price that *Homo sapiens* pays for language: a resolution of the central paradox in the origin of the species. Brain Res Rev 31:118–129.

Cruz JR, Carlsson B, García B, Gebre-Medhin M, Hofvander Y, Urrutia JJ, Hanson LA. 1982. Studies on human milk: III: Secretory IgA quantity and antibody levels against *Escherichia coli* in colostrum and milk from underprivileged and privileged mothers. Pediatr Res 16:272–276.

Culot L, Liedo-Ferrer Y, Hoelscher O, Muñoz Lazo FJJ, Huynen M-C, Heymann EW. 2011. Reproductive failure, possible maternal infanticide, and cannibalism in wild moustached tamarins, *Saguinus mystax*. Primates 52:179–186.

Cunnane SC. 2005. Survival of the fattest: the key to human brain evolution. Singapore: World Scientific Publishing.

Cunnane SC, Crawford MA. 2003. Survival of the fattest: fat babies were the key to evolution of the large human brain. Comp Biochem Physiol A: Mol Integr Physiol 136(1):17–26.

Cupp CJ, Uemura E. 1980. Age-related changes in prefrontal cortex of *Macaca mulatta*: quantitative analysis of dendritic branching patterns. Exp Neurol 69:143–163.

Curia G, Papouin T, Séguéla P, Avoli M. 2009. Downregulation of tonic GABAergic inhibition in a mouse model of fragile X syndrome. Cereb Cortex 19:1515–1520.

Czank C, Mitoulas L, Hartmann PE. 2007. Human milk composition: fat. In: Hale T, Hartmann P, editors. Textbook of human lactation. Amarillo, TX: Hale. 75–84.

Dabbs JM, Karpas AE, Dyomina N, Juechter J, Roberts A. 2002. Experimental raising or lowering of testosterone level affects mood in normal men and women. Soc Behav Pers 30(8):795–806.

Dabbs JM, Morris R. 1990. Testosterone, social class, and antisocial behavior in a sample of 4,462 men. Psychol Sci 1(3):209–211.

Dahlberg F, editor. 1981. Woman the gatherer. New Haven, CT: Yale University Press.

Dai L, Carter CS, Ying J, Bellugi U, Pournajafi-Nazarloo H, Korenberg JR. 2012. Oxytocin and vasopressin are dysregulated in Williams syndrome, a genetic disorder affecting social behavior. PLoS ONE 7:e38513.

Daly M, Wilson M. 1995. Discriminative parental solicitude: a biological perspective. J Marr Fam 42:377–388.

Daly SE, Hartmann PE. 1995. Infant demand and milk supply: part 2: the short-term control of milk synthesis in lactating women. J Hum Lact 11(1):27–37.

Daly SE, Owens RA, Hartmann PE. 1993. The short-term synthesis and infant-regulated removal of milk in lactating women. Exp Physiol 78(2):209–220.

Daniels J, Krahenbuhl G, Foster C, Gilbert J, Daniels S. 1977. Aerobic responses of female distance runners to submaximal and maximal exercise. Ann NY Acad Sci. 301:726–733.

Dart RA. 1925. *Australopithecus africanus*: the man-ape of South Africa. Nature 115:195–199.

Dart RA. 1929. *Australopithecus africanus* and his place in human nature. Johannesburg, South Africa: University of Witwatersrand Archives. Unpublished manuscript.

Darwin C. 1871. The descent of man, and selection in relation to sex. New York: Appleton.

Dave DM, Fernandez JM. 2015. Rising autism prevalence: real or displacing other mental disorders? evidence from demand for auxiliary healthcare workers in California. Econ Inq 53(1):448–468.

Dean C. 2006. Tooth microstructure tracks the pace of human life-history evolution. Proc Roy Soc A 273:2799–2808.

Decety J, Svetlova M. 2012. Putting together phylogenetic and ontogenetic perspectives on empathy. Dev Cogn Neurosci 2:1–24.

DeFelipe J. 1997. Types of neurons, synaptic connections and chemical characteristics of cells immunoreactive for calbindin-D28K, parvalbumin and calretinin in the neocortex. J Chem Neuroanat 14:1–19.

DeFelipe J, López-Cruz PL, Benavides-Piccione R, Bielza C, Larrañaga P, Anderson S, Burkhalter A, Cauli B, Fairén A, Feldmeyer D, et al. 2013. New insights into the classification and nomenclature of cortical GABAergic interneurons. Nat Rev Neurosci 14:202–216.

Dehaene-Lambertz G, Hertz-Pannier L, Dubois J. 2006. Nature and nurture in language acquisition: anatomical and functional brain-imaging studies in infants. Trends Neurosci 29(7):367–373.

Dementieva YA, Vance DD, Donnelly SL, Elston LA, Wolpert CM, Ravan SA, DeLong GR, Abramson RK, Wright HH, Cuccaro ML. 2005. Accelerated head growth in early development of individuals with autism. Pediatr Neurol 32(2):102–108.

Deoni SC, Dean DC, Piryatinsky IO, Waskiewicz N, Lehman H, Han, M, Dirks H. 2013. Breastfeeding and early white matter development: a cross-sectional study. Neuroimage 15:77–86.

Derntl B, Windischberger C, Robinson S, Kryspin-Exner I, Gur RC, Moser E, Habel U. 2009. Amygdala activity to fear and anger in healthy young males is associated with testosterone. Psychoneuroendocrinol 34(5):687–693.

DeSilva JM. 2009. Functional morphology of the ankle and the likelihood of climbing in early hominins. Proc Natl Acad Sci USA 106:6567–6572.

DeSilva JM. 2011. A shift toward birthing relatively large infants early in human evolution. Proc Natl Acad Sci USA 108:1022–1027. doi:10.1073/pnas.1003865108.

DeSilva JM, Lesnik J. 2006. Chimpanzee neonatal brain size: implications for brain growth in *Homo erectus*. J Hum Evol 51:207–212.

DeSilva JM, Lesnik J. 2008. Brain size at birth throughout human evolution: a new method for estimating neonatal brain size in hominins. J Hum Evol 55:1064–1074.

Desmond MM, Franklin RR, Vallbona C, Hill RM, Plumb R, Arnold H, Watts J. 1963. The clinical behavior of the newly born: I: the term baby. J Pediatr 62:307–325.

Dettmer AM, Suomi SJ, Hinde K. 2013. Nonhuman primate models of mental health: early life experiences affect developmental trajectories. In: Narvaez N, Valentino K, Fuentes A, McKenna JJ, Gray P, editors. Ancestral landscapes in human evolution. Oxford: Oxford University Press. 42–58.

Dettwyler KA. 2004. When to wean: biological versus cultural perspectives. Clin Obstetr Gynecol 47:712–723.

Developmental Disabilities Monitoring Network. 2014. Prevalence of autism spectrum disorder among children aged 8 years: autism and developmental disabilities monitoring network, 11 sites, United States, 2010. MMWR 63(2):1.

Dewey KG. 2003. Is breastfeeding protective against child obesity? J Hum Lact
19(1):9–18.

Diaz-Munoz SL, DuVal EH, Krakauer AH, Lacey EA. 2014. Cooperating to compete:
altruism, sexual selection and causes of male cooperation. Anim Behav
88:67–78.

Diekhof EK, Wittmer S, Reimers L. 2014. Does competition really bring out the
worst? testosterone, social distance and inter-male competition shape paro-
chial altruism in human males. PLoS ONE 9(7):e98977.

Dienske H. 1986. A comparative approach to the question of why human infants
develop so slowly. In: Else JG, Lee PC, editors. Primate ontogeny, cognition,
and social behavior. Cambridge: Cambridge University Press. 145–154.

Digby L. 2000. Infanticide by female mammals: implications for the evolution of
social systems. In: van Schaik CP, Janson CH, editors. Infanticide by males
and its implications. Cambridge: Cambridge University Press. 423–446.

Digby L, Ferrari SF. 1994. Multiple breeding females in free-ranging groups of *Callithrix jacchus*. Int J Primatol 15:389–397.

Digby L, Ferrari SF, Saltzman W. 2011. Callitrichines: the role of competition in
cooperatively breeding species. In: Campbell C, Fuentes A, MacKinnon K,
Bearder S, Stumpf R, editors. Primates in perspective. 2nd ed. Oxford:
Oxford University Press. 91–107.

Digby L, Saltzman W. 2009. Balancing cooperation and competition in callitrichid
primates: examining relative risk of infanticide across species. In: Ford
SM, Porter LJ, Davis L, editors. The smallest anthropoids: the marmoset/
callimico radiation. New York: Springer. 135–153.

Digiacomo RF, Shaughnessy PW, Tomlin SL. 1978. Fetal-placental weight relationships in the rhesus (*Macaca mulatta*). Biol Reprod 18:749–753.

Dinstein I, Pierce K, Eyler L, Solso S, Malach R, Behrmann M, Courchesne E.
2011. Disrupted neural synchronization in toddlers with autism. Neuron
70:1218–1225.

Dixson AF, George L. 1982. Prolactin and parental behavior in a male new-world
primate. Nature 299(5883):551–553.

Dobbing J, Sands J. 1973. Quantitative growth and development of human brain.
Arch Disease Child 48:757–767.

Dobzhansky T. 1962. Mankind evolving. New Haven, CT: Yale University Press.

Dombrowski SM. 2001. Quantitative architecture distinguishes prefrontal cortical
systems in the rhesus monkey. Cereb Cortex 11:975–988.

Dominguez-Bello MG, Costello EK, Contreras M, Magris M, Hidalgo G, Fierer N,
Knight R. 2010. Delivery mode shapes the acquisition and structure of the

initial microbiota across multiple body habitats in newborns. Proc Natl Acad Sci USA 107:11971–11975.

Doneray H, Orbak Z, Yildiz L. 2009. The relationship between breast milk leptin and neonatal weight gain. Acta Paediatr 98(4):643–647.

Donovan SM, Odle J. 1994. Growth factors in milk as mediators of infant development. Ann Rev Nutr 14:147–167.

Doyle TF, Bellugi U, Korenberg JR, Graham J. 2004. "Everybody in the world is my friend": hypersociability in young children with Williams syndrome. Am J Med Genet A124:263–273.

Driscoll C. 2005. Killing babies: Hrdy on the evolution of infanticide. Biol Philos 20:271–289.

Dryden IL, Mardia K. 1998. Statistical shape analysis. New York: Wiley.

Duffy FH, Shankardass A, McAnulty GB, Als H. 2013. The relationship of Asperger's syndrome to autism: a preliminary EEG coherence study. BMC Med 11. doi:10.1186/1741-7015-11-175.

Duffy KG, Wrangham RW, Silk JB. 2007. Male chimpanzees exchange political support for mating opportunities. Curr Biol 17(15):R586–R587.

Dufour DL, Sauthier ML. 2002. Comparative and evolutionary dimensions of the energetics of human pregnancy and lactation. Am J Hum Biol 14:584–602.

Dulac C, O'Connell A, Wu Z. 2014. Neural control of maternal and paternal behaviors. Science 345:765–770.

Dunbar RIM. 1995. The mating system of callitrichid primates: I: conditions for the coevolution of pair bonding and twinning. Anim Behav 50:1057–1070.

Dunbar RIM, Shultz S. 2007. Evolution in the social brain. Science 317(5843):1344–1347.

Dundar NO, Anal O, Dundar B, Ozkan H, Caliskan S, Büyükgebiz A. 2005. Longitudinal investigation of the relationship between breast milk leptin levels and growth in breast-fed infants. J Pediatr Endocrinol Metab 18(2):181–187.

Dunsworth HM. 2006. *Proconsul heseloni* feet from Rusinga island, Kenya. PhD diss., Pennsylvania State University.

Dunsworth HM, Warrener AG, Deacon T, Ellison PT, Pontzer H. 2012. Metabolic hypothesis for human altriciality. Proc Natl Acad Sci USA 109:15212–15216.

Edelstein RS, van Anders SM, Chopik WJ, Goldey KL, Wardecker BM. 2014. Dyadic associations between testosterone and relationship quality in couples. Horm Behav 66:401–407.

Edwards DA, Wetzel K, Wyner DR. 2006. Intercollegiate soccer: saliva cortisol and testosterone are elevated during competition, and testosterone is related to status and social connectedness with teammates. Physiol Behav 87(1):135–143.

Edwards G. 1758. Gleanings of natural history, exhibiting figures of quadrupeds, birds, insects, plants, etc., most of which have not, till now, been either figured or described. Vol. 8. London: Royal College of Physicians.

Eide MG, Øyen N, Skjærven R, Nilsen ST, Bjerkedal T, Tell GS. 2005. Size at birth and gestational age as predictors of adult height and weight. Epidemiol 16(2):175–181. doi:10.1097/01.ede.0000152524.89074.bf.

Eisert R, Potter CW, Ofteda, OT. 2013. Brain size in neonatal and adult Weddell seals: costs and consequences of having a large brain. Mar Mammal Sci 30:184–205.

Eliasson S, Jorgensen C. 2014. Extra-pair mating and evolution of cooperative neighborhoods. PLoS ONE 9(7):e99878.

Ellison PT. 2001a. On fertile ground: a natural history of human reproduction. Cambridge, MA: Harvard University Press.

Ellison PT. 2001b. Reproductive ecology and human evolution. New York: Aldine de Gruyter.

Ellison PT. 2009. Developmental plasticity in a biocultural context. Am J Hum Biol 21:1.

Elston GN. 2007. Specialization of the neocortical pyramidal cell during primate evolution. In: Preuss TM, Kaas JH, editors. The evolution of nervous systems. Vol. 4, The evolution of primate nervous systems. New York: Elsevier. 191–242.

Emlen ST. 1995. An evolutionary theory of the family. Proc Natl Acad Sci USA 92:8092–8099.

Epple G. 1970. Maintenance, breeding and development of marmoset monkeys (Callitrichidae) in captivity. Folia Primatol 12:56–76.

Epstein HT. 1973. Possible metabolic constraints on human brain weight at birth. Am J Phys Anthropol 39:135–136.

Etkin W. 1954. Social behavior and the evolution of man's mental faculties. Am Nat 88:129–142.

Evans KL, Hampson E. 2014. Does risk-taking mediate the relationship between testosterone and decision-making on the Iowa gambling task? Pers Indiv Differ 61:57–62.

Fagiolini M, Pizzorusso T, Berardi N, Domenici L, Maffei L. 1994. Functional postnatal development of the rat primary visual cortex and the role of visual experience: dark rearing and monocular deprivation. Vis Res 34(6):709–720.

Fairbanks LA, Hinde K. 2013. Behavioral response of mothers and infants to variation in maternal conditions: adaptation, compensation and resilience. In: Clancy KBH, Hinde K, Rutherford JN, editors. Building babies: primate development in proximate and ultimate perspective. New York: Springer. 281–302.

Falk D. 2004. Prelinguistic evolution in early hominins: whence motherese? Behav Brain Sci 27:491–541.

Falk D. 2009. Finding our tongues: mothers, infants and the origins of language. New York: Pertheus.

Falk D. 2012. The role of mothers and infants in prelinguistic evolution. In: Tallerman M, Gibson KR, editors. The Oxford handbook of language evolution. Oxford: Oxford University Press. 318–321.

Falk D. 2014. Interpreting sulci on hominin endocasts: old hypotheses and new findings. Front Hum Neurosci 8. http://dx.doi.org/10.3389/fnhum.2014.00134.

Falk D. 2016. Evolution of brain and culture: the neurological and cognitive journey from Australopithecus to Albert Einstein. J Anthropol Sci 94:1–14. doi:10.4436/jass.94027.

Falk D, Redmond JC Jr, Guyer J, Conroy GC, Recheis W, Weber GW, Seidler H. 2000. Early hominid brain evolution: a new look at old endocasts. J Hum Evol 38:695–717.

Falk D, Schofield EP. Forthcoming. Aspies rising: the evolution of Asperger syndrome. Albuquerque: University of New Mexico Press.

Falk D, Zollikofer CP, Morimoto N, Ponce de León MS. 2012. Metopic suture of Taung (*Australopithecus africanus*) and its implications for hominin brain evolution. Proc Natl Acad Sci USA 109(22):8467–8470.

Fardig JA. 1980. A comparison of skin-to-skin contact and radiant heaters in promoting neonatal thermoregulation. J Nur Midwif 25(1):19–28.

Farrar MJ. 1990. Discourse and the acquisition of grammatical morphemes. J Child Lang 17(3):607–624.

Feldman R. 2004. Mother-infant skin-to-skin contact (kangaroo care): theoretical, clinical, and empirical aspects. Inf Young Child 17:145–161.

Feldman R, Eidelman A, Sirota L, Weller A. 2002. Comparison of skin-to-skin (kangaroo) and traditional care: parenting outcomes and preterm infant development. Pediatr 110:16–26.

Feldman R, Weller A, Sirota L, Eidelman AI. 2003. Testing a family intervention hypothesis: the contribution of mother-infant skin-to-skin contact (kangaroo care) to family interaction, proximity, and touch. J Fam Psychol 17:94–107.

Ferber R. 2006. Solve your child's sleep problems. New York: Simon and Schuster.

Ferber R, McClay Davis I, Williams DS. 2003. Gender differences in lower extremity mechanics during running. Clin Biomech 18:350–357.

Ferguson CA. 1978. Talking to children: a search for universals. In: Greenberg J, editor. Universals of human language. Stanford, CA: Stanford University Press. 176–189.

Ferguson JE, Sistrom CL. 2000. Can fetal-pelvic disproportion be predicted? Clin Obstetr Gynecol 43:247–264.

Fernald A. 1994. Human maternal vocalizations to infants as biologically relevant signals: an evolutionary perspective. In: Bloom P, editor. Language acquisition core readings. Cambridge, MA: MIT Press. 51–94.

Fernandez-Duque E, Valeggia CR, Mendoza SP. 2009. The biology of paternal care in human and nonhuman primates. Ann Rev Anthropol 38:115–130.

Fernandez-Guasti A, Kruijver FP, Fodor M, Swaab DF. 2000. Sex differences in the distribution of androgen receptors in the human hypothalamus. J Comp Neurol 425(3):422–435.

Ferrero DM, Moeller LM, OsakadaT, Horio N, Li Q, Dheeraj SR, Chichy A, Spehr M, Touhara K, Liberies SD. 2013. A juvenile mouse pheromone inhibits sexual behaviour through the vomeronasal system. Nature 502:368–371. doi:10.1038/nature12579.

Ferry A, Hespos SJ, Waxman SR. 2013. Nonhuman primate vocalizations support categorization in very young human infants. Proc Natl Acad Sci USA 110:15231–15235.

Fewtrell MS. 2011. Breast-feeding and later risk of CVD and obesity: evidence from randomised trials. P Nutr Soc 70(4):472–477.

Field T. 1995. Infant massage therapy. In: Field TM, editor. Touch in early development. Mahwah, NJ: Erlbaum. 105–114.

Field T. 1996. Attachment and separation in young children. Ann Rev Psychol 47:541–561.

Field T. 1998. Touch therapy effects on development. Int J Beh Dev 22:779–797.

Field T. 2001. Massage therapy facilitates weight gain in preterm infants. Cur Dir Psych Sci 10:51–54.

Field T, Scafidi F, Schanberg S. 1987. Massage of preterm newborns to improve growth and development. Pediatr Nurs 13(6):385–387.

Field T, Schanberg SM, Scafidi F, Bauer CR, Vega-Lahr N, Garcia R, Nystrom J, Kuhn CM. 1986. Tactile/kinesthetic stimulation effects on preterm neonates. Pediatr 77:654–658.

Fields DA, Demerath EW. 2012. Relationship of insulin, glucose, leptin, IL-6 and TNF-alpha in human breast milk with infant growth and body composition. Pediatr Obesity 7:304–312.

Fildes VA. 1986. Breasts, bottles and babies: a history of infant history of feeding. Edinburgh: Edinburgh University Press.

Finlay BL, Darlington RB. 1995. Linked regularities in the development and evolution of mammalian brains. Science 268(5217):1578–1584.

Finlay BL, Darlington RB, Nicastro N. 2001. Developmental structure in brain evolution. Behav Brain Sci 24:283–308.

Finlay BL, Workman AJ. 2013. Human exceptionalism. Trends Cogn Sci 17:199–201.

Fiser J, Aslin RN. 2002. Statistical learning of new visual feature combinations by infants. Proc Natl Acad Sci USA 99:15822–15826.

Fite JE, Patera KJ, French JA, Rukstalis M, Hopkins EC, Ross CN. 2005. Opportunistic mothers: female marmosets (*Callithrix kuhlii*) reduce their investment in offspring when they have to and when they can. J Hum Evol 49:122–142.

Flechsig P. 1901. Developmental myelogenetic localisation of the cerebral cortex in the human subject. Lancet 2:1027–1029.

Flechsig P. 1920. Anatomie des menschlichen gehirns und rückenmarks auf myelogenetischer grundlage. Leipzig: Thieme.

Fleming A, Corter C, Stallings J, Steiner M. 2002. Testosterone and prolactin are associated with emotional responses to infant cries in new fathers. Horm Behav 42(4):399–413.

Flinn M, Ponzi D, Muehlenbein M. 2012. Hormonal mechanisms for regulation of aggression in human coalitions. Hum Nat 23(1):68–88.

Foley R. 1996. The adaptive legacy of human evolution: a search for the environment of evolutionary adaptedness. Evol Anthropol 6:194–203.

Forste R, Weiss J, Lippincott E. 2001. The decision to breastfeed in the United States: does race matter? Pediatr 108:291–296.

Fox SA, Vayro J, Potvin-Rosselet E, Cortty A, Sicotte P. 2014. Males who are potential sires show affiliation and tolerance towards infants in *Colobus villerosus* (abstract). Am J Phys Anthropol 58(Suppl):120.

Fragaszy DM, Bard K. 1997. Comparison of development and life history in *Pan* and *Cebus*. Int J Primatol 18:683–701.

Fragaszy DM, Visalberghi E, Fedigan LM. 2004. The complete capuchin: the biology of the genus *Cebus*. Cambridge: Cambridge University Press.

Frank LG, Glickland SE. 1994. Giving birth through a penile clitoris: parturition and dystocia in the spotted hyaena (*Crocuta crocuta*). J Zool 234(4):659–665.

Frodi AM, Lamb ME, Leavitt LA, Donovan CM, Neff C, Sherry D. 1978. Fathers' and mothers' responses to the faces and cries of normal and premature infants. Dev Psychol 14(5):40–49.

Fuentes A, Wyczalkowski MA, MacKinnon KC. 2010. Niche construction through cooperation: a nonlinear dynamics contribution to modeling facets of the evolutionary history in the genus *Homo*. Curr Anthropol 51(3):435–444.

Fukumoto A, Hashimoto T, Ito H, Nishimura M, Tsuda Y, Miyazaki M, Mori K, Arisawa K, Kagami S. 2008. Growth of head circumference in autistic infants during the first year of life. J Autism Dev Disord 38(3):411–418.

Garber P. 1997. One for all and breeding for one: cooperation and competition as a tamarin reproductive strategy. Evol Anthropol 7:187–199.

Garber PA, Moya L, Malaga C. 1984. A preliminary field study of the moustached tamarin monkey (*Saguinus mystax*) in northeastern Peru: questions concerned with the evolution of a communal breeding system. Folia Primatol 42:17–32.

Garwicz M, Christensson M, Psouni E. 2009. A unifying model for timing of walking onset in humans and other mammals. Proc Natl Acad Sci USA 106:21889–21893.

Geddes DT, Aljazaf KM, Kent JC, Prime DK, Spatz DL, Garbin CP, Lai CT, Hartmann PE. 2012. Blood flow characteristics of the human lactating breast. J Hum Lact 28(2):145–152.

Gelstein S, Yeshuran Y, Rozenkrantz L, Shushan S, Frumin I, Roth Y, Sobel N. 2011. Human tears contain chemosignal. Science 331:226–230.

German JB, Freeman SL, Lebrilla CB, Mills DA. 2008. Human milk oligosaccharides: evolution, structures and bioselectivity as substrates for intestinal bacteria. Nestle Nutr Workshop Ser Pediatr Prog 62:205–218, discussion 218–222. doi:10.1159/000146322.

Gerra G, Avanzini P, Zaimovic A, Sartori R, Bocchi C, Timpano M, Zambelli U, Delsignore R, Gardini F, Talarico E, Brambilla F. 1999. Neurotransmitters, neuroendocrine correlates of sensation-seeking temperament in normal humans. Neuropsychobiology 39(4):207–213.

Gesquiere LR, Learn NH, Simao MC, Onyango PO, Alberts SC, Altmann J. 2011. Life at the top: rank and stress in wild male baboons. Science 333(6040):357–360.

Gettler LT. 2010. Direct male care and hominin evolution: why male-child interaction is more than a nice social idea. Am Anthropol 112:7–21. doi:10.1111/j.1548-1433.2009.01193.x.

Gettler LT. 2014. Applying socioendocrinology to evolutionary models: fatherhood and physiology. Evol Anthropol 23(4):146–160.

Gettler LT, Agustin SS, Kuzawa CW. 2010. Testosterone, physical activity, and somatic outcomes among Filipino males. Am J Phys Anthropol 142:590–599.

Gettler LT, McDade TW, Agustin SS, Feranil AB, Kuzawa CW. 2013. Do testosterone declines during the transition to marriage and fatherhood relate to men's sexual behavior? evidence from the Philippines. Horm Behav 64(5):755–763.

Gettler LT, McDade TW, Agustin SS, Feranil AB, Kuzawa CW. 2014. Testosterone, immune function, and life history transitions in Filipino males (*Homo sapiens*). Int J Primatol 35(3–4):787–804.

Gettler LT, McDade TW, Agustin SS, Feranil AB, Kuzawa CW. 2015. Longitudinal perspectives on fathers' residence status, time allocation, and testosterone in the Philippines. Adapt Hum Behav Physiol 1:124–149.

Gettler LT, McDade TW, Feranil AB, Kuzawa CW. 2011. Longitudinal evidence that fatherhood decreases testosterone in human males. Proc Natl Acad Sci USA 108(29):16194–16199.

Gettler LT, McKenna JJ. 2010. Never sleep with baby? or, keep me close but keep me safe: eliminating inappropriate "safe infant sleep" rhetoric in the United States. Curr Ped Rev 1:1–6.

Gettler LT, McKenna JJ, Agustin SS, McDade TW, Kuzawa CW. 2012. Does cosleeping contribute to lower testosterone levels in fathers? evidence from the Philippines. PLoS ONE 7(9):e41559.

Gettler LT, Oka RC. 2016. Aging US males with multiple sources of emotional social support have low testosterone. Horm Behav 78:32–42.

Gibson KR. 1991. Myelination and behavioral development: a comparative perspective on neoteny, altriciality, and intelligence. In: Gibson KR, Petersen AC, editors. Brain maturation and cognitive development: comparative and cross-cultural perspectives. New York: Aldine de Gruyter. 22–63.

Gicdd JN, Blumenthal J, Jeffries NO, Castellanos FX, Liu H, Zijdenbos A. 1999. Brain development during childhood and adolescence: a longitudinal MRI study. Nature Neurosci 2(10):861–863.

Gillberg C, de Souza L. 2002. Head circumference in autism, Asperger syndrome, and ADHD: a comparative study. Dev Med Child Neurol 44(5):296–300.

Gillman MW. 2002. Breast-feeding and obesity. J Pediatr 141(6):749–750.

Gillman MW. 2010. Early infancy as a critical period for development of obesity and related conditions. Nestle Nutr Workshop Ser Pediatr Program 65:13–20.

Gillman MW, Mantzoros CS. 2007. Breast-feeding, adipokines, and childhood obesity. Epidemiol 18(6):730–732.

Gillman MW, Rifas-Shiman SL, Camargo CA, Berkey CS, Frazier AL, Rockett HR, Field AE, Colditz GA. 2001. Risk of overweight among adolescents who were breastfed as infants. JAMA 285(19):2461–2467.

Glocker ML, Langleben DD, Ruparel K, Loughead JW, Valdez JN, Griffin MD, Sachser N, Gur RC. 2009. Baby schema modulates the brain reward system in nulliparous women. Proc Natl Acad Sci USA 106(22):9115–9119.

Goetz SM, Tang L, Thomason ME, Diamond MP, Hariri AR, Carré JM. 2014. Testosterone rapidly increases neural reactivity to threat in healthy men: a novel two-step pharmacological challenge paradigm. Biol Psychiatr 76(4):324–331. doi:10.1016/j.biopsych.2014.01.016.

Gogtay N, Giedd JN, Lusk L, Hayashi KM, Greenstein D, Vaituzis AC, Nugent TF, Herman DH, Clasen LS, Toga AW, et al. 2004. Dynamic mapping of human cortical development during childhood through early adulthood. Proc Natl Acad Sci USA 101:8174–8179.

Goldizen AW. 1988. Tamarin and marmoset mating systems: unusual flexibility. Trends Ecol Evol 3(2):36–40.

Goldizen AW. 1990. A comparative perspective on the evolution of tamarin and marmoset social systems. Int J Primatol 11(1):63–83.

Gonzalez PN, Bernal V, Perez SI. 2009. Geometric morphometric approach to sex estimation of human pelvis. Forensic Sci Int 189:68–74.

Goodall J. 1986. The chimpanzees of Gombe. Cambridge, MA: Harvard University Press.

Gopnik A, Meltzoff A, Kuhl P. 1999. The scientist in the crib. New York: Perennial.

Gordon I, Zagoory-Sharon O, Leckman JF, Feldman R. 2010. Prolactin, oxytocin, and the development of paternal behavior across the first six months of fatherhood. Horm Behav 58:513–518.

Goren CC, Sarty M, Wu PY. 1975. Visual following and pattern discrimination of face-like stimuli by newborn infants. Pediatr 56:544–549.

Goudriaan AE, Lapauw B, Ruige J, Feyen E, Kaufman J, Brand M, Vingerhoets G. 2010. The influence of high-normal testosterone levels on risk-taking in healthy males in a 1-week letrozole administration study. Psychoneuroendocrinol 35(9):1416–1421.

Gould SJ. 1975. Allometry in primates with emphasis on scaling and the evolution of the brain. Contrib Primatol 5:244–292.

Gould SJ. 1977. Ontogeny and phylogeny. Cambridge, MA: Harvard University Press.

Gould SJ. 1991. Exaptation: a crucial tool for evolutionary psychology. J Soc Issues 47:43–65.

Grabowski MW. 2013. Hominin obstetrics and the evolution of constraints. Evol Biol 40:57–75.

Grabowski MW, Polk JD, Roseman CC. 2011. Divergent patterns of integration and reduced constraint in the human hip and the origins of bipedalism. Evol 65:1336–1356.

Graetz E. 1968. Studien über das mittelamerikanische Krallenafchen Oedipomidas spixi. Sitzungsh, Ges Naturf Freunde 8(1):29–40.

Grand TI. 1992. Altricial and precocial mammals: a model of neural and muscular development. Zoo Biol 11:3–15.

Grandin T. 1995. Thinking in pictures and other reports from my life with autism. New York: Vintage.

Gray L, Watt L, Blass EM. 2000. Skin to skin contact is analgesic in healthy newborns. Pediatr 105(1):e14. http://www.ncbi.nlm.nih.gov/pubmed/10617751.

Gray PB. 2003. Marriage, parenting, and testosterone variation among Kenyan Swahili men. Am J Phys Anthropol 122(3):279–286.

Gray PB, Anderson K. 2010. Fatherhood: evolution and human paternal behavior. Cambridge, MA: Harvard University Press.

Gray PB, Campbell BC. 2009. Human male testosterone, pair bonding and father-hood. In: Ellison PT, Gray PB, editors. Endocrinology of social relation-ships. Cambridge, MA: Harvard University Press. 270–293.

Gray PB, Campbell BC, Marlowe FW, Lipson SF, Ellison PT. 2004a. Social variables predict between-subject but not day-to-day variation in the testosterone of US men. Psychoneuroendocrinol 29(9):1153–1162.

Gray PB, Chapman JF, Burnham TC, McIntyre MH, Lipson SF, Ellison PT. 2004b. Human male pair bonding and testosterone. Hum Nature 15(2):119–131.

Gray PB, Ellison PT, Campbell BC. 2007. Testosterone and marriage among Ariaal men of northern Kenya. Curr Anthropol 48(5):750–755.

Gray PB, Kahlenberg SM, Barrett ES, Lipson SF, Ellison PT. 2002. Marriage and fatherhood are associated with lower testosterone in males. Evol Hum Behav 23:193–201.

Gray PB, Yang CJ, Pope HG. 2006. Fathers have lower salivary testosterone levels than unmarried men and married non-fathers in Beijing, China. Proc R Soc B 273(1584):333–339.

Green C, Dissanayake C, Loesch D. 2015. A review of physical growth in children and adolescents with autism spectrum disorder. Dev Rev 36:156–178.

Green MF, Horan WP. 2010. Social cognition in schizophrenia. Curr Dir Psychol Sci 19:243–248.

Green RE, Krause J, Briggs AW, Maricic T, Stenzel U, Kircher M, Patterson N, Li H, Zhai W, Fritz MHY, et al. 2010. A draft sequence of the Neandertal genome. Science 328:710–722.

Greenough WT, Black JE, Wallace CS. 1987. Experience and brain development. Child Dev 58:539–559.

Gregg J, Wynne-Edwards K. 2005. Placentophagia in naive adults, new fathers, and new mothers in the biparental dwarf hamster, *Phodopus cambelli*. Psychobiol 47(20):179–188.

Grinker RR. 2008. Unstrange minds: remapping the world of autism. Boston, MA: Da Capo.

Grodzinsky Y, Nelken I. 2014. Neuroscience: the neural code that makes us human. Science 343(6174):978–979.

Grummer-Strawn LM, Mei Z, Centers for Disease Control, Prevention Pediatric Nutrition Surveillance. 2004. Does breastfeeding protect against pediatric overweight? analysis of longitudinal data from the Centers for Disease Control and Prevention Pediatric Nutrition Surveillance system. Pediatr 113(2):e81–e86.

Guastella AJ, Mitchell PB, Dadds MR. 2008. Oxytocin increases gaze to the eye region of human faces. Biol Psychiatr 63:3–5.

Gupta JK, Nikodem C. 2000. Case report: maternal posture in labour. Eur J Obstet Gyn R B 92:273–277.

Gurven M, Winking J. 2008. Collective action in action: prosocial behavior in and out of the laboratory. Am Anthropol 110(2):179–190.

Hachey DL, Silber GH, Wong WW, Garza C. 1989. Human lactation: II: endogenous fatty acid synthesis by the mammary gland. Pediatr Res 25(1):63–68.

Hagen DR, Shuey CP, Watkins JL. 1984. Restriction of uterine space reduces litter size in feral ossabaw swine. Biol Reprod 30:423–426.

Haile-Selassie Y, Saylor BZ, Deino A, Alene M, Latimer BM. 2010. New hominid fossils from Woranso-Mille (central Afar, Ethiopia) and taxonomy of early *Australopithecus*. Am J Phys Anthropol 141:406–417.

Haith MM. 1980. Rules that babies look by: the organization of newborn visual activity. Hillsdale, NJ: Erlbaum.

Hall AJ, Masel A, Bell K, Halliday JA, Shaw DC, VandeBerg JL. 2001. Characterization of baboon (*Papio hamadryas*) milk proteins. Biochem Genet 30(1–2):59–71.

Hallmayer J, Cleveland S, Torres A, Phillips J, Cohen B, Torigoe T, Miller J,

Fedele A, Collins J, Smith K, et al. 2011. Genetic heritability and shared environmental factors among twin pairs with autism. Arch Gen Psychiatr 68(11):1095–1102.

Halverson HM. 1937a. Studies of the grasping responses of early infancy: I. J Genet Psychol 51:371–392.

Halverson HM. 1937b. Studies of the grasping responses of early infancy: II: clinging strength. J Genet Psychol 51:393–424.

Halverson HM. 1937c. Studies of the grasping responses of early infancy: III: relation of activity and posture to grasping. J Genet Psychol 51:425–449.

Hamilton BE, Martin JA, Ventura SJ. 2011. Births: preliminary data for 2010. Natl Vital Stat Rep 60(2):1–25. www.cdc.gov/nchs/data/nvsr/nvsr60/nvsr60_02.pdf.

Hammond KA, Diamond J. 1997. Maximal sustained energy budgets in humans and animals. Nature 386:457–462.

Hamner SR, Seth A, Delp SL. 2010. Muscle contributions to propulsion and support during running. J Biomech 43:2709–2716.

Hanson K, Hrvoj-Mihic B, Semendeferi K. 2014. A dual comparative approach: integrating lines of evidence from human evolutionary neuroanatomy and neurodevelopmental disorders. Brain Behav Evol 84:135–155.

Harcourt A, Stewart K. 2007. Gorilla society: what we know and don't know. Evol Anthropol 16(4):147–158.

Hardyment C. 1983. Dream babies: child care from Locke to Spock. London: Jonathan Cape.

Hare B. 2014. Bonobos are xenophilic (abstract). Am J Phys Anthropol 58 (Suppl):251.

Hare B, Melis AP, Woods V, Hastings S, Wrangham R. 2007. Tolerance allows bonobos to outperform chimpanzees on a cooperative task. Curr Biol 17:1–6.

Hare B, Wobber V, Wrangham R. 2012. The self-domestication hypothesis: evolution of bonobo psychology due to selection against aggression. Anim Behav 83:573–585. doi:10.1016/j.anbehav.2011.12.007.

Harlow HF. 1958. The nature of love. Am Psychol 13:573–685.

Harlow HF, Dodsworth RO, Harlow MK. 1965. Total social isolation in monkeys. Proc Natl Acad Sci USA 54:90–97.

Harlow HF, Suomi SJ. 1971. Social recovery by isolation-reared monkeys. Proc Natl Acad Sci USA 68(7):1534–1538.

Harris JA, Rushton JP, Hampson E, Jackson DN. 1996. Salivary testosterone and self-report aggressive and pro-social personality characteristics in men and women. Aggressive Behav 22(5):321–331.

Harris KD, Mrsic-Flogel TD. 2013. Cortical connectivity and sensory coding. Nature 503(7474):51–58.

Harris RA, Tardif SD, Vinar T, Wildman DE, Rutherford JN, Rogers J, Worley KC, Aagaard KM. 2014. Evolutionary genetics and implications of small size and twinning in callitrichine primates. Proc Natl Acad Sci USA 111:1467–1472.

Hart D, Sussman R. 2005. Man the hunted; primates, predators and human evolution. Boulder, CO: Westview.

Harvey PH. 1992. Life-history patterns. In: Jones S, Martin R, Pilbeam D, editors. The Cambridge encyclopedia of human evolution. Cambridge: Cambridge University Press. 95–97.

Harvey PH, Clutton-Brock TH. 1985. Life history variation in primates. Evol 39:559–581.

Harvey PH, Pagel M. 1988. Diversity in the brain sizes of newborn mammals. BioScience 40:116–122.

Hassiotou F, Beltran A, Chetwynd E, Stuebe AM, Twigger AJ, Metzger P, Trengove N, Lai CT, Filgueira L, Blancafort P, et al. 2012. Breastmilk is a novel source of stem cells with multilineage differentiation potential. Stem Cells 30(10):2164–2174.

Hassiotou F, Hartmann PE. 2014. At the dawn of a new discovery: the potential of breast milk stem cells. Adv Nutr 5(6):770–778.

Hatt J-M, Zollikofer CPE, Thali MJ, Kircher PR, Morimoto N, Ponce de León MS. 2013. The Virtual Ape Project: more than a source of anatomy for veterinarians, anthropologists and primatologists. Paper presented at: 45th Annual Meeting of the American Association of Zoo Veterinarians, Salt Lake City, UT.

Häusler M, Schmid P. 1995. Comparison of the pelves of Sts 14 and AL 288-1: implications for birth and sexual dimorphism in australopithecines. J Hum Evol 29:363–383.

Hausman BL 2003. Mother's milk: breastfeeding controversies in American culture. London: Routledge.

Hawkes K. 1991. Showing off: test of a hypothesis about men's foraging goals. Ethol Sociobiol 12:29–54.

Hawkes K. 1997. Hadza women's time allocation, offspring provisioning and the evolution of long postmenopausal life spans. Curr Anthropol 38:551–577.

Hawkes K, Coxworth JE. 2013. Grandmothers and the evolution of human longevity. Evol Anthropol 22(6):294–302.

Hawkes K, O'Connell JF, Blurton Jones NG. 1989. Hardworking Hadza grandmothers. In: Standen V, Foley R, editors. Comparative socioecology: the behavioral ecology of humans and other mammals. London: Basil Blackwell. 341–366.

Hawkes K, O'Connell JF, Blurton Jones NG. 2014. More lessons from the Hadza about men's work. Hum Nature 25(4):596–619. doi:10.1007/s12110-014-9212-5.

Hawkes K, O'Connell JF, Blurton Jones NG, Alvarez H, Charnov EL. 1998. Grandmothering, menopause, and the evolution of human life histories. Proc Natl Acad Sci USA 95:1336–1339.

Hawkes K, O'Connell JF, Coxworth J. 2010. Family provisioning is not the only reason men hunt. Curr Anthropol 52(2):259–264.

Hawkes K, Paine RR, editors. 2006. The evolution of human life history. Santa Fe, NM: SAR Press.

Hegner RE, Wingfield JC. 1987. Effects of experimental manipulation of testosterone levels on parental investment and breeding success in male house sparrows. Auk 104(3):462–469.

Hendry S, Schwark H, Jones E, Yan J. 1987. Numbers and proportions of GABA-immunoreactive neurons in different areas of monkey cerebral cortex. J Neurosci 7:1503–1519.

Henrich J, Gil-White FJ. 2001. The evolution of prestige: freely conferred deference as a mechanism for enhancing the benefits of cultural transmission. Evol Human Behav 22(3):165–196.

Henrich J, Heine SJ, Norenzayan A. 2010. Beyond WEIRD: towards a broad-based behavioral science. Behav Brain Sci 33(2–3):111–135.

Hens SM, Konigsberg LW, Jungers WL. 2000. Estimating stature in fossil hominids: which regression model and reference sample to use? J Hum Evol 38:767–784.

Hermans EJ, Putman P, Van Honk J. 2006. Testosterone administration reduces empathetic behavior: a facial mimicry study. Psychoneuroendocrinol 31(7):859–866.

Herndon JG, Tigges J, Anderson DC, Klumpp SA, McClure HM. 1999. Brain weights throughout the lifespan of the chimpanzee. J Comp Neurol 409:567–579.

Hershkovitz P. 1977. Living new world monkeys (Platyrrhini). Vol. 1. Chicago, IL: University of Chicago Press.

Herting MM, Gautam P, Spielberg JM, Kan E, Dahl RE, Sowell ER. 2014. The role of testosterone and estradiol in brain volume changes across adolescence: a longitudinal structural MRI study. Hum Brain Mapp 35(11):5633–5645.

Hewett TE. 2005. Biomechanical measures of neuromuscular control and valgus loading of the knee predict anterior cruciate ligament injury risk in female athletes: a prospective study. Am J Sports Med 33:492–501.

Hewett TE. 2006. Anterior cruciate ligament injuries in female athletes: part 1: mechanisms and risk factors. Am J Sports Med 34:299–311.

Hewlett BS, editor. 1992. Father-child relations: cultural and biosocial contexts. New York: Aldine de Gruyter.

Hewlett BS, Lamb M, editors. 2005. Hunter-gatherer childhoods. Piscataway, NJ: Aldine/Transaction.

Hewlett BS, Winn S. 2014. Allomaternal nursing in humans. Curr Anthropol 55(2):1–30.

Hilário RR, Ferrari SF. 2009. Four breeding females in a free-ranging group of buffy-headed marmosets (*Callithrix flaviceps*). Folia Primatol 81:31–40.

Hill J, Inder T, Neil J, Dierker D, Harwell J, Van Essen D. 2010. Similar patterns of cortical expansion during human development and evolution. Proc Natl Acad Sci USA 107:13135–13140.

Hill K, Hurtado AM. 2009. Cooperative breeding in South American hunter-gatherers. Proc Roy Soc B 276(1674):3863–3870. doi:10.1098/rspb.2009.1061.

Hinde K. 2009. Richer milk for sons but more milk for daughters: sex-biased investment during lactation varies with maternal life history in rhesus macaques. Am J Hum Biol 21(4):512–519.

Hinde K. 2012. Mother's fat sends love letter to baby via the milk express: mammals suck milk. http://mammalssuck.blogspot.com/2012/06/mothers-fat-sends-love-letter-to-baby.html.

Hinde K. 2013. Lactational programming of infant behavioral phenotype. In: Clancy KBH, Hinde K, Rutherford JN, editors. Building babies: primate development in proximate and ultimate perspective. New York: Springer. 187–207.

Hinde K, Capitanio JP. 2010. Lactational programming? mother's milk energy predicts infant behavior and temperament in rhesus macaques (*Macaca mulatta*). Am J Primatol 72(6):552–559.

Hinde K, Carpenter AJ, Clay JS, Bradford BJ. 2014. Holsteins favor heifers, not bulls: biased milk production programmed during pregnancy as a function of fetal sex. PLoS One 9(2):e86169.

Hinde K, German JB. 2012. Food in an evolutionary context: insights from mother's milk. J Sci Food Agric 92(11):2219–2223.

Hinde K, Milligan LM. 2011. Primate milk: proximate mechanisms and ultimate perspectives. Evol Anthropol 20(1):9–23. doi:10.1002/evan.20289.

Hinde K, Power ML, Oftedal OT. 2009. Rhesus macaque milk: magnitude, sources, and consequences of individual variation over lactation. Am J Phys Anthropol 138(2):148–157.

Hirata S, Fuwa K, Sugama K, Kusunoki K, Takeshita H. 2011. Mechanism of birth in chimpanzees: humans are not unique among primates. Biol Letters 7:686–688.

Hirschenhauser K, Winkler H, Oliveira RF. 2003. Comparative analysis of male androgen responsiveness to social environment in birds: the effects of mating system and paternal incubation. Horm Behav 43(4):508–519.

Hoage RJ. 1982. Social and physical maturation in captive lion tamarins, *Leontopithecus rosalia* (primates: Callitrichidae). Smithson Contrib Zool 354. doi:10.5479/si.00810282.354.

Hofer MA. 1994. Early relationships as regulators of infant physiology and behavior. Acta Paediatr Suppl 1(397):9–18.

Hoffman KA, Mendoza SP, Henness M, Mason WA. 1995. Responses of infant titi monkeys, *Callicebus moloch*, to removal of one or both parents: evidence for parental attachment. Dev Psychobiol 28(7):399–407.

Hofman MA. 1983. Evolution of brain size in neonatal and adult placental mammals: a theoretical approach. J Theoret Biol 105:317–332.

Hofman MA. 2014. Evolution of the human brain: when bigger is better. Front Neuroanat 8:15. doi:10.3389/fnana.2014.00015.

Holliday M. 1971. Metabolic rate and organ size during growth from infancy to maturity and during late gestation and early infancy. Pediatr 47:169–172.

Holloway RL, Broadfield, DC, Yuan MS. 2004. The human fossil record. Vol. 3, Brain endocasts: the paleoneurological evidence. Hoboken, NJ: Wiley-Liss.

Holt AB, Cheek DB, Mellits ED, Hill D. E. 1975. Brain size and the relation of the primate to the nonprimate. In: Cheek DB, editor. Fetal and postnatal cellular growth: hormones and nutrition. New York: Wiley. 23–44.

Holt PG, Jones CA. 2000. The development of the immune system during pregnancy and early life. Allergy 55:688–697.

Hoogland J. 1994. Nepotism and infanticide among prairie dogs. In: Parmigiano S, vom Saal F, editors. Infanticide and parental care. Chur, Switzerland: Harwood Academic. 321–337.

Hooper AEC, Gangestad SW, Thompson ME, Bryan AD. 2011. Testosterone and romance: the association of testosterone with relationship commitment and satisfaction in heterosexual men and women. Am J Hum Biol 23(4):553–555.

Houseknecht KL, McGuire MK, Portocarrero CP, McGuire MA, Beerman K. 1997. Leptin is present in human milk and is related to maternal plasma leptin concentration and adiposity. Biochem Biophys Res Commun 240(3):742–747.

Hrdy SB. 1977. The langurs of Abu: female and male strategies of reproduction. Cambridge, MA: Harvard University Press.

Hrdy SB. 1979. Infanticide among animals: a classification, review and examination of the reproductive implications of females. Ethol Sociobiol 1:13–40.

Hrdy SB. 1981. The woman that never evolved. Cambridge, MA: Harvard University Press.

Hrdy SB. 1999. Mother Nature: a history of mothers, infants and natural selection. New York: Pantheon.

Hrdy SB. 2000. The optimal number of fathers: evolution, demography and history in the shaping of female mate preferences. Ann NY Acad Sci 907:75–96.

Hrdy SB. 2008. Cooperative breeding and the paradox of facultative fathering. In: Bridges R, editor. The neurobiology of the parental mind. New York: Academic. 405–414.

Hrdy SB. 2009. Mothers and others: the evolutionary origins of empathy and mutual understanding. Cambridge, MA: Harvard University Press.

Hrdy SB. 2010. Estimating the prevalence of shared care and cooperative breeding in the order Primates: an appendix to Mothers and Others: the evolutionary origins of mutual understanding (2009). http://nebula.wsimg.com/ 1b6aeb533ca713bb1528073d9c65926c?AccessKeyId=EFCDB7266BB382DCA1 11&disposition=0.

Hrdy SB. 2016. Development plus social selection in the emergence of "emotionally modern humans." In: Meehan CL, Crittenden AM, editors. Origins and implications of the evolution of childhood. Santa Fe, NM: SAR Press.

Hrvoj-Mihic B, Bienvenu T, Stefanacci L, Muotri A, Semendeferi K. 2013a. Evolution, development, and plasticity of the human brain: from molecules to bones. Front Hum Neurosci 7:707.

Hrvoj-Mihic B, Marchetto MCN, Gage FH, Semendeferi K, Muotri AR. 2014. Novel tools, classic techniques: evolutionary studies using primate pluripotent stem cells. Biol Psychiatr 75(12):929–935.

Hrvoj-Mihic B, Stefanacci L, Hanson KL, Korenberg JR, Muotri AR, Halgreen E, Jacobs B, Semendeferi K. 2013b. Morphology of pyramidal neurons in Williams syndrome. Paper presented at: 43rd Annual Meeting of the Society for Neuroscience, San Diego, CA (abstract).

Huck M, Fernandez-Duque E. 2013. When dads help: male behavioral care during primate infant development. In: Clancy KBH, Hinde K, Rutherford JN, editors. Building babies: primate development in proximate and ultimate perspective. New York: Springer. 361–385.

Huerta-Enochian GS, Katz VL, Fox LK, Hamlin JA, Kollath JP. 2006. Magnetic resonance–based serial pelvimetry: do maternal pelvic dimensions change during pregnancy? Am J Obstet Gynecol 194:1689–1694.

Humle T, Snowdon CT. 2008. Socially biased learning in the acquisition of a complex foraging task in juvenile cotton-top tamarins (*Saguinus oedipus*). Anim Behav 75:267–277.

Hutsler JJ, Zhang H. 2010. Increased dendritic spine densities on cortical projection neurons in autism spectrum disorders. Brain Res 1309:83–94.

Insel TR. 2003. Is social attachment an addictive disorder? Physiol Behav 79:351–357.

Insull W, Hirsch J, James T, Ahrens EH. 1959. The fatty acids of human milk: II: alterations produced by manipulation of caloric balance and exchange of dietary fats. J Clin Invest 38(2):443–450.

Irish JD, Guatelli-Steinberg D, Legge SS, de Ruiter DJ, Berger LR. 2013. Dental morphology and the phylogenetic "place" of Australopithecus sediba. Science 340. doi:10.1126/science.1233062.

Irons WG. 1998. Adaptively relevant environments vs. the environment of evolutionary adaptedness. Evol Anthropol 6:194–204.

Isler K, Kirk EC, Miller JMA, Albrecht GA, Gelvin BR, Martin RD. 2008. Endocranial volumes of primate species: scaling analyses using a comprehensive and reliable data set. J Hum Evol 55:967–978.

Isler K, van Schaik C. 2009. The expensive brain: a framework for explaining evolutionary changes in brain size. J Hum Evol. 57:392–400.

Isler K, van Schaik C. 2012. Allomaternal care, life history and brain size evolution in mammals. J Hum Evol 63(1):52–63.

Jaarsma P, Welin S. 2012. Autism as a natural human variation: reflections on the claims of the neurodiversity movement. Health Care Anal 20(1):20–30.

Jacobs B, Driscoll L, Schall M. 1997. Life-span dendritic and spine changes in areas 10 and 18 of human cortex: a quantitative Golgi study. J Comp Neurol 386:661–680.

Jacobs B, Schall M, Prather M, Kapler E, Driscoll L, Baca S, Jacobs J, Ford K, Wainwright M, Treml M. 2001. Regional dendritic and spine variation in human cerebral cortex: a quantitative Golgi study. Cereb Cortex 11:558–571.

Jaeggi AV, De Groot E, Stevens JM, van Schaik CP. 2013. Mechanisms of reciprocity in primates: testing for short-term contingency of grooming and food sharing in bonobos and chimpanzees. Evol Human Behav 34(2):69–77.

Jaeggi AV, Gurven M. 2013. Reciprocity explains food sharing in humans and other primates independent of kin selection and tolerated scrounging: a phylogenetic meta-analysis. Proc Biol Sci 280(1768):20131615.

Jaeggi AV, Stevens JM, van Schaik CP. 2010. Tolerant food sharing and reciprocity is precluded by despotism among bonobos but not chimpanzees. Am J Phys Anthropol 143(1):41–51.

Jaeggi AV, van Schaik CP. 2011. The evolution of food sharing in primates. Behav Ecol Sociobiol 65:2125–2140.

Jandó G, Mikó-Baráth E, Markó K, Hollódy K, Török B, Kovacs I. 2012. Early-onset binocularity in preterm infants reveals experience-dependent visual development in humans. Proc Natl Acad Sci USA 109(27):11049–11052.

Järvinen-Pasley A, Bellugi U, Reilly J, Mills DL, Galaburda A, Reiss AL, Korenberg JR. 2008. Defining the social phenotype in Williams syndrome: a model for linking genes, the brain, and behavior. Dev Psychopathol 20:1–35.

Jasienska G, Jasienski M, Ellison PT. 2012. Testosterone levels correlate with the number of children in human males, but the direction of the relationship depends on paternal education. Evol Human Behav 33(6):665–671.

Jelliffe DB, Jelliffe EF. 1978. The volume and composition of human milk in poorly nourished communities: a review. Am J Clin Nutr 31(3):492–515.

Jerison HJ. 1991. Brain size and the evolution of mind (James Arthur lecture on the evolution of the human brain). New York: American Museum of Natural History.

Johnson LD, Petto AJ, Schgal PK. 1991. Factors in the rejection and survival of captive cotton top tamarins (*Saguinus oedipus*). Am J Primatol 25:91–102.

Johnson RT, Burk JA, Kirkpatrick LA. 2007. Dominance and prestige as differential predictors of aggression and testosterone levels in men. Evol Human Behav 28(5):345–351.

Jones KE, Bielby J, Cardillo M, Fritz SA, O'Dell J, Orme CDL, Safi K, Sechrest W, Boakes EH, Carbone C, et al. 2009. PanTHERIA: a species-level database of life history, ecology, and geography of extant and recently extinct mammals. Ecol 90. doi:10.1890/08-1494.1.

Jordan B. 1993. Birth in four cultures: a cross-cultural investigation of childbirth in Yucatan, Holland, Sweden, and the United States. Long Grove, IL: Waveland.

Joseph R. 2000. The evolution of sex differences in language, sexuality, and visual-spatial skills. Arch Sex Behav 29(1):35–66.

Julian T, McKenry PC. 1989. Relationship of testosterone to men's family functioning at mid-life: a research note. Aggressive Behav 15(4):281–289.

Jusczyk PW, Houston DM, Newsome M. 1999. The beginnings of word segmentation in English-learning infants. Cognit Psychol 39(3–4):159–207.

Kaplan H, Hill K, Lancaster J, Hurtado AM. 2000. A theory of human life history evolution: diet, intelligence, and longevity. Evol Anthropol 9(4):156–185.

Karatas Z, Durmus Aydogdu S, Dinleyici EC, Colak O, Dogruel N. 2011. Breastmilk ghrelin, leptin, and fat levels changing foremilk to hindmilk: is that important for self-control of feeding? Eur J Pediatr 170(10):1273–1280.

Karmiloff K, Karmiloff-Smith A. 2001. Pathways to language: from fetus to adolescent. Cambridge, MA: Harvard University Press.

Karmiloff-Smith A, Grant J, Berthoud I, Davies M, Howlin P, Udwin O. 1997. Language and Williams syndrome: how intact is "intact"? Child Dev 68:246–262.

Kaufmann WE, Moser HW. 2000. Dendritic anomalies in disorders associated with mental retardation. Cerebral Cortex 10(10):981–991.

Kawai M. 1965. Newly acquired pre-cultural behavior of the natural troop of Japanese monkeys on Koshima islet. Primates 6(1):1–30.

Kempe V, Brooks, P. 2001. The role of diminutives in the acquisition of Russian gender: can elements of child-directed speech aid in learning morphology? Lang Learn 51:221–256.

Kent JC, Mitoulas LR, Cregan MD, Ramsay DT, Doherty DA, Hartmann PE. 2006. Volume and frequency of breastfeedings and fat content of breast milk throughout the day. Pediatr 117(3):e387–e395.

Ketterson ED, Nolan V, Wolf L, Ziegenfus C. 1992. Testosterone and avian life histories: effects of experimentally elevated testosterone on behavior and correlates of fitness in the dark-eyed junco (*Junco hyemalis*). Am Nat 140:980–999.

Keyes KM, Susser E, Cheslack-Postava K, Fountain C, Liu K, Bearman PS. 2012. Cohort effects explain the increase in autism diagnosis among children born from 1992 to 2003 in California. Int J Epidemiol 41(2):495–503.

Khaitovich P, Lockstone HE, Wayland MT, Tsang TM, Jayatilaka SD, Guo AJ, Zhou J, Somel M, Harris LW, Holmes E, et al. 2008. Metabolic changes in schizophrenia and human brain evolution. Genome Biol 9. http://doi.org/10.1186/gb-2008-9-8-r124.

Kinnally EL. 2013. Genome-environment in neurobiobehavioral development. In: Clancy KBH, Hinde K, Rutherford JN, editors. Building babies: primate development in proximate and ultimate perspective. New York: Springer. 155–168.

Kinney HC, Thach BT. 2009. The sudden infant death syndrome. N Engl J Med 361(8):795–805.

Kirkham NZ, Slemmer JA, Johnson SP. 2002. Visual statistical learning in infancy: evidence for a domain general learning mechanism. Cognition 83:B35–B42.

Klaus MH, Kennell JH. 1982. Parent-infant bonding. St. Louis, MO: Mosby.

Klei L, Sanders SJ, Murtha MT, Hus V, Lowe JK, Willsey AJ, Moreno-De-Luca D, Yu TW, Fombonne E, Geschwind D, et al. 2012. Common genetic variants, acting additively, are a major source of risk for autism. Mol Autism 3(1):9–13.

Kleiman DG, Malcolm JR. 1981. The evolution of male parental investment in mammals. In: Gubernick DJ, Klopfer PH, editors. Parental care in mammals. London: Plenum. 347–387.

Klingberg T, Vaidya CJ, Gabrieli JDE, Moseley ME, Hedehus M. 1999. Myelination and organization of the frontal white matter in children: a diffusion tensor MRI study. NeuroReport 10:2817–2821.

Knickmeyer RC, Gouttard S, Kang C, Evans D, Wilber K, Smith, JK, Gilmore JH. 2008. A structural MRI study of human brain development from birth to 2 years. J Neurosci 28(47):12176–12182.

Knott C. 2001. Female reproductive ecology of the apes: implications for human evolution. In: Ellison PT, editor. Reproductive ecology and human evolution. New York: Aldine de Gruyter. 429–463.

Knott C. 2015. Infant carrying in orangutans: implications for human evolution. Am J Phys Anthropol 156:192.

Kochetkova V. 1978. Paleoneurology. New York: Wiley.

Kochunov P, Duff Davis M. 2010. Development of structural MR brain imaging protocols to study genetics and maturation. Methods 50:136–146.

Koldovsky O. 1994. Hormonally active peptides in human milk. Acta Paediatr Suppl 402:89–93.

Koletzko B, Beyer J, Brands B, Demmelmair H, Grote V, Haile G, Gruszfeld D, Rzehak P, Socha P, Weber M, et al. 2013. Early influences of nutrition on postnatal growth. Nestle Nutr Inst Workshop Ser 71:11–27.

Koletzko B, von Kries R. 2001. Are there long term protective effects of breast feeding against later obesity? Nutr Health 15(3–4):225–236.

Koletzko B, von Kries R, Monasterolo RC, Subias JE, Scaglioni S, Giovannini M, Beyer J, Demmelmair H, Anton B, Gruszfeld D, et al. 2009. Infant feeding and later obesity risk. Adv Exp Med Biol 646:15–29.

Kong A, Frigge ML, Masson G, Besenbacher S, Sulem P, Magnusson G, Gudjonsson SA, Sigurdsson A, Jonasdottir A, Wong WS, et al. 2012. Rate of de novo mutations and the importance of father's age to disease risk. Nature 488(7412):471–475.

Konner M. 2010. How childhood has evolved. Chron High Educ (May 9).

Konner M. 2011. The evolution of childhood: relationships, emotion, mind. Cambridge MA: Belknap.

Konner M, Worthman C. 1980. Nursing frequency, gonadal function, and birth spacing among !Kung hunter-gatherers. Science 207(4432):788–791.

Kornienko O, Clemans KH, Out D, Granger DA. 2014. Hormones, behavior, and social network analysis: exploring associations between cortisol, testosterone, and network structure. Horm Behav 66(3):534–544.

Kraft TS, Venkataraman VV, Dominy NJ. 2014. A natural history of human tree climbing. J Hum Evol 71:105–118.

Kramer KL, Ellison PT. 2010. Pooled energy budgets: resituating human energy-allocation trade-offs. Evol Anthropol 19(4):136–147.

Kramer KL, Otárola-Castillo E. 2015. When mothers need others: the impact of hominin life history evolution on cooperative breeding. J Hum Evol 84:16–24.

Krantz GS. 1968. Brain size and hunting ability in earliest man. Curr Anthropol 9:450–451.

Krauss AN, Auld P. 1975. Metabolic rate of neonates with congenital heart disease. Arch Disease Child 50:539–541.

Krogman W. 1951. The scars of human evolution. Sci Am 185:54–57.

Kruger DJ, Fitzgerald CJ. 2011. Reproductive strategies and relationship preferences associated with prestigious and dominant men. Pers Indiv Differ 50(3):365–369.

Kuhl PK. 2000. A new view of language acquisition. Proc Natl Acad Sci USA 97(22):11850–11857.

Kuhl PK. 2004. Early language acquisition: cracking the speech code. Nat Rev Neurosci 5(11):831–843.

Kuhl PK, Coffey-Corina S, Padden D, Dawson G. 2005. Links between social and linguistic processing of speech in preschool children with autism: behavioral and electrophysiological measures. Dev Sci 8(1):F1–F12.

Kurki HK. 2007. Protection of obstetric dimensions in a small-bodied human sample. Am J Phys Anthropol 133:1152–1165.

Kurki HK. 2013. Skeletal variability in the pelvis and limb skeleton of humans: does stabilizing selection limit female pelvic variation? Am J Hum Biol 25:795–802.

Kuwahata H, Adachi I, Fujita K, Tomonaga M, Matsuzawa T. 2004. Development of schematic face preference in macaque monkeys. Behav Process 66:17–21.

Kuzawa C. 1998. Adipose tissue in human infancy and childhood: an evolutionary perspective. Yearb Phys Anthropol 41:177–209.

Kuzawa CW, Chugani HT, Grossman LI, Lipovich L, Muzik O, Hof PR, Wildman DE, Sherwood CC, Leonard WR, Lange N. 2014. Metabolic costs and evolutionary implications of human brain development. Proc Natl Acad Sci USA 111:13010–13015.

Kuzawa CW, Gettler LT, Muller MN, McDade TW, Feranil AB. 2009. Fatherhood, pairbonding, and testosterone in the Philippines. Horm Behav 56(4):429–435.

Kuzawa CW, Quinn EA. 2009. Developmental origins of adult function and health: evolutionary hypotheses. Ann Rev Anthropol 38:131–147.

Lacruz RS, Rozzi FR, Bromage TG. 2005. Dental enamel hypoplasia, age at death, and weaning in the Taung child. S Afr J Sci 101:567–569.

Lai MC, Lombardo MV, Chakrabarti B, Baron-Cohen S. 2013. Subgrouping the autism "spectrum": reflections on DSM-5. PLoS Biology 11(4):e1001544.

Lancaster J. 1978. Carrying and sharing in human evolution. Hum Nat 1:82–89.

Lancaster JB. 1985. Evolutionary perspectives on sex differences in the higher primates. In: Rossi AS, editor. Gender and the life course. Hawthorne, NY: Aldine de Gruyter. 3–27.

Lancaster JB, Lancaster CS. 1983. Parental investment: the hominid investment. In: Ortner D, editor. How humans adapt: a biocultural odyssey: proceedings of the Seventh International Smithsonian Symposium. Washington, DC: Smithsonian Institution Press. 33–66.

Lancaster JB, Lancaster CS. 1987. The watershed: changes in parental investment and family formation strategies in the course of human evolution. In: Lancaster JB, Altmann J, Rossi A, Sherrod L, editors. Parenting across the life span. Hawthorne, NY: Aldine. 187–205.

Lapiz MDS, Fulford A, Muchimapura S, Mason R, Parker T, Marsden CA. 2003. Influence of postweaning social isolation in the rat on brain development, conditioned behavior, and neurotransmission. Neurosci Behav Physiol 33(1):13–29.

LaVelle M. 1995. Natural selection and developmental sexual variation in the human pelvis. Am J Phys Anthropol 98:59–72.

Lawrence PR, Nohria N. 2002. Driven: how human nature shapes our choices. Cambridge, MA: Harvard Business School Press.

Leckman J, Kuint J, Eidelman A. 1999. The nature of the mother's tie to her infant: maternal bonding under conditions of proximity, separation and potential loss. J Child Psychol Psychiatr 40(6):929–939.

Lee RB. 1980. Lactation, ovulation, infanticide, and women's work: a study of hunter-gatherer population regulation. In: Cohen MN, Malpass RS, Klein HG, editors. Biosocial mechanisms of population regulation. New Haven, CT: Yale University Press. 321–348.

Lee RB, DeVore I, editors. 1968. Man the hunter. Chicago, IL: Aldine.

Leigh SR. 2004. Brain growth, life history, and cognition in primate and human evolution. Am J Primatol 62:139–164.

Lenhard MS, Johnson TRC, Weckbach S, Nikolaou K, Friese K, Hasbargen U. 2010. Pelvimetry revisited: analyzing cephalopelvic disproportion. Eur J Radiol 74:e108–e112.

Leonard WR, Robertson ML, Snodgrass J, Kuzawa CW. 2003. Metabolic correlates of hominid brain evolution. Comp Biochem Physiol A: Mol Integr Physiol 136:5–15.

Leutenegger W. 1973. Maternal-fetal weight relationships in primates. Folia Primatol 20:280–293.

Leutenegger W. 1978. Scaling of sexual dimorphism in body size and breeding system in primates. Nature 272:610–611.

Leutenegger W. 1979. Evolution of litter size in primates. Am Naturalist 114:525–531.

Leutenegger W. 1982. Encephalization and obstetrics in primates, with particular reference to human evolution. In: Armstrong E, Falk D, editors. Primate brain evolution: methods and concepts. New York: Plenum. 85–96.

Leutenegger W. 1987. Neonatal brain size and neurocranial dimensions in Pliocene hominids: implications for obstetrics. J Hum Evol 16:291–296.

Levitt P. 2003. Structural and functional maturation of the developing primate brain. J Pediatr 143:S35–S45.

Levy O. 2007. Innate immunity of the newborn: basic mechanisms and clinical correlates. Nat Rev Immunol 7:379–390.

Lewis DA, Curley AA, Glausier JR, Volk DW. 2012. Cortical parvalbumin interneurons and cognitive dysfunction in schizophrenia. Trends Neurosci 35:57–67.

Lewton KL. 2012. Evolvability of the primate pelvic girdle. Evol Biol 39:126–139.

Ley SH, Hanley AJ, Sermer M, Zinman B, O'Connor DL. 2012. Associations of prenatal metabolic abnormalities with insulin and adiponectin concentrations in human milk. Am J Clin Nutr 95(4):867–874.

Lieberman DE. 2015. Human locomotion and heat loss: an evolutionary perspective. Comp Physiol 5(1):99–117.

Liston WA. 2003. Rising caesarean section rates: can evolution and ecology explain some of the difficulties of modern childbirth? J R Soc Med 96:559–561.

Liu H-M, Kuhl, PK, Tsao, F-M. 2003. An association between mothers' speech clarity and infants' speech discrimination skills. Developmental Sci 6:F1–F10.

Liu X, Somel M, Tang L, Yan Z, Jiang X, Guo S, Yuan Y, He L, Oleksiak A, Zhang Y, et al. 2012. Extension of cortical synaptic development distinguishes humans from chimpanzees and macaques. Genome Res 22:611–622.

Locke R. 2002. Preventing obesity: the breast milk–leptin connection. Acta Paediatr 91(9):891–894.

Long JA. 2012. Dawn of the deed. Chicago, IL: University of Chicago Press.

Lonnerdal B, Forsum E, Gebre-Medhin M, Hambraeus L. 1976. Breast milk composition in Ethiopian and Swedish mothers: II: Lactose, nitrogen, and protein contents. Am J Clin Nutr 29:1134–1141.

Lordkipanidze D, Vekua A, Ferring R, Rightmire GP, Zollikofer CPE, Ponce de León MS, Agusti J, Kiladze G, Mouskhelishvili A, Nioradze M, et al. 2006. A fourth hominin skull from Dmanisi, Georgia. Anat Rec 288A:1146–1157.

Lovejoy CO. 1981. The origin of man. Science 211(4480):341–350.

Lovejoy CO. 2009. Reexamining human origins in the light of *Ardipithecus ramidus*. Science 326(5949):74e1–74e8.

Lovejoy CO, Heiple KG, Burstein AH. 1973. The gait of *Australopithecus*. Am J Phys Anthropol 38:757–779.

Lovejoy CO, Suwa G, Simpson SW, Matternes JH, White TD. 2009a. The great divides: *Ardipithecus ramidus* reveals the postcrania of our last common ancestor with African apes. Science 326:100–106.

Lovejoy CO, Suwa G, Spurlock L, Asfaw B, White TD. 2009b. The pelvis and femur of *Ardipithecus ramidus*: the emergence of upright walking. Science 326:71e1–71e6.

Ludington-Hoe SM, Hosseini R, Torowicz DL. 2005. Skin-to-skin contact (kangaroo care) analgesia for preterm infant heel stick. AACN Clin Issues 16(3):373–387.

Lukas D, Clutton-Brock T. 2013. The evolution of social monogamy in mammals. Science 341(6145):526–530.

Lyle HF, Smith EA. 2014. The reputational and social network benefits of prosociality in an Andean community. Proc Natl Acad Sci USA 111(13):4820–4825.

Lynch M. 2007. The frailty of adaptive hypotheses for the origins of organismal complexity. Proc Natl Acad Sci USA 104:8597–8604.

Magill C, Ashley G, Freeman K. 2013. Ecosystem variability and human habitats in eastern Africa. Proc Natl Acad Sci USA 110(4):1167–1174.

Maharaj D. 2010. Assessing cephalopelvic disproportion: back to the basics. Obstetr Gynecol Surv 65:387–395.

Mallinson JJC. 1965. Notes on the nutrition, social behavior and reproduction of Hapalidae in captivity. Int Zoo Yearb 5:137–140.

Malone N, Fuentes A. 2009. The ecology and evolution of hylobatid communities: causal and contextual factors underlying inter- and intraspecific variation. In: Lappan S, Whittaker DJ, editors. The gibbons: new perspectives on small ape socioecology and population biology. New York: Springer. 241–264.

Mandel DR, Jusczyk PW, Pisoni DB. 1995. Infants' recognition of the sound patterns of their own names. Psychol Sci 6:314–317.

Mangold-Wirz K. 1966. Cerebralisation und ontogenesemodus bei eutherien. Cells Tissues Organs 63:449–508.

Maningat PD, Sen P, Rijnkels M, Sunehag AL, Hadsell DL, Bray M, Haymond MW. 2009. Gene expression in the human mammary epithelium during lactation: the milk fat globule transcriptome. Physiol Genomics 37(1):12–22.

Mann AE. 1972. Hominid and cultural origins. Man 7:379–386.

Mann J. 1992. Nurturance or negligence? maternal psychology and behavioral preference among preterm twins. In: Barkow J, Cosmides L, Tooby J, editors. The adapted mind. New York: Oxford University Press. 367–390.

Manuck SB, Marsland AL, Flory JD, Gorka A, Ferrell RE, Hariri AR. 2010. Salivary testosterone and a trinucleotide (CAG) length polymorphism in the androgen receptor gene predict amygdala reactivity in men. Psychoneuroendocrinol 35(1):94–104.

Marchal F. 2000. A new morphometric analysis of the hominid pelvic bone. J Hum Evol 38:347–365.

Marchetto MC, Carromeu C, Acab A. Yu D, Yeo GW, Mu Y, Chen G, Gage FH, Muotri AR. 2010. A model for neural development and treatment of Rett syndrome using human induced pluripotent stem cells. Cell 143(4):527–539.

Marín O. 2012. Interneuron dysfunction in psychiatric disorders. Nat Rev Neurosci 13:107–120.

Marin-Padilla M. 1970. Prenatal and early postnatal ontogenesis of the human motor cortex: a Golgi study: I: the sequential development of the cortical layers. Brain Res 23(2):167–183.

Markram H, Toledo-Rodriguez M, Wang Y, Gupta A, Silberberg G, Wu C. 2004.

Interneurons of the neocortical inhibitory system. Nat Rev Neurosci 5(10):793–807.

Marlowe FW. 2001. Male contribution to diet and female reproductive success among foragers. Curr Anthropol 42:755–760.

Marlowe FW. 2003. A critical period for provisioning by Hadza men: implications for pair bonding. Evol Hum Behav 24:217–229.

Marlowe FW. 2005. Hunter-gatherers and human evolution. Evol Anthropol 14(2):54–67.

Marlowe FW. 2006. Central place provisioning: the Hadza as an example. In: Hohmann G, Robbins MM, Boesch C, editors. Feeding ecology in apes and other primates: ecological, physical and behavioral aspects. Cambridge: Cambridge University Press. 359–377.

Marlowe FW. 2007. Hunting and gathering: the human sexual division of foraging labor. Cross Cult Res 41(2):170–195.

Marlowe FW. 2010. The Hadza: hunter-gatherers of Tanzania. Berkeley: University of California Press.

Marlowe FW, Berbesque JC. 2012. The human operational sex ratio: effects of marriage, concealed ovulation, and menopause on mate competition. J Hum Evol 63(6):834–842.

Marshall AJ, Hohmann G. 2005. Urinary testosterone levels of wild male bonobos (*Pan paniscus*) in the Lomako forest, Democratic Republic of Congo. Am J Primatol 65(1):87–92.

Martin EMB, Burkart JM. 2013. Common marmosets preferentially share difficult to obtain food items. Folia Primatol 84:281–282.

Martin LJ, Spicer DM, Lewis MH, Gluck JP, Cork LC. 1991. Social deprivation of infant rhesus monkeys alters the chemoarchitecture of the brain: I: subcortical regions. J Neurosci 11(11):3344–3358.

Martin LJ, Woo JG, Geraghty SR, Altaye M, Davidson BS, Banach W, Dolan LM, Ruiz-Palacios GM, Morrow AL. 2006. Adiponectin is present in human milk and is associated with maternal factors. Am J Clin Nutr 83(5):1106–1111.

Martin MA, Sela DA. 2013. Infant gut microbiota: developmental influences and health outcomes. In: Clancy KBH, Hinde K, Rutherford JN, editors. Building babies: primate development in proximate and ultimate perspective. New York: Springer. 233–256.

Martin RD. 1983. Human brain evolution in an ecological context: fifty-second James Arthur lecture on the evolution of the human brain. New York: American Museum of Natural History.

Martin RD. 1990. Primate origins and evolution. Princeton, NJ: Princeton University Press.

Martin RD. 1992. Primate reproduction. In: Jones S, Martin R, Pilbeam D, editors. The Cambridge encyclopedia of human evolution. Cambridge: Cambridge University Press. 86–90.

Martin RD. 1996. Scaling of the mammalian brain: the maternal energy hypothesis. News Physiol Sci 11:149–156.

Martin RD. 1998. Comparative aspects of human brain evolution: scaling, energy costs and confounding variables. In: Jablonski NG. Aiello LC, editors. The origin and diversification of language. San Francisco: California Academy of Science. 35–68.

Martin RD. 2003. Human reproduction: a comparative background for medical hypotheses. J Reprod Immunol 59:111–135.

Martin RD. 2007. The evolution of human reproduction: a primatological perspective. Am J Phys Anthropol 134:59–84.

Martin RD. 2013. How we do it: the evolution and future of human reproduction. New York: Basic.

Martin RD, MacLarnon AM. 1990. Reproductive patterns in primates and other mammals: the dichotomy between altricial and precocial offspring. In: DeRousseau CJ, editor. Primate life history and evolution. New York: Wiley-Liss. 47–79.

Mascaro J, Hackett PD, Gouzoules H, Lori A, Rilling JK. 2013a. Behavioral and genetic correlates of the neural response to crying among human fathers. Soc Cogn Affect Neur. doi:10.1093/scan/nst166.

Mascaro JS, Hackett PD, Rilling JK. 2013b. Testicular volume is inversely correlated with nurturing-related brain activity in human fathers. Proc Natl Acad Sci USA 110(39):15746–15751.

Matthiesen A-S, Ransjö-Arvidson A-B, Nissen E, Uvnäs-Moberg K. 2001. Postpartum maternal oxytocin release by newborns: effects of infant hand massage and sucking. Birth 28:13–19. doi:10.1046/j.1523-536x.2001.00013.x.

Mattila M-L, Kielinen M, Jussila K, Linna S-L, Bloigu R, Ebeling H, Moilanen I. 2007. An epidemiological and diagnostic study of Asperger syndrome according to four sets of diagnostic criteria. J Am Acad Child Adol Psychiatr 46(5):636–646.

Mazur A. 1995. Biosocial models of deviant behavior among male army veterans. Biol Psychol 41(3):271–293.

Mazur A. 2009. The age-testosterone relationship in black, white, and

Mexican-American men, and reasons for ethnic differences. Aging Male 12(2–3):66–76.

Mazur A. 2014. Testosterone of young husbands rises with children in the home. Andrology 2(1):125–129.

Mazur A, Michalek J. 1998. Marriage, divorce, and male testosterone. Soc Forces 77(1):315–330.

McDade TW. 2005. The ecologies of human immune function. Ann Rev Anthropol 34:495–521.

McDade TW, Worthman CM. 1998. The weanling's dilemma reconsidered: a biocultural analysis of breastfeeding ecology. J Dev Behav Pediatr 19(4):286–299.

McFarlin SC, Barks SK, Tocheri MW, Massey JS, Eriksen AB, Fawcett KA, Stoinski TS, Hof PR, Bromage TG, Mudakikwa A, et al. 2013. Early brain growth cessation in wild Virunga mountain gorillas (*Gorilla beringei beringei*). Am J Primatol 75:450–463.

McGrew WC. 1979. Evolutionary implications of sex differences in chimpanzee predation and tool use. In: Hamburg DA, McCown E, editors. The great apes. Menlo Park, CA: Benjamin Cummings. 441–464.

McIntyre M, Gangestad SW, Gray PB, Chapman JF, Burnham TC, O'Rourke MT, Thornhill R. 2006. Romantic involvement often reduces men's testosterone levels—but not always: the moderating role of extrapair sexual interest. J Pers Soc Psychol 91(4):642–651.

McKenna JJ. 1986. An anthropological perspective on the sudden infant death syndrome (SIDS): the role of parental breathing cues and speech breathing adaptations. Med Anthropol 10:9–53.

McKenna JJ, Ball H, Gettler LT. 2007. Mother-infant co-sleeping, breastfeeding and sudden infant death syndrome: what biological anthropology has discovered about normal infant sleep and pediatric sleep medicine. Yearb Phys Anthropol 50:133–161.

McKenna JJ, Gettler L. 2007. Aspects of mother-infant co-sleeping with breastfeeding in the western industrialized context: a biocultural perspective. In: Hale TW, Hartmann PE, editors. Textbook of human lactation. Amarillo, TX: Hale. 271–302.

McKenna JJ, Gettler LT. 2012. It's dangerous to be an infant: on-going relevance of John Bowlby's environment of evolutionary adaptedness (the EEA) in promoting healthier births, safer maternal-infant sleep, and breastfeeding in a contemporary western industrial context. In: Narvaez D, Panksepp J, Schore A, Gleason T, editors. Evolution, early experience and human development: from research to practice and policy. New York: Oxford University Press. 439–452.

McKenna JJ, Gettler LT. 2016. There is no such thing as infant sleep, there is no such thing as breastfeeding, there is only breastsleeping. Acta Paediatr 105:17–21.

McKenna JJ, Mosko S. 1990. Evolution and the sudden infant death syndrome (SIDS): part III: infant arousal and parent-infant co-sleeping. Hum Nat 1:291–330.

McKenna JJ, Mosko S. 2000. Mother infant cosleeping: toward a new scientific beginning. In: Byard R, Krous H, editors. Sudden infant death syndrome: problems, puzzles, possibilities. New York: Arnold. 258–272.

McKenna JJ, Mosko S, Richard C, Drummond S. 1997. Bed sharing promotes breast-feeding. Pediatr 100:214–219.

McKenna JJ, Mosko S, Richard C, Drummond S, Hunt L Cetal M, Arpaia J. 1994. Mutual behavioral and physiological influences among solitary and co-sleeping mother-infant pairs: implications for SIDS. Early Hum Dev 38:182–201.

McKenna JJ, Thoman E, Anders T, Sadeh A, Schechtman V, Glotzbach S. 1993. Infant-parent co-sleeping in evolutionary perspective: implications for understanding infant sleep development and the sudden infant death syndrome (SIDS). Sleep 16:263–282.

McLachlan RI, Wreford NG, O'Donnell L, de Kretser DM, Robertson DM. 1996. The endocrine regulation of spermatogenesis: independent roles for testosterone and FSH. J Endocrinol 148(1):1–9.

Meehan CL. 2005. The effects of residential locality on parental and alloparental investment among the Aka of the Central African Republic. Hum Nat 16:58–80.

Meehan CL, Crittenden AM, editors. 2016. Origins and implications of the evolution of childhood. Santa Fe, NM: SAR Press.

Meehan CL, Hawks S. 2013. Cooperative breeding and attachment among the Aka foragers. In: Quinn N, Mageo J, editors. Attachment reconsidered: cultural perspectives on a western theory. New York: Palgrave. 85–113.

Melnik BC, John SM, Schmitz G. 2013. Milk is not just food but most likely a genetic transfection system activating mTORC1 signaling for postnatal growth. Nutr J 12. doi:10.1186/1475-2891-12-103.

Meltzoff AN, Moore MK. 1977. Imitation of facial and manual gestures by human neonates. Science 198(4312):75–78.

Mercuri E, Baranello G, Romeo DM, Cesarini L, Ricci D. 2007. The development of vision. Early Hum Dev 83:795–800.

Mesgarani N, Cheung C, Johnson K, Chang EF. 2014. Phonetic feature encoding in human superior temporal gyrus. Science 343(6174):1006–1010.

Meyer M, Kircher M, Gansauge MT, Li H, Racimo F, Mallick S, Schraiber JG, Jay F, Prüfer K, de Filippo C, et al. 2012. A high-coverage genome sequence from an archaic Denisovan individual. Science 338(6104):222–226.

Meyer-Lindenberg A, Mervis CB, Berman KF. 2006. Neural mechanisms in Williams syndrome: a unique window to genetic influences on cognition and behaviour. Nat Rev Neurosci 7:380–393.

Miller DJ, Duka T, Stimpson CD, Schapiro SJ, Baze WB, McArthur MJ, Sherwood CC. 2012. Prolonged myelination in human neocortical evolution. Proc Natl Acad Sci USA 109:16480–16485.

Miller EM, McConnell DS. 2015. Milk immunity and reproductive status among Ariaal women of northern Kenya. Ann Hum Biol 42(1):76–83.

Milligan, LA. 2013. Do bigger brains mean better milk? In: Clancy KBH, Hinde K, Rutherford JN, editors. Building babies: primate development in proximate and ultimate perspective. New York: Springer. 209–231.

Milligan LA, Gibson SV, Williams LE, Power ML. 2008. The composition of milk from Bolivian squirrel monkeys (*Saimiri boliviensis boliviensis*). Am J Primatol 70(1):35–42.

Milsom SR, Blum WF, Gunn AJ. 2008. Temporal changes in insulin-like growth factors I and II and in insulin-like growth factor binding proteins 1, 2, and 3 in human milk. Horm Res 69(5):307–311.

Miralles O, Sanchez J, Palou A, Pico C. 2006. A physiological role of breast milk leptin in body weight control in developing infants. Obesity 14(8):1371–1377.

Mitani JC. 2009. Male chimpanzees form enduring and equitable social bonds. Anim Behav 77(3):633–640.

Mitani JC, Watts, D. 1997. The evolution of non-maternal caretaking among anthropoid primates: do helpers help? Behav Ecol Sociobiol 40:213–230.

Mitchell EA, Thompson JMD. 1995. Cosleeping increases the risks of the sudden infant death syndrome, but sleeping in the parent's bedroom lowers it. In: Rognum TO, editor. Sudden infant death syndrome in the nineties. Oslo: Scandinavian University Press. 266–269.

Mizuno Y, Takeshita H, Matsuzawa T. 2006. Behavior of infant chimpanzees during the night in the first 4 months of life: smiling and suckling in relation to behavioral state. Infancy 9:221–240.

Mohammad MA, Haymond MW. 2013. Regulation of lipid synthesis genes and milk fat production in human mammary epithelial cells during secretory activation. Am J Physiol Endocrinol Metab 305(6):e700–e716.

Monnot M. 1999. Function of infant-directed speech. Hum Nat: Int Bios 10:415–443.

Montagu A. 1961. Neonatal and infant immaturity in man. JAMA 178:56–57.

Montagu A. 1986. Touching: The human significance of the skin. 3rd ed. New York: Harper and Row.

Moon RY. 2011. SIDS and other sleep-related infant deaths: expansion of recommendations for a safe infant sleeping environment. Pediatr 128:e1341–e1367.

Moore DR. 1985. Postnatal development of the mammalian central auditory system and the neural consequences of auditory deprivation. Acta Oto-Laryngol 99(S421):19–30.

Morein B, Blomqvist G, Hu K. 2007. Immune responsiveness in the neonatal period. J Comp Pathol 137:S27–S31.

Morimoto N, Ponce de León MS, Nishimura T, Zollikofer CPE. 2011. Femoral morphology and femoropelvic musculoskeletal anatomy of humans and great apes: a comparative virtopsy study. Anat Rec 294:1433–1445.

Mosko S, Richard C, McKenna J. 1997. Infant arousals during mother-infant bedsharing; implications for infant sleep and SIDS research. Pediatr 100(5):841–849.

Mosko S, Richard C, McKenna J, Drummond S. 1996. Infant sleep architecture during bedsharing and possible implications for SIDS. Sleep 19:677–684.

Moujahid A, D'Anjou DA, Graña M. 2014. Energy demands of diverse spiking cells from the neocortex, hippocampus, and thalamus. Front Comp Neurosci 41(8):1–12.

Mountcastle VB. 1979. An organizing principle for cerebral function: the unit module and the distributed system. In: Schmitt FO, Worden FG, editors. The neurosciences: fourth study program. Cambridge, MA: MIT Press. 21–42.

Muehlenbein MP, Bribiescas RG. 2005. Testosterone-mediated immune functions and male life histories. Am J Hum Biol 17:527–558.

Muehlenbein MP, Watts DP, Whitten P. 2004. Dominance rank and fecal testosterone levels in adult male chimpanzees (*Pan troglodytes schweinfurthii*) at Ngogo, Kibale national park, Uganda. Am J Primatol 64:71–82.

Mueller NT, Bakacs E, Combellick J, Grigoryan Z, Dominguez-Bello MG. 2015. The infant microbiome development: mom matters. Trends Molec Med 21:109–117.

Muir D. 2000. Early ontogeny of locomotor behaviour: a comparison between altricial and precocial animals. Brain Res Bull 53:719–726.

Mulle J, Penagarikano O, Warren ST. 2007. Path to understanding the pathophysiology of fragile X syndrome. Future Neurol 2:567–575.

Muller F, O'Rahilly R. 2006. The amygdaloid complex and the medial and lateral ventricular eminences in staged human embryos. J Anat 208:547–564.

Muller MN, Marlowe FW, Bugumba R, Ellison PT. 2009. Testosterone and paternal care in East African foragers and pastoralists. Proc R Soc B 276(1655):347–354.

Muller MN, Mitani JC. 2005. Conflict and cooperation in wild chimpanzees. Adv Study Behav 35:275–331.

Muller MN, Wrangham RW. 2004. Dominance, aggression and testosterone in wild chimpanzees: a test of the challenge hypothesis. Anim Behav 67:113–123.

Nathanielsz PW, Vaughan CC. 2001. The prenatal prescription. New York: HarperCollins.

Nathavitharana KA, Catty D, McNeish AS. 1994. IgA antibodies in human milk: epidemiological markers of previous infections? Arch Dis Child 71:F192–F197.

Navarete A, van Schaik CP, Isler K. 2011. Energetics and the evolution of human brain size. Nature 480:91–93.

Naya DE, Spangenberg L, Naya H, Bozinovic F. 2013. How does evolutionary variation in basal metabolic rates arise? a statistical assessment and a mechanistic model. Evol 67(5):1463–1476.

Neilson JP, Verkuyl DA, Bannerman C. 2005. Tape measurement of symphysis-fundal height in twin pregnancies. BJOG 95(10):1054–1059.

Nelson RC, Brooks CM, Pike NL. 1977. Biomechanical comparison of male and female distance runners. Ann NY Acad Sci 301:793–807.

Neu J, Rushing J. 2011. Cesarean versus vaginal delivery: long-term infant outcomes and the hygiene hypothesis. Clin Perinatol 38:321–331.

Neubauer SH. 1990. Lactation in insulin-dependent diabetes. Prog Food Nutr Sci 14(4):333–370.

Neubauer SH, Hublin J-J. 2012. The evolution of human brain development. Evol Biol 39:568–586. doi:10.1007/s11692-011-9156-1.

Neville MC, Morton J. 2001. Physiology and endocrine changes underlying human lactogenesis II. J Nutr 131(11):3000S–3008S.

Newburg DS, Walker WA. 2007. Protection of the neonate by the innate immune system of developing gut and of human milk. Pediatr Res 61:2–8.

Newburg DS, Woo JG, Morrow AL. 2010. Characteristics and potential functions of human milk adiponectin. J Pediatr 156(2 Suppl):S41–S46.

Newman JD. 2004. Motherese by any other name: mother-infant communication in non-hominin mammals. Behav Brain Sci 27(4):519–520.

Newman JD. 2007. Neural circuits underlying crying and cry responding in mammals. Behav Brain Res 182(2):155–165.

Newman T, Lengyel C, Pavlicev M, Muglia LJ. 2014. Human evolution, genomics and birth timing: new approaches for investigating preterm birth. NeoReviews 15:e17–e27.

Noakes DE, Parkinson TJ, England, GCW. 2001. Arthur's veterinary reproduction and obstetrics. 8th ed. Edinburgh: Saunders.

Noë R, Sluijter AA. 1995. Which adult male savanna baboons form coalitions? Int J Primatol 16(2):77–105.

Nommsen LA, Lovelady CA, Heinig MJ, Lönnerdal B, Dewey KG. 1991. Determinants of energy, protein, lipid, and lactose concentrations in human milk during the first 12 mo[nths] of lactation: the DARLING study. Am J Clin Nutr 53(2):457–465.

Nommsen-Rivers LA, Chantry CJ, Peerson JM, Cohen RJ, Dewey KG. 2010. Delayed onset of lactogenesis among first-time mothers is related to maternal obesity and factors associated with ineffective breastfeeding. Am J Clin Nutr 92(3):574–584.

Nommsen-Rivers LA, Dolan LM, Huang B. 2012. Timing of stage II lactogenesis is predicted by antenatal metabolic health in a cohort of primiparas. Breastfeed Med 7(1):43–49.

Numan M, Insel T. 2003. The neurobiology of parental behavior. New York: Springer.

Nunes S, Fite JE, French JA. 2000. Variation in steroid hormones associated with infant care behaviour and experience in male marmosets (*Callithrix kuhlii*). Anim Behav 60:857–865.

Nunes S, Fite JE, Patera KJ, French JA. 2001. Interactions among paternal behavior, steroid hormones, and parental experience in male marmosets (*Callithrix kuhlii*). Horm Behav 39(1):70–82.

Oblak AL, Gibbs TT, Blatt GJ. 2009. Decreased GABA(A) receptors and benzodiazepine binding sites in the anterior cingulate cortex in autism. Autism Res 2:205–219.

Oblak AL, Gibbs TT, Blatt GJ. 2010. Decreased GABA(B) receptors in the cingulate cortex and fusiform gyrus in autism. J Neurochem 114:1414–1423.

Oblak AL, Rosene DL, Kemper TL, Bauman ML, Blatt GJ. 2011. Altered posterior cingulate cortical cyctoarchitecture, but normal density of neurons and interneurons in the posterior cingulate cortex and fusiform gyrus in autism. Autism Res 4:200–211.

Ochs E. 1982. Talking to children in Western Samoa. Lang Soc 11:77–104.

Ochs E, Schieffelin B. 1984. Language acquisition and socialization: three developmental stories. In: Schweder R, LeVine R, editors. Culture theory: mind, self, and emotion. Cambridge: Cambridge University Press. 176–322.

O'Connell CA, DeSilva JM. 2013. Mojokerto revisited: evidence for an intermediate pattern of brain growth in *Homo erectus*. J Hum Evol 65:156–161.

O'Connell JF, Hawkes K, Blurton Jones NG. 1999. Grandmothering and the evolution of *Homo erectus*. J Hum Evol 36:461–485.

O'Connor DB, Archer J, Wu FCW. 2004. Effects of testosterone on mood, aggression, and sexual behavior in young men: a double-blind, placebo-controlled, cross-over study. J Clin Endocrinol Metab 89(6):2837–2845.

Oftedal OT. 2012. The evolution of milk secretion and its ancient origins. Animal 6(3):355–368.

Okamoto-Barth S. 2012. Social and cognitive development in humans and chimpanzees from a comparative perspective. Paper presented at: Multiple perspectives on the evolution of childhood, School for Advanced Research seminar, Santa Fe, NM.

O'Malley AJ, Arbesman S, Steiger DM, Fowler JH, Christakis NA. 2012. Egocentric social network structure, health, and pro-social behaviors in a national panel study of Americans. PLoS ONE 7(5):e36250.

Orekhova EV, Stroganova TA, Nygren G, Tsetlin MM, Posikera IN, Gillberg C, Elam M. 2007. Excess of high frequency electroencephalogram oscillations in boys with autism. Biol Psychiatr 62:1022–1029.

Ouss L, Saint-Georges C, Robel L, Bodeau N, Laznik MC, Crespin GC, Chetouani M, Bursztejn C, Golse B, Nabbout R, et al. 2014. Infant's engagement and emotion as predictors of autism or intellectual disability in West syndrome. Eur Child Adolesc Psychiatr 23(3):143–149.

Overpeck MD, Brenner RA, Trumble AC, Trifiletti LB, Berendes HW. 1998. Risk factors for infant homicide in the United States. New Engl J Med 339:1211–1216.

Ozarda Y, Gunes Y, Tuncer GO. 2012. The concentration of adiponectin in breast milk is related to maternal hormonal and inflammatory status during 6 months of lactation. Clin Chem Lab Med 50(5):911–917.

Ozonoff S, Young GS, Goldring S, Greiss-Hess L, Herrera AM, Steele J, Macari S, Hepburn S, Rogers SJ. 2008. Gross motor development, movement abnormalities, and early identification of autism. J Autism Dev Disord 38(4):644–656.

Padawer R. 2014. The recovered. New York Times Magazine. August 3:20–27, 46–47.

Pakkenberg B, Gundersen HJG. 1997. Neocortical neuron number in humans: effect of sex and age. J Comp Neurol 384:312–320.

Palombit RA. 2000. Infanticide and the evolution of male-female bonds in animals. In: van Schaik C, Janson CR, editors. Infanticide by males and its implications. Cambridge: Cambridge University Press. 239–268.

Palombit RA. 2012. Infanticide: male strategies and female counterstrategies. In: Mitani JC, Call J, Kappeler PM, Palombit RA, Silk JB, editors. The evolution of primate societies. Chicago, IL: University of Chicago Press. 433–468.

Palombit RA, Seyfarth RM, Cheney DL. 1997. The adaptive value of "friendships" to female baboons: experimental and observational evidence. Anim Behav 54(3):599–614.

Palou M, Picó C, McKay JA, Sánchez J, Priego T, Mathers JC, Palou A. 2011. Protective effects of leptin during the suckling period against later obesity may be associated with changes in promoter methylation of the hypothalamic pro-opiomelanocortin gene. Br J Nutr 106(5):769–778.

Pang WW, Hartmann PE. 2007. Initiation of human lactation: secretory differentiation and secretory activation. J Mammary Gland Biol Neoplasia 12(4):211–221.

Pappano DJ. 2013. The reproductive trajectories of bachelor geladas. PhD diss., University of Michigan.

Parish AR, de Waal F. 2000. The other "closest living relative": how bonobos (Pan paniscus) challenge traditional assumptions about females, dominance, intra- and intersexual interactions, and hominid evolution. Ann NY Acad Sci 907(1):97–113.

Passingham RE. 1975. Change in the size and organization of the brain in man and his ancestors. Brain Behav Evol 11:73–90.

Passingham RE. 1982. The human primate. San Francisco, CA: Freeman.

Passingham RE. 1985. Rates of brain development in mammals including man. Brain Behav Evol 26:167–175.

Paulozzi L. 2002. Variation in homicide risk during infancy: United States, 1989–1998. MMWR 51(109):187–189.

Paus T, Zijdenbos A, Worsley K, Collins DL, Blumenthal J, Giedd JN. 1999. Structural maturation of neural pathways in children and adolescents: in vivo study. Science 283:1908–1911.

Peaker M, Wilde CJ. 1996. Feedback control of milk secretion from milk. J Mammary Gland Biol Neoplasia 1(3):307–315.

Perez-Gomez J, Rodriguez GV, Ara I, Olmedillas H, Chavarren J, González-Henriquez JJ, et al. 2007. Role of muscle mass on sprint performance: gender differences? Eur J Appl Physiol 102:685–694.

Perini T, Ditzen B, Fischbacher S, Ehlert U. 2012. Testosterone and relationship quality across the transition to fatherhood. Biol Psychol 90(3):186–191.

Perrigo G, vom Saal F. 1994. Behavioral cycles and the neural timing of infanticide and parental behavior in male house mice. In: Parmigiano S, vom Saal F, editors. Infanticide and parental care. Chur, Switzerland: Harwood Academic. 365–396.

Perrin JS, Herve PY, Leonard G, Perron M, Pike GB, Pitiot A, Richer L, Veillette S, Pausova Z, Paus T. 2008. Growth of white matter in the adolescent brain: role of testosterone and androgen receptor. J Neurosci 28(38):9519–9524.

Petanjek Z, Judas M, Kostovic I, Uylings HBM. 2008. Lifespan alterations of basal dendritic trees of pyramidal neurons in the human prefrontal cortex: a layer-specific pattern. Cereb Cortex 18:915–929.

Petanjek Z, Judas M, Simic G, Rasin MR, Uylings HBM, Rakic P, Kostovic I. 2011. Extraordinary neoteny of synaptic spines in the human prefrontal cortex. Proc Natl Acad Sci USA 108:13281–13286.

Peterson CC, Nagy KA, Diamond J. 1990. Sustained metabolic scope. Proc Natl Acad Sci USA 87:2324–2328.

Peterson CK, Harmon-Jones E. 2012. Anger and testosterone: evidence that situationally-induced anger relates to situationally-induced testosterone. Emotion 12(5):899–902.

Pfefferbaum A, Mathalon DH, Sullivan EV, Rawles JM, Zipursky RB, Lim KO. 1994. A quantitative magnetic resonance imaging study of changes in brain morphology from infancy to late adulthood. Arch Neurol 51(9):874–887.

Pickering TR, Clarke RJ, Moggi-Cechi J. 2004. Role of carnivores in the accumulation of the Sterkfontein member 4 hominid assemblage: a taphonomic reassessment of the complete hominid fossil sample 1936–1999. J Hum Evol 125:1–15.

Pico C, Oliver P, Sanchez J, Miralles O, Caimari A, Priego T, Palou A. 2007. The intake of physiological doses of leptin during lactation in rats prevents obesity in later life. Int J Obesity 31(8):1199–1209.

Pinhasi R, Higham TF, Golovanova LV, Doronichev VB. 2011. Revised age of late Neanderthal occupation and the end of the Middle Paleolithic in the northern Caucasus. Proc Natl Acad Sci USA 108:8611–8616.

Pinto-Correia C. 1997. The ovary of Eve: egg and sperm and preformation. Chicago, IL: University of Chicago Press.

Piperata BA. 2009. Variation in maternal strategies during lactation: the role of the biosocial context. Am J Hum Biol 21:817–827.

Pitt R. 1978. Warfare and hominid brain evolution. J Theor Biol. 72:551–575.

Plavcan JM, Lockwood CA, Kimbel WH, Lague MR, Harmon EH. 2005. Sexual dimorphism in *Australopithecus afarensis* revisited: how strong is the case for a human-like pattern of dimorphism? J Hum Evol 48:313–320.

Plooij FX. 1984. The behavioral development of free-living chimpanzee babies and infants. Norwood, NJ: Ablex.

Plunkett J, Doniger S, Orabona G, Morgan T, Haataja R, et al. 2011. An evolutionary genomic approach to identify genes involved in human birth timing. PLoS Genet 7(4):e1001365.

Pollet TV, van der Meij L, Cobey KD, Buunk AP. 2011. Testosterone levels and their associations with lifetime number of opposite sex partners and remarriage in a large sample of American elderly men and women. Horm Behav 60(1):72–77.

Ponce de León MS, Golovanova L, Doronichev V, Romanova G, Akazawa T, Kondo O, Ishida H, Zollikofer CPE. 2008. Neanderthal brain size at birth provides insights into the evolution of human life history. Proc Natl Acad Sci USA 105:13764–13768.

Pond CM. 1992. An evolutionary and functional view of mammalian adipose tissue. Proc Nutr Soc 51(3):367–377.

Pontzer H, Brown MH, Raichlen DA, Dunsworth H, Hare B, Walker K, Luke A, Dugas L, Durazo-Arviz R, Schoeller D, et al. Forthcoming. Metabolic acceleration and the evolution of human brain size and life history. Nature.

Pontzer H, Raichlen DA, Gordon AD, Schroepfer-Walker KK, Hare B, O'Neill MC, Muldoon KM, Dunsworth HM, Wood BM, Isler K, et al. 2014. Primate energy expenditure and life history. Proc Natl Acad Sci USA 111:1433–1437.

Pontzer H, Raichlen DA, Shumaker RW, Ocobock C, Wiche SA. 2010. Metabolic adaptation for low energy throughput in orangutans. Proc Natl Acad Sci USA 107(32):14048–14052.

Pope HG, Kouri EM, Hudson JI. 2000. Effects of supraphysiologic doses of testosterone on mood and aggression in normal men: a randomized controlled trial. Arch Gen Psychiatr 57(2):133–140.

Porter JT, Johnson CK, Agmon A. 2001. Diverse types of interneurons generate thalamus-evoked feed forward inhibition in the mouse barrel cortex. J Neurosci 21:2699–2710.

Portmann A. 1939. Nesthocker und Nestflucker als Entwicklungszustande von verschiedener Wertigkeit bei Vogeln und Saugern. Rev Suisse Zool 46:385–390.

Portmann A. 1990. A zoologist looks at humankind. Judith Schaefer, translator. New York: Columbia University Press. Original edition, New York: Columbia University Press, 1944.

Posner G, Black A, Jones G, Dy J, Oppenheimer L. 2013. Oxorn-Foote human labor and birth. 6th ed. New York: McGraw-Hill.

Potts R. 1996. Humanity's descent: The consequences of ecological instability. New York: Avon.

Powe CE, Knott CD, Conklin-Brittain N. 2010. Infant sex predicts breast milk energy content. Am J Hum Biol 22(1):50–54.

Power ML, Oftedal OT, Tardif SD. 2002. Does the milk of callitrichid monkeys differ from that of larger anthropoids? Am J Primatol 56(2):117–127.

Power ML, Verona CE, Ruiz-Miranda C, Oftedal OT. 2008. The composition of milk from free-living common marmosets (*Callithrix jacchus*) in Brazil. Am J Primatol 70(1):78–83.

Powers CM. 2010. The influence of abnormal hip mechanics on knee injury: a biomechanical perspective. J Orthop Sports Phys Ther 40:42–51. doi:10.2519/jospt.2010.3337.

Prentice AA. 1995. Regional variation in the composition of human milk. In: Jensen RG, editor. Handbook of milk composition. New York: Academic. 115–221.

Prentice AA, Prentice AM, Whitehead RG. 1981a. Breast-milk fat concentrations of rural African women: 1: Short-term variations within individuals. Br J Nutr 45(3):483–494.

Prentice AA, Prentice AM, Whitehead RG. 1981b. Breast-milk fat concentrations of rural African women: 2: Long-term variations within a community. Br J Nutr 45(3):495–503.

Prentice AM, Goldberg G R, Prentice A. 1994. Body mass index and lactational performance. Eur J Clin Nutr 48(Suppl 3):S78–S89.

Prentice AM, Moore SE, Collinson AC, O'Connell MA. 2002. Leptin and undernutrition. Nutr Rev 60(10, pt. 2):S56–S67.

Prentice AM, Prentice AA. 1988. Energy costs of lactation. Ann Rev Nutr 8:63–79.

Prentice AM, Roberts SB, Prentice A, Paul AA, Watkinson M, Watkinson AA, Whitehead RG. 1983. Dietary supplementation of lactating Gambian women: I. Effect on breast-milk volume and quality. Hum Nutr Clin Nutr 37(1):53–64.

Pretorius E, Steyn M, Scholtz Y. 2006. Investigation into the usability of geometric morphometric analysis in assessment of sexual dimorphism. Am J Phys Anthropol 129:64–70.

Provine RR, Krosnowski KA, Brocato NW. 2009. Tearing: breakthrough in human emotional signaling. Evol Psychol 7(1):52–56.

Prudom SL, Broz CA, Schultz-Darken N, Ferris CT, Snowdon, C, Ziegler T. 2008. Exposure to infant scent lowers serum testosterone in father common

marmosets (*Callithrix jacchus*). Biol Letters 4(6):603–605. doi:1098/
rsbl.2008.0358.

Prüfer K, Racimo F, Patterson N, Jay F, Sankararaman S, Sawyer S, Heinze A,
Renaud G, Sudmant PH, de Filippo C, et al. 2014. The complete
genome sequence of a Neanderthal from the Altai mountains. Nature
505(7481):43–49.

Pye C. 1991. The acquisition of K'iché Maya. In: Slobin I, editor. The crosslinguistic
study of language acquisition. Vol. 3. Hillsdale, NJ: Erlbaum. 221–308.

Quinn EA. 2013. No evidence for sex biases in milk macronutrients, energy, or
breastfeeding frequency in a sample of Filipino mothers. Am J Phys
Anthropol 152(2):209–216.

Quinn EA, Diki Bista K, Childs G. 2016. Milk at altitude: human milk macronutrient
composition in a high-altitude-adapted population of Tibetans. Am J Phys
Anthropol 159(2):233–243.

Quinn EA, Largado F, Borja JB, Kuzawa CW. 2014. Maternal characteristics associated with milk leptin content in a sample of Filipino women and associations with infant weight for age. J Hum Lact 31:273–281.

Quinn EA, Largado F, Power M, Kuzawa CW. 2012. Predictors of breast milk macronutrient composition in Filipino mothers. Am J Hum Biol 24(4):533–540.

Rabinowicz T, de Courten-Myers GM, Petetot JMC, Xi GH, de los Reyes E. 1996.
Human cortex development: estimates of neuronal numbers indicate major
loss late during gestation. J Neuropathol Exper Neuro 55:320–332.

Radinsky LB. 1979. The fossil record of primate brain evolution (James Arthur lecture on the evolution of the human brain). New York: American Museum
of Natural History.

Rafacz ML, Margulis S, Santymire RM. 2012. Hormonal correlates of paternal care
differences in the Hylobatidae. Am J Primatol 74:247–260.

Rakic P. 1988. Defects of neuronal migration and the pathogenesis of cortical malfor-
mations. Prog Brain Res 73:15–37.

Rakic P, Bourgeois JP, Eckenhoff MF, Zecevic N, Goldmanrakic PS. 1986. Concurrent overproduction of synapses in diverse regions of the primate cerebral
cortex. Science 232:232–235.

Rakic P, Kornack DR. 2007. The development and evolutionary expansion of the
cerebral cortex in primates. Evol Nervous Syst 4:243–259.

Ramsay DT, Mitoulas LR, Kent JC, Larsson M, Hartmann PE. 2005. The use of
ultrasound to characterize milk ejection in women using an electric breast
pump. J Hum Lact 21(4):421–428.

Ramsbottom R, Nute MG, Williams C. 1987. Determinants of five kilometre running performance in active men and women. Brit J Sports Med 21:9–13.

Rapaport LG. 2006. Provisioning in wild golden lion tamarins (*Leontopithecus rosalia*): benefits to omnivorous young. Behav Ecol 17:212–221.

Rapaport LG. 2011. Progressive parenting behavior in wild golden lion tamarins. Behav Ecol 22(4):745–754.

Rapaport LG, Brown GR. 2008. Social influences on foraging behavior in young primates: learning what, where, and how to eat. Evol Anthropol 17(4):189–201. doi:10.1002/evan.20180.

Rapaport LG, Kloc B, Warneke M, Mickelberg J, Ballou J. 2013. Do mothers prefer helpers? birth sex-ratio adjustment in captive callitrichines. Anim Behav 85:1295–1303. doi:10.1016/janbehav.2013.03.018.

Rasmussen KM. 1992. The influence of maternal nutrition on lactation. Ann Rev Nutr 12:103–117.

Rasmussen KM, Hilson JA, Kjolhede CL. 2001. Obesity may impair lactogenesis II. J Nutr 131(11):3009S–3011S.

Raznahan A, Wallace GL, Antezana L, Greenstein D, Lenroot R, Thurm A, Gozzi M, Spence S, Martin A, Swedo SE. 2013. Compared to what? early brain overgrowth in autism and the perils of population norms. Biol Psychiatr 74(8):563–575.

Redfield A. 1970. A new aid to aging immature skeletons: development of the occipital bone. Am J Phys Anthropol 33:207–220.

Reed DL, Light JE, Allen JM, Kirchman JJ. 2007. Pair of lice lost or parasites regained: the evolutionary history of anthropoid primate lice. BMC Biol 5. http://doi.org/10.1186/1741-7007-5-7.

Reed WL, Clark ME, Parker PG, Raouf SA, Arguedas N, Monk DS, Snajdr E, Nolan V, Ketterson ED. 2006. Physiological effects on demography: a long-term experimental study of testosterone's effects on fitness. Am Nat 167(5):667–683.

Reichman BL, Chessex P, Putet G, Verellen GJ, Smith JM, Heim T, Swyer PR. 1982. Partition of energy metabolism and energy cost of growth in the very low-birth-weight infant. Pediatr 69:446–451.

Reilly J, Losh M, Bellugi U, Wulfeck B. 2004. "Frog, where are you?": narratives in children with specific language impairment, early focal brain injury, and Williams syndrome. Brain Lang 88:229–247.

Reite M, Field T, editors. 1985. Psychobiology of attachment and separation. New York: Academic.

Reite M, Seiler C, Short R. 1978a. Loss of your mother is more than loss of a mother. Am J Psychiatr 135:370–371.

Reite M, Short R, Kaufman IC, Stynes AJ, Pauley JD. 1978b. Heart rate and body temperature in separated monkey infants. Biol Psychiatr 13:91–105.

Reno PL, Meindl RS, McCollum M, Lovejoy CO. 2003. Sexual dimorphism in *Australopithecus afarensis* was similar to that of modern humans. Proc Natl Acad Sci USA 100:9404–9409.

Rhoads RE, Grudzien-Nogalska E. 2007. Translational regulation of milk protein synthesis at secretory activation. J Mammary Gland Biol Neoplasia 12(4):283–292.

Richard C, Mosko S, McKenna J. 1998. Apnea and periodic breathing in the bedsharing infant. J App Physio 84(4):1374–1380.

Ridley M. 1995. Pelvic sexual dimorphism and relative neonatal brain size really are related. Am J Phys Anthropol 97:197–200.

Rilling JK. 2013. The neural and hormonal bases of human parental care. Neuropsychologia 51:731–747.

Rilling JK, Young LJ. 2014. The biology of mammalian parenting and its effect on offspring social development. Science 345:742–743.

Rinaman L. 2007. Visceral sensory inputs to the endocrine hypothalamus. Front Neuroendocrinol 28(1):50–60.

Riskin A, Almog M, Peri R, Halasz K, Srugo I, Kessel A. 2012. Changes in immunomodulatory constituents of human milk in response to active infection in the nursing infant. Pediatr Res 71(2):220–225.

Rissech C, Garcìa M, Malgosa A. 2003. Sex and age diagnosis by ischium morphometric analysis. For Sci Int 135:188–196.

Rivinus HA, Katz SH. 1971. Evolution: newborn behavior and maternal attachment. Comments Contemp Psychiatr 1:95–104.

Robbins MM, Czekala NM. 1997. A preliminary investigation of urinary testosterone and cortisol levels in wild male mountain gorillas. Am J Primatol 43(1):51–64.

Roberts EK, Lu A, Bergman TJ, Beehner JC. 2012. A Bruce effect in wild geladas. Science 335(6073):1222–1225.

Roberts SB, Cole TJ, Coward WA. 1985. Lactational performance in relation to energy intake in the baboon. Am J Clin Nutr 41:1270–1276.

Robson SL, van Schaik CP, Hawkes K. 2006. The derived features of human life history. In: Paine RL, Hawkes K, editors. The evolution of human life history. Santa Fe, NM: SAR Press. 17–44.

Robson SL, Wood B. 2008. Hominin life history: reconstruction and evolution. J Anat 212:394–425.

Rolian C, Lieberman DE, Hallgrimsson B. 2010. The coevolution of human hands and feet. Evol 64(6):1558–1568.

Ronay R, von Hippel W. 2010. The presence of an attractive woman elevates testosterone and physical risk taking in young men. Soc Psychol Pers Sci 1(1):57–64.

Rosenberg KR. 1992. The evolution of modern human childbirth. Yearb Phys Anthropol 35:89–124.

Rosenberg KR, Trevathan WR. 1995. Bipedalism and human birth: the obstetrical dilemma revisited. Evol Anthropol 4:161–168.

Rosenberg KR, Trevathan WR. 2001. The evolution of human birth. Sci Am 285(5):72–77.

Rosenberg KR, Trevathan WR. 2002. Birth, obstetrics and human evolution. Brit J Obstetr Gynaecol 109:1199–1206.

Rosenberg KR, Trevathan WR. 2007. An anthropological perspective on the evolutionary context of preeclampsia in humans. J Reprod Immunol 76:91–97.

Rosenblum LA, Kaufman IC. 1968. Variations in infant development and response to maternal loss in monkeys. Am J Orthopsychiatr 38(3):418–426.

Ross C. 2001. Park or ride? evolution of infant carrying in primates. Int J Primatol 22:749–771.

Ross CN, French JA, Orti G. 2007. Germ-line chimerism and parental care in marmosets (*Callithrix kuhlii*). Proc Natl Acad Sci USA 104:6278–6282.

Ross CN, Maxwell HR, French JA. 2005. A comparison of pre- and post-partum urinary hormone profiles of abusive and non-abusive marmoset mothers, *Callithrix kuhlii*. Paper presented at: Annual Meeting of the American Society of Primatologists (abstract 73). https://www.asp.org/meetings/abstractDisplay.cfm?abstractID=920confEventID=1087.

Rothe H. 1975. Influence of newborn marmosets' (*Callithrix jacchus*) behaviour on expression and efficiency of maternal and paternal care. Fifth International Congress of Primatology, Nagoya 1974:315–320.

Rozzi SL, Lephart SM, Gear WS, Fu FH. 1999. Knee joint laxity and neuromuscular characteristics of male and female soccer and basketball players. Am J Sports Med 27:312–319.

Rubenstein JLR, Merzenich MM. 2003. Model of autism: increased ratio of excitation/inhibition in key neural systems. Genes Brain Behav 2:255–267.

Ruff CB. 1995. Biomechanics of the hip and birth in early *Homo*. Am J Phys Anthropol 98:527–574.

Ruff CB. 1998. Evolution of the hominid hip. In: Strasser E, Fleagle J, Rosenberger A, McHenry HM, editors. Primate locomotion: recent advances. New York: Plenum. 449–469.

Ruff CB. 2010. Body size and body shape in early hominins: implications of the Gona pelvis. J Hum Evol 58:166–178.

Ruff CB, Trinkaus E, Holliday TW. 1997. Body mass and encephalization in Pleistocene *Homo*. Nature 387:173–176.

Rutherford J. 2013. The primate placenta as an agent of developmental and health trajectories across the life course. In: Clancy KBH, Hinde K, Rutherford J, editors. Building babies: primate development in proximate and ultimate perspective. New York: Springer. 531–578.

Rutherford JN, Tardif SD. 2008. Placental efficiency and intrauterine resource allocation strategies in the common marmoset pregnancy. Am J Phys Anthropol 137:60–68.

Sacher GA, Staffeldt EF. 1974. Relation of gestation time to brain weight for placental mammals: implications for the theory of vertebrate growth. Am Nat 108:593–615.

Sackett DL, Strauss SE, Richardson WS, Rosenberg W, Haynes RB. 2000. Evidence based medicine: how to practice and teach EBM. 2nd ed. Edinburgh: Churchill Livingstone.

Saint-Georges C, Chetouani M, Cassel R, Apicella F, Mahdhaoui A, Muratori F, Laznik MC, Cohen D. 2013. Motherese in interaction: at the cross-road of emotion and cognition? (a systematic review). PLoS ONE 88(10):e78103.

Saito A, Nakamura K. 2011. Oxytocin changes primate paternal tolerance to offspring in food transfer. J Comp Physiol A 197:329–337.

Sakaguchi K, Oki M, Honma S, Hasegawa T. 2006. Influence of relationship status and personality traits on salivary testosterone among Japanese men. Pers Indiv Differ 41(6):1077–1087.

Sakai T, Hirata S, Fuwa K, Sugama K, Kusunoki K, Makishima H, Eguchi T, Yamada S, Ogihara N, Takeshita H. 2012. Fetal brain development in chimpanzees versus humans. Curr Biol 22(18):R791 R792.

Sakai T, Mikami A, Tomonaga M, Matsui M, Suzuki J, Hamada Y, Tanaka M, Miyabe-Nishiwaki T, Makishima H, Nakatsukasa M, et al. 2011. Differential prefrontal white matter development in chimpanzees and humans. Curr Biol 21:1397–1402.

Salafia CM, Yampolsky M. 2009. Metabolic scaling law for fetus and placenta. Placenta 30:468–471.

Saltzman W, Abbott DH. 2005. Diminished maternal responsiveness during pregnancy in multiparous female common marmosets. Horm Behav 47:151–163.

Salvador A, Suay F, Martinez-Sanchis S, Simon VM, Brain PF. 1999. Correlating testosterone and fighting in male participants in judo contests. Physiol Behav 68(1–2):205–209.

Samuelsen GB, Larsen KB, Bogdanovic N, Laursen H, Graem N, Larsen, JF. 2003. The changing number of cells in the human fetal forebrain and its subdivisions: a stereological analysis. Cereb Cortex 13:115–122.

Sánchez SM, Ziegler TE, Snowdon CT. 2014. Both parents respond equally to infant cues in the cooperatively breeding common marmoset (*Callithrix jacchus*). Anim Behav 97:95–103.

Sannen A, Van Elsacker L, Heistermann M, Eens M. 2004. Urinary testosterone-metabolite levels and dominance rank in male and female bonobos (*Pan paniscus*). Primates 45(2):89–96.

Sapienza P, Zingales L, Maestripieri D. 2009. Gender differences in financial risk aversion and career choices are affected by testosterone. Proc Natl Acad Sci USA 106(36):15268–15273.

Sapolsky RM. 1983. Endocrine aspects of social instability in the olive baboon (*Papio anubis*). Am J Primatol 5:365–379.

Savino F, Benetti S, Liguori SA, Sorrenti M, Cordero Di Montezemolo L. 2013. Advances on human milk hormones and protection against obesity. Cell Mol Biol 59(1):89–98.

Savino F, Fissore MF, Liguori SA, Oggero R. 2009a. Can hormones contained in mothers' milk account for the beneficial effect of breast-feeding on obesity in children? Clin Endocrinol 71(6):757–765.

Savino F, Liguori SA. 2008. Update on breast milk hormones: leptin, ghrelin and adiponectin. Clin Nutr 27(1):42–47.

Savino F, Liguori SA, Fissore MF, Oggero R. 2009b. Breast milk hormones and their protective effect on obesity. Int J Pediatr Endocrinol 2009:327505. http://doi.org/10.1155/2009/327505.

Savino F, Lupica MM, Benetti S, Petrucci E, Liguori SA, Cordero Di Montezemolo L. 2012a. Adiponectin in breast milk: relation to serum adiponectin concentration in lactating mothers and their infants. Acta Paediatr 101(10):1058–1062.

Savino F, Petrucci E, Nanni G. 2008. Adiponectin: an intriguing hormone for paediatricians. Acta Paediatr 97(6):701–705.

Savino F, Sorrenti M, Benetti S, Lupica MM, Liguori SA, Oggero R. 2012b. Resistin and leptin in breast milk and infants in early life. Early Hum Dev 88:779–782.

Scelza BA. 2010. Fathers' presence speeds the social and reproductive careers of sons. Curr Anthropol 51(2):295–303.

Schack-Nielsen L, Michaelsen KF. 2006. Breast feeding and future health. Curr Opin Clin Nutr Metab Care 9(3):289–296.

Schack-Nielsen L, Michaelsen KF. 2007. Advances in our understanding of the biology of human milk and its effects on the offspring. J Nutr 137(2):503S–510S.

Schade JP, Van Groenou WB. 1961. Structural organization of human cerebral cortex. Acta Anat 47:74–111.

Schenker N, Zilles K, Semendeferi K. 2008. A comparative quantitative analysis of cytoarchitecture and minicolumnar organization in Broca's area in humans and great apes. J Comp Neurol 510:117–128.

Schieffelin BB. 1990. The give and take of everyday life: language socialization of Kaluli children. Cambridge: Cambridge University Press.

Schino G, Troisi A. 2005. Neonatal abandonment in Japanese macaques. Am J Phys Anthropol 126:447–452.

Schlaug G, Armstrong E, Schleichner A, Zilles K. 1993. Layer V pyramidal cells in the adult human cingulate cortex. Anat Embryol 187:515–522.

Schmidt KL, Cohn JF. 2001. Human facial expressions as adaptations: evolutionary questions in facial expression research. Yearb Phys Anthropol 44:3–24.

Schone RA, Silven M. 2007. Natural parenting: back to basics in infant care. Evol Psychol 5(1):102–183.

Schradin C, Anzenberger G. 2005. Mothers, not fathers, determine the delayed onset of male carrying in Goeldi's monkey (*Callimico goeldii*). J Hum Evol 45:389–399.

Schradin C, Yuen C. 2011. Hormone levels of male African striped mice change as they switch between alternative reproductive tactics. Horm Behav 60(5):676–680.

Schueler J, Alexander B, Hart AM, Austin K, Larson-Meyer DE. 2013. Presence and dynamics of leptin, GLP-1, and PYY in human breast milk at early postpartum. Obesity 21(7):1451–1458.

Schultz AH. 1940. Growth and development of the chimpanzee. Contrib Embryol 28:1–63.

Schultz AH. 1941. Growth and development of the orang-utan. Contrib Embryol 29:57–111.

Schultz AH. 1949. Sex differences in the pelves of primates. Am J Phys Anthropol 7:887–964.

Schultz AH. 1969. The life of primates. London: Weidenfeld Nicolson.

Schulz KM, Molenda-Figueira HA, Sisk CL. 2009. Back to the future: the organizational-activational hypothesis adapted to puberty and adolescence. Horm Behav 55(5):597–604.

Schumann CM, Bloss CS, Barnes CC, Wideman GM, Carper RA, Akshoomoff N, Pierce K, Hagler D, Schork N, Lord C, et al. 2010. Longitudinal magnetic resonance imaging study of cortical development through early childhood in autism. J Neurosci 30(12):4419–4427.

Schuster S, Hechler C, Gebauer C, Kiess W, Kratzsch J. 2011. Leptin in maternal serum and breast milk: association with infants' body weight gain in a longitudinal study over 6 months of lactation. Pediatr Res 70(6):633–637.

Scott JR, et al., editors. 1994. Danforth's obstetrics and gynecology. 7th ed. Philadelphia, PA: Lippincott.

Sear R, Mace R. 2008. Who keeps children alive? a review of the effects of kin on child survival. Evol Hum Behav 29(1):1–18.

Seidel E, Silani G, Metzler H, Thaler H, Lamm C, Gur R, Kryspin-Exner I, Habel U, Derntl B. 2013. The impact of social exclusion vs. inclusion on subjective and hormonal reactions in females and males. Psychoneuroendocrinol 38(12):2925–2932.

Sellen DW. 2007. Evolution of infant and young child feeding: implications for contemporary public health. Ann Rev Nutr 27:123–148.

Semendeferi K, Armstrong E, Schleicher A, Zilles K, Van Hoesen GW. 2001. Prefrontal cortex in humans and apes: a comparative study of area 10. Am J Phys Anthropol 114:224–241.

Semendeferi K, Teffer K, Buxhoeveden D, Park MS, Bludau S, Amunts K, Travis K, Buckwalter J. 2011. Spatial organization of neurons in the frontal pole sets humans apart from great apes. Cereb Cortex 21:1485–1497.

Senghas A, Kita S, Ozyurek A. 2004. Children creating core properties of language: evidence from an emerging sign language in Nicaragua. Science 305(5691):1779–1782.

Senut B, Pickford M, Gommery D, Mein P, Cheboi K, Coppens Y. 2001. First hominid from the Miocene (Lukeino formation, Kenya). CR Acad Sci IIA 332(2):137–144.

Shankle WR, Rafii MS, Landing BH, Fallon JH. 1999. Approximate doubling of numbers of neurons in postnatal human cerebral cortex and in 35 specific cytoarchitectural areas from birth to 72 months. Pediatr Dev Pathol 2:244–259.

Sherwood CC, Raghanti MA, Stimpson CD, Spocter MA, Uddin M, Boddy AM. 2010. Inhibitory interneurons of the human prefrontal cortex display conserved evolution of the phenotype and related genes. Proc Biol Sci 277:1011–1020.

Shorten A, Donsante J, Shorten B. 2002. Birth position, accoucheur, and perineal outcomes: informing women about choices for vaginal birth. Birth 29(1):18–27.

Shur MD. 2008. Hormones associated with friendship between adult male and lactating female olive baboons. PhD diss., Rutgers University.

Sidman RL, Rakic P. 1973. Neuronal migration, with special reference to developing human brain: review. Brain Res 62:1–35.

Silk JB, Brosnan SF, Henrich J, Lambeth SP, Shapiro, S. 2013. Chimpanzees share food for many reasons: the role of kinship, reciprocity, social bonds and harassment on food transfers. Anim Behav 85:941–947.

Simpson GG. 1967. The meaning of evolution: a study of the history of life and of its significance for man. New Haven, CT: Yale University Press.

Simpson SW, Quade J, Levin NE, Butler R, Dupont-Nivet G, et al. 2008. A female *Homo erectus* pelvis from Gona, Ethiopia. Science 322:1089–1092.

Singh D, Young RK. 1995. Body weight, waist-to-hip ratio, breasts, and hips: role in judgments of female attractiveness and desirability for relationships. Ethol Sociobiol 16:483–507.

Singhal A, Farooqi IS, O'Rahilly S, Cole TJ, Fewtrell M, Lucas A. 2002. Early nutrition and leptin concentrations in later life. Am J Clin Nutr 75(6):993–999.

Siret M. 1778. Observations sur l'ouistiti, espece de sagouin. J Phys (Paris) 12(2):453–454.

Slocum S. 1975. Woman the gatherer: male bias in anthropology. In: Reiter R, editor. Toward an anthropology of women. New York: Monthly Review Press. 36–50.

Small M. 1991. Alloparental behavior in Barbary macaques (*Macaca sylvanus*). Anim Behav 39:297–306.

Small MF. 1998. Our babies, ourselves: how biology and culture shape the way we parent. New York: Anchor.

Smit EN, Martini IA, Mulder H, Boersma ER, Muskiet FA. 2002. Estimated biological variation of the mature human milk fatty acid composition. Prostaglandins Leukot Essent Fatty Acids 66(5–6):549–555.

Smith AC, Tirado Hirrera E. R, Buchanon-Smith HM, Heymann EW. 2001. Multiple breeding females and allo-nursing in a wild group of moustached tamarins (*Saguinus mystax*). Neotrop Primates 9(2):67–69.

Smith BH, Tompkins RL. 1995. Toward a life history of the Hominidae. Ann Rev Anthropol 24:257–279.

Smith EA. 2004. Why do good hunters have higher reproductive success? Hum Nat 15(4):343–364.

Smith LK, Lelas JL, Kerrigan DC. 2002. Gender differences in pelvic motions and center of mass displacement during walking: stereotypes quantified. J Women Health Gend Based Med 11:453–458.

Smith RJ. 2009. Use and misuse of the reduced major axis for line-fitting. Am J Phys Anthropol 140:476–486.

Smith TM. 2013. Teeth and human life-history evolution. Ann Rev Anthropol 42:191–208.

Smith TM, Tafforeau P, Reid DJ, Pouech J, Lazzari V, Zermeno JP, Guatelli-Steinberg D, Olejniczak AJ, Hoffman A, Radovčić J, et al. 2010. Dental evidence for ontogenetic differences between modern humans and Neanderthals. Proc Natl Acad Sci USA 107:20923–20928.

Smith-Kirwin SM, O'Connor DM, De Johnston J, Lancey ED, Hassink SG, Funanage VL. 1998. Leptin expression in human mammary epithelial cells and breast milk. J Clin Endocrinol Met 83(5):1810–1813.

Smuts BB, Gubernick DJ. 1992. Male-infant relationships in nonhuman primates: paternal investment or mating effort? In: Hewlett BS, editor. Father-child relations: cultural and biosocial contexts. New York: Aldine de Gruyter. 1–30.

Snowdon CT, Pieper BA, Boe CY, Cronin KA, Kurian AV, Ziegler TE. 2011. Variation in oxytocin is related to variation in affiliative behavior in monogamous, pairbonded tamarins. Horm Behav 58(4):614–618.

Sobolewski ME, Brown JL, Mitani JC. 2012. Territoriality, tolerance and testosterone in wild chimpanzees. Anim Behav 84(6):1469–1474.

Soltis J. 2004. The signal functions of early infant crying. Behav Brain Sci 27(4):443–490.

Sowell ER, Thompson PM, Holmes CJ, Jernigan TL, Toga AW. 1999. In vivo evidence for post-adolescent brain maturation in frontal and striatal regions. Nature Neurosci 2(10):859–861.

Spek AA, Velderman E. 2013. Examining the relationship between autism spectrum disorders and technical professions in high functioning adults. Res Autism Spec Dis 7(5):606–612.

Spitz RA. 1945. Hospitalism: an inquiry into the genesis of psychiatric conditions in early childhood. Psychoanal Study Child 1:53–74.

Spitz RA. 1951. The psychogenic diseases in infancy: an attempt at their etiologic classification. Psychoanal Study Child 6:255–275.

Spocter MA, Hopkins WD, Barks SK, Bianchi S, Hehmeyer AE, Anderson SM, Sherwood CC. 2012. Neuropil distribution in the cerebral cortex differs between humans and chimpanzees. J Comp Neurol 520(13):2917–2929.

Sponheimer M, Alemseged Z, Cerling TE, Grine FE, Kimbel WH, Leakey MG, Lee-Thorp JA, Manthi FK, Reed KE, Wood BA, et al. 2013. Isotopic evidence of early hominin diets. Proc Natl Acad Sci USA 110:10513–10518.

Squire L, Berg D, Bloom F, du Lac S, Ghosh A, Spitzer N. 2008. Fundamental neuroscience. Boston, MA: Academic.

Stallings JF, Fleming AS, Worthman CM, Steiner M, Corter C, Coote M. 2001. The effects of infant cries and odors on sympathy, cortisol, and autonomic responses. Parent-Sci Prac 1:71–100.

Stanton SJ, Liening SH, Schultheiss OC. 2011. Testosterone is positively associated with risk taking in the Iowa gambling task. Horm Behav 59(2):252–256.

Stanton SJ, Wirth MM, Waugh CE, Schultheiss OC. 2009. Endogenous testosterone levels are associated with amygdala and ventromedial prefrontal cortex responses to anger faces in men but not women. Biol Psychol 81(2):118–122.

Starkweather K, Hames R. 2012. A survey of non-classical polyandry. Hum Nat 23:149–172.

Stevens EE, Patrick TE, Pickler R. 2009. A history of infant feeding. J Perinat Educ 18(2):32–39.

Stewart MW, Stewart LA. 1991. Modification of sleep respiratory patterns by auditory stimulation: indications of techniques for preventing sudden infant death syndrome? Sleep 14:241–248.

Stiles J, Jernigan TL. 2010. The basics of brain development. Neuropsychol Rev 20:327–348.

Stoller M. 1995. The obstetric pelvis and mechanism of labor in nonhuman primates. PhD thesis, University of Chicago.

Storey AE, Walsh CJ, Quinton RL, Wynne-Edwards KE. 2000. Hormonal correlates of paternal responsiveness in new and expectant fathers. Evol Hum Behav 21:79–95.

Strathearn L, Mamun AA, Najman JM, O'Callaghan M. 2009. Does breastfeeding protect against substantiated child abuse and neglect? Pediatr 123(2):483–493.

Striedter GF. 2005. Principles of brain evolution. Sunderland, MA: Sinauer.

Stutz A. 2014. Embodied niche construction in the hominin lineage: semiotic structure and sustained attention in human embodied cognition. Front Psychol 5:1–19.

Surbeck M, Deschner T, Schubert G, Weltring A, Hohmann G. 2012. Mate competition, testosterone and intersexual relationships in bonobos, *Pan paniscus.* Anim Behav 83(3):659–669.

Suwa G, Asfaw B, Kono RT, Kubo D, Lovejoy CO, White TD. 2009. The *Ardipithecus ramidus* skull and its implications for hominid origins. Science 326:68e1–68e7. doi:10.1126/science.1175825.

Swamy GK, Ostbye T, Skjaerven R. 2008. Association of preterm birth with long-term survival, reproduction, and next-generation preterm birth. JAMA 299(12):1429–1436. doi:10.1001/jama.299.12.1429. Erratum in JAMA 300(2):170–171.

Sweeney CG, Curran E, Westmoreland SV, Mansfield, KG, Vallender EJ. 2012. Quantitative molecular assessment of chimerism across tissues in marmosets and tamarins. BMC Genomics 13. http://doi.org/10.1186/1471-2164-13-98.

Symons D. 1982. Another woman that never evolved. Q Rev Biol 57:297–300.

Szatmari P, Bryson S, Duku E, Vaccarella L, Zwaigenbaum L, Bennett T, Boyle MH. 2009. Similar developmental trajectories in autism and Asperger syndrome: from early childhood to adolescence. J Child Psychol Psychiatr 50(12):1459–1467.

Tague RG. 1989. Variation in pelvic size between males and females. Am J Phys Anthropol 80:59–71.

Tague RG. 1991. Commonalities in dimorphism and variability in the anthropoid pelvis, with implications for the fossil record. J Hum Evol 21:153–176.

Tague RG. 1992. Sexual dimorphism in the human bony pelvis, with a consideration of the Neandertal pelvis from Kebara cave, Israel. Am J Phys Anthropol 88:1–21.

Tague RG. 2005. Big-bodied males help us recognize that females have big pelves. Am J Phys Anthropol 127:392–405.

Tague RG, Lovejoy CO. 1986. The obstetric pelvis of AL-288-1 (Lucy). J Hum Evol 15:237–255.

Tague RG, Lovejoy CO. 1998. AL 288-1: Lucy or Lucifer: gender confusion in the Pliocene. J Hum Evol 35:75–94.

Tanguay PE. 2011. Autism in DSM-5. Am J Psychiatr 168(11):1142–1144.

Tanner N, Zihlman A. 1976. Women in evolution: part I: innovation and selection in human origins. Signs 1:585–608.

Tardif S, Ross C, Smucny D. 2013. Building marmoset babies: trade-offs and cutting bait. Dev Primatol Progr Prosp 37:169–183.

Tardif SD, Smucny DA, Abbott DH, Mansfield K, Schultz-Darken N, Yamamoto ME. 2003. Reproduction in captive common marmosets (*Callithrix jacchus*). Comp Med 53:364–368.

Teffer K, Buxhoeveden D, Stimpson CD, Fobbs AJ, Schapiro SJ, Baze WB, McArthur MJ, Hopkins WD, Hof P, Sherwood CC, et al. 2013. Developmental changes in the spatial organization of neurons in the neocortex of humans and chimpanzees. J Comp Neurol 521(18):4249–4259.

Teffer K, Semendeferi K. 2012. Human prefrontal cortex: evolution, development, and pathology. Prog Brain Res 195:191–218.

Thibault V, Guillaume M, Berthelot G, El Helou N, Schaal K, Quinquis L, Nassif H, Tafflet M, Escolana, S Hermine, O, Toussaint JF. 2010. Women and men in sport performance: the gender gap has not evolved since 1983. J Sports Sci Med 9:214–223.

Thiessen E, Saffran, JR. 2007. Learning to learn: acquisition of stress-based strategies for word segmentation. Lang Learn Dev 3:75–102.

Thoman EB, Graham SE. 1986. Self-regulation of stimulation by premature infants. Pediatr 78:855–860.

Thompson ME. 2013. Comparative reproductive energetics of human and nonhman primates. Ann Rev Anthropol 42:287–304.

Thorburn GD, Hollingworth SA, Hooper SB. 1991. The trigger for parturition in sheep: fetal hypothalamus or placenta? J Dev Physiol 15(2):71–79.

Tilden CD, Oftedal OT. 1997. Milk composition reflects pattern of maternal care in prosimian primates. Am J Primatol 41(3):195–211.

Tirado-Herrera E, Knogge C, Heymann EW. 2000. Infanticide in a group of wild saddle-back tamarins, *Saguinus fuscicollis*. Am J Primatol 50:153–157.

Tomasello M. 1999. The human adaptation for culture. Ann Rev Anthropol 28:509–529.

Tomasello M. 2009. Why we cooperate. Cambridge, MA: Boston Review Books.

Tomicić S, Johansson G, Voor T, Björkstén B, Böttcher MF, Jenmalm MC. 2010. Breast milk cytokine and IgA composition differ in Estonian and Swedish mothers: relationship to microbial pressure and infant allergy. Pediatr Res 68(4):330–334.

Tomonaga M. 2007. Visual search for orientation of faces by a chimpanzee (*Pan troglodytes*): face-specific upright superiority and the role of facial configural properties. Primates 48:1–12.

Trainor BC, Marler CA. 2002. Testosterone promotes paternal behaviour in a monogamous mammal via conversion to oestrogen. Proc R Soc B 269(1493):823–829.

Travers MT, Barber MC, Tonner E, Quarrie L, Wilde CJ, Flint DJ. 1996. The role of prolactin and growth hormone in the regulation of casein gene expression and mammary cell survival: relationships to milk synthesis and secretion. Endocrinol 137(5):1530–1539.

Travis K, Ford K, Jacobs B. 2005. Regional dendritic variation in neonatal human cortex: a quantitative Golgi study. Dev Neurosci 27:277–287.

Trevarthen C, Aitken, KJ. 2001. Infant intersubjectivity: research, theory and clinical application. J Child Psychol Psychiatr 42:3–48.

Trevathan WR. 1983. Maternal "en face" orientation during the first hour after birth. Am J Orthopsychiatr 53:92–99.

Trevathan WR. 1987. Human birth: an evolutionary perspective. Hawthorne, NY: Aldine de Gruyter. Reissued in 2011 by Transaction, New Brunswick, NJ.

Trevathan, WR. 1988. Fetal emergence patterns in evolutionary perspective. Am Anthropol 90:674–681.

Trevathan WR. 2010. Ancient bodies, modern lives: how evolution has shaped women's health. New York: Oxford University Press.

Trevathan WR. 2015. Primate pelvic anatomy and implications for birth. Phil Trans R Soc B 370. doi:10.1098/rstb.2014.0065.

Trevathan WR, McKenna JJ. 1994. Evolutionary environments of human birth and infancy: insights to apply to contemporary life. Child Environ 11(2):88–104.

Trevathan, WR, Rosenberg, KR. 2000. The shoulders follow the head: postcranial constraints on human childbirth. J Hum Evol 396:583–586.

Trevathan WR, Smith EO, McKenna JJ, editors. 2007. Evolutionary medicine and health. Oxford: Oxford University Press.

Treviño-Garza C, Bosques-Padilla FJ, Estrada-Zúñiga CM, Mancillas-Adame L, Villarreal-Pérez JZ, Abrego-Moya V, Argente J. 2010. Typical leptin fall is mitigated by breastfeeding in female infants. Arch Med Res 41(5):373–377.

Tricker R, Casaburi R, Storer TW, Clevenger B, Berman N, Shirazi A, Bhasin S. 1996. The effects of supraphysiological doses of testosterone on angry behavior in healthy eugonadal men: a clinical research center study. J Clin Endocrinol Metab 81(10):3754–3758.

Trinkaus E. 1984. Neandertal pubic morphology and gestation length. Curr Anthropol 25:509–513.

Trivers R. 1985. Social evolution. San Francisco, CA: Benjamin Cummings.

Trumble BC, Cummings DK, O'Connor KA, Holman DJ, Smith EA, Kaplan HS, Gurven MD. 2013. Age-independent increases in male salivary testosterone during horticultural activity among Tsimane forager-farmers. Evol Human Behav 34(5):350–357.

Trumble BC, Jaeggi AV, Gurven M. 2015. Evolving the neuroendocrine physiology of human and primate cooperation and collective action. Phil Trans R Soc B 370(1683). doi:10.1098/rstb.2015.0014.

Trumble BC, Smith EA, O'Connor KA, Kaplan HS, Gurven MD. 2014. Successful hunting increases testosterone and cortisol in a subsistence population. Proc R Soc B 281(1776):1–8.

Tsai LY. 2013. Asperger's disorder will be back. J Autism Dev Disord 43(12):2914–2942.

Tsai LY, Ghaziuddin M. 2014. DSM-5 ASD moves forward into the past. J Autism Dev Disord 44(2):321–330.

Tsao FM, Liu HM, Kuhl PK. 2004. Speech perception in infancy predicts language development in the second year of life: a longitudinal study. Child Dev 75(4):1067–1084.

Turke P. 2013. Altriciality, neoteny and pleiotropy. In: Summers K, Crespi B, editors. Human social evolution. Oxford: Oxford University Press. 171–181.

Turner S, Gould L, Duffus DA. 2005. Maternal behavior and infant congenital limb malformation in a free-ranging group of *Macaca fuscata* on Awaji island, Japan. Int J Primatol 26:1435–1457.

Ulfig N, Setzer M, Bohl J. 2003. Ontogeny of the human amygdala. Ann NY Acad Sci 285:22–33.

Uvnäs-Moberg K. 1989. Physiological and psychological effects of oxytocin and prolactin in connection with motherhood with special reference to food intake and the endocrine system of the gut. Acta Physiol Scand Suppl. 583:41–48.

Uvnäs-Moberg K. 2003. The oxytocin factor: tapping the hormone of calm, love, and healing. Cambridge, MA: Da Capo.

Uvnäs-Moberg K, Widstrom AM, Marchini G, Winberg J. 1987. Release of GI hormones in mother and infant by sensory stimulation. Acta Paediatr Scand 76:851–860.

Uysal FK, Onal EE, Aral YZ, Adam B, Dilmen U, Ardicolu Y. 2002. Breast milk leptin: its relationship to maternal and infant adiposity. Clin Nutri 21(2):157–160.

van Anders SM. 2013. Beyond masculinity: testosterone, gender/sex, and human social behavior in a comparative context. Front Neuroendocrinol 34(3):198–210.

van Anders SM, Goldey KL. 2010. Testosterone and partnering are linked via relationship status for women and "relationship orientation" for men. Horm Behav 58(5):820–826.

van Anders SM, Goldey KL, Kuo PX. 2011. The steroid/peptide theory of social bonds: integrating testosterone and peptide responses for classifying social behavioral contexts. Psychoneuroendocrinol 36(9):1265–1275.

van Anders SM, Hamilton LD, Watson NV. 2007. Multiple partners are associated with higher testosterone in North American men and women. Horm Behav 51(3):454–459.

van Anders SM, Tolman RM, Volling BL. 2012. Baby cries and nurturance affect testosterone in men. Horm Behav 61(1):31–36.

van Anders SM, Watson NV. 2006. Relationship status and testosterone in North American heterosexual and non-heterosexual men and women: cross-sectional and longitudinal data. Psychoneuroendocrinol 31(6):715–723.

van Anders SM, Watson NV. 2007. Testosterone levels in women and men who are single, in long-distance relationships, or same-city relationships. Horm Behav 51(2):286–291.

van Honk J, Montoya ER, Bos PA, van Vugt M, Terburg D. 2012. New evidence on testosterone and cooperation. Nature 485(7399):e4–e5.

van Honk J, Schutter DJ, Bos PA, Kruijt AW, Lentjes EG, Baron-Cohen S. 2011. Testosterone administration impairs cognitive empathy in women depending on second-to-fourth digit ratio. Proc Natl Acad Sci USA 108(8):3448–3452.

van Honk J, Tuiten A, Verbaten R, van den Hout M, Koppeschaar H, Thijssen J, de Haan E. 1999. Correlations among salivary testosterone, mood, and selective attention to threat in humans. Horm Behav 36(1):17–24.

van Lawick-Goodall J. 1967. Mother-offspring relationship in free-ranging chimpanzees. In: Morris, D, editor. Primate ethology. New Brunswick, NJ: Rutgers University Press. 287–346.

van Schaik CP, Isler K. 2012. Life-history evolution in primates. In: Mitani JC, Call J, Kappeler PM, Palombit RA, Silk JB, editors. The evolution of primate societies. Chicago, IL: University of Chicago Press. 220–244.

van Schaik CP, Janson C, editors. 2000. Infanticide by males and its implications. Cambridge: Cambridge University Press.

van Wingen G, Mattern C, Verkes RJ, Buitelaar J, Fernandez G. 2010. Testosterone reduces amygdala-orbitofrontal cortex coupling. Psychoneuroendocrinol 35(1):105–113.

Venkataraman VV, Kraft TS, Dominy NJ. 2013. Tree climbing and human evolution. Proc Natl Acad Sci USA 110:1237–1242.

Vennemann M, Bajanowski T, Jorch G, Mitchell E. 2009. Does breastfeeding reduce the risk of sudden infant death syndrome? Pediatr 123:e406–e410.

Villalpando S, del Prado M. 1999. Interrelation among dietary energy and fat intakes, maternal body fatness, and milk total lipid in humans. J Mammary Gland Biol Neoplasia 4(3):285–295.

Villalpando SF, Butte NF, Wong WW, Flores-Huerta S, Hernandez-Beltran MJ, Smith EO, Garza C. 1992. Lactation performance of rural Mesoamerindians. Eur J Clin Nutr 46(5):337–348.

Vinicius L. 2005. Human encephalization and developmental timing. J Hum Evol 49:762–776.

Vitzthum VJ. 2001. Why not so great is still good enough: flexible responsiveness in human reproductive functioning. In: Ellison P, editor. Reproductive ecology and human evolution. New York: Aldine de Gruyter. 179–202.

Volman I, Toni I, Verhagen L, Roelofs K. 2011. Endogenous testosterone modulates prefrontal-amygdala connectivity during social emotional behavior. Cereb Cortex 21(10):2282–2290.

von Koenigswald GHR. 1936. Ein fossiler hominide aus dem Altpleistocän Ostjavas. De Ingenieur in Nederlandsch-Indie 8:149–158.

von Rueden C, Gurven M, Kaplan H. 2008. The multiple dimensions of male social status in an Amazonian society. Evol Human Behav 29(6):402–415.

von Rueden C, Gurven M, Kaplan H. 2011. Why do men seek status? fitness payoffs to dominance and prestige. Proc R Soc B 278(1715):2223–2232.

von Rueden CR, Trumble BC, Emery Thompson M, Stieglitz J, Hooper PL, Blackwell AD, Kaplan HS, Gurven M. 2014. Political influence associates with cortisol and health among egalitarian forager-farmers. Evol Med Public Health 2014(1):122–133.

Vrba E. 1998. Multiphasic growth models and the evolution of prolonged growth exemplified by human brain evolution. J Theoret Biol 140:227–239.

Walker A. 2009. The strength of great apes and the speed of humans. Curr Anthropol 50(2):229–234.

Walker R, Flinn MV, Hill K. 2010. Evolutionary history of partible paternity in lowland South America. Proc Natl Acad Sci USA 107(45):19195–19200.

Wall-Scheffler CM. 2012. Energetics, locomotion, and female reproduction: implications for human evolution. Ann Rev Anthropol 41:71–85.

Wall-Scheffler CM, Geiger K, Steudel-Numbers KL. 2007. Infant carrying: the role of increased locomotor costs in early tool development. Am J Phys Anthropol 133:841–846.

Wall-Scheffler CM, Myers MJ. 2013. Reproductive costs for everyone: how female loads impact human mobility strategies. J Hum Evol 64:448–456.

Walrath D. 2003. Rethinking pelvic typologies and the human birth mechanism. Curr Anthropol 44:5–31.

Ward CV. 2002. Interpreting the posture and locomotion of *Australopithecus afarensis*: where do we stand? Yearb Phys Anthropol 119:185–215.

Warrener AG, Lewton KL, Pontzer H, Lieberman DE. 2015. A wider pelvis does not increase locomotor costs in humans, with implications for the evolution of childbirth. PLoS ONE 10(3). doi:10.1371/journal.pone.0118903.

Washburn S. 1960. Tools and human evolution. Sci Am 203:3–15.

Washburn SL, Lancaster CS. 1968. The evolution of hunting. In: Lee RB, DeVore I, editors. Man the hunter. Chicago, IL: Aldine-Atherton. 293–303.

Watson RE, DeSesso JM, Hurtt ME, Cappon GD. 2006. Postnatal growth and morphological development of the brain: a species comparison. Birth Defects Res 77:471–484.

Watts DP. 1998. Coalitionary mate guarding by male chimpanzees at Ngogo, Kibale national park, Uganda. Behav Ecol Sociobiol 44(1):43–55.

Watts ES. 1990. Evolutionary trends in primate growth and development. In: DeRousseau CJ, editor. Primate life history and evolution, New York:Wiley-Liss. 89–104.

Weaver LT. 2011. How did babies grow 100 years ago? Eur J Clin Nutr 65(1):3–9.

Weaver TD. 2002. A multi-causal functional analysis of hominid hip morphology. PhD diss., Stanford University.

Weimer AK, Schatz AM, Lincoln A, Ballantyne AO, Trauner DA. 2001. "Motor" impairment in Asperger syndrome: evidence for a deficit in proprioception. J Dev Behav Pediatr 22(2):92–101.

Weiner S, Monge J, Mann A. 2008. Bipedalism and parturition: an evolutionary imperative for cesarean delivery? Clin Perinatol 35(3):469–478.

Welker KM, Lozoya E, Campbell JA, Neumann CS, Carré JM. 2014. Testosterone, cortisol, and psychopathic traits in men and women. Physiol Behav 129:230–236.

Wells JC. 2000. Environmental temperature and human growth in early life. J Theor Biol 204(2):299–305.

Wells JC. 2003. The thrifty phenotype hypothesis: thrifty offspring or thrifty mother? J Theor Biol 221(1):143–161.

Wells JC. 2012a. The capital economy in hominin evolution. Curr Anthropol 53(S6):S466–S478.

Wells JC. 2012b. Ecogeographical associations between climate and human body composition: analyses based on anthropometry and skinfolds. Am J Phys Anthropol 147(2):169–186.

Wells JC. 2012c. Ecological variability and human evolution: a novel perspective on life history change. Evol Anthropol 21:277–288.

Wells JC. 2014 Adaptive variability in the duration of critical windows of plasticity: implications for the programming of obesity. Evol Med Public Health 2014(1):109–121.

Wells JC, DeSilva JM, Stock JT. 2012. The obstetric dilemma: an ancient game of Russian roulette, or a variable dilemma sensitive to ecology? Am J Phys Anthropol 149(S55):40–71.

Wells JC, Stock JT. 2007. The biology of the colonizing ape. Am J Phys Anthropol 45:191–222.

Wermke K, Leising D, Stellzig-Eisenhauer A. 2007. Relation of melody complexity in infants' cries to language outcome in the second year of life: a longitudinal study. Clin Linguist Phon 21(11–12):961–973.

West-Eberhard MJ. 2003. Developmental plasticity and evolution. Oxford: Oxford University Press.

Weyand PG, Sternlight DB, Bellizzi MJ, Wright S. 2000. Faster top running speeds are achieved with greater ground forces not more rapid leg movements. J Appl Physiol 89:1991–1999.

Weyermann M, Beermann C, Brenner H, Rothenbacher D. 2006. Adiponectin and leptin in maternal serum, cord blood, and breast milk. Clin Chem 52(11):2095–2102.

Weyermann M, Brenner H, Rothenbacher D. 2007. Adipokines in human milk and risk of overweight in early childhood: a prospective cohort study. Epidemiol 18(6):722–729.

Whitcome KK, Shapiro LJ, Lieberman DE. 2007. Fetal load and the evolution of lumbar lordosis in bipedal hominins. Nature 450:1075–1078.

White CR, Seymour RS. 2003. Mammalian basal metabolic rate is proportional to body mass$^{2/3}$. Proc Natl Acad Sci USA 100:4046–4049.

Whitmore TJ, Trengove NJ, Graham DF, Hartmann PE. 2012. Analysis of insulin in human breast milk in mothers with type 1 and type 2 diabetes mellitus. Int J Endocrinol 2012. doi:10.1155/2012/296368.

Whittier CA, Milligan LA, Nutter FB, Cranfield MR, Power ML. 2011. Proximate composition of milk from free-ranging mountain gorillas (*Gorilla beringei beringei*). Zoo Biol 30(3):308–317.

Wibral M, Dohmen T, Klingmuller D, Weber B, Falk A. 2012. Testosterone administration reduces lying in men. PLoS ONE 7(10):e46774.

Widström AM, Lilja G, Aaltomaa-Michalias P, Dahllöf A, Lintula M, Nissen E. 2011. Newborn behaviour to locate the breast when skin-to-skin: a possible method for enabling early self-regulation. Acta Paediatr 100(1):79–85.

Wiesel TN. 1982. The postnatal development of the visual cortex and the influence of environment. Biosci Rep 2(6):351–377.

Wiessner P. 1982. Risk, reciprocity and social influences on !Kung San economics. In: Leacock E, Lee R, editors. Politics and history in band societies. Cambridge: Cambridge University Press. 171–190.

Wingfield JC, Hegner RE, Ball GF, Duffy AM. 1990. The "challenge hypothesis": theoretical implications for patterns of testosterone secretion, mating systems, and breeding strategies. Am Nat 136:829–846.

Wirth MM, Schultheiss OC. 2007. Basal testosterone moderates responses to anger faces in humans. Physiol Behav 90(2):496–505.

Wittman AB, Wall LL. 2007. The evolutionary origins of obstructed labor: bipedalism, encephalization, and the human obstetric dilemma. Obstet Gynecol Surv 62:739–748.

Wobber V, Hare B, Maboto J, Lipson S, Wrangham R, Ellison PT. 2010a. Differential changes in steroid hormones before competition in bonobos and chimpanzees. Proc Natl Acad Sci USA 107(28):12457–12462. Wobber V, Wrangham R, Hare B. 2010b. Bonobos exhibit delayed development of social behavior and cognition relative to chimpanzees. Curr Biol 20(3):226–230.

Wolff PH. 1969. The natural history of crying and other vocalizations in early infancy. In: Ross B, editor. Determinants of infant behavior. London: Methuen. 81–109.

Wonders CP, Anderson SA. 2006. The origin and specification of cortical interneurons. Nat Rev Neurosci 7:687–696.

Woo JG, Guerrero ML, Altaye M, Ruiz-Palacios GM, Martin LJ, "Dubert-Ferrandon A," Newburg DS, Morrow AL. 2009. Human milk adiponectin is associated with infant growth in two independent cohorts. Breastfeed Med 4(2):101–109.

Woo JG, Guerrero ML, Guo F, Martin LJ, Davidson BS, Ortega H, Ruiz-Palacios

GM, Morrow AL. 2012. Human milk adiponectin affects infant weight trajectory during the second year of life. J Pediatr Gastroenterol Nutr 54(4):532–539.

Wood BM, Marlowe FW. 2013. Household and kin provisioning by Hadza men. Hum Nat 24:280–317.

Woolridge M. 1995. Baby-controlled breastfeeding: biocultural implications. In: Stuart-Macadam P, Dettwyler K, editors. Breastfeeding: biocultural perspectives. New York: Aldine de Gruyter. 217–242.

Worthman CM, Konner MJ. 1987. Testosterone levels change with subsistence hunting effort in !Kung San men. Psychoneuroendocrinol 12(6):449–458.

Wrangham R, Conklin-Brittain N. 2003. Cooking as a biological trait. Comp Biochem Physiol A: Mol Integr Physiol 136:35–46.

Wright ND, Bahrami B, Johnson E, Di Malta G, Rees G, Frith CD, Dolan RJ. 2012. Testosterone disrupts human collaboration by increasing egocentric choices. Proc R Soc B 279(1736):2275–2280.

Wroblewski EE, Murray CM, Keele BF, Schumacher-Stankey JC, Hahn BH, Pusey AE. 2009. Male dominance rank and reproductive success in chimpanzees, *Pan troglodytes schweinfurthii*. Anim Behav 77(4):873–885.

Wu Z, Autrey AE, Bergan JF, Watabe-Uchida M, Dulac C. 2014. Galanin neurons in the medial preoptic area govern parental behaviour. Nature 509:325–330.

Wynne-Edwards KE, Timonin ME. 2007. Paternal care in rodents: weakening support for hormonal regulation of the transition to behavioral fatherhood in rodent animal models of biparental care. Horm Behav 52(1):114–121.

Yagil R, Amir H, Abu-Rabiya Y, Etzion Z. 1986. Dilution of milk: a physiological adaptation of mammals to water stress. J Arid Environ 11:243–247.

Yamamoto S, Tanaka M. 2009. How did altruism and reciprocity evolve in humans? perspectives from experiments on chimpanzees (*Pan troglodytes*). Interact Stud 10(2):150–182. doi:10.1075/is.10.2.04yam.

Yerkes RM, Tomlin MI. 1935. Mother-infant relations in chimpanzees. J Comp Psychol 20:321–348.

Yizhar O, Fenno LE, Prigge M, Schneider F, Davidson TJ, O'Shea DJ, Sohal VS, Goshen I, Finkelstein J, Paz JT, et al. 2011. Neocortical excitation/inhibition balance in information processing and social dysfunction. Nature 477:171–178.

Yuhas R, Pramuk K, Lien EL. 2006. Human milk fatty acid composition from nine countries varies most in DHA. Lipids 41(9):851–858.

Zak PJ, Kurzban R, Ahmadi S, Swerdloff RS, Park J, Efremidze L, Redwine K, Morgan K, Matzner W. 2009. Testosterone administration decreases generosity in the ultimatum game. PLoS ONE 4(12):e8330.

Zanolli C, Bondioli L, Manni F, Rossi P, Macchiarelli R. 2011. Gestation length, mode of delivery and neonatal line thickness variation. Hum Biol 83(6):695–713.

Zeba M, Jovanovic-Milosevic N, Petanjek Z. 2008. Quantitative analysis of basal dendritic trees of layer IIIc pyramidal neurons in different areas of adult human frontal cortex. Coll Antropol 32:161–169.

Zethraeus N, Kocoska-Maras L, Ellingsen T, von Schoultz B, Hirschberg AL, Johannesson M. 2009. A randomized trial of the effect of estrogen and testosterone on economic behavior. Proc Natl Acad Sci USA 106(16):6535–6538.

Ziegler TE, Jacoris S, Snowdon CT. 2004b. Sexual communication between breeding male and female cotton-top tamarins (*Saguinus oedipus*), and its relationship to infant care. Am J Primatol 64:57–69.

Ziegler TE, Prudom SL, Zahed SR, Parlow AF, Wegner FH. 2009. Prolactin's mediative role in male parenting in parentally experienced marmosets (*Callithrix jacchus*). Horm Behav 56:436–443.

Ziegler TE, Schultz-Darken NJ, Scott JJ, Snowdon CT, Ferris CF. 2005. Neuroendocrine response to female ovulatory odors depends upon social condition in male common marmosets, *Callithrix jacchus*. Horm Behav 47(1):56–64.

Ziegler TE, Snowdon CT. 2000. Preparental hormone levels and parenting experience in male cotton-top tamarins, *Saguinus oedipus*. Horm Behav 38(3):159–167.

Ziegler TE, Washabaugh KF, Snowdon CT. 2004a. Responsiveness of expectant male cottontop tamarins, *Saguinus oedipus*, to mate's pregnancy. Horm Behav 45:84–92.

Zihlman AL. 1981. Women as shapers of the human adaptation. In: Dahlberg F, editor. Woman the gatherer. New Haven, CT: Yale University Press. 75–120.

Zihlman AL. 1989. Woman the gatherer: the role of women in early hominid evolution. In: Morgan S, editor. Gender and anthropology: critical reviews for teaching and research. Washington, DC: American Anthropological Association. 23–43.

Zikopoulos B, Barbas H. 2013. Altered neural connectivity in excitatory and inhibitory cortical circuits in autism. Front Hum Neurosci 7. doi:10.3389/fnhum.2013.00609.

Zimmerman R. 2011. Women's tears send chemical message, lowering men's sexual arousal. WBUR's CommonHealth. http://commonhealth.wbur.org/2011/01/womens-tears-mens-sexual-arousal.

Zollikofer CPE, Ponce de León MS, Lieberman DE, Guy F, Pilbeam D, Likius A, Mackaye HT, Vignaud P, Brunet M. 2005. Virtual cranial reconstruction of *Sahelanthropus tchadensis*. Nature 434:755–759.

Participants in the School for Advanced Research advanced seminar "Costly and Cute: How Helpless Newborns Made Us Human," co-chaired by Wenda Trevathan and Karen Rosenberg, May 11–15, 2014. *Standing in back row, from left:* Holly M. Dunsworth, Lee T. Gettler, Wenda R. Trevathan, Jeremy M. DeSilva, Sarah B. Hrdy, James J. McKenna, Christoph P. E. Zollikofer, and Katerina Semendeferi. *Standing in front row, from left:* E. A. Quinn, Karen R. Rosenberg, Marcia Ponce de León, and Dean Falk. Photograph by William Geoghegan.

Jeremy M. DeSilva
Department of Anthropology, Dartmouth College

Holly M. Dunsworth
Department of Sociology and Anthropology, University of Rhode Island

Dean Falk
Senior Scholar, School for Advanced Research and Department of Anthropology, Florida State University

Lee T. Gettler
Department of Anthropology, University of Notre Dame

Kari L. Hanson
Department of Anthropology, University of California, San Diego

Sarah B. Hrdy
Professor Emerita, University of California, Davis

James J. McKenna
Department of Anthropology, University of Notre Dame

Marcia Ponce de León
Anthropological Institute, University of Zurich

E. A. Quinn
Department of Anthropology, Washington University in St. Louis

Karen R. Rosenberg
Department of Anthropology, University of Delaware

Katerina Semendeferi
Department of Anthropology, University of California, San Diego

Wenda R. Trevathan
Department of Anthropology, New Mexico State University

Christoph P. E. Zollikofer
Anthropological Institute, University of Zurich